J. W. Leonard

The industries of Saint Louis. Her relations as a center of trade, manufacturing establishments and business houses

J. W. Leonard

**The Industries of Saint Louis. Her relations as a center of trade, manufacturing establishments and business houses**

ISBN/EAN: 9783337336301

Printed in Europe, USA, Canada, Australia, Japan

Cover: Foto ©ninafisch / pixelio.de

More available books at **www.hansebooks.com**

⟵≡ OF ≡⟶

# SAINT LOUIS.

---•••---

HER RELATIONS AS A CENTER OF TRADE.

---•••---

MANUFACTURING ESTABLISHMENTS AND
BUSINESS HOUSES.

ST. LOUIS, MO.
J. M. ELSTNER & CO., PUBLISHERS.
1887.

# PREFACE.

The object of this volume is to set forth the inherent and acquired advantages of St. Louis with reference to traffic and industry, and the extent to which these resources have been utilized in the development of the material interests of the city. The author has essayed to briefly sketch such points of antecedent history as are necessary to explain the city's industrial growth and indicate the steps in her progress, and to present such a view of the present as will convey a faithful idea of the greatness of St. Louis as a commercial and manufacturing center.

In the pursuit of this result, information has been sought from the best available sources, and every endeavor has been made to secure accuracy. It is therefore believed that the statements and statistics contained in the book are in every instance as nearly correct as careful scrutiny could render them.

Trusting that the utility of the book may be regarded as sufficient to compensate for whatever may be the shortcomings of its literary style, the author leaves its merits to be judged by the discriminating public.

J. W. LEONARD.

*St. Louis, June, 1887.*

# CONTENTS.

Progress in the Past .................. . 9
The Present and Future .......... 14
Trade and Commerce: The Exchanges .................. 20
Transportation Facilities .................. 26
Exports and Imports .......... .................. 33
Merchants and Traders .................. 34
Leading Manufactures .................. 43
Banking and Finance .................. 51
Real Estate and Building .................. 52
The Municipality .................. 54
Exposition and Music Hall .................. 58
The Public Parks .................. 61
The St Louis Press .................. 65
Representative Houses .................. 71
East St. Louis .................. 244
Index .................. 245

## PROMINENT ILLUSTRATIONS.

Representative Men.—Ex-Gov. E. O. Stanard; Gen. John W. Noble; Frank Gaiennie, President of the Merchants' Exchange; Geo. Taylor, President of the Cotton Exchange .................. 1
Blair and Benton Monuments, St. Louis Club House .................. 7
Entrance to Tower Grove Park .................. 15
Chamber of Commerce .................. 20
Bird's-eye View of the Bridge .................. 27
Odd Fellows' Building .................. 53
St. Louis Art Museum; Liederkranz Hall .................. 55
Exposition and Music Hall .................. 58
Scenes in Tower Grove Park .................. 59
The Republican Building .................. 63
New Business Blocks.—The Commercial Block and the Laclede Building .................. 210

BLAIR MONUMENT.

BENTON MONUMENT.

ST LOUIS CLUB HOUSE.

# PROGRESS IN THE PAST.

## ADVANCE OF ST. LOUIS FROM A FRENCH TRADING POST TO A GREAT METROPOLIS.

THERE is no lack of evidence of the fact that the spot upon which St. Louis now stands, and the country contiguous to it, formed the habitation, centuries ago, of races now extinct or represented only by a debased progeny, long since transplanted to other climes. The inquiry into the traits and characteristics of the Mound Builders and the measure of their advancement from barbarism, while interesting to the ethnologist or antiquarian, has no material bearing upon the history of St. Louis, which began, so far as the present has any important connection with it, one hundred and twenty-three years ago.

The record of the city since then has been one of steady and sturdy growth. Originally established as a fur trading post, and aspiring to nothing greater for nearly half a century, the town began to develop, after the American occupation, a position as an important distributive point, and to assume, as population and productiveness increased in the vicinity, the place for which she was so eminently fitted by her incomparable location and the physical advantages which had been so bountifully bestowed upon her by Nature. Later, by deliberate but sure and substantial advancement, the manufacturing interests of the city grew from small beginnings to gigantic proportions, and the city of to-day, one of the greatest, wealthiest and most prosperous on the continent, and the undisputed metropolis of the Mississippi Valley, is the result of the patient but sanguine industry, the sagacious improvement of opportunities, the energy and enterprise of her progressive citizens.

As an appropriate introduction to the presentation of the facts and statistics of the present, it will be proper to briefly sketch a few of the salient features of the city's early history, showing the progressive stages of the wonderful development of a primitive hamlet into a city of the first class.

### PIONEER DAYS.

DeSoto crossed the Mississippi in 1541; Marquette sailed down it to the mouth of the Arkansas River in 1673, and La Salle explored its entire length in 1682. All these events, with the inspiring narratives of those who participated in them, offered the stimulus and prepared the way for the settlement of the Mississippi Valley and, as a consequence, of St. Louis, its center and metropolis.

St. Louis had its origin in the adventurous and enterprising spirit of a business man, bound on a business errand. The firm of Maxent, Laclede & Co., of New Orleans, obtained in 1762, from the Governor General of Louisiana, a grant of exclusive control of the fur trade with the Missouri and other tribes of Indians inhabiting this region. The youngest member of the firm, Pierre Laclede Liguest, commonly called, after the French fashion, by his middle name of "Laclede," was sent to choose a site for a trading post in what was then known as Northern Louisiana. He selected and named St. Louis, returning to Fort de Chartres for the winter. In February, 1764, Laclede sent his young companion and clerk, Auguste Chouteau, ahead of him, and the latter arrived with his men on the 14th of February, and the following day the trees were felled for the first log huts which were the germs of a great city.

### SPANISH DOMINION.

Although the portion of Louisiana west of the Mississippi had been ceded to Spain by Louis XV two years before, the new colony had not heard of it, and it was not until 1770 that Spanish authority was asserted by the arrival, with a small body of Spanish troops, of Don Pedro Piernas, who took charge as governor. He was succeeded by Cruzat, who was followed in 1778 by Fernando de Leyba. During the latter's administration, on the day of the feast of Corpus Christi, May 25, 1780, the town was attacked by Indians. The war of the Revolution was then in progress, and the attack was charged to English influence. Governor Leyba was suspected, perhaps unjustly, of complicity in the affair, and was shortly afterward removed, his place being taken by Cruzat, who had been his predecessor. After Cruzat's second term, the governorship was successively held by Manuel Perez, Zenon Trudeau and Charles Dehault Delassus. In the latter part of 1803 the Territory of Louisiana was ceded back by Spain to France, but the same year Jefferson's purchase of Louisiana took place. Formal possession was taken by the United States Government, represented by Captain Amos Stoddard, March 10, 1804.

### TERRITORIAL TIMES.

From the time of the change of government the growth of the village was more rapid, and its industries became more numerous. In 1808 Joseph Charless issued the first newspaper, the *Missouri Gazette*, the name of which was afterward changed to the *Missouri Republican*. In the same year the first incorporation of the town occurred, the municipal government being vested in five trustees.

Up to 1811 the peltry and fur trade was almost the sole industry of the people. There are feeble records of small beginnings in other directions, but they were entirely confined to supplying the local needs. Laclede had established a small grist mill, a small brew house began to make porter and ale in 1810, and a few tradesmen supplied the simple wants of the town in other directions, but the fur trade was still the principal object of the existence of the place.

In 1811 the first brick house, a two-story structure at the corner of Main and Spruce streets, was built for the mercantile firm of Berthold & Chouteau. Soon after a small trade began to develop in lead and hemp. In 1812 the first shop for the manufacture of saddles, bridles and harness was opened; nails were manufactured in 1814, and in 1816 pottery was made. The same year saw the incorporation of the Bank of St. Louis. In 1817 there were twenty-one business houses in St. Louis and manufactures of copper and tin and of tobacco were begun. In 1819 the first foundry and first saw mill were started.

The first steamboat to reach St. Louis was the "Zebulon M. Pike," from Louisville, which landed at the foot of Market street August 2, 1817. In a year or two, however, the steamboat ceased to be an object of curiosity, and the principal commerce of the city found its outlet and inlet by the Mississippi and its tributaries. The first boat for New Orleans, the "Franklin," left in June, 1818, and the same year the first steamboat went up the Missouri River.

The population of the town grew from 1,100 in 1810 to 2,000 in 1815 and to 4,000 in 1820. The latter year saw the end of the struggle which had agitated the country in regard to the admission of Missouri to the sisterhood of States, the Missouri Compromise Bill being approved March 6, 1820, and the State Constitution being adopted July 19, following.

## ST. LOUIS AS A CITY.

In 1822 St. Louis became a city, a charter being granted by the Legislature and Dr. William Carr Lane being chosen as Mayor. From that time the pursuits of the citizens became more diversified. All kinds of tradesmen began to establish their shops, coal and lead sought a market in the city, and it had become the most important point in what was then "The Far West." A branch of the Bank of the United States was opened in 1829; meat packing for local consumption was inaugurated in 1832, and in 1833 a marine railway for repairing steamboats was put in operation. In 1835 the *Missouri Republican* was first issued as a daily, and in 1837 gas was in use, the steamboat "North St. Louis" was successfully launched, and fire-brick manufacture was commenced.

The panic of 1837 here, as elsewhere, prostrated business for a time. Some of the banks suspended payment, and the Bank of the State of Missouri passed a resolution "that the bank will in future receive from and pay only to individuals her own notes and specie on the notes of specie-paying banks." This resolution caused great financial stringency and severe loss to many. St. Louis, however, showed great recuperative power and was not so badly injured by the panic as were the majority of the cities of the country.

The growth of the city from its incorporation was steady and continuous. In 1839 a new charter was granted to the city, and at the next election Dr. Lane, who had been the first mayor of the city under its original charter from the State in 1822, was elected to a second term. In 1840, the population of the city was 16,469.

## INDUSTRIAL GROWTH.

A contemporary writer summarizes the manufacturing industries of the city in 1841 as follows: Two foundries; twelve stove, grate, tin and copper manufactories; twenty-seven blacksmiths and housesmiths; two white lead, red lead and litharge manufactories; one castor oil factory; twenty cabinet and chair factories; two establishments for making linseed oil; three factories for the manufacture of lead pipe; fifteen tobacco and cigar manufactories; eleven coopers; nine hatters; twelve saddle, harness and trunk manufactories; fifty-eight boot and shoe shops that manufactured; six grist mills; six breweries; a glass-cutting establishment; a brittania manufactory; a type foundry; an oil cloth factory; a sugar refinery; a chemical and fancy soap manufactory; a pottery and stoneware manufactory; an establishment for cutting and beautifying marble; two tanneries, and several establishments for the manufacture of plows and other agricultural implements.

In the next ten years the advance of the city in industrial matters was very great. A cotton factory was started in 1844, and in 1846 glass, woolen, soap, candle and starch manufactures had been introduced. About eighteen foundries were then in operation, and a number of flouring mills, machine shops, etc. The next year saw the completion of the first telegraph line connecting St. Louis with the Atlantic coast, and the first establishments for the manufacture of wood and willow ware and furniture; and in 1849 the first saw factory was started.

## YEARS OF DISASTER.

On the night of May 17, 1849, the greatest calamity that had yet befallen St. Louis occurred. A fire, believed to be incendiary, broke out on board the steamboat " White Cloud," lying between Wash and Cherry streets. The flames were quickly communicated to other boats, many of them the largest and finest engaged in the St. Louis trade, and some just arrived and others ready to depart with full loads. Freight was piled up on the levee, and this was soon in a blaze. A row of frame shanties between Vine and Locust streets were ignited, and the fire spread until fifteen blocks were destroyed in whole or in part. Twenty-three steamers were destroyed, and the aggregate loss of property was estimated as follows by the City Assessor: Stock and merchandise in store and on wharf, $5,000,000; steamboats and merchandise on board, $600,000; buildings burned, $502,290, a total of $6,102,-290. Thousands were thrown out of employment by the fire and the indirect damage could not be calculated.

The same year St. Louis suffered from the cholera epidemic to an alarming degree. It had escaped from the visitation of the same disease in 1832 with comparatively light mortality; but, in the period beginning in December, 1848, and continuing through 1849 and 1850, a total of 5,157 deaths from the disease occurred. The disease was at its height in the summer of 1849, the deaths in June of that year amounting to 1,259, and in July, to 1.804.

### A DECADE OF PROGRESS.

In spite of these calamities the population of the city increased steadily, and in 1850, the government census placed the population of the city at 56,803, and two years later a sheriff's census made it 94,819. Much of this increase was the result of the heavy German immigration which followed the revolution of 1848. In three years 34,218 Germans arrived in St. Louis, about two-thirds of whom remained here. This acquisition has been an important factor in the development of the industries of the city, and has proved a valuable element of its citizenship, contributing largely to its progress and stability.

The first ground for railway construction was broken July 4, 1851, and a train was run from St. Louis to Franklin, over the First Division of the Missouri Pacific, July 19, 1853. Prosperous years followed, and in 1860, with a population of 160,773, St. Louis was the largest, as well as the most prosperous of all the cities of the West.

### THE CIVIL WAR.

The outbreak of hostilities in 1861 was regarded as a severe blow to St. Louis. The South was her best customer, and the cutting off of communication with the lower Mississippi deprived her of a large and lucrative trade. Later on, however, the strategic advantages of the city's location served to open to its commerce other channels of activity. It became the supply point for the Union army operating in Missouri, Arkansas and Tennessee.

The times of the war were particularly exciting and full of dramatic incident in St. Louis. Her proximity to the scenes of conflict, and the fact that the city became the base of the operations of the armies of the Southwest made it the theatre of important events. Many of the citizens of St. Louis took part in the struggle, and acquitted themselves with distinction upon the field.

In 1863, the territory occupied by the Union army had widened, and the steamboats were given employment and many new ones built to supply the increased demand for their services. The wholesale merchants sought their supplies in New York, instead of in New Orleans, and manufacturers in most lines found an increased demand for their products. The suspension of trade relations with the South led to the extension of the business territory of St. Louis to the West, and when peace was restored, the population of the city had greatly increased, the market for her goods and products had been considerably enlarged, her steamboat interest had expanded, her manufacturing establishments had increased in number and become more diversified, and all the fields of industry and commerce had been widened.

### RECENT DEVELOPMENTS.

It is in the years of peace that have elapsed since the close of the war that St. Louis has made the most rapid strides. The city had at the time of the cessation of hostilities about 200,000 inhabitants. Its population has steadily ncreased until it is now about 500,000. The great and unprecedented development of the Mississippi Valley, with its wealth of agricultural, mineral and industrial resources, has given an impetus to the trade of the city, which has advanced, step by step, to its present proud and commanding position as a busy center of distribution and production.

The great Mississippi Bridge, begun in 1865, was completed in 1874, and is a monument to the skill and ingenuity of one of St. Louis' most distinguished citizens, the late Capt. J. B. Eads, whose work at the mouth of the Mississippi, in deepening the channel, has also proved of immense benefit to St. Louis by facilitating the means of direct export by that route. The great bridge gave the city a direct connection with the entire railway system of the East.

The means of communication with the entire country have been greatly improved in the past twenty years. The Pacific Coast has been brought into connection with the city by several rail routes. Railroads to Texas and Mexico have made them tributary, in a commercial sense, to St. Louis, and they now are an important part of her trade territory.

The greatest advancement has been in the direction of manufactures, which have become more varied. Old establishments have grown, and new ones have been successfully introduced, making the city a great productive as well as a distributive center.

A marked improvement is apparent in the character and value of the buildings and in the general appearance of the city. The new Chamber of Commerce, the Custom House, the Exposition Building and nearly all the fine business blocks and handsome residence structures which are the leading architectural features of the city have been erected within the last twenty years. Improvements in paving, in water supply, in sanitation and in all the elements which go to constitute a metropolitan city of this advanced age, have been introduced, and in all the conveniences and refinements of business and social intercourse the history of the recent past has been one of constant progress.

# THE PRESENT AND FUTURE.

## STATUS OF THE CITY OF TO-DAY—HER PROSPERITY, ADVANTAGES AND PROSPECTS.

VOLUMES full of incident and interesting narration might be written, portraying scenes and events of past history in which St. Louis has been concerned, but they would be foreign to the purpose of this work, which is to present the facts showing her standing in commerce and the productive industries.

The city in area embraces 61.37 square miles, or 39,276¼ acres. It is 17 miles in length from north to south and 6⅝ miles from the river to the western boundary; and it has 19.15 miles of river front. It is situated as to natural advantages more favorably than any interior city of the continent. The Missouri flows into the Mississippi twenty-one miles above the city, and the junction of the Illinois River with the Father of Waters is only twenty-four miles above St. Louis. The city is centrally located both as to the Mississippi Valley and the country at large, and has waterways to the north, south and west as well as to the sea. It is in the heart of the greatest food-producing region of the continent, and is central to a boundless wealth of minerals. Around it, within a radius of fifty miles, are vast supplies of coal, iron, granite, building stone, and earths adapted to the manufacture of glass. Productive lead mines are in the vicinity and seek St. Louis as a point of manufacture and distribution.

The greatness of St. Louis in the present, and her brilliant prospects for the future do not, however, depend upon any geographical accident. The favorable location of the city is a great advantage, of course, but the genius of the age is one that surmounts obstacles, and since the introduction of railways many places otherwise hopelessly beyond the possibility of becoming important, have been developed into thriving and populous municipalities.

### RESULTS OF ENTERPRISE.

The citizens of to-day have made St. Louis great by supplementing her natural advantages with all the aids of modern progress. As a railway center she has connections with all parts of the continent. The West, the Southwest, Mexico, and all the Southern States within the reach of the Mississippi sell their products and buy their supplies in her markets. In the Northwest she combats Chicago on its own ground with increasing success, and in many lines of industry has a lucrative trade with the country to the East.

The merchants and manufacturers of St. Louis have all the enterprise and push necessary to prosperity in this age of competition, and have made the city prominent in every important line of industry, and the leader in many. It is one of the greatest grain, flour and hay markets, and the largest horse and mule market on the continent,

ENTRANCE TO TOWER GROVE PARK.

the leading cotton market of all the interior cities and a most important center of distribution for wool, hides and every description of agricultural produce. It leads all American cities in the manufacture of tobacco, of saddlery, of fire clay products, of chemicals and in many other lines of productive industry. It is the largest in hardware dealings, and only second to New York in the drug and grocery trade; and it is not surpassed by any city of the West in the volume of its transactions in all important jobbing lines.

The trade of the city grows from year to year, each season showing a material gain in trade territory acquired, and an increase in the aggregate of business transacted. Steady progress is made in the acquisition of trade facilities and the inauguration of new enterprises of commercial importance.

### ELEMENTS OF SUCCESS.

In the past attempts have been made to arouse a national sentiment favorable to the removal of the federal capital from Washington to St. Louis. While the central position of the city gave great plausibility to the arguments of the enthusiastic and well-meaning gentlemen who were the advocates of the measure, it met with no great favor in the country at large, and has ceased to be seriously discussed.

No such expedient, however, is necessary to insure a steady increase in the already matchless prosperity of the city. Her merchants and manufacturers have long since learned that natural facilities are not all the prerequisites to the city's commercial and industrial progress; and they are waging a successful war with the business men of competitive cities, and combating for every inch of disputed trade territory. They are making a valiant fight against the many freight discriminations which have proven the greatest obstacle to their energetic and earnest endeavors to promote the city's commercial growth, and with the aid given them by the recent passage of the Interstate Commerce Bill by Congress will doubtless win the battle. The building of the Merchants' Bridge will remove the obstacle of excessive tolls across the Mississippi, and there is every prospect that, at no distant day, the city will be free from all unnatural checks imposed upon her commerce.

A material point that has been gained is the general acquiescence of the business community of St. Louis in the fact that physical and geographical advantages are only a factor in the commercial progress of a city, and that enterprise and push are necessary to utilize them for the benefit of business. There was a time when St. Louis was charged with an ultra-conservatism amounting to inertness in her business methods. Her business men are still conservative in the sense of refraining from rash, reckless or dubious speculations, and conducting their affairs upon a basis which comprehends the payment of dollar for dollar, owning what they pretend to own, and operating upon capital not encumbered by mortgages. But whatever justification there may have been in the past for a charge of slow methods against any portion of her business community, there is none now, and progressiveness and energy are conspicuous in the business life of the city.

### A PRODUCING CENTER.

The main point of advantage in the present situation, and the brightest promise for the future, is found in the fact that recent development has been most conspicuous in the line of manufactures. St. Louis is not only a mart—it is a vast and busy workshop. Each succeeding year records an increase in its mills, it forges and its factories. The products of industry are not only bought, sold and handled in the city—they are made here. Old manufacturing establishments are enlarging their facilities and increasing their output; new ones are springing up almost daily. For progress in this direction, this city has more abundant resources than any location in the West. Every description of raw material for any line of manufacture which is to be found in North America can be procured in abundance within easy reach of St. Louis.

As a center of production the advantages of the city as a market for the purchase of materials and the distribution of the manufactured product are emphasized and given assurance of stability; and more encouragement for the future of the city is to be found in the steady increase and the expanding diversification of her manufactures, than from any other fact.

A writer, about five years ago, after enumerating the States and Territories forming the commercial back country of St. Louis (to which Mexico has since been added,) said : " When it is considered, therefore, that this city has such surroundings as have been here described; that she is the very center of the most productive agricultural region of the earth; that she is in immediate proximity and of convenient access to an inexhaustible deposit of the purest iron ore in the world; that she is at the head of navigation from the South, and at the foot of navigation from the North; that she is sustained and impelled forward by the immense illimitable trade of the Father of Waters and his tributaries; that she has the material around her for building up the most extensive and profitable manufacturing establishments that the world has ever known; that all the necessaries of life, the cereal grains and pork particularly, are produced in all the region round-about in such profusion that living must always be cheap, and that, consequently, she can support her population, though it should increase to almost indefinite limits; when all these facts are considered, who can feel disposed to set boundaries to her future progress?

" It will be seen in view of the territory thus tributary to St. Louis that she draws from a greater variety of resources, from a greater extent of country, that she is the center of more mineral wealth, more agricultural resources, and that she has the opportunity and is fast endowing herself with the instrumentalities for obtaining a vaster internal commerce than any city of the Union. Her manufactures are varied in kind and character, and conducted with less expense than those of any of her sister cities. Her population has been steadily swelled by the influx of immigration; her wares and merchandise find their market in every hamlet of the country, and compete in Europe with those of older countries."

### PRESENT PROSPERITY.

In the past few years many gratifying signs of increased business and material gain in commercial importance have become apparent. Among these is the steady growth of the city as a market for cotton, a business almost wholly acquired in the past twenty years, the gross receipts of the staple having increased from 19,838 bales in the season of 1866-67 to 244.598 bales in 1875-76, and 472,471 in 1885-86, while the through shipments have quadrupled and the net receipts nearly doubled in the past ten years. Increased facilities for reaching the cotton fields and the great inducements offered by St. Louis factors have combined to bring about this gratifying result, and the city has advanced to a position far in advance of any other interior city as a market for cotton.

In another important direction St. Louis has recently shown great activity. This is as a mining center. It is natural and in accordance with the necessities of the situation that the vast mining regions of the West should center their operations in the market at some point nearer to the mines than New York; and this business is rapidly being transferred to St. Louis. The building of railways throughout the mining regions has rendered them accessible, and the vast improvements in machines and implements for mining and reduction works have greatly cheapened the cost of production, and many mines which a few years ago, on account of the low grade or refractory nature of their ores, were considered practically valueless are now productive and good paying properties. Much St. Louis capital is invested in the mines themselves, interesting the city in stocks of the mining companies; but it is not only in this direction that the commerce of the city is benefited by this enhanced development. In the manufacture and sale of improved machinery, tools and supplies for mining and reduction works, and in the general trade which is intimately connected with those industries, the city profits by the increased intimacy of the business relations of St. Louis with the mining camps of the West.

St. Louis has had to deal with injurious discriminations against her commerce in freight rates, but the prospects for the future are bright. Competing lines with equal terminal facilities will bring rates to a fair basis, and with an equal show in the race for trade, she need fear no competitor in commerce or manufacture.

# TRADE AND COMMERCE.

## ORGANIZATIONS FOR THE PROMOTION OF THE BUSINESS INTERESTS OF THE CITY.

ST. LOUIS, like all other important business centers, has a number of organizations which exert an influence for the welfare of the city in its trade relations.

Some are intended to regulate and benefit specified industries, while others, having a wider scope, are devoted to the interests of the entire mercantile community, to adding to the facilities for business in all directions, and to shaping the commercial policy of the city.

These organizations are numerous, and it is only possible here to mention the larger and more important of them. All, however, the smaller as well as the larger, are aids to the business progress and development of the city.

**The Merchants' Exchange.**—This important commercial organization, having a total membership of 3,312, exerts a powerful influence for the good of the business community. Daily market reports are received by wire not only from all the important trade points in the United States but also from those of Europe. Through its committees the exchange attends to the classification and inspection of grain, flour, provisions and other commodities; represents the mercantile community in matters relating to transportation, river improvement and the extension of trade; and exerts its influence for the procurement of such State and federal legislation as is found to be necessary in behalf of the business interests of the country at large and the city in particular.

The first exchange organized in St. Louis was the Chamber of Commerce, which was formed in 1836. In 1849 an organization known as the Merchants' Exchange was organized, and in the same year the Millers' Exchange was formed. Later the two were united and acted in conjunction with the Chamber of Commerce, occupying the same building.

A new exchange building was erected on Main street and formally opened in 1857. When the time of war came, dissensions which had been engendered by political excitement caused a rupture and led to the organization of "The Union Merchants' Exchange of St. Louis" in 1862, and in the same year the Chamber of Commerce went out of existence. In course of time the Union Exchange absorbed the members of the others, retaining its title until 1875, when the name was changed to that of "The Merchants' Exchange of St. Louis." In the preamble to the rules and by-laws then adopted the object of the association is declared to be "to advance the commercial character and promote the manufacturing interests of the city of St. Louis; to inculcate just and equitable principles of trade, establish and maintain uniformity in the commercial usages of the city, acquire, preserve, and disseminate valuable business information, and to avoid and adjust, as far as practicable, the controversies and misunderstandings which may arise between individuals engaged in trade."

The need of more commodious quarters for the exchange led to the organization, in 1871, of the St. Louis Chamber of Commerce Association, under the auspices of which the present spacious and elegant structure fronting on Third, Pine and Chestnut streets, was built and formally opened, with imposing ceremonies, on 21st of December, 1875. Mr. Rufus J. Lackland has been President of the Chamber of Commerce Association from its organization; the Vice-Presidents are Messrs. Charles Green and Adolphus Meier and Mr. George H. Morgan is Secretary and Treasurer.

The Merchants' Exchange has exerted great influence in behalf of the trade of the city. It has been managed by merchants of the highest order and standing, and it justly occupies a prominent position among the commercial bodies of the country.

In the compilation and dissemination of valuable trade information and statistics, the Secretary of the Exchange, George H. Morgan, has shown a rare discrimination, thoroughness and ability which fully justify his retention in his honorable position for the twenty-two years during which he has discharged the duties of the post. The statistics used in this work are for the most part compiled from his complete and exhaustive statement of the trade and commerce of St. Louis.

The following are the officers of the Exchange for the year 1887: President, Frank Gaiennie; Vice-Presidents, Louis Fusz and Thomas Booth; Directors 1887, Henry C. Haarstick, Charles W. Isaacs. E. P. Bronson, Peter Nicholson, M. M. McKeen; Directors 1887-8, S. W. Cobb, P. P. Connor, Wm. T. Anderson, A. Nedderhut and S. R. Francis; Secretary and Treasurer, Geo. H. Morgan; Caller, Joseph P. Carr; Doorkeeper, James P. Newell.

**The Cotton Exchange.**—Another organization which has exerted an important influence in extending the trade and commerce of St. Louis is the Cotton Exchange. This body, which was originally known as the Cotton Association, was organized at a meeting held on October 17, 1873, the name, however, being changed to its present style of the "St. Louis Cotton Exchange," on its incorporation in the following year. At the first regular meeting of the directory, held in 1875, the present Secretary, C. W. Simmons, was elected to the position which he has filled ever since with marked efficiency, securing the respect and commendation of all who have had dealings with him.

Since the organization of this important body, and as a direct result of its earnest and intelligent efforts, the cotton trade of the city has developed from comparative insignificance to primary importance. The Exchange occupied rented premises until May 4, 1882, when with appropriate ceremony the present handsome and imposing structure was formally opened and occupied. This building, which is located at the southwest corner of Main and Walnut streets, was erected by the Cotton Exchange Building Company, is five stories in height, and fronts 85 feet on Main street and 135 feet on Walnut street.

As a result of the efforts of the Exchange and its members, the cotton trade of St. Louis has been brought to its present gratifying position of the largest in volume of any interior city in the country. In 1870-71 the receipts of cotton in this city were only 20,270 bales. In the season of 1885-86 the receipts amounted to 472,471 bales, while the present season gives promise of a still larger aggregate.

The membership of the Cotton Exchange embraces nearly all the cotton factors and dealers of the city. The organization has been managed from its inception upon enlightened and intelligent methods, by officers having the interests of the market at heart. The present executive of the Exchange, President George Taylor, is a very large handler of the staple, thoroughly informed as to the details of the trade, and possessed of ripe judgment and great administrative ability. The statistical labors of Secretary Simmons are an important aid to the carrying out of the purposes of the organization. The figures in regard to the cotton trade of the city, found elsewhere in this work, are compiled from his report. The officers of the Exchange for 1887 are: President, George Taylor; Vice-President, George B. Emmons; Secretary and Treasurer, C. W. Simmons; Directors: John M. Gilkeson, Jerome Hill, Thomas H. West, R. F. Phillips, John A. Senter, L. Frank and C. S. Freeborn.

Intimately connected with the Cotton Exchange, and acting in harmony with it, is the St. Louis Wool and Fur Exchange, of which August Taussig is President and Julius Rashky, Secretary and Treasurer. This Association was established in 1880 to regulate the methods of transactions in wool and furs in this city, and to promote harmony and good fellowship among the members of the trade. The organization is not incorporated, but those belonging to it hold their meetings in the Cotton Exchange, of which they are all members.

**Live Stock Exchange.**—The St. Louis Live Stock Exchange, which has its offices at the National Stock Yards, was organized October 20, 1885, and has a membership of about one hundred. The object of the organization is the promotion and development of the live stock industry in all its branches, the promulgation and enforcement of correct and uniform principles in all transactions pertaining to the buying and selling of live stock, and the protection of the interests involved.

The organization of the Exchange has proved a great benefit to the live stock trade of this market, and indirectly to the feeders and shippers of stock who patronize St. Louis. It has reformed a great many local abuses in the care and manner of handling stock, and by the influence which naturally followed a consolidation of the trade in this Association, has procured a great many advantages for the country shipper. It has also, by a strict enforcement of its rules, eliminated from the business everyone and everything of a suspicious or disreputable character, and placed the trade on a sounder and more reliable basis than ever before. Since its organization, nearly all the principal live stock markets have formed similar associations, all of which, as far as can be learned, have been equally successful in benefitting the live stock interests of the country.

The present officers of the Exchange are: President, W. L. Cassidy; Vice-President, C. M. Keys; Secretary and Treasurer, W. J. Broderick; Directors, Samuel Scaling, W. D. Little, E. J. Senseney, T. J. Daniel, C. C. Daly, R. P. Lindsay, J. G. Cash, C. C. Brown and R. H. Mann.

**The Mechanics' Exchange.**—Several attempts, more or less successful, had been made in the direction of the organization of an exchange for mechanics and artisans before 1856, in which year was formed an organization known as "The Mechanics' and Manufacturers' Exchange," of which the present "Mechanics' Exchange," incorporated September 20, 1875, is the development and outgrowth.

The objects of the association are declared by its constitution to be "the promotion of mechanical and industrial interests in the city of St. Louis, to inculcate just and equitable principles of trade, to establish and maintain uniformity in the commercial usages of said city, to acquire, preserve and disseminate valuable business information, and also to adjust, as far as practicable, controversies and misunderstandings arising between individuals engaged in the various industrial pursuits."

The membership of the Exchange, which is large, includes many of the leading builders, mechanics, dealers in builders' supplies, etc., of the city, and the organization has been of great benefit and enjoys a steady prosperity. The office and rooms of the Exchange are located at No. 9 North Seventh street, and its executive officers for the present year are: President, James H. Keefe; First Vice-President, Mark Hudson; Second Vice-President, Thos. F. Hayden; Treasurer, Wm. S. Stamps; Secretary, Richard Walsh; Directors, Daniel Evans, James Duross, F. C. P. Tiedemann, P. J. Woodlock, P. Nagle, Thos. J. Kelly, Henry E. Roach, Thos. H. Rich, Jos. F. Nuelle, J. H. Daues, P. Kirby and W. B. Philibert.

**The Associated Wholesale Grocers.**—This corporation, comprising thirty members engaged in the wholesale grocery business, was organized in 1884 for the purpose, as recited in the preamble to its constitution, of promoting good fellowship among themselves, and for mutual benefit in their business affairs. These purposes have been subserved and the association has been useful in advancing the interests of the trade. The officers for the present year are: President, Peter Nicholson; Vice-President, Jacob Furth; Secretary and Treasurer, W. E. Schweppe; Directors, Peter Nicholson, Jacob Furth, W. E. Schweppe, J. R. Holmes, E. G. Scudder, F. H. Beims and L. J. Peck.

**St. Louis Real Estate and Stock Exchange.**—The premises occupied by this association are at Nos. 14 and 16 North Seventh street. It was organized in 1877 and incorporated in 1881. The object of the organization is to provide facilities for agents to meet and discuss matters pertaining to real estate; to provide and keep on bulletin boards, for public inspection, a record of houses, rooms and stores for rent and property for sale, and to furnish the housekeeper, real estate buyer and public generally with information regarding realty in the city. The Exchange furnishes to its members an institution where public and private sales of real estate, stocks, and other property can be conducted.

The Exchange is one of the most prosperous business organizations in the city, and has a large and steadily increasing membership, comprising many of the most prominent dealers in realty. The present officers of the Exchange are: President, James S. Farrar; Vice-President, Leon L. Hull; Secretary and Treasurer, these gentlemen, with the following four others, composing the Board of Directors: J. T. Percy, T. F. Farrelly, John G. Priest and Marcus A. Wolff.

**Merchants' and Manufacturers' Association.**—This important organization, which was formed some three years ago, has exerted a wide influence in behalf of the general interests of the business of the city, and to promote the welfare of the commercial and manufacturing community in all legitimate ways. A special subject in which it takes an active and abiding interest is the correction of discriminations by railroads in rates to the injury of the commerce of the city, exerting a potent influence toward securing from the State and National Legislatures such corrective action as may secure to the city a just and equalized tariff on all common carrier lines.

The officers of the Association are: President, John R. Holmes; First Vice-President, Wm. M. Senter; Second Vice-President, V. O. Saunders; Third Vice-President, E. F. Williams; Secretary, J. J. Wertheimer; Assistant Secretary, John G. Shelton. The office of the Association is at 518 Washington avenue.

**The St. Louis Furniture Exchange.**—This Association, organized in 1879, has forty members connected with the furniture trade and kindred occupations. The objects of the organization are stated to be to "secure and promulgate among its members the best information obtainable regarding the standing, habits and reliability of the various dealers to whom the goods of its members are likely to be sold, and thus not only protect the interest of its members, but also advance the interest of well-meaning and prudent dealers. It also aims to secure just and equitable rates of transportation and insurance." Jacob Kaiser is President; A. H. Dreyer, Secretary, and J. G. Koppelman, Treasurer of this organization.

**St. Louis Furniture Manufacturers' Association.**—This organization was formed in 1886, about the time that extensive strikes had been inaugurated, in order that those engaged in the manufacture of furniture and chairs might meet and discuss matters for their mutual benefit and protection, the Furniture Exchange being largely composed of gentlemen belonging to other trades. The Association has twenty-one members, and Alb. Borumueller is President; Daniel Aude, Treasurer, and J. W. Tremayne, Secretary.

**Implement and Vehicle Manufacturers' Association.**—This organization is devoted to the interest of the manufacturing industries mentioned in its corporate title, and serves a useful purpose in facilitating the discussion and adjustment of matters of mutual concern among those engaged in these lines. The officers of the Association are: A. Mansur, President; D. W. Haydock and Wm. Koenig, Vice-Presidents; T. W. Haydock, Treasurer, and G. K. Oyler, Secretary.

## OTHER BUSINESS ORGANIZATIONS.

Although there have been and now are a number of other organizations, all useful in their way, the foregoing comprise the principal ones now in active existence, having for their object the extension or protection of trade and manufacture.

**Board of Fire Underwriters.**—The membership of this useful organization embraces three local joint stock insurance companies, fifty-eight other domestic companies and twenty-four United States branches of foreign companies. The officers of the Board are: President, James A. Waterworth; Vice-President, John R. Triplett; Secretary, C. T. Aubin; Assistant Secretary, A. C. Acton, and Treasurer, James E. Cowan.

**Board of Underwriters (Marine.)**—The companies represented by this Board are the Marine Insurance Company and the Citizens' Insurance Company, of St. Louis; Boatman's Fire and Marine, Pittsburgh; St. Paul Fire and Marine, Minnesota; Enterprise Fire and Marine, Cincinnati; Louisville Underwriters, Kentucky; Phenix Fire and Marine, Brooklyn; Boston Marine, Massachusetts; Insurance Company of North America, Philadelphia; Commercial Fire and Marine, San Francisco; Western Assurance Company, Toronto, Canada; and the Greenwich Insurance Company, of New York.

The present officers of the Board are: President, Howard A. Blossom; Vice-President, John P. Harrison; Secretary and Adjuster, James Barnard; Inspector of Hulls, Silas Adkins. The Board, which was incorporated in 1860 by an act of the legislature, maintains a well disciplined Salvage Corps, and has performed valuable service in the protection of property and the adjustment of marine losses.

# TRANSPORTATION FACILITIES.

## RAILROAD SYSTEMS AND WATER ROUTES ACCELERATING THE CITY'S COMMERCE.

IN facilities for transportation by rail and river, St. Louis is the most advantageously situated city on the continent. Fifteen railroads enter this city, which, with their connections give its commerce easy access to every railroad point in all directions. Converging from St. Louis as a center, vast trunk lines stretch out in every direction; and other railroads recognize the central importance of the city by their anxiety to secure terminals here. The river affords great facilities for and greater possibilities of aid to the commerce of the city, is a convenient outlet for a direct export trade, and must remain a permanent source of profitable and expanding business.

## THE RAILWAY LINES.

Each year marks a distinct gain in the shipping facilities of St. Louis by rail routes. By their aid even Mexico has been made tributary to her commerce, and in every direction these vast arms of trade stretch out and radiate from the city, which is so situated on the track of traffic between the East and the West, that it must ever maintain its central point of vantage. Every enterprise in the direction of new East and West lines must necessarily consider St. Louis as an important factor in its plans, and the future gives certain promise of an increase in railroad facilities from year to year. Every railroad built in the West must tap one or more of the trunk lines centering at St. Louis, and add to the trade facilities of the city.

**The Missouri Pacific.**—This road, with its leased and operated lines, includes more than six thousand miles of railway located in Missouri, Arkansas, Texas, Indian Territory, Kansas and Nebraska; and connecting St. Louis with those States and Colorado, Old and New Mexico, and all the States of the West. Included under the Missouri Pacific management are the Missouri Pacific proper, the Missouri, Kansas and Texas, and the St. Louis, Iron Mountain and Southern Railroads, with a number of branches and leased lines connected with each of these. It forms a part of the Gould system, and is one of the most prosperous and important routes in the country.

**The Wabash, St. Louis and Pacific.**—This system, which has passed into the control of the Courts, has recently been divided, the lines between St. Louis and Kansas City, Council Bluffs and Des Moines, west of the Mississippi, and the lines between Detroit and Logansport, and Indianapolis and Michigan City, east of the Mississippi, being still operated by the Wabash, St. Louis and Pacific Railway Company in connection with the Gould syndicate, with the headquarters at St.

BIRD'S-EYE VIEW OF THE BRIDGE.

Louis. The other portion of the road, east of the Mississippi, is operated separately, with Gen. McNulta as Receiver, and extends from East St. Louis to Chicago, 286 miles, and to Toledo, 436 miles. The Wabash, St. Louis and Pacific operates about 900 miles west of the Mississippi.

**The St. Louis and San Francisco.**—One of the most important routes to the business of the city is the St. Louis and San Francisco Railway, which also operates the Central Division of the Atlantic and Pacific Railway, completed to Sapulpa, I. T. The company has a line via Fort Smith, Ark., to Paris, Tex., which only lacks a few miles of completion, at this writing, and will be ready for business, through to Paris, in June of the present year. The company also has lines to Halstead and Bluff City, Kansas, and a number of smaller branches. The Texas line will be pushed from Paris to a connection with the Houston and Texas Central, which will give St. Louis a route able to compete with those now controlling the bulk of the Texas business. The country traversed by this line is of the greatest importance to the commerce of the city, and the St. Louis and San Francisco does an immense business in the transportation of cotton, grain and the other valuable products, vegetable and mineral, of Texas, Arkansas, Kansas and Indian Territory. It is ably and aggressively managed, and its interests being identical with those of St. Louis, has maintained liberal relations with the merchants and manufacturers of the city.

**The Chicago and Alton.**—This road makes an air line connection between St. Louis and Chicago, and has a Missouri Division from St. Louis to Kansas City. It forms one of the most important items in the shipping facilities, is under enlightened and efficient management, and has one of the finest tracks and most complete equipments, both for freight and passenger traffic, in the country.

**The Vandalia Line.**—This is the name by which is known the St. Louis, Vandalia, Terre Haute and Indianapolis Railroad, and which is the connection of the Pennsylvania Railroad system. It is the shortest route from this city to Pittsburgh, Philadelphia and New York, and also a favorite route for Cincinnati via the Cincinnati, Indianapolis, St. Louis and Chicago Railway; and, in addition, has a line to Chicago, via the Illinois Central. It is over this line that the fast mail from the East arrives.

**The Ohio and Mississippi.**—This road was the first to reach the Mississippi River from the East, having been completed from Cincinnati to St. Louis in 1857. It has branches to Shawneetown and Springfield, Ill., and Louisville, Ky. In connection with the Baltimore and Ohio Railroad, it forms a direct line to Washington and Baltimore, and by its Erie connection to New York. It is a valuable aid to the commerce of St. Louis in freight traffic with Southern Illinois and Indiana.

**The Indianapolis and St. Louis.**—This line, which extends from St. Louis to Cleveland, Ohio, is under the control of the Columbus, Cincinnati and Indianapolis Railroad, known as the "Bee Line." Its eastern connections are with the Lake Shore and New York Central systems.

**The Chicago, Burlington and Quincy.**—This extensive system comprises a mileage in Missouri, Iowa, Nebraska, Minnesota and Illinois of over 5,000. It forms a valuable outlet for the trade of St. Louis, west to Denver and north as far as St. Paul. The system embraces the Chicago, Burlington and Quincy proper; the Hannibal and St. Joseph; Chicago, Burlington and Northern; Burlington and Missouri River, and a number of leased and operated lines. It reaches St. Louis on the east by the Indianapolis and St. Louis track, and on the west by the St. Louis, Keokuk and Northwestern.

**The St. Louis, Keokuk and Northwestern.**—This road is a part of the Chicago, Burlington and Quincy system, and extends from Keokuk, Iowa, to St. Peters, Mo., where it connects with the St. Louis, Wabash and Pacific, over the tracks of which road it reaches St. Louis. During 1888 it is contemplated to complete the road from St. Peters to St. Louis, giving the Chicago, Burlington and Quincy system a complete and independent route into the city.

**The Cairo Short Line.**—This is the best known name of the line extending from East St. Louis southward to Du Quoin, Ill., with a branch thence east to Eldorado. The corporate name of the company is the St. Louis, Alton and Terre Haute Railroad Company, the main line of which, from St. Louis to Terre Haute, Ind., is leased to the Indianapolis and St. Louis Railroad Company. The former company has recently acquired the St. Louis Southern Railroad, formerly known as the St. Louis Coal Road, branching from the Cairo Short Line at Pinckneyville, Ill., and crossing the Illinois Central at Carbondale. This connection is a very important one, as the St. Louis Southern reaches the Big Muddy and Cartersville coal fields. The Cairo Short Line is the Illinois Central connection for St. Louis, and part of the Great Jackson Route for the South.

**The Mobile and Ohio.**—This line extends from St. Louis to Mobile, Ala. Its main line is from Mobile to Cairo, Ill., and connection is made with St. Louis over the St. Louis and Cairo, which was changed last year from a narrow gauge to a standard gauge road and leased by the Mobile and Ohio. It is an important outlet for the trade of St. Louis with the Southeast.

**The Louisville and Nashville.**—This system is the greatest in the section southeast of the Mississippi River, reaching from St. Louis, via Evansville, Nashville and Montgomery to Mobile and New Orleans, and having leased lines and connections covering all the Southern States east of the Mississippi. It affords St. Louis an additional route to the Atlantic seaboard through its connection, at Lexington, Ky., with the Chesapeake and Ohio Railroad, to Newport News.

**The St. Louis, Arkansas and Texas.**—This road, which was originally a narrow gauge, known as the Texas and St. Louis, or "Cotton Belt Route," was changed to standard gauge during the past year. At present its business in and out of St. Louis is done under traffic agreements with the Mobile and Ohio, between St. Louis and Como, the Iron Mountain between St. Louis and Belmont Crossing, and the Cairo Short Line and Illinois Central via Du Quoin, Ill. The company, however, is preparing to secure an independent entrance to St. Louis by extending its road from Maldon, Mo., to this city. Southward the line extends to Mount Pleasant, Tex., from which point construction is in progress to Sherman, Tex. Other projected extensions of this road are from Magnolia, Ark., to Shreveport, La., and from Cotton Center, Ark., to Little Rock. This line is a valuable adjunct to the cotton trade of St. Louis, and important for the facilities it offers for the shipment of every description of merchandise from this city to a large portion of its most important trade territory.

**The Toledo, Kansas City and St. Louis.**—This road, forming an important part of the transportation systems centering in St. Louis, is a direct line from this city to Toledo, Ohio, 450 miles, and reaches many portions of Illinois, Indiana and Ohio by the shortest routes.

**The Illinois and St. Louis.**—This road extends from the east side of the river to Belleville, 15 miles, and has branches, including the Venice and Carondelet Belt Line, which are 28 miles in length. Notwithstanding its restricted mileage, it is of great importance to St. Louis, as it taps the principal coal fields in the territory in Illinois adjacent to St. Louis. This road, with its connections, is operated by the Wiggins Ferry Company, and does an immense business.

## OTHER RAILROAD ENTERPRISES.

With the exception of a few local and suburban roads, and the bridge and tunnel line, the roads above enumerated comprise the railways now completed, and through which the vast trade and traffic of St. Louis finds its outlet and inlet by rail routes to every point of the compass. Through them every part of the continent is brought into close connection with its most central city. Other definite railroad enterprises of interest to St. Louis are in a tangible shape, which affords immediate promise of an important augmentation of the railroad facilities of the city. Among these is the St. Louis, Kansas City and Colorado Railroad, now extending from the western limits of the city, and rapidly being constructed to Union. It is intended to push this road far into Kansas, with a branch to Kansas City. Consolidated with this road is the Central Railroad of Missouri. which has concluded to abandon the "Alton" route and build direct. This system will be of great benefit to St. Louis, opening to its market easy access from the valley of the Missouri and points on the Central Railroad of Missouri.

The St. Louis and Edwards County Railroad will tap an important coal region in Illinois, and form a most useful addition to the means of obtaining a cheap coal supply.

The Atchison, Topeka and Santa Fe will soon, it is expected, extend its lines to this city, forming another important link between St. Louis, the Southwest, and Mexico. The St. Louis and Central Illinois, running from Springfield, Ill., to Grafton, Ill., contemplates an extension to Alton, Ill., from which point it will connect with St. Louis, either by traffic arrangements with existing lines, or by an independent route of its own.

**St. Louis Merchants' Bridge Company.**—A sketch of the railroad facilities and prospects of St. Louis would be incomplete without a reference to this company, which was incorporated in May, 1886, under the auspices of the Merchants' Exchange, and secured from Congress, at its recent session, a franchise for a high bridge. Back of the company are ample resources, and the construction of the new bridge at the earliest practicable date is assured, when the necessary terminal facilities are obtained. This bridge will be a great boon to the interest of St. Louis, affording relief from excessive bridge tolls and an easy means for the entrance into the city of any railroad desiring to reach St. Louis from any direction.

This city has suffered in the past from injurious discriminations in freight rates in favor of competing cities. It is believed that the Interstate Commerce Bill, passed at the last session of Congress, will operate favorably to the interests of St. Louis, and tend to remove the arbitrary barriers interposed in the path of her commercial progress.

## RIVER TRANSPORTATION.

In convenient situation as to inland water routes, St. Louis is more favorably located than any other city on the continent, being practically at the junction of the Missouri and Illinois rivers with the Mississippi. The commerce of the upper river terminates at St. Louis, and that of the lower river originates here. Even prior to the advent of railroad building in the West the city became important because of its facilities for transportation by the rivers.

The work done under the direction of the late Capt. J. B. Eads at the mouth of the Mississippi gave a new impetus to river traffic by making feasible a connection with ocean navigation, and opening up the grain movement via New Orleans and the jetties, giving an outlet by the way of the Gulf of Mexico for the exporting of the products of the great West. For the complete accomplishment of this great work upon a scale commensurate with the necessities of the situation, further improvement of the river channel by the Government is needed; but when it is done it will reduce the cost of transportation of the surplus product to foreign markets to a minimum, and add to the business importance of St. Louis, which will be the natural point of shipment for this immense exported surplus.

The rivers serve a most useful purpose in behalf of the commerce of the city by restricting discriminations in freight rates between St. Louis and all those points easily reached by water, and rail rates must, so far as competing points are concerned, be kept within reasonable bounds by the competition of steamboats and barges.

The rapid and constant increase of railroad lines in every direction took away from the river lines the monopoly of the carrying business they formerly enjoyed, but the more bulky freights, and all those which will not justify the extra expense of rail transportation still seek the water routes.

The Missouri River trade has most felt the effect of the competition of the railroads, and the only regular traffic up that river from St. Louis, is that carried on by seven steamboats and three tow boats, none of which go higher than Kansas City.

A prosperous trade is still carried on to points on the Upper Mississippi from St. Louis to St. Paul by packet lines, raft boats and tow boats. Besides this traffic, the rafting of lumber down the river from the Upper Mississippi above Minneapolis, the Minnesota, St. Croix, Chippewa, Black and Wisconsin Rivers, is of immense value to the Mississippi Valley. During 1886 the amount received at St. Louis reached 140,000,000 feet of lumber, nearly 7,000,000 feet of logs and 86,500,000 pieces of shingles, laths and pickets.

On the Lower Mississippi shipments are increasing as a result of the enhanced facilities for through grain trade. There is also a considerable traffic with Ohio River points and a steadily increasing one with the Cumberland and Tennessee Rivers.

The volume of the river business of St. Louis cannot be better exhibited than by the following table, showing the amount of freight in tons received at and shipped from St. Louis in 1886 by the rivers:

| | RECEIVED. | SHIPPED. |
|---|---|---|
| Upper Mississippi River | 140,880 | 46,190 |
| Lower Mississippi River | 173,610 | 431,945 |
| Illinois River | 88,010 | 5,175 |
| Missouri River | 32,620 | 24,255 |
| Ohio River | 116,885 | 26,060 |
| Cumberland and Tennessee Rivers | 18,200 | 25,075 |
| Red and Ouachita Rivers | | 3,195 |
| Total tons 1886 | 570,205 | 561,895 |
| " " 1885 | 479,065 | 534,175 |
| " " 1884 | 520,350 | 514,910 |

The extent of the direct export trade of this city via New Orleans and the jetties is shown in the fact that last year the shipment of bulk grain by river to New Orleans for export amounted to 8,834,924 bushels.

The principal steamboat and barge lines running out of St. Louis are: The New Orleans "Anchor" Line, from St. Louis to Vicksburg, New Orleans and intermediate points; the St. Louis and Mississippi Valley Transportation Company, steamers and barges, also between this city and New Orleans; the "Diamond Jo" packets between St. Louis and St. Paul; the St. Louis and St. Paul Packet Company;. the St. Louis and Kansas City "Electric" Packet Company; the St. Louis and Clarksville Packet Company; the Naples Packet Company, to Illinois River points; Gray's Iron Line and Brown's Line, to Pittsburgh and Wheeling, on the Ohio River; and the St. Louis and Tennessee River Packet Company, and the Evansville,. Paducah and Tennessee Packet Company, on the Cumberland and Tennessee rivers.

## EXPORTS AND IMPORTS.

As before stated, the bulk grain exported from St. Louis via New Orleans in 1886 amounted to 8,834,924 bushels. In addition to this the exports to foreign countries by Atlantic seaports were very large. It is not possible to give a fair idea of the amount in figures, as much is shipped to seaboard cities on local bills of lading; but even the amount sent abroad on through bills of lading makes an important showing for the commerce of St. Louis. Included in the commodities thus shipped were: Corn, 105,410 bushels; flour, 173,840 barrels; cotton, 146,467 bales; tobacco, 1,952 hhds.; meats, 3,153,872 lbs.; tallow, 912,600 lbs.; lard, 23,803 lbs.; walnut lumber, 1.008 tons, bran, 542 tons; grease, 44,800 lbs.; beer 670 casks; dried apples, 430,976 lbs.; bone black, 200 tons; live hogs, 9,010; sundries, 1.900,369 lbs.

The direct importations of the city from foreign countries in 1886 were worth, in foreign values, $3,315,187, upon which duties were paid amounting to $1,517,905.73, these amounts being exclusive of packages remaining in bond. Leading among the imports were articles with foreign values as follows: Chemicals, $105,705; china and earthenware, $131,547; glass and glassware, $124,259; hops, $142,803; manufactures of iron and steel, $554,910; of cotton, $184,118; of linen, $90,297; of wool, $165,165; sugar, $711,766; tobacco and cigars, $118,354; wines and spirits, $101,737; cutlery, $86,986; fire arms, $68,765. In addition to these articles the direct importations included ale and beer, anvils, art works, books and printed matter, bricks and tiles, barley, breadstuffs, brushes, cements, lime and plaster, cork, dairy and meat products, druggists' sundries and fancy goods, files, fish, glue, gunpowder, percussion caps, hair and manufactures of hair, jewelers' merchandise, manufactures of leather, india rubber, metals, paper, silks and wood, musical instruments, nuts and fruits, oils, paints, colors, philosophical instruments, rice, seeds, spices, varnishes, vegetables, etc.

Of course the figures given above do not convey anything like an approximate idea of the amount of imported goods brought to St. Louis. Many of the large importing houses in this city have branches in eastern seaports, where the duties are paid, and the articles so received do not figure in the returns of the Custom House in this city. So with exports, much of the traffic of St. Louis is carried on through agents in Atlantic ports, from which goods are shipped to Europe and elsewhere.

# MERCHANTS AND TRADERS.

## BUSINESS TRANSACTED BY THE WHOLESALE DEALERS AND JOBBERS OF ST. LOUIS.

IT IS NOT possible to distinguish, with anything like accuracy, between the transactions of merchants and manufacturers. In the majority of cases manufacturers sell their own product to a greater or less extent, and have traveling men representing them on the road, selling direct to the wholesale or retail trade. Many business houses originally started for the purpose of doing a wholesaling or jobbing trade have found it to their interest to add a manufacturing department in some of the lines they handle.

In treating of the various industries of the city, the several lines which are connected with the business of the city as a point of distribution will be first noticed.

## THE GRAIN TRADE.

The central position of St. Louis in the most productive section of the country gives it great importance as a center of distribution for grain and other products of agriculture, and causes its transactions in the various cereals to reach an enormous volume. All the necessary facilities for a great grain market are to be found in the city. With an elevator capacity increased to 13,000,000 bushels in bulk and about half a million in sacks, and the Mississippi river and a vast railroad system as feeders, the only drawback to a steady and continuous annual increase in the transactions of the city as a center of receipt and distribution for grain has been the discriminations in freight rates from the West in favor of other markets. An important step in the correction of these discriminations has been taken by the passage of the Interstate Commerce Law. The building of the new Merchants' Bridge, by admitting competing lines to equal terminal facilities with those already in the city will also, in all probability, prove a great benefit in this direction.

In regard to the grain trade for the year 1886, the report of the Merchants' Exchange makes a favorable showing, with the single exception of corn, in which there was a decrease in receipts. The total receipts of grain for the year aggregated 39,100,923 bushels, and the shipments 17,595,754 bushels. Including flour reduced to wheat, the receipts equaled 42,918,799 bushels, and the shipments 27,690,878 bushels.

The year 1886 was marked by an interruption to traffic in the spring season by strikes, first on the Missouri Pacific system and afterward on the roads terminating in East St. Louis, and trade in all lines was considerably affected, and both receipts and shipments of all commodities were doubtless decreased by the partial suspension of traffic.

**Wheat.**—The wheat crop of 1886 was very large, and the business of the St. Louis market in that cereal increased in a ratio corresponding with the increase in the crop over that of 1885, the receipts of wheat for the past year being 12,309,364 bushels, against 10,690,677 bushels received in the preceding year. The States from which St. Louis draws her principal supplies of wheat are Arkansas, Tennessee, Kentucky, Illinois, Missouri, Kansas and Nebraska, and the increase in receipts was general from all sources, but especially from Tennessee and Kentucky. The shipments of the year were 2,429,462 bushels. They were less to Eastern seaboard points, but greater by 700,000 bushels for export via New Orleans. The demand from city mills took 8,133,055 bushels, in the manufacture of 1,807,956 barrels of flour.

**Corn.**—The corn crop of 1886 fell off considerably from that of the preceding year, and the decrease in receipts at St. Louis was in still greater proportion, the discrimination in freight rates in favor of competing cities diverting much of the supply to other points. The removal of this obstacle will doubtless regain to St. Louis its leading position as a corn market. The receipts for the year were 16,387,071 bushels, of which 11,859,405 bushels came from west of the Mississippi. The shipments for the year were 11,848,995 bushels, of which 7,501,730 bushels went to New Orleans by the barge line for export, while 103,550 bushels went to Europe direct via Atlantic cities, 1,693,160 bushels went east for a market, 1,614,979 went south by rail for consumption, 875,649 bushels went south by river to local points, 48,315 bushels went north by rail and river, and 11,612 bushels went west by rail and the Missouri river. A large amount was required for the manufacture of the 415,420 barrels of corn meal, and 70,869 barrels of hominy and grits turned out by the city mills in 1886.

**Oats and Rye.**—The oat crop of 1886 was not so large as in the previous year, but there was an increase of 43,386 bushels in the receipts at St. Louis, which amounted to 7,426,915 bushels, received about equally from the west, north and east. The shipments amounted to 2,764,922 bushels, most of which went to the Southern States for consumption.

The receipts of rye for the year were 726,798 bushels, an increase of 90,158 bushels over the preceding year, the bulk of receipts being from the West. The shipments, which were mostly to the East and local points for consumption, amounted to 636,640 bushels, an increase of 299,622 bushels over the shipments for 1885.

**Barley.**—The receipts of barley for the year were 2,529,731 bushels, nearly all of which was taken by maltsters and brewers in this city for the manufacture of beer and ale. Most of the receipts were from Iowa, Wisconsin, Minnesota and Canada.

At the close of the year the stocks of grain in store in public elevators amounted in bushels to: Wheat, 4,411,912; corn, 1,254,818; barley, 100,982; oats, 578,220; rye, 23,973.

**Cotton.**—St. Louis is the largest interior cotton market in the Union, its accessibility by both rail and river, and the superior facilities it possesses for handling the staple being recognized as the main factors in securing for it its prominence in the cotton trade. The cotton year ends August 31, and the figures for the season of 1885-86 showed a gratifying increase in receipts over those for the preceding year. The gross receipts for the year were 472,471 bales, and the gross shipments 464,156 bales, an increase in receipts of 181,517 bales, and in shipments of 173,299 bales, as shown by the report of the Cotton Exchange. The present season gives promise of an equally prosperous cotton business, the gross receipts for the seven months from September 1, 1886 to April 1, 1887, aggregating 404,120 bales, and the shipments during the same period 380,336 bales.

The sources of supply for cotton coming to St. Louis are Arkansas and Texas, from which States 90 per cent. of the cotton shipped to this market is received, the remainder coming from Mississippi, Tennessee, Missouri, Indian Territory, Kentucky and Louisiana, in the order named.

In the direction of shipments there has been a steady annual increase in the amount shipped eastward by rail for consumption, while the amount for export shows a corresponding decrease. The stock of cotton on hand at the close of the year was 9,924 bales, a larger stock than was ever before carried over into a new cotton year.

The annual report of the Cotton Exchange for 1885-86 sums up the advantages which this market holds out to the planter and merchant of the South for the consignment of his cotton as follows: "The certainty of liberal and fair dealing by the factors, the competition of buyers from all the manufacturing centers, favorable freight rates to and from all points, freedom from expense at the warehouses, and their superior facilities for handling the fleecy staple, its protection from fire and the elements, and from pilferers; and last, but not least, the planter and merchant can here lay in his supplies of flour, meats and groceries, clothing, agricultural implements, bagging and ties, mules, and all other necessary articles at a far greater advantage than at any other cotton market."

**Wool.**—In setting forth the condition of the wool market in St. Louis, no clearer statement can be made than that embraced in the report of the Secretary of the Cotton Exchange, which says: "In the Spring of 1885, efforts were made by the Cotton Exchange and parties interested largely in the wool business for the development of St. Louis as a wool market, and a committee was appointed to invite the National Wool Growers' Association to hold their next annual convention here, and the effort was successful and the convention was held here May 27th and 28th, and was presided over by Hon. Columbus Delano of Ohio, the President of the association, and attended by a large number of gentlemen interested in that great industry."

"Stimulated by the success of this meeting, the Association of Missouri Wool Growers appointed St. Louis as the place to hold their annual meeting, and in connection with the National Sheep Shearing Association held a very successful meeting from April 7th to 10th, (1886), which was an occasion of great interest, and gave universal satisfaction to the large number of the friends of the wool interest who attended. These meetings have had the effect intended, and St. Louis to-day is attracting the attention of the trade from all parts of the country, and has become the leading wool market of the West."

The total receipts of wool for 1886 were 18,563,614 pounds, and the shipments 17,825,630. This was somewhat less than the business for the previous year, in which the wool clip was much larger, but with that exception is largely in excess of the annual aggregate of transactions in wool for the past eight years.

**Hides, Furs, Etc.**—When Laclede first located St. Louis, he chose it as the best place in which to carry on a trade in furs. This was the earliest industry of the city, and still remains an important one. The receipts of peltries and furs in 1886 amounted to 18,889 bundles, which is a larger number than any recorded in the Merchants' Exchange report for any previous year.

The hide business of St. Louis is of great importance, the volume of annual transactions in this line being very large. In 1886 the receipts amounted to 19,978,698 pounds, received from Texas, Colorado, New Mexico, Kansas, Arkansas and other States tributary to the St. Louis hide market. This amount was augmented by the slaughtering of cattle here to such an extent that, in addition to the large amount consumed by local tanneries, etc., there were shipped from this city, principally eastward, a total of 23,407,160 pounds.

St. Louis steadily maintains her lead as a hide market, being favorably situated within easy reach of the centers of production, and having every facility for handling, shipping and warehousing. In addition to hides, St. Louis, during 1886, received 49,894 rolls of leather, most of which went into consumption by local factories of boots and shoes, saddlery, etc.

## LIVE STOCK.

Several causes combined to make the receipts of live stock at the Union and National stock yards somewhat less in 1886 than in the preceding year, among which may be named the strike upon the railroads of the Southwest, which shut off the supply for nearly three months, and the severe drouth that prevailed so generally throughout the range country, which had a serious effect in materially reducing the runs of grass cattle.

**Cattle.**—The total receipts of cattle for 1886 amounted to 377,550 head, a falling off of 8,770 head as compared with the receipts of the preceding year. The shipments were 212,958 head, or 20,201 less than in 1885, this decrease, however, being largely due to the increase in the dressed beef industry at the National yards, which, while it reduced the comparative shipments of cattle on the hoof, assisted materially in keeping up values and making a ready market for cattle. On the whole the falling off in receipts was not serious, and was the result of exceptional causes not affecting the future of St. Louis as a live stock market.

**Hogs.**—The receipt of hogs for 1886 amounted to 1,264,471. This was a falling off of 191,064 head from the figures for the preceding year, but was largely due to a material shortage in the crop. The railroad strikes also diverted many thousands of hogs from this market. The shipments were 520,362, a decrease of 269,125 head from 1885, in which the shipments reached the largest figure since 1881. But while the shipments of hogs were decreased the demand from packers was heavier, and the provision trade was very prosperous, as will be seen by reference to the article on the subject elsewhere, and the summer packing season of 1886 consumed 125,996 more hogs than that of the previous year.

**Sheep.**—The receipts of sheep for the year amounted to 328,985 head, the falling off of 33,873 head from the figures for 1885 being due to the abandonment of the business of wool growing by many owing to the low prices that it obtained in that year. Prices for sheep averaged somewhat higher in 1886, and the demand of the dressed beef works for good, fat stock had a tendency to keep them up and make an active market. The shipments for the year amounted to 202,728 head.

**Horses and Mules.**—St. Louis is the leading horse and mule market in America, and the trade shows a steady increase. During 1886 a total of 42,032 head were received by rail and river, but this fails to exhibit the total volume of this important trade, as vast numbers of horses and mules are raised within driving distance of the city, and are brought to market on the hoof. The government purchases of mules are made in this city, and buyers from all points make their headquarters here. The shipments to all points last year reached an aggregate of 39,793 head, an increase of 4,188 head over the figures for 1885. The situation o St. Louis is admirably adapted to the continuance and increase of its foremost position as a market for horses and mules. It is located in the center of the region of production of the largest and best animals in the country, and its rail and river routes give the city an unapproachable advantage as a point for their receipt, sale and distribution.

**Produce.**—As a market for the sale and shipment of all products of the soil St. Louis is not surpassed by any city of the continent, and in all the leading articles coming under this head its receipts and shipments are very large. In dried fruits the receipts in sacks and barrels for 1886 were 99,567, and the shipments 114,079, an increase over the previous year of 3,505 sacks and barrels in receipts, and in shipments of 57,572 sacks and barrels. This is an industry for which St. Louis has unrivaled facilities and in which she is steadily gaining an increased trade.

In potatoes the ascertained receipts in bushels amounted to 812,950, and the shipments to 1,780,544 bushels. The large discrepancy in the comparative amount of receipts and shipments is explained by the fact that fully one-half of the potatoes received in the market come by wagons, and that no account is taken of produce received in that way. The principal market for potatoes is found in the Southern States.

The receipts of onions in 1886 in sacks and barrels amounted to 33,732, and of bushels in bulk to 134,500. The shipments were 73,602 sacks and barrels.

In green apples the receipts were 240,934 barrels, and the shipments 191,299 barrels. Large quantities of apples are brought in by wagons, of which no data can be obtained. Large amounts are dried in the city and shipped in that form. The shipments are mostly Southward.

In dairy products the receipts of butter for the year 1886 were 8,605,230 lbs., and the shipments 2,557,238 lbs. Of cheese 128,882 boxes were received, and 99,883 boxes were shipped.

Of white beans 45,420 sacks and barrels were received, an increase of 8,242 over the previous year, and 56,239 sacks and barrels were shipped. Of hay the receipts were 85,078 tons, and the shipments 30,006 tons. Of bran 110,763 sacks and 366 cars in bulk were received, and 767,856 sacks and 335 cars were shipped. Of buckwheat the receipts were 1,274 sacks, and of buckwheat flour 2,906 barrels. Hops were received to the amount of 8,834 bales; cranberries 5,728 barrels; oranges and lemons 103,812 boxes. Besides these articles a number of others amounting to a considerable trade, but of which no account is kept, were received and shipped in large quantities, such as feathers, peanuts, ginseng and other roots, etc.

**Leaf Tobacco.**—St. Louis being the largest of all cities in the manufacture of tobacco, as will be seen by reference to the statistics given elsewhere in this work, her market for leaf tobacco is a very important one, about 75 per cent. of the receipts going into manufacture here. Thus, in 1886 the receipts were 32,113 hhds. and the shipments 8,135 hhds. Of the amount received 15,715 hhds. were consigned to manufacturers direct, in addition to which 8,997 hhds. were delivered to manufacturers from warehouses. The receipt for 1886 were larger than in any previous year, being 632 hhds. more than in 1885, and larger by several thousands than in any year before that.

**Coal and Coke.**—There is no surer way of gauging the growth of a city's population and manufactures, than by comparison of its receipts of coal. Tested by this standard, the showing made by St. Louis is very gratifying. Thus, the coal received in the city, including anthracite reduced to bushels, amounted in 1881 to 44,720,175 bushels; in 1882, 47,750,375 bushels; in 1883, 50,687,225 bushels; in 1884, 52,349,600 bushels; in 1885, 53,387,064 bushels, and in 1886 the receipts were 61,258,525 bushels, included in which were 70,000 tons of anthracite. In addition to this there were 5,463,950 bushels of coke received during the year. Thus it will be seen that there has been a steady gain, year by year, in the receipts of coal, indicating an increase of population and an expansion of productive activity in the line of manufactures.

**Lumber.**—The situation of St. Louis is peculiarly adapted to fill, in an advantageous manner, the requisites of a prosperous lumber market. From the great white pine producing regions of Wisconsin and Minnesota, the upper Mississippi acts as a feeder to the St. Louis market, while from the south the lower Mississippi and its tributaries perform a similar service in supplying the diversified timber products of the extensive forests in that section. The railroad lines centering at St. Louis from timber points in every direction, also bring a vast amount of lumber, and the aggregate receipts by all these various routes foot up an enormous total.

The railroad strikes in the early part of 1886 had a depressing effect on the lumber trade, but later in the year it recuperated, and the demands for building and railroad construction became active. Stocks were greatly reduced by a prolonged low water season and by a fire in one of the largest yards which destroyed about forty million feet in one day. The total receipts of white pine by the upper Mississippi river were 124,154,170 feet, and of cottonwood lumber by the same route, 3,925,500 feet, and by the lower Mississippi the receipts of poplar were 8,420,462 feet, and of other lumber 2,788,422 feet, including yellow pine, ash, oak, cyprus, gum, hickory, sycamore and walnut lumber, part of the latter coming from the Missouri River. The total amount of lumber of all kinds received by rail was 391,-908,000 feet, swelling the total of receipts of lumber from all sources to 531,196,554 feet. To this must be added logs, received by river in rafts, the superficial measurement of which was 6,609,930 feet, equivalent to about 26,000,000 feet of board measure. In other lumber products the receipts were: Shingles, 55,136,000; lath, 37,254,000; pickets, 862,330.

### OTHER PRODUCTS.

In many other lines besides those above enumerated St. Louis is a leading market of receipt and distribution. In lead, one of the prominent articles in which St. Louis is a heavy handler, the receipts for 1886 exceeded those of any previous year except 1882, aggregating 1,138,854 pigs. The shipments were 561,544 pigs, the remainder being used in the manufacture of white lead, etc., of which mention is made elsewhere in this work.

In salt the receipts were 51,992 sacks, 400,358 barrels and 247,160 bushels in bulk and the shipments 11,658 sacks, 396,437 barrels, and 56,924 bushels in bulk, of which 14,948 sacks, 327,701 barrels and 45,360 bushels came from Michigan direct and the remainder from various points.

This city is a prominent market for flax seed, the receipts for 1886 being 5,578 sacks and 353,651 bushels and the shipments 3,165 sacks and 50,163 bushels. The difference between the receipts and shipments represents an important industry, the remainder being consumed in the mills. In cotton seed the receipts were 7,697 tons and of cotton seed meal 883 tons, and 6,179 tons of cotton seed meal were shipped. In grass and other seeds the receipts were 85,892 sacks.

Other dealings in important articles were 81,612 packages of fish received; nails, 908,817 kegs received, 583,628 kegs shipped; oils, 139,814 barrels and 5,058 tanks received. In ores 164,199 tons of iron were received and 263,574 shipped; 32,425 tons of zinc arrived and the shipments amounted to 12,050 tons as well as 595,481 slabs of zinc and spelter. Other receipts were rosin, 33,742 barrels; railroad iron 193,069 tons; staves 5,095 cars and 460,000 pieces; tar and pitch 5,096 barrels; turpentine 18,912 barrels; tin 110,977 boxes.

## THE JOBBING TRADES.

The importance of St. Louis as a central source of supply for the entire Mississippi Valley and the great West is shown in an immense volume of transactions in all jobbing lines. The jobbers of St. Louis are prospering and steadily adding to their trade territory and the volume of their transactions. A brief review of the more important branches of mercantile industry carried on in this city will doubtless prove interesting.

**Groceries.**—A recent writer estimates the volume of the sales of groceries in 1886 from this city at $75,000,000, an increase of $15,000,000 over the sales of 1885. Part of this increase was due to the general advance in prices which occurred in the latter part of the year. The early part of the year was marked by the occurrence of the great railroad strikes, which had a discouraging effect upon business in all lines, and in none more than in the grocery trade. In the last part of the year, however, a general revival was noticed in all lines of goods handled, which has been continued through the Winter and Spring, with every prospect that the present year will be the most prosperous for grocers in the history of the city.

There has been a notable extension of the trade territory of the city in the last few years, and Texas, Illinois, Missouri, Arkansas, Mississippi, Kansas, Nebraska, Colorado, Indian Territory, New Mexico and Arizona all deal largely with the grocers of St. Louis. The trade to Mexico is steadily increasing, and is especially heavy in canned goods of every description, and Iowa and Minnesota to the Northwest, and Georgia and Alabama to the Southeast also add to the volume of the business of the city.

As a coffee market St. Louis does a much larger business than any other interior city of the country, and probably of the world, the receipts of last year amounting to 240,685 bags, and the shipments to 205,135 bags. In sugar 32,887 hhds., 242,075 bbls., 792 boxes and 105,580 bags were received, and 771 hhds., 330,349 bbls., and 2,463 bags were shipped. In molasses the receipts were 27,720 bbls. and 3,281 kegs, and the shipments were 24,141 bbls. and 18,810 kegs. In rice 72,079 sacks and barrels were received and 41,571 packages were shipped. Of tea 43,518 packages were received during the year. In the year's shipments were 75,417 boxes of candles and 345,303 boxes of soap.

Intimately connected with the grocery trade of the city are many establishments engaged in canning, the manufacture of vinegar, baking powders, soap and household preparations, which do a large and steadily increasing business, as well as a great many commission dealers who handle lines coming under the head of groceries.

There are about thirty large exclusively wholesale grocery houses in the city, none working on a less capital than $100,000 and many possessing several times that amount, besides a number of thrifty smaller concerns and dealers in special lines such as provisions, flour, etc. This market offers to purchasers of groceries advantages not equaled by any other in the West, in the large number of houses and the heavy and diversified stocks carried, the amount invested in the business in St. Louis being larger than in any other western city.

**Dry Goods.**—The vast territory covered by the jobbing house of St. Louis in the line of dry goods makes the demand upon its resources very heavy, but it is met by an investment of $15,000,000 in the business and annual sales amounting to about five times that figure. The past year, which began unpropitiously in this as in other lines, developed into the best ever known in the history of the trade in St. Louis.

This activity has been more pronounced during the Spring season of the present year, which promises even better results than its predecessor.

The wholesalers of St. Louis have of late years made an aggressive fight for trade territory with competing cities with the result of a rapid extension of their business. In addition to the large trade from the West and Southwest, the South is yearly becoming a better customer for goods in this line, the rapid improvement going on in the Southern States tending to an increase in purchases.

The dry goods trade of St. Louis is steadily growing and country merchants who formerly bought their stocks in New York have abandoned that market, as the goods can be purchased to equal advantage in this city and a great saving in time and freight expenses is made. The houses engaged in the business in this city have ample capital and keep fully up with the times in the selection and assortment of their stocks, carrying full lines of all the latest novelties in fabrics as well as in staple goods.

In notions, millinery and other lines intimately related to the dry goods trade the city has a vast business and many houses with large resources are engaged in these branches of trade. In the number of houses engaged in the dry goods and kindred trades St Louis is ahead of all western cities, and all are doing a prosperous business.

**Hats and Caps.**—In this department of trade St. Louis leads all western cities. Over $1,000,000 in capital is invested in the business and the annual transactions will aggregate in the neighborhood of $4,000,000. Larger and better stocks are carried in this city than in any other in the western country, and the aggressive methods of the merchants engaged in the line have secured for it the custom of an extensive business territory, and a trade that is expanding in volume with each successive year.

**Hardware.**—The business done by the hardware trade of St. Louis is very large, over $3,000,000 being invested, while the volume of annual transactions in the line is not less than $15,000,000. In the Southwestern States this city has almost a monopoly of the hardware business, its central location and facilities for distribution throughout this region giving it an advantage with which other markets are unable to compete. The establishments engaged in this line in St. Louis are for the most part large and well stocked. The hardware merchants of the city are very aggressive in their efforts to increase the trade of St. Louis in this branch of commercial enterprise, and have invaded territory claimed by competing centers and made it their own until this city now sells hardware north to the Lakes, west to the Pacific and south to the Gulf on both sides of the Mississippi, the Republic of Mexico also being a customer of growing importance.

This vast trade, won by St. Louis merchants in the face of strong competition, the city has every facility for retaining. A very large quantity of the goods pertaining to the line are manufactured here, the raw material being abundant in the immediate vicinity. The year 1886 marked a material increase in the hardware trade of the city, the volume of transactions for the year being fully 20 per cent. greater than in 1885. This prosperous state of things has been continued through the Winter and Spring seasons, and the prospects are favorable for the present year to prove better than any ever before experienced in this market. Intimately connected with this trade are a number of manufactures of iron, steel, etc., which are mentioned in a special manner elsewhere in this work.

**Provisions and Packing.**—St. Louis occupies an important position as a packer and dealer in hog products, ranking third among the important packing points of the country. The total shipments for 1886 amounted to 174,907,899 lbs., which includes barrels of pork reduced to pounds, hams, meats and lard. The packing of the season of 1885-6 was 369,130 hogs of average gross weight of 257.21 lbs. The summer packing of 1886 was 370,000 hogs averaging 245 lbs. gross, the largest packing, with one exception, ever done in the summer season in this city. In detail the receipts of hog products for the year were pork, 6,667 bbls.; hams, 4,564,875 lbs.; meats, 62,288,459 lbs.; lard, 11,924,131 lbs., and the shipments 46,816 bbls. pork; 35,748,854 lbs. hams; 81,553,875 lbs. meats, and 48,710,130 lbs. lard.

### TRADE IN OTHER LINES.

Many other important branches of industry are so intimately connected with manufacturing, that they will be treated separately. In addition to these the city has an important trade in all lines of the necessities of life and the luxuries of advanced civilization. In glass, chinaware and crockery, this is the leading market of the West, a very large amount of capital being invested in the business, and the annual trade in the line reaching an enormous volume.

The present trade outlook is bright, all lines reporting an increased demand and a tendency toward better prices than have prevailed for a number of years past. In cutlery, musical instruments, watches, clocks, jewelry, books, paper and stationery, oils, wall papers, sewing machines. art goods, nuts and fruits, broom corn, leather and shoe findings, mathematical and surgical instruments, feed, varnishes, paints and colors, rubber goods. fire proof safes. fish, game and poultry, vegetables of all kinds, flowers and seeds, and all the various commodities pertaining to the stock of a metropolitan market, a heavy trade is done. In short, St. Louis offers to the country merchant inducements for trade which are not excelled, in any department, by any city on the continent, and in many lines positively superior to any market in the land.

# LEADING MANUFACTURES.

## FACTS AND FIGURES IN REGARD TO THE PRODUCTIVE INDUSTRIES OF THE CITY.

GREAT as is the importance of the business of buying and selling the products of the soil, and handling the commodities received from localities far and near, it is in productive industry that the prosperity and greatness of a city receives its main support and encouragement. To shape the raw material into the manufactured product; to add to the sum of existing wealth by creative energy, and to supply the varied wants of humanity by the combined forces of labor and capital is to give to a city a permanency and stability which can be achieved in no other way.

St. Louis is admirably situated for the prosecution of all departments of manufacture. In close proximity to a boundless store of all the useful metals, with vast supplies of coal almost at her gates, with a limitless profusion of food products near at hand for the sustenance of any possible increase of population, and with a market, comprising the entire Mississippi Valley and the Great West, prepared to tax even these wonderful facilities to their utmost limit, every circumstance coincides to promote enterprise and encourage industry in every branch of productive activity.

In the brief historical review introducing this work, it has been shown how St. Louis early turned her attention to manufactures. The initial enterprises in that direction were necessarily crude, and confined to the endeavor to supply the limited wants of a sparse and frugal population. But, with a development the rapidity of which eclipses all previous history, a market has grown up around her, the frontier has been wiped out and a few primitive settlements have been changed to a vast and mighty empire, throbbing with activity and animated by sturdy industry.

Nature had selected St. Louis as the site for the workshop from which this immense accretion of humanity should draw the tools for its labor, the supplies for its myriad wants, and the means of luxury which its advanced state of civilization demanded. This selection was approved by the judgment and utilized by the energy of those who in part foresaw the great possibilities of the future, and step by step the creative industries of the city have flourished and expanded in unison with the growth of the Mississippi Valley and the West, and far beyond the expectations of even the most hopeful of those who saw the beginning of this great development.

It would not be possible, within the limits of a single volume, to state in detail all the many facts in connection with the manufacturing operations conducted in the city. A brief review of the condition of the leading industries in this year of 1887 is here given, and much further information will be found in the concluding chapter of this work, where special reference is made to leading corporations and firms engaged in the varied manufactures carried on in this city.

**Iron and Steel.**—The vast deposits of iron found in various portions of Missouri have been utilized in the creation of a great industry requiring immense capital and giving employment to an army of workmen. There are more establishments engaged in the various departments of iron and steel manufacture in St. Louis than in any other western city, and these industries exert a wide influence in enhancing the business interests of the city.

The depression in all the iron industries of the country in 1884 and 1885, which was generally ascribed to overproduction, has passed away, and in the latter part of 1886 the demand became more active and prices advanced. This reaction has continued during the Spring season, and the outlook is encouraging for a steady demand at moderately good prices for some time to come. A renewed impetus to railroad building and an increased demand for rolling stock has had much to do with producing this renewal of activity both in iron for car, bridge and track construction, and in steel rails.

It is not only in iron for railroad construction purposes that this healthy reaction is felt, but it extends to all branches of iron manufacture. There are many shops in this city engaged in the manufacture of boilers, engines, pumping and mining machinery, agricultural machines and implements, building fronts, etc., and in all there is a notable increase in the demand over the past few years. There is no truer index of the times than iron manufactures, which are among the first to feel depression or to indicate a general enhancement of the business welfare. In all these lines of industry, St. Louis has the advantage of location, both as to the means of procurement of the raw material and the efficient distribution of the manufactured product. The capital invested in them cannot be even approximately estimated. It amounts up to many millions and represents a large and most important trade to the city.

Outside of the heavier branches of this great industry, St. Louis is a heavy producer in many other lines of iron manufacture. The city is notably in the lead of all western cities in the manufacture of stoves, in which a capital of considerably over $2,000,000 is invested with an annual output approximating 200,000 stoves and ranges, while in stove furnishings, stamped goods, tinware, etc., this city also maintains an advanced position.

In the manufacture of circular saws, St. Louis is not excelled, if equalled, by any other city in the Union, and circular and gang saws of St. Louis make are to be found in all the leading saw mills of the country. Plumbers and gas fitters' goods are also manufactured in this city in great quantities, some of the largest concerns in this department of industry being located here, and their market extending over the entire West and South.

In addition to the large amount of agricultural machinery and implements made here, all of the leading makers of such articles are represented in the city, the convenient location of which as related to the most productive agricultural region of the country makes it the best point for the distribution and sale of this character of goods. The same is true of wire fencing, which is manufactured here in large quantities, as well as being a leading market for the sale of goods manufactured elsewhere.

A partial idea of the magnitude of the iron interests of the city both in the sale of ore and the large proportions of the manufacturing industries may be given by the statement that although the stocks on hand in the beginning of 1886 were very large, the receipts of iron and steel during the year were 81,947 tons, while of pig iron 154,719 tons were received and 50,771 tons were shipped, and of iron ore the receipts were 164,199 tons and the shipments 263,574 tons.

## THE INDUSTRIES OF ST. LOUIS. 45

**Flour, Meal, Etc.**—This is an industry of great proportions and vast importance to St. Louis, which is only exceeded by Minneapolis in output. There are sixteen mills in the city, with a capacity of 12,200 barrels of flour each twenty-four hours. In addition to the city mills there are eleven mills adjacent to the city, owned and operated by St. Louis millers and with a daily capacity of about 7,000 barrels. The season of 1886 was, however, a very discouraging one to the millers of this city. They labored under the great drawback of being the especial victims of most injurious freight discriminations in favor of competing markets, especially Minneapolis, by which they were practically deprived of the Eastern and European markets. This, combined with a decreased demand from the South, reduced receipts, and caused a falling off of 33,000 barrels in amount manufactured by the city mills from the preceding year which was only partly offset by an increase of 11,000 barrels over the products of 1885 by the suburban mills.

The amount manufactured by the city mills last year, one of the largest being shut down for four months, was 1,807,956 barrels while the output of the suburban mills was 798,380 barrels, making a total of 2,606,336 barrels, against a total output of 2,628,941 barrels manufactured in 1885. The amount of flour handled by millers and dealers in 1886 was 848,417 barrels received, 1,807,956 barrels manufactured in the city mills and 542,010 sold and shipped direct from country mills, a total of 3,198,383 barrels. The direction of the shipments, which amounted to a total of 2,243,361 barrels, was in barrels or their equivalent in sacks 173,840 direct for export, 214,408 to Eastern points by rail and water, to Southern points 1,249,242 by rail and 577,920 by water, 10,599 to Western points, and 17,352 to Northern points. The demand from the city mills took 8,133,055 bushels of wheat in the manufacturing of the year.

In regard to the freight discriminations before referred to, the millers justly claim that they can only work their mills to full capacity on as cheap freights per mile as others pay. As a correction to this check upon the flour industry of St. Louis, it is confidently believed that the Inter-State Commerce Bill will prove adequate to the situation and that under a proper enforcement of its provisions the milling trade of St. Louis will be greatly aided and put upon a footing of equitable freight rates.

In the manufacture of corn meal, etc., St. Louis also does a large business. Three mills manufactured a total of 415,420 barrels of corn meal in 1886; two mills made 70,869 barrels of hominy and grits, and two manufactured 6,696 barrels of rye flour. The shipments for the year were 466,791 barrels, nearly all the product going to the South. The shipments of hominy and grits were 61,150 barrels. In addition to these manufactures there must be accounted as belonging to this department of trade the receipt of 110,763 sacks and 366 cars in bulk of bran and shipstuffs, and the shipment of 767,856 sacks and 335 cars.

**Tobacco.**—The receipts and shipments of leaf tobacco have been given on a former page of this work. In the manufacture of tobacco, St. Louis is the leading city of the world, and is steadily gaining in the volume of her production in this important industry. In 1886, the amount manufactured was 32,448,936 pounds, not including snuff, against 28,517,401 pounds in 1885. The Merchants' Exchange report for 1886, says in regard to this industry: "The production has steadily increased during the past ten years, and there is no indication of a diminution in the yearly increase in the future. In 1886, the output of St. Louis was one-sixth of the entire product of the nine hundred and ninety-six factories of the United States, and of the value of $11,500,000. It exceeded the amount manufactured by the four other tobacco cities of the West combined, viz: Chicago, Cincinnati, Louisville and Detroit, and leaving out Virginia and New Jersey, was greater than all the remainder of the United States. There are now seventeen establishments in St. Louis, some of which are as extensive as any in the country, and whose brands are well known and command a large portion of the trade in all parts of the land."

The great growth of the manufacture of tobacco in this city is shown by the totals for the past five years, being 17,121,199 pounds in 1882; 23,780,508 in 1883; 22,581.762 in 1884; 28,475,323 in 1885, and 32,448,936 in 1886. The product in 1886 paid to the government in taxes the large sum. of $2,484,204.41. In detail the manufacture for the past year was: plug chewing tobacco, 27,916,600 pounds; fine cut, 240,567 pounds; smoking tobacco, 4,291,679 pounds; to which must be added the manufacture of 46,919 pounds of snuff, paying a tax of $3,589.80.

The manufacture of cigars is also extensively carried on in St. Louis, the product last year amounting to a total of 43,586,000 cigars, and paying a tax of $130,-759.09.

The present season promises well for the tobacco trade of the city and will probably show a gratifying increase in the amount of business, several factories having in contemplation an increase in their capacity.

**Saddlery, Harness, Etc.**—In this branch of industry St. Louis is far in advance of any city in the country, both in number of establishments engaged in the business, the amount of capital invested, number of hands employed and the amount and value of the product. About $2,000,000 is invested in this business and the products amount to about twice that sum annually. The advantageous location of the city for distribution to the West and South, from whence the greatest demand comes for this class of goods, has been utilized by the manufacturers of saddlery and harness who have made St. Louis the greatest in this line of production.

There is no line for which St. Louis is more surely headquarters than in this. The business of the past year showed a decided and gratifying increase, while that of the spring of the present year gives indication that 1887 will prove the most prosperous of any known to the trade. A recent writer, speaking upon this subject says: "The establishment of jobbing houses in small cities in the West and South, which have grown wonderfully in population during the past few years, has not hurt the St. Louis trade scarcely at all, for the reason that all the saddle trees and fine harness still have to be procured in this city. Formerly St. Louis sent East for bits, buckles, spurs and other saddlery hardware, but for the past four or five years all hardware necessary for saddlery has been manufactured in this city, and nearly the entire West and Southwest are supplied from here. Another promising tributary of trade for St. Louis is Mexico. For the past couple of years several prominent firms here have been almost supplying the Mexican capital in this line, and are very hopeful of capturing the entire trade of that country. One of the most notable facts is, that during the past year the saddle trade has been falling off, and the harness trade increasing in proportion. The reason given for this change is that so many cheap buggies are now being made that horseback riding is losing its former popularity."

There are ninety-two harness and saddlery manufactories in St. Louis, and included in the number are the largest in the country. Some of the leading firms are noted elsewhere in this work.

**Boots and Shoes.**—About $5,000,000 is invested in the jobbing and manufacturing of boots and shoes in St. Louis, the annual sales footing up about $12,000,000. The receipts of boots and shoes during 1886 amounted to 302,445 cases, and during the year ten large local houses were engaged in manufacturing. In the superior grades of ladies' and gentlemen's footwear this city is rapidly taking the lead as a manufacturing center. The trade in boots and shoes from this city has steadily increased for several years past, both in the extent of the territory covered and the volume of sales. The jobbers have pushed their trade into the Northwest where a few years ago they did but little business. In Indiana, Illinois, Iowa, Kansas, Nebraska, Minnesota and Dakota, the St. Louis merchants practically control the field, especially in the first five named.

Many of the larger houses here rank in capital and resources with the most extensive in the land, and in the volume of trade in this line St. Louis ranks third among American cities. The spring trade of 1887 has opened auspiciously, and the manufacturers and jobbers predict that the year will prove the best in the history of the trade. St. Louis is increasing her business in this important line of industry more rapidly than any competing city, and the outlook for its future is very bright.

**Building Materials.**—In all the vast and varied industries pertaining to building in all its branches, St. Louis exhibits a great and ever growing activity. The development of the Southwest is accompanied by a constantly increasing demand for homes, public buildings and business structures. As time advances the buildings which served to fill the frugal wants of pioneer communities are discarded to make room for more imposing edifices, and the lofty iron and stone fronts of to-day mark the advance from the log huts which sufficed to gratify the limited ambitions of the sturdy, but unassuming first settlers.

In all the advantages of natural location and means of supply of the raw material, St. Louis occupies a peculiarly fortunate position. In the supply of lumber of all kinds the forests of the South and of the Northwest alike find easy means to place their wealth at the disposal of the St. Louis artisan. Granite is found in various localities contiguous to St. Louis in inexhaustible supply and in quality the Missouri product, in gray and red, is noted far and near for its durability, its great beauty, its susceptibility to the finest polish, and its unexcelled adaptability to all the diversified uses to which this stone can be put, whether for architectural or ornamental purposes, or for the making of roads and bridges.

In the manufacture of brick the materials are here in limitless supply and of quality far better than any in the West, so much so that St. Louis brick invades the territory of competing cities and is in heavy demand wherever quality enters into the calculation. In this industry a large amount of capital is invested and thousands of laborers and mechanics are given employment.

In sash, doors, blinds, mouldings, etc., this city maintains the leading position, and a large number of firms and corporations are engaged in this department of industry. A reference has been made elsewhere to the statistics of the lumber supply of the city, and in all classes of hardwood lumber it is the most important market in the country, fixing the prices upon that class of lumber product.

In sewer pipe, retorts, fire brick, fire clay, etc., St. Louis is peculiarly fortunate in the possession of a finer quality and more generous supply of the raw material than any other city in the Union. This supply has been utilized in the building up in this city of more extensive establishments for the manufacture of these useful and necessary commodities than are to be found at any other point. A large capital is invested, and thousands of men are employed in this business, which has for its trade territory all the country west of the Ohio River. A more adequate idea of the extent of this industry may be gleaned from a subsequent portion of this work, where leading firms engaged in this department are noted.

Another important branch of business connected with building is glass, in which, both as a productive and distributive point, St. Louis has no rival. The supply of sand adapted for the purposes of glass making is inexhaustible, and in quality is better than any found in the world. This bountiful provision of Nature, coupled with the ample supply of coal and fire clay in the vicinity, gives every facility for manufacture, and enables the firms engaged in the business to produce a superior article at a minimum of cost, and supply a territory practically embracing the entire country. Connected with this industry also are several establishments for the manufacture of ornamental and silver glass, all of which are doing a prosperous business.

The industries engaged in the manufacture of iron work for building fronts and other architectural purposes have been already mentioned; to which may be added the entire range of industries in connection with galvanized iron for roofing, cornices, etc., in which St. Louis is heavily and profitably engaged, and in which her product is notably of the best quality.

In the manufacture of sheet lead and lead pipe, a number of prosperous firms are engaged. In the manufacture of white lead, red lead, etc., this is one of the most important producing points in the country, the shipments of white lead for 1886, having amounted to 21,298,216 pounds, in addition to which a very large amount was used in the manufacture of ready mixed paints, itself a business in which St. Louis holds an important position as a source of supply for all the country west to and including the Pacific Coast States and Territories. In the manufacture of oils, varnishes, etc., St. Louis also ranks as a leader.

**Drugs and Chemicals.**—In this line St. Louis stands foremost among American cities, with the possible exception of New York, both in the extent of its manufactures and the volume of its sales. Several of the largest wholesale houses in the country are located here, and the amount of capital invested will not fall short of $4,000,000, while the annual sales foot up nearly $15,000,000. In the manufacture of chemicals a number of firms of great capital and resources are engaged, while others devote their attention to the production of special articles, such as ammonia, castor oil, glycerine, etc. In these lines of manufacture and distribution, the market is by no means local, the demand for many of the commodities extending even beyond national limits to Canada, Mexico, Australia and the Sandwich Islands, while in this country the large capital and great facilities of the St. Louis merchants enable them to compete successfully with those of other centers of trade on their own ground.

**Furniture.**—This business has steadily increased year after year until it now ranks as one of the most important of the industries of St. Louis, between sixty and seventy factories, employing some five thousand men, being engaged in the manufacture of furniture of all grades, from the cheapest to the finest, and aggregating in value about $8,000,000 annually. The prominence of St. Louis as a leading market for the supply of hardwood lumber gives the city a great advantage in this manufacture, and the furniture made here finds a ready market throughout the Mississippi Valley, Texas, Mexico and all the Southern States. This industry includes not only the manufacture of household furniture in general, but a specially large business in the manufacture of chairs for all purposes, including reclining chairs for railroads, and also extensive enterprises engaged in the manufacture of office furniture, desks, counters, show cases, and everything belonging to the line.

**Brewing.**—St. Louis is one of the leading cities of the Union in the manufacture of beer, its leading breweries being the largest in the country, and the product being admitted to be of the finest quality made. In 1886, the beer manufactured in this city amounted to 1,280,091 barrels, or 39,682,821 gallons, upon which the internal revenue collections were $1,116,817.34. About $12,000,000 is invested in business by the brewers and maltsters of St. Louis, and the receipt of 2,529,731 bushels of barley, of which only 215,357 bushels were shipped, indicates the use of over 2,250,000 bushels of that grain in the manufacture of beer during the year. The industry gives employment to thousands of men, not only directly in the breweries, but also in the malt houses, cooper shops, ice harvesting, etc. The brewers of St. Louis lead in the bottling trade for export, and send more beer to foreign countries than is shipped by any other American city.

**Vehicles.**—Both in manufacture and in the sale of vehicles of every description, St. Louis does a very large business, as will be seen by reference to the description of the leading establishments in this line, printed elsewhere in this work. In the sale of carriages and buggies, St. Louis and Cincinnati do about half the entire business of the country, these two cities being about equal in the volume of their trade in this line, New York, Chicago and other places having a comparatively small share in the business of shipping carriages and buggies. To quote a recent writer: "St. Louis has sold carriages in New York State, and even in Vermont, while its trade with Charleston, South Carolina, and other southern points is very extensive. Numbers of vehicles are sold in the extreme northern portions of Michigan and Wisconsin, and large shipments are regularly made to California and Oregon. In fact the carriage trade of St. Louis extends from the Atlantic to the Pacific and from the Gulf to the Canadian line."

In addition to the manufacture and sale of the lighter vehicles, St. Louis has a large business in wagons, street cars, omnibuses, etc., having prosperous factories engaged in all these lines and shipping to all parts of the country.

**Bags, Ropes, Etc.**—The rapid and healthy increase of the trade of St. Louis in cotton, noted elsewhere, has induced a like growth in the manufacture of bagging for baling purposes, and the manufacture of this article in this city reached a total of about 16,000,000 yards, a marked increase over all former years. The Merchants' Exchange report states that "the manufacture of other places also finds a market here to a large extent and the business shows a large gain from year to year. The central position of this market is shown by the fact that fully one-third of the bagging required to cover the cotton crop is supplied from this point."

In 1886 the receipts of hemp and tow were 645 bales, of flax tow 2,038 bales, and of jute 65,192 bales. This vast amount of material was used in the manufacture of rope, which is also a prosperous industry here, as well as the manufacture of bagging. Besides the bagging made for cotton, there is a large business carried on in the manufacture of sacks for grain, etc.

**Clothing.**—This line of manufacture is showing renewed activity, and to the many establishments already engaged in this line a number have been added in the past few years. The industry is a very large one, not only in jeans and other of the standard grades, but also the finer qualities and the trade extends all over the South and Southwest. About $2,000,000 of capital is employed in the business, between 4,000 and 5,000 people are employed, and the annual sales approximate $5,000,000.

**Distilling.**—The distilling business is largely carried in this city, which is a center of distribution for liquors throughout the Southwest. In 1886 there were 60,133 barrels of highwines and whiskies received and 99,087 barrels of whisky shipped. There were 534,784 bushels of grain mashed and distilled in 1886 and 2,334,701 gallons of spirits distilled. Allowing for alcohol withdrawn for scientific purpose, allowance for leakage, etc., there were taxes paid on 2,291,586 gallons amounting to $2,062,426.50. Of spirits there were rectified or compounded during the year 2,455,-687.09 gallons and gauged by United States Gaugers 9,601,110.32 gallons. These figures show a slight falling off from the previous year, but still indicate a large business.

**Native Wines, Etc.**—Missouri is yearly increasing in importance as a wine growing State and a number of firms are engaged in the manufacture of wines. The largest of these produces a quality of champagne which is a favorite not only in this country but also enjoys a reputation in Europe which necessitates a considerable export trade. The sale of Missouri wines is increasing from season to season and gives encouragement for the increased production of wine grapes.

### OTHER MANUFACTURES.

In addition to the many departments of industry above referred to, St. Louis leads the world in wooden and willow ware, including the manufacture of tubs, pails, kegs, churns, wash-boards, ax and pick handles, buckets, etc., and every description of basket.

There are in this city and doing a prosperous business, box factories, trunk factories, establishments for wood carving and turning, picture frame factories and a number other industries that utilize the immense lumber supply of St. Louis.

In the manufacture of crackers, St. Louis is the largest producer in the West, competing with other cities in the Northwestern country, while the Southern and Southwestern territory is peculiarly its own.

In printing, lithography, and all the related occupations, this city does a large business. Type and printers' machinery are largely manufactured here, and the city is the recognized headquarters for the South and Southwest in all lines of stationery, stationers' sundries, blank-book manufacture, etc.

In brief, without any attempt to further particularize individual branches of industry, it may be said that in all the enterprises of productive energy St. Louis holds her place among the leading and most vigorous. Each year marks some gain made in the sum of her industries and shows some advance in the aggregate of her productive usefulness. All the advantages of climatic, topographical and social influences are here to encourage effort and to approve enterprise. The present holds out encouragement and the future promises success. St. Louis has all the facilities for prosperity in creative industry and she has men with judgment and ability to make the most of the grand opportunities her situation offers.

# OTHER BUSINESS FACTS.

## BANKING AND FINANCIAL PROSPERITY—REAL ESTATE AND BUILDING IN ST. LOUIS.

IT is an apparent and encouraging fact that at no time in the history of St. Louis has the condition of its banks been more sound and prosperous than at the present. The number of banks in the city is less than at any time during the past twenty years, but the aggregate of business done is much larger, and the amounts of capital and surplus of the twenty-two banks now in existence, of their deposits, of their loans, bonds and exchange maturing, etc., are larger than were the aggregates of the same items for thirty-two banks ten years ago.

Of the St. Louis banks seventeen are operated under State charter, and five are National banks. The aggregate of capital and surplus at the beginning of the present year was $14,941,771, an increase of $288,119 over the statement of the same item for twenty-three banks a year previously; and the aggregate of clearings for 1886 was $810,795,062, and of balances $149,968,903, an increase in clearings of $51,664,637 and in balances of $22,420,948 over the aggregates for 1885, or 8.4 per cent. on clearings and balances combined. The increase in deposits during the year was $3,524,462, the aggregate at the beginning of the present year being $47,501,397, of which $9,200,334 was time deposits, and $38,301,063 was demand deposits.

The revival of business in 1886, which was generally felt by the commercial and manufacturing community, is emphasized by this showing of increased activity in banking transactions, there being no more accurate barometer of the state of trade than the reports of the Clearing House. This activity has continued during the first four months of the present year, with a gratifying prospect of an even more favorable showing when the annual statements are made up at its close.

All of the banks in St. Louis are old, firmly established institutions, no new enterprises of that character having been inaugurated during the past twelve or fifteen years. Age is a valuable asset to a bank, and especially is this true, when, as is the case with those of this city, added years have been accompanied by a steadily increasing prosperity. Banks have gone out of existence from time to time from various causes, but those now conducting business in this city have been tried by experience and have shown their stability by passing with ease and safety through crises which have proved too strong for other and less substantial institutions. Reference to the financial history of a number of the leading banks may be found in a later portion of this work.

Intimately associated with banking, the Money Order Division of the St. Louis Post Office makes an important showing for 1886, during which 283,552 domestic orders, 3,021 international orders, and 190,521 postal notes were paid, aggregating $5,047,981.76; and 52,529 domestic orders, 7,492 international orders, and 19,106 postal notes were issued, amounting to a total of $1,032.611.99. The remittances received from depository offices footed up $5,797,036.96 and those sent from this office to New York were $1,762,500.

## REAL ESTATE AND BUILDING.

The business in real estate transactions has taken on a steadily increasing activity during the past few months, and is now more lively than for several years previously. Last year was not a good one, either for the real estate dealers or the builders. The strikes in the early part of the year caused a temporary depression in all business, and as real estate is the last interest to react from troubles of that character, the general revival which other industries experienced was not felt by the real estate market until some months later. Many causes may be assigned for this, the uncertainty of the labor situation in the Spring, when building operations are usually most active, being one of the principal ones. By the time confidence had been restored the season for building was nearing its close, and as a consequence the market was flat until about the beginning of the present year.

While the market in 1886 was dull in the aggregate, there were individual transactions which were among the largest ever closed in the city. One sale of property on Washington avenue was made for $475,000, and other very valuable properties changed hands.

Early in the present year the inquiries in regard to real estate began to be more active, and these inquiries were followed by a steady increase of sales, and a noticeable rise in prices. This has been particularly the case with West End residence property, in which the transactions have been more numerous and at better prices than at any previous time in the history of that locality.

In 1886 building permits were issued for 1,825 buildings; and 1,732 new brick and stone structures, valued at $5,916,958; and 491 new frame buildings, valued at $405,892, were erected. Additions and alterations to the value of $707,949 were made to existing buildings. These figures indicate a falling off from those of the previous year which may be ascribed to causes already enumerated. In the present year, however, there has been a revival in this as in other lines, and the architects and builders of the city are busy, while the character of the buildings now in course of erection or under contract is greatly improved.

The signs of the times indicate an increased confidence on the part of capital, and a disposition to place it upon permanent investment. The money put into the improvements now going on is, for the most part, that of St. Louis investors, but there is, nevertheless, a good demand for properties from Eastern capitalists, to whom investments here offer inducements greatly superior to anything to be found in the seaboard cities.

### ODD FELLOWS' BUILDING.

A number of handsome business and other structures will soon be added to the architectural attractions of the city. Conspicuous among these is the Odd Fellows' Building now being erected at the corner of Olive and Ninth streets, shown in the accompanying illustration, and which is particularly notable as being built of Missouri red granite, showing the beauty and fine surface of this superior stone and the fine polish of which it is susceptible. Among other buildings which will

form notable additions to the list of the more imposing business structures of the city are the Mercantile Library, at the corner of Broadway and Locust streets; the new office building, at the corner of Fourth and Olive streets; the Commercial Block, at the corner of Sixth and Olive streets, and a new nine-story railroad office building, at the corner of Seventh and Chestnut streets. In addition to these are many others for business purposes, while in fine residences this promises to be one of the busiest years in the history of the city.

The activity now manifest in the real estate and building circles of the city does not indicate what is generally called a "boom," which too often means a season of feverish excitement, unduly inflated prices, and reckless speculation. In St. Louis the advance has been from prices below up to the actual, reasonable value of the property. The active demand for property is mostly for building purposes and indicates the confidence of the people in the belief that St. Louis is now entering upon a period of greatly enhanced prosperity.

# THE MUNICIPALITY.

## HOW IT IS GOVERNED—FACTS IN RELATION TO ITS BUSINESS AND SOCIAL LIFE.

THE area of the city has been given in a former chapter of this work. Many changes have been made, from time to time, in the methods of the city's government, from the time of its original incorporation, until the present system was adopted, by the ratification by the people, in 1876, of what is known as the "Scheme and Charter," severing the municipal relations of the city with St. Louis County, and blending its government, both as to city and county functions, into one.

The "Scheme and Charter," setting forth the organic rights of the city government and limiting its power of taxation, was prepared by thirteen freeholders elected for that purpose in pursuance of an act of the Legislature. By its provisions, the legislative powers of the city are vested in two houses, one known as the Council and the other designated as the House of Delegates. The members of the Council, numbering thirteen, are chosen on a general ticket, elected from the city at large, and those of the House of Delegates, twenty-eight in number, one from each of the wards of the city.

The executive department of the city consists of the Mayor and elective department officers and boards. These are elected for four years, and the present incumbents of these offices, who hold until their successors are elected in 1889, are: Mayor, David R. Francis; Comptroller, Robert A. Campbell; Treasurer, Fred F. Espenschied; Auditor, A. J. Smith; Register, D. O'Connell Tracy; Collector, H. Clay Sexton; Marshal, Martin Nieser; President of Board of Assessors, John J. O'Brien; Coroner, Samuel H. Frazer, M. D.; Sheriff, Henry F. Harrington; Recorder of Deeds, William A. Hobbs; President Board of Public Improvements, Henry Flad; President of Council (Acting Mayor), W. R. Allen; Inspector of Weights and Measures, Andrew Haley.

In addition to these officers, elected by the people, there are appointive officers and boards having charge of streets; the water supply; harbors and wharves; public parks; public buildings; inspection of boilers; law department, etc. The Health Department is composed of an appointed Commissioner and a Board. The Police Board is appointed by the Governor of the State, the Mayor being President *ex-officio*. The heads of the Fire Department are appointed by the Mayor, by and with the advice and consent of the upper house of the Municipal Assembly.

PUBLIC BUILDINGS.

St. Louis has a large number of public buildings, befitting its size and importance. The City Hall, which occupies the block bounded by Market, Tenth, Chestnut and Eleventh streets, has very few architectural pretensions, but it is a very large building and accommodates most of the city offices. The Court House, in

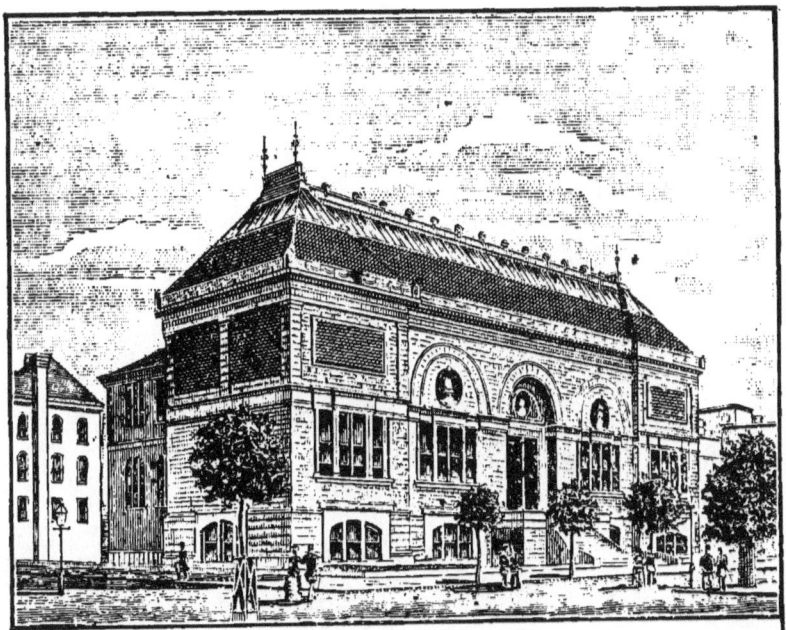

ST. LOUIS ART MUSEUM.

LIEDERKRANZ HALL.

which are the offices of the Collector, Sheriff, Recorder of Deeds, Court of Appeals, Probate Court, Circuit Courts and Law Library, is on the block bounded by Market, Chestnut and Fourth streets and Broadway.

The "Four Courts," an imposing structure between Clark avenue and Spruce street and Eleventh and Twelfth streets, was so named, it is said, by one of the judges, a native of Ireland, because of its general resemblance to the Four Courts at Dublin. As a matter of fact only three courts are held there, the Criminal Court, Court of Criminal Correction and the Police Court of the First District, the remainder of the building being devoted to the uses of the Police Department. In the rear of the building is the City Jail, and the Morgue occupies the southwest corner of the yard. The cost of the building was $755,000, and of the ground $125,000.

The Water Works were the first, on a large scale, in America, that were built with settling basins, into which water is pumped by two high service engines, having a daily capacity of 41,500,000 gallons. The water, after being pumped, is allowed to stand from eighteen to twenty hours before it is again pumped into the reservoir at Compton Hill, which has a capacity of 60,000,000 gallons, and an elevation of water line of 176 feet above the city directrix.

The Armory, built at a cost of $50,000, is on Pine street, between Seventeenth and Eighteenth streets, and its hall is not surpassed, for drilling purposes, in the country. The city has numerous other buildings, which are used for school, library, hospital and other purposes, and there are in the city a number of university and college buildings.

The Custom House and Post Office, built at an expense to the government of about $6,000,000, is one of the finest public buildings in the country. The sub-basement is used for the machinery and steam-heating apparatus, and the basement and first floor by the Post Office. The second floor is occupied by the Custom House, Internal Revenue Department, and Sub-Treasury, the Steamboat, Lighthouse and Post Office Inspectors and Pension Examiners. On the third floor are the United States Court rooms, the judges' private offices, the grand and petit jury rooms, the offices of the United States Engineers and the Railway Mail Service. The dome is devoted to the use of the United States Signal Service.

## MUNICIPAL STATISTICS.

The financial condition of the city is a healthy one, and its credit is excellent. The refunding of the bonds of the city at $3\frac{1}{2}$ per cent. is proving a success. At the close of the fiscal year ending April 11, 1887, there was a balance in the treasury amounting to $1,422,037.04. The bonded debt was $22,105,000, a reduction during the year of $837,000. The total rate of taxation, which has been levied for many years past is $2.55 on the $100, of which $1 is for municipal, 40 cents for State, and 40 cents for school purposes, and 75 cents for interest and public debt revenue. The refunding of the debt will reduce taxation, and at $3\frac{1}{2}$ per cent. will effect a saving of $118,070 per annum. The total collections of the year were $6,800,469.10. The Board of Assessors return a total valuation of taxable property of $215,199,090 as against $211,555,390 in the preceding year.

During the year 8.62 miles of granite pavement were laid, making a total of 30.93 miles of granite pavement in the city. The total expenditure of the public sewer system for the year was $94,852.76, and the length of public sewer built was 21,835 feet, and 62,115 feet of district sewers were built in twenty-one districts at a cost to property owners of $129,062.15. The total length of public sewers is 54.77 miles and of district sewers 208.25 miles. The total expenditure of the street department was $983,703.10; that of the fire department, $422,539.56; of fire and police telegraph, $29,798.67; and of the health department, $343,699.53.

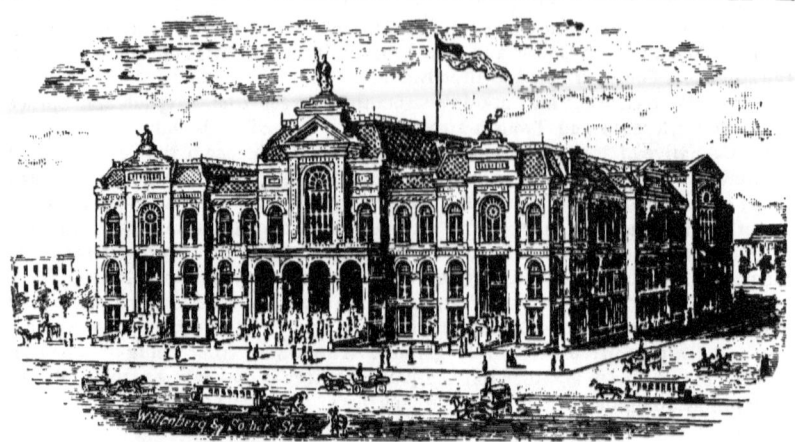

**Exposition and Music Hall.**—St. Louis has for many years been celebrated for the magnificence of its autumnal festivities, and the grand and effective scale upon which the annual fair is conducted. This attraction, however, continues only six days, and exhibitors from a distance, in many instances, regarded the expense as too great for a display lasting so short a time. As a consequence it was resolved to build a structure which should serve for an Exposition to last for forty days exclusive of Sundays, and also to build a Music Hall to be used as a large auditorium. In less than three weeks from the time the enterprise took definite shape, $500,000 was subscribed, and additional funds were provided as they became necessary. The Municipal Assembly leased Missouri Park to the St. Louis Exposition and Music Hall Association for a term of fifty years, and the Exposition Building was erected in time for the Exposition of 1884, the Music Hall being added the following year. The entire length of the building is 445 feet by a frontage on Olive street of 336 feet. The cost of the building was $750,000. Every appliance and adjunct necessary for success has been provided, including a number of powerful engines and 1.300 horse power boiler capacity to propel the machinery exhibit. The building is lighted by fifty-five powerful arc lights and 4,600 incandescent lights, while the front is illuminated by six arc lights and 1,960 gas jets of various colors.

The Expositions of 1885 and 1886 were even more successful than that of 1884, and the management are making preparations for still greater success the coming Autumn. During the Exposition the Grand Army of the Republic will hold its Annual Encampment in this city, and will doubtless attract to the city a crowd as great or greater than that drawn here by the Knights Templar Triennial Conclave of 1886.

The Music Hall, which is one of the largest in the country, is from the front to the footlights 126 feet by 84 feet in width, and from the floor to the ceiling is 80 feet, the seating capacity being about 4,000. The stage is 120 feet deep by 84 feet wide, and is provided with commodious dressing rooms. The acoustic properties of the hall are excellent, and it has been a great success. There is also a smaller hall in the north part of the building, known as Entertainment Hall, which has a seating capacity of 1,300.

The management of the Exposition and Music Hall Association has been noted for its ability and the energy of its efforts in behalf of the enterprise. The officers of the association for 1887 are: President, Sam M. Kennard; First Vice-President,

SCENES IN TOWER GROVE PARK.

E. O. Stanard; Second Vice-President, D. M. Houser; Treasurer, R. M. Scruggs; Secretary, J. H. Johnston; Assistant Secretary, E. P. Davies; Directors, Sam M. Kennard, E. O. Stanard, D. M. Houser, R. M. Scruggs, C. H. Turner, Ellis Wainwright, L. Methudy, Joseph Specht, Joseph Hill, L. D. Kingsland, C. H. Sampson, Jerome Hill, and J. Cliff Richardson.

The Public Parks.—Nothing is more important to the health and enjoyment of the residents of a city than a generous system of public parks. In this necessary provision St. Louis is particularly fortunate, both in the number and acreage of its breathing spots, which are laid out with beauty not excelled by the parks of any city on the continent.

Forest Park contains 1,371.94 acres, and has twenty-one miles of drives. It is situated in the western limits of the city, and is reached by the Wabash. St. Louis and Pacific Railway. It is one of the most beautiful as well as the largest, of the city's parks, and in addition to other attractions has a race track one mile in length, a number of artificial lakes, and fine bronze statues of Edward C. Bates and Frank P. Blair.

Tower Grove Park, for which the city is indebted to the munificence of Henry Shaw, contains 276.76 acres, and is one of the finest driving parks in the city. It is situated on Grand avenue, between Arsenal and Magnolia avenues. It is kept with great care, has beautiful flower beds and foliage, and contains a number of fine specimens of statuary, including monuments to Shakespeare, Columbus, Humboldt, Mozart and others.

O'Fallon Park contains 158.32 acres, and was purchased in 1875, at a cost of $239,063.35. It has some five miles of drives and is a popular resort for all ages and sexes.

Carondelet Park (New Limit) contains 180 acres, and is located between Kansas and Loughborough avenues, extending westwardly from Ninth street in South St. Louis. It has several miles of improved drives and a skating pond.

Lafayette Park, which contains 29.94 acres, is one of the most beautifully laid out in the city. It lies between Lafayette, Park, Mississippi and Missouri avenues. It has fine shaded walks and a large pond supplied with water from a fountain. This park contains statues of Washington and Thomas H. Benton.

Twelve other smaller parks are located in different parts of the city, all of them being of incalculable benefit in affording recreation for the people.

Shaw's Garden, or to speak more correctly, the Missouri Botanical Garden, adjoins Tower Grove Park, and has no superior—if, indeed, it has an equal—in the world. It contains every variety of flowers, vines, shrubs and trees. These beautiful grounds are the property of Henry Shaw, and have been willed to the city of St. Louis. The garden is open to visitors every week day.

## OTHER ELEMENTS OF PROGRESS.

St. Louis has an excellent school system which offers the advantages of education to all the children brought up within her limits. The public schools are conducted upon the most approved principles of teaching, while the high schools offer to the ambitious youth the opportunity for securing instruction in higher branches of knowledge. In addition to the public schools are those of the Catholic Church and others belonging to the several religious denominations.

Fine church edifices abound, all shades of belief being sheltered in elegant structures which add greatly to the architectural attractions of the city.

In social life there is every means provided for the pursuit of instruction or pleasure. The St. Louis Club House, an illustration of which is found elsewhere, is the home of one of the leading organizations, but there are many others devoted to social intercourse, to art, to music, to literature and to the various objects which indicate the intelligence and enlightenment of the people.

From a sanitary standpoint St. Louis is a desirable place to live. Comparative vital statistics show it to be a very healthy city, in fact the last comparative table showed that St. Louis was, with one exception, the healthiest city in the Union, Cincinnati only excelling it by a small decimal in its favor.

In short, St. Louis is a live, vigorous and progressive modern city, endowed with many natural advantages to which are added all the improvements which art or science has discovered to aid progress in business, in social life and in the pursuit of happiness.

THE REPUBLICAN BUILDING.

# THE ST. LOUIS PRESS.

## SKETCH OF THE METROPOLITAN NEWSPAPERS AND THE MEN WHO MAKE THEM.

THE American people are the greatest newspaper readers in the world, and as a result of the application of the law of supply and demand, newspapers are both more numerous and of better quality in the United States than in any other country. In all the elements of enterprise, of restless activity, of argus-eyed newsgathering, and of intelligent comment upon passing events, the newspapers of St. Louis are fully up to the highest standard of American journalism.

The press of the city has exercised a great influence in promoting its interests in every useful direction, and in aiding its progress toward the advanced position it holds among the great cities of the country.

The leading dailies in St. Louis are the "Missouri Republican," the "Globe-Democrat," the "Post-Dispatch" and the "Evening Chronicle," published in the English language, and the "Anzeiger des Westens," the "Westliche Post" and "Amerika," German papers.

**The Missouri Republican.**—This paper, the oldest in the city, was established as the "Missouri Gazette," in July, 1808, by Joseph Charless. It took a prominent part in the early history of the city, and its files preserved to posterity many of the interesting incidents of those days which would otherwise have been lost. In 1822 the name of the paper was changed to the "Missouri Republican." In 1827 George Knapp entered the office as an apprentice to the printing trade and continued his connection with it as journeyman, pressman, foreman and proprietor until his death a few years ago, the publishing firm owning the paper being still known as George Knapp & Co. The "Gazette" in its infancy was an enthusiastic supporter of Thomas Jefferson, and later, when the Whig party was formed, the "Republican" advocated the doctrine of that party, becoming Democratic after the Whig party went out of existence. It has since grown in influence as a representative of Democratic principles and a leader in the counsels of that party. The building occupied by the "Republican" is the most massive and beautiful of all the newspaper buildings in the city, and was erected, at great cost, in 1873. After George Knapp died, William Hyde became managing editor, and held that position until 1885, when he was succeeded by Frank R. O'Neill, Mr. Hyde shortly afterward being appointed Postmaster, which position he still holds. Under the management of Mr. O'Neill the paper has made rapid improvement and is now without a superior in the country as a news gatherer. Its editorial page exhibits marked ability, being scholarly without pedantry and incisive without coarseness or vituperation. Its editorial staff, which ably seconds the efforts of Managing Editor O'Neill, consists of Messrs. C. N. Howell, Wm. V. Byers and D. M. Grissom. R. M. Yost is city editor; Henry B. Wandell, night and telegraph editor; Capt. Bellairs, sporting editor; Mr. Lowenstein, dramatic and literary editor; Shepard Knapp, river editor; Wm. A. Kehoe, commercial editor; John T. McEnnis and O'Brien Moore, staff correspondents, and a full staff of reporters. The business management of the paper is in charge of Mr. Dumont G. Jones.

**The Globe-Democrat.**—The "St. Louis Democrat" was established in 1853, by Wm. McKee and Wm. Hill, and soon took rank as a leading and popular newspaper. It had men of note on its staff, including, at different times, Gen. Frank P. Blair and B. Gratz Brown. Originally Democratic, it espoused the cause of Abraham Lincoln in 1860, and was afterward a strong Republican paper. Mr. George W. Fishback became a partner in 1857, and Mr. Houser, who had risen from newsboy to bookkeeper, was taken into the firm in 1865. In 1872 differences arose between the partners, leading to litigation and finally resulting in the sale of the paper to Mr. Fishback. The same year Messrs. McKee and Houser established the "St. Louis Globe," which acquired great popularity. Mr. Joseph B. McCullagh, who had already made a National reputation on Cincinnati and Chicago newspapers, was given the editorial charge, and built up its reputation and influence until it became known and admired throughout the Southwest. The "Democrat" was afterward purchased and consolidated with the "Globe," the name being changed to the "Globe-Democrat." Upon the death of Mr. McKee, Mr. Houser succeeded to the presidency of the company, a position which he still holds, and in which he displays an executive ability which has been a potent factor in the wonderful success the paper has since achieved.  The complete and exhaustive manner in which the entire news of the day is presented in its columns, and the logical manner in which important issues are discussed, have given to the "Globe-Democrat" a distinctive personality that has secured for it the largest circulation in the West, and a wide influence in shaping public opinion throughout the Union. Mr. McCullagh, the editor, enjoys a merited distinction as one of the great journalists of the country. The officers of the publishing company are: D. M. Houser, President; J. B. McCullagh, Vice-President; S. Ray, Secretary and Treasurer; Will M. Houser, Cashier. The staff is composed of J. B. McCullagh, editor-in-chief; Henry King, associate editor; Charles A. Taylor, night editor; John C. Martin, city editor; N. C. Burke, telegraph editor, and twenty-five reporters.

**The Post-Dispatch.**—The place filled by the evening paper is an important

one. It brings the news fresh, upon the same day that it occurs. By the busy, the morning paper can only be superficially scanned but in the evening both time and inclination are available for reading. Those having leisure also look for the evening paper, which supplements or anticipates the morning journal. The "Post-Dispatch" fills all the requirements of a first-class afternoon paper, and is everywhere regarded as one of the best in the country. The paper is the result of the purchase in 1876, by Hon. Joseph Pulitzer, of several newspapers the name of two of which were hyphenated in the "Post-Dispatch" which was the result of the consolidation. Messrs. Pulitzer and John A. Dillon were the editors until 1879, when the latter retired and was succeeded by Col. John A. Cockerill, who remained as managing editor until he went to New York to take a similar position on the New York "World" of which Mr. Pulitzer is also proprietor, and Mr. Dillon returned to the "Post-Dispatch," of which he is now editor-in-chief. The completeness of its reports of the general news of the world, the thoroughness with which its bright staff of reporters gathers up every item of local news, and the crispness and independence of its editorial columns, have made the "Post-Dispatch" a great and merited success, and a pride to the city. The building occupied by the paper is shown in the accompanying illustration, but about September next the paper will be moved to the new building to be erected at 513 Olive street. In addition to Mr. Dillon the following compose the editorial force: Samuel Williams, associate editor; Henry W. Moore, managing editor; John F. Magner, city editor; Leon Witzig, telegraph editor; George S. Johns, dramatic and literary editor, and a large staff of reporters and correspondents. Ignaz Kappner is the business manager and D. W. Woods, cashier.

The Evening Chronicle.—This paper was established July 3, 1880, by a company which also owns the Cincinnati "Evening Post," the Detroit "News," and the Cleveland, O., "Evening Press." It was designed to fill the demand of all great cities for a paper which will give all the news in a condensed form at a low price. In July, 1886, Mr. Milton A. McRae, who had made a great success of the Cincinnati "Post" was placed in charge of the "Chronicle" as managing director. Under his supervision the circulation of the paper has largely increased. In March last, the price of the paper was reduced from two cents to one cent. The paper is bright, newsy and interesting, and is rapidly extending its influence. E. W. Scripps is president of the Chronicle Publishing Company; Milton A. McRae, managing director, and E. E. Vincent, business manager. The editorial staff is Wm. A. Carpenter, managing editor; H. B. Kantner, associate editor; Wilbur C. Fant, city editor, and Maj. W. H. Current, telegraph editor. A full staff of reporters supplies the local news, of which a specialty is made. All the departments are filled with marked ability, and the condensation is judiciously done.

## THE GERMAN PRESS.

The large number of citizens of German birth or descent, who reside in St. Louis and the region of which it is the center, has led to the establishment here of several newspapers printed in the German language, and which are of recognized prominence and influence among the German-speaking people of America.

Amerika.—This paper was established in 1872 by the German Literary Society, and has since enjoyed the favor of a large and increasing circle of readers. Dr. Edward Preuss, its editor, has been connected with the paper from its inception, first as assistant editor, and since 1878 in his present position, and has contributed largely to its success by the force and elegance of his editorial work. The paper is Democratic in politics, and publishes morning, Sunday and weekly editions.

**Anzeiger des Westens.**—This is the oldest German paper in the city, its first number having appeared on October 31, 1835, from which time it was regularly published until in 1863, owing to losses caused by the war, the publication was suspended for about five months, when its publication was resumed by the Independent Press Association, under the title of "Der Neue Anzeiger des Westens," with Carl Daenzer as editor and manager. Afterward the word "Neue" was dropped from the title, and the publication has been continued with increasing success and influence until the present time. Its editorial matter is thoughtful and scholarly, and it is a recognized exponent of Democratic principles. Its news columns are well conducted and complete, and it enjoys a large circulation. Carl Daenzer is President and Treasurer of the Association; Chas. Speck, Vice-President; Edward C. Kehr, Secretary; and John Schroers, Business Manager. Mr. Daenzer is editor-in-chief; Ernst Schierenberg, associate editor; F. E. Osthaus, city editor, and Carl Leman, telegraph editor.

**Westliche Post.**—This great and influential newspaper was originally established in 1857, and in 1864 Theodore Plate became its publisher, and Dr. Emil Preetorius its editor-in-chief, with whom Arthur Olshausen and Hon. Carl Schurz became associated in proprietorship in 1867. The paper removed to its present commodious premises in 1874. Dr. Preetorius still remains at the head of the paper as editor, and as President of the publishing company, being the principal proprietor of the company. He is a very able man, distinguished for his forcible and logical style and elegance of diction. The paper is Republican in politics, and in all the attributes of advanced journalism is the peer of the best newspapers in the land. Felix Coste is Secretary and Treasurer of the company; Oscar Hoefer, business manager; Ferdinand Harrsen and E. D. Kargan, associate editors; G. E. Serviere, city editor, and A. Barron, telegraph editor.

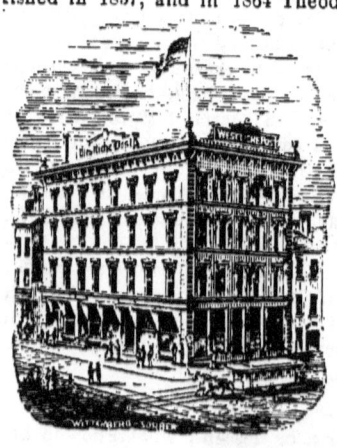

### OTHER PUBLICATIONS.

There are many other publications worthy of extended mention if space permitted. The "Sunday Sayings" is a bright paper which contains a large amount of valuable and interesting reading matter, and is a popular Sunday visitor to thousands of the citizens of St. Louis. Among other publications are the Critic, the Mining News, Le Patriote, a French weekly, besides a host of journals representing all the religious denominations, society papers, agricultural, railway, school and trade papers, etc., and the St. Louis Magazine, edited by A. N. DeMenil, and other monthlies.

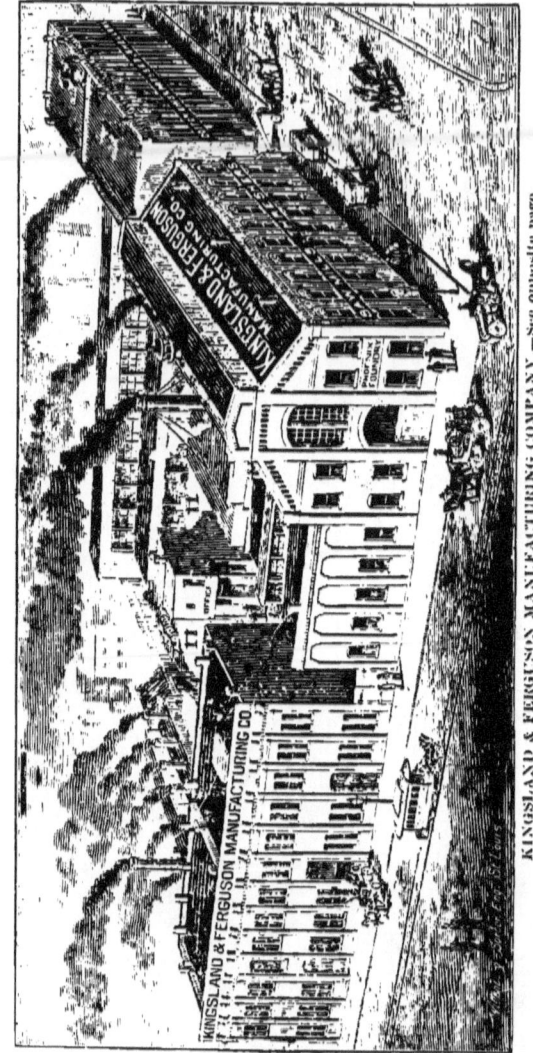

KINGSLAND & FERGUSON MANUFACTURING COMPANY.—See opposite page.

# REPRESENTATIVE HOUSES.

## SKETCHES OF LEADING MERCHANTS, MANUFACTURERS AND BUSINESS FIRMS.

IN this concluding chapter it is intended to present the history and present status of leading commercial and manufacturing corporations and firms, whose capital, energy and enterprise have been most important factors in the development of the resources and expansion of the trade of the city, and in her advancement to her present proud position as the great mercantile and industrial center of the Mississippi Valley. Only such houses have been mentioned as have reputations above suspicion, and whatever the list may lack of being complete is not chargeable to any bias on the part of the editor or publishers. But comparatively few of the large retail houses of the city have been given a place in the work, which is intended for wider circulation than their merely local patronage would justify.

**Kingsland & Ferguson Manufacturing Company.**—D. K. Ferguson, President; L. D. Kingsland, Vice-President; E. W. Douglas, Secretary; Agricultural and Saw Mill Machinery; 1521 North Eleventh street.—This great establishment has a history covering more than half a century, having been established in 1835 as a branch of the Pittsburgh firm of Kingsland & Lightner, the senior member of which, Mr. Lawrence Kingsland, started the first blast furnace in Pittsburgh. Mr. George Kingsland, his son, had charge of the branch here, and in 1844, on the death of Mr. Lawrence Kingsland, the connection with the Pittsburgh concern ceased, and Mr. George Kingsland, with Mr. D. K. Ferguson, established the firm of Kingsland & Ferguson. In 1874, upon the death of Mr. George Kingsland, his son, Mr. L. D. Kingsland, succeeded to his interest in the firm, and the business was incorporated under its present style. Mr. E. W. Douglas, who came from Pittsburgh in 1863, and had been employed by the firm, acquired an interest in the business in 1868. Since 1856 the works have been located on North Eleventh street, and now, with the numerous additions made from time to time, cover the two blocks extending from Eleventh to Thirteenth streets on Mullanphy street. These works have a complete outfit of the latest improved machinery and plant adapted to the manufacture of agricultural and saw mill machinery, and four hundred men are employed. The company manufacture threshers, portable and stationary engines, circular saw mills, head blocks, shafting and pulleys, edgers, swing saws, cord wood mills, saw mill supplies, corn and wheat mills, cane mills, evaporators, corn and cob crushers, corn shellers, agricultural and traction engines, cotton gins, cotton gin condensers and feeders, cotton presses, castings of every description, and many other specialties, which are named in their complete catalogue. Their business extends to all parts of the world, and is especially large in the United States, Mexico and Central and South America. They have recently shipped a saw mill to New Zealand, and orders from other far-off quarters of the globe frequently demonstrate how wide is the celebrity of this great industrial establishment. A specialty of the firm is a thresher especially adapted to Mexico, the company having sent an expert mechanic to that country to devise some practical machine. They make a thresher, with engine, for Mexico for $1.600, while the competing English thresher costs $10,000. They have a very large business in Mexico and South America, and were the first to seek that trade. They have agencies in the city of Mexico, Chihuahua, and other leading cities. Mr. Ferguson, the President, has been with the works since boyhood, and is a prominent figure in the business life of St. Louis. He is President of the Mechanics' Bank and otherwise prominent in important enterprises. Mr. Kingsland, the Vice-President, is the grandson of the founder of the business, to which he has been reared from youth, and is interested in many enterprises for the purpose of improving the trade relations of this country with Mexico. Mr. Douglas is also a thoroughly practical and experienced man and valuable in his position as secretary. The management of the company's affairs befits its greatness, and its success and prominent standing is due to the great care and close attention which has been devoted to every detail throughout its long and honorable history.

**The Equitable Life Assurance Society of the United States.**—Ben. May, Manager for Missouri, Kansas, Texas and Arkansas; J. S. Kendrick, Cashier; St. Louis Branch, Equitable Building, corner of Sixth and Locust streets.—

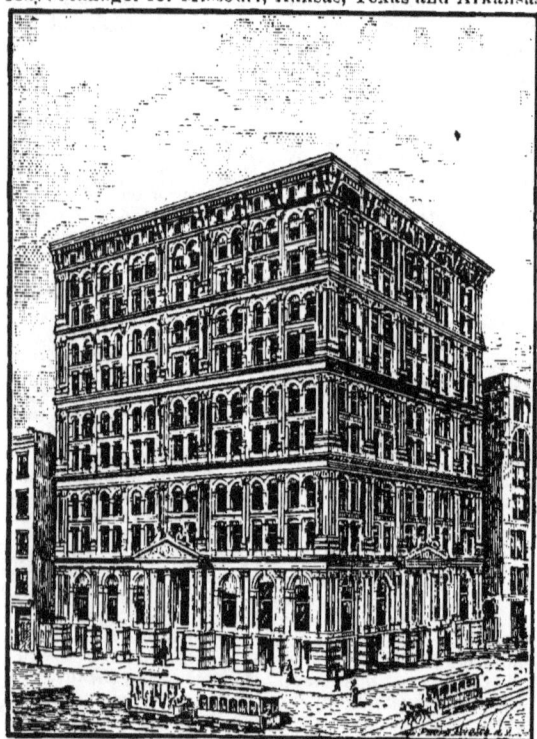

Established in 1859, the history of the Equitable Life Assurance Society of the United States has been one of steadily increasing prosperity, and it now, in the twenty-eighth year of its existence, exceeds in actual surplus, premium income, and the amount of assurance in force on its books, every other life assurance company, and may be justly regarded as the largest and strongest life assurance corporation in the world. Its growth has been steady, each year showing a marked improvement over the preceding one. The total assets of the company at the time of its last annual statement were $75,510,-472, while its total liabilities, including legal reserve on all existing policies, 4 per cent standard, amounted to $59,154,597, leaving a total undivided surplus over 4 per cent. reserve of $16,355,875.76. The company wrote new assurance in 1886 amounting to $111,540,203, as against $96,011,378 in the previous year, an increase of $15,528,825. At the beginning of the present year, the company had outstanding assurance of $411,779,098, an increase over the preceding year of $54,440,852. The premium income of the Equitable in 1886 was larger than that of any other company, amounting to $16,272,154.62, an increase over the preceding year of $2,810,-475.40; while during the same year the increase in the assets of the company was $8,957,085.26, and in its surplus, on the 4 per cent. basis, $2,493,636.63. Upon the New York State standard of 4½ per cent. interest, the surplus is, as computed, $20,495,175.76. These figures are given in detail as showing that the Equitable Life Assurance Society of the United States is in its excess of accumulated funds over liabilities, and in stability and progress, the foremost of all the assurance companies in existence. The headquarters of the society are in New York. The office of the

Southwestern department is located in the Equitable Building, at the corner of Sixth and Locust streets, which building they own, and which is one of the finest, largest and most complete buildings in the city; eleven stories or 158 feet high from the sidewalk to top cornice, and 100x130 feet in area, elegant in all its appointments, fitted with all modern conveniences, and fireproof. From 1859 to the present time, the Equitable has written $160,000,000 more assurance than any other company in the world, and has paid out to policy holders, during that period, over $100,000,000. This vast business has been secured by a happy combination of conservatism and enterprise. The Southwestern department furnishes a larger share of the new business than any other department, and does about double as much as any other company in the same territory—comprising the States of Missouri, Kansas, Texas and Arkansas—writing during 1886 more than $12,000,000 of new assurance. There were only five companies in the United States whose entire new business in 1886 exceeded that of the Southwestern department of the Equitable. A prominent feature of the Society's methods of assurance is its Free Tontine Policy, combining all the advantages and guarantees which can safely and properly be united in one form of policy. It is without restriction on travel, residence and occupation, after the first year; it is incontestable after two years; it is payable immediately upon the death of the assured; it is non-forfeiting (having a surrender value in paid-up assurance) after three years, and retains all the advantages peculiar to tontine assurance, including the largest return in dividends, and a choice of six methods of settlement. Through no other channel can so safe and so profitable an investment be made for the benefit of the family, as is offered in the Free Tontine Policy of the Equitable Life Assurance Society of the United States.

**E. O. Stanard Milling Company.**—E. O. Stanard, President; E. P. Bronson, Vice-President; W. K. Stanard, Secretary; Manufacturers of Roller Process Flour; Office, Chamber of Commerce.—The old and prominent firm of E. O. Stanard & Co., established in 1857, was succeeded in January, 1886, by the present incorporation. The office of the company is located in the Chamber of Commerce building, and their city mills, the "Eagle Steam Mills," are at the corner of Main and Dickson streets. They also own and operate the Alton City Mills, at Alton, Ill. The daily capacity of their mills amounts to 2,500 barrels. They also own and operate two large grain elevators at Jerseyville, Ill., with a capacity of 150,000 bushels of grain. The product of their mills is of the best quality; their "Eagle Steam" and "Roller Process Royal Patent" brands being in high favor with the trade and consumers. They sell chiefly South, although they have also a considerable export business to Havana, Glasgow and London. Their "Royal Patent" and "Eagle" brands are also well known and in demand in the East, where they compete successfully with the product of the Minneapolis millers, notwithstanding the advantage of cheap freights heretofore possessed by the latter. The high standing possessed by this house has been maintained through thirty years by meritorious goods and honorable dealings.

**The Water, Light and Power Company.**—Grant Tilden, President; N. W. Perkins, Jr., Secretary; F. Wm. Raeder, Engineer; Engineers and Contractors; 47 Turner Building, 304 N. Eighth street.—This company was incorporated in May, 1886, for the purpose of carrying on the business of engineers and contractors for the construction of water works on franchise from cities, supplying water at a stipulated price per hydrant for fire protection, and also supplying consumers by meters or upon such arrangements as can be agreed upon. They also put in electric light and gas plants in connection with the water works, where satisfactory arrangements can be made. Although of recent incorporation, the company has made a number of contracts in the States of Kansas, Arkansas, Illinois and other parts of the West. They have ample means, and every facility for carrying on their business, and are prepared to make contracts for supplying water works of any desired capacity on the most favorable terms.

**The Anchor Line.**—St. Louis to Vicksburg and New Orleans; John A. Scudder, President; Theo. C. Zeigler, Secretary; I. M. Mason, Superintendent; D. T. Prather, Freight Agent; Office on the Wharfboat, Foot of Pine street.—That steamboating has been brought to a higher degree of perfection on the Mississippi River than on any other in the world has long been an acknowledged fact. Even the hypercritical European travelers who have come to this country and returned to write books, more or less uncomplimentary, have invariably forgotten themselves and changed their tone to eulogy when writing of the comfort, the elegance, the speed and luxury of the floating palaces of the Father of Waters. While the advent of the extensive railroad systems of the South and West has diverted much of the traffic from the river, those who wish to travel with comfort and enjoy themselves en route still prefer the luxury of the better class of steamboats, such as those of the Anchor Line; and for freight these steamboats offer advantages with which railroads can not compete. The Anchor Line is a consolidation of the St. Louis and Vicksburg Anchor Line, originally chartered in 1859 as the St. Louis and Memphis Packet Company, with the St. Louis and New Orleans Anchor Line, incorporated in 1878. The consolidation was effected in 1883. The Anchor Line is the largest freight and passenger line on the river, and the only one now carrying passengers South. It has now six boats running to New Orleans, viz: "City of St. Louis," Capt. James O'Neal; "City of Baton Rouge," Capt. Horace Bixby; and "City of New Orleans," Capt. A. J. Carter, and three others. It has five boats running to Vicksburg: "City of Vicksburg," Capt. Ralph J. Whitledge; "City of Cairo," Capt. A. S. Lightner; "City of Providence," Capt. Geo. Carvell; "Belle of Memphis," Capt. Geo. Baker; and "Arkansas City," Capt. H. W. Brolaski. The company also has a packet, "E. C. Elliott," Capt. G. W. Lennox, running three times a week to Grand Tower, and keeps two boats in reserve, one of which Capt. Dan Able, late of the "City of Vicksburg," will command. All of these steamers are of the finest build, equipped with the best machinery, and offering unequaled accommodation both for freight and passenger transportation, while their commanders are selected with care from the most experienced navigators of the river. Boats of the Anchor Line leave St. Louis for St. Joseph, Rodney, Waterproof. Natchez, Bayou Sara. Baton Rouge and New Orleans, Wednesdays and Saturdays at 5 o'clock P. M. For Cape Girardeau. Cairo, Memphis, Helena, Greenville, Arkansas City and Vicksburg, Tuesdays, Thursdays and Saturdays at 5 o'clock P. M; and the Steamer "Elliott" for Ste. Genevieve, St. Marys, Chester, Wittenburg and Grand Tower, leaves Tuesdays, Thursdays and Saturdays at 4 o'clock P. M. The Anchor Line agents are Thos. W. Shields, Cairo, Ill.; Adriance Storm, Memphis, Tenn.; E. C. Carroll, Vicksburg, Miss.; and J. B. Woods, New Orleans, La. The President of the company, Capt. John A. Scudder, has long been identified with the steamboat interest. He was one of the original incorporators of the St. Louis and Memphis Packet Co. in 1859, and to his energy, experience and good judgment is due, in a large measure, the great prosperity which the present Anchor Line. as the successor of that company, has enjoyed, and its growth into the most successful of all inland navigation companies. Mr. Theo C. Zeigler, the secretary, has been connected with the Anchor Line and the companies out of which it grew, for upwards of twenty years, and has given its affairs efficient attention. Superintendent Mason. who was formerly Sheriff of St. Louis has held his present office with the company since January 1885, bringing to it a high order of executive ability; and Mr. Prather is a thorough business man who attends closely and with efficiency to the duties of freight agent.

Connected with the business of the company, and owned by it. is the Anchor Line Store, which, in addition to supplying the company, does a large general business in ship chandlers' and engineers' supplies, manila cordage, tackle blocks, oakum, and everything pertaining to vessel outfitting. The store is six stories high, with a frontage of 40 feet at 118 North Commercial street. and running back 115 feet to a like frontage at 110 North Levee. The store is under the efficient management of Mr. W. H. Langdale, carries a large stock, and possesses unexcelled facilities for advantageous dealing in every description of supplies for vessels.

**Frank Gaiennie.**—Commission Merchant; 308 Chamber of Commerce.—One of the most prominent and successful commission merchants of the city is Mr. Frank Gaiennie, President of the Merchants' Exchange. He came to St. Louis in 1873 from New Orleans, and established the firm of Gaiennie & Marks, in the commission business, making a specialty of the provision trade. Mr. Marks soon retired and Mr. Gaiennie has since conducted the business for himself. His trade is located principally in the South, where he has a large and extensive list of customers. Since his arrival in St. Louis he has been an active and energetic citizen and devoted his time, attention and finances to matters of public interest and the enlargement of commercial facilities. He has been vigorously and actively identified with the scheme for establishing a Central and South American steamship line from New Orleans, and has aided with his personal powers every movement for the good of St. Louis or its commerce. He has been a director of the Merchants' Exchange, Vice-President of that body and is now its President. In December last he was nominated and elected to that distinguished and honorable position without opposition. It was a unanimous action on the part of the members of that organization. Mr. Gaiennie is also a member of the Board of Police Commissioners of St. Louis, to which he was appointed for a term of four years by Gov. Marmaduke in 1885. "The Industries of St. Louis" would be incomplete without this short biographical sketch.

**Hamilton-Brown Shoe Company.**—A. D. Brown, President; E. F. Williams, Vice-President; R. F. Spencer, Secretary; Manufacturers and Jobbers of Boots and Shoes Exclusively for Cash; Corner of Tenth street and Washington avenue.— The admitted prominence of St. Louis as a manufacturing and distributing center for boots and shoes is largely due to the energy and enterprise of this house, much

the largest in its line in the West. The business was established in 1872 by Hamilton & Brown, the former of whom had been with the house of Appleton, Noyes & Co. in the same line, while Mr. Brown had conducted a general merchandise business at Columbus, Miss. The incorporation of the business under its present style occurred January 1, 1884; and the trade of the house, already large, has steadily increased since then, until in 1886 the sales aggregated $2,500,000. The present year gives promise of a still greater volume of business, as the manufacturing capacity of the company has been greatly augmented. As manufacturers the company confine themselves to ladies', misses' and children's shoes, and make a specialty of a one-price shoe, in glazed Dongola, kid and goat, to be sold to the consumer at $2.50. Of these they sold

$250,000 worth in 1886, and during the present year are finding for them a greatly increased demand. In addition to the lines of their own manufacture the company are very large jobbers of men's and boys' boots and shoes, and rubber goods, in which latter line they are agents for the Western and Garden State Rubber Companies. The vast operations of the house give employment in selling, manufacturing, etc., to three hundred people, in addition to which twenty-five traveling salesmen represent the company in a trade territory embracing the States of Missouri, Illinois, Indiana, Kentucky, Tennessee, Mississippi, Georgia, Alabama, Louisiana, Texas, Arkansas, Kansas, Iowa, Nebraska, Colorado and New Mexico. The block occupied by the company is an imposing six story and basement structure, the first, second, third and fourth stories of which are used for stock and salesrooms, the fifth and sixth for manufacturing purposes, and the basement for rubber goods. The factory floors are fitted with all the requisite modern machinery and equipments, and the entire building is well lighted from three sides and equipped with elevators and every convenience and accessory calculated to facilitate the business. A perfect system is maintained throughout and intelligent supervision is given to every detail. Mr. Williams, the Vice-President of the company, was a traveler for the house before he acquired an interest, and Secretary Spencer became a member of the company as a recognition of his business attainments and efficient services. Messrs. Brown and Williams are President and Vice-President, respectively, of the Pitchfork Land and Cattle Company, with a capital of $300,000, operating a Texas ranch of over 100,000 acres, and owning about 15,000 head of cattle. President Brown is also a Director of the Exposition and otherwise identified with important business enterprises. A striking feature of the company's methods is its adherence to the cash system, upon which all its transactions are conducted. The good customer does not pay an extra margin of profit to make up losses on bad debts. Results have proven the wisdom of the system. The Hamilton-Brown Shoe Company is justly regarded with the highest confidence by the trade throughout the South and West. Its stock is immense in size, unequaled in assortment, and unsurpassed in quality. Its resources are practically unlimited and its facilities the best. Its great prosperity is the result of superior management and honorable methods.

**Wiggins Ferry Company.**—John Scullin, President; F. L. Ridgely, Vice-President; H. L. Clark, Secretary and Treasurer: H. W. Gays, Manager; Corner Third and Chestnut streets.—In 1795, Capt. James S. Piggott, a revolutionary soldier who had located on the present site of East St. Louis, made a road and bridge over Cahokia Creek and established a ferry from the Illinois to the Missouri shore. On the 15th of August, 1797, he petitioned Commander Zenon Trudeau, then representing the Spanish Crown in the government of St. Louis, for the exclusive right to collect ferriage at this point, which was granted, and a ferry house was built on the Missouri side. After the death of Capt. Piggott in 1799, there was much litigation over the ferry right, but it was finally settled in favor of the heirs of Capt. Piggott, whose interests finally passed by transfer into the hands of Samuel Wiggins, who received a charter in 1819, and afterward sold his interests to a company, of which his brother, William C. Wiggins, who had managed the ferry for many years, was a member. In 1853, the original Wiggins charter expired, and a perpetual charter for ferry purposes was granted to Andrew Christy, William C. Wiggins, Adam L. Mills, Lewis V. Bogy and Napoleon B. Mulliken. The capital stock of the company is of a par value of $1,000,000, although it has rated much above par for many years. The company has extensive freight yards in St. Louis, located on the river front and Mound street, Chouteau avenue and Carroll street. It also operates the East St. Louis Connecting Railway, the Venice and Carondelet Belt Railway, the Illinois and St. Louis Railway Terminal, the Wiggins Car Transfer, the Madison County Car Transfer, and the Illinois and St. Louis Car Transfer. The steamboat interests of the company consist of six ferry boats, four car transfer boats, two tugs, five car transfer barges and five ferry landing barges. The company operates a ferry from Carr street, St. Louis, to the opposite shore in East St. Louis, and one from Spruce street, St. Louis, to the opposite shore in East St. Louis. The car transfer is operated between Mound street, St. Louis, and opposite shore in East St. Louis, and from Chouteau avenue and Carroll street, St. Louis, and opposite shore in East St. Louis; direct connections being made between all roads terminating in East St. Louis and those terminating in St. Louis. The company employs 150 men in its river interests. The business of the East St. Louis Connecting Railway and the Venice and Carondelet Belt Railway is principally switching cars between connecting roads terminating in East St. Louis and the car transfers, elevators and warehouses located on their tracks, giving constant employment to a force of seventy-five men. The growth of this great enterprise from the canoes used by Capt. Piggott in 1795, to the present magnificent equipment, is one of the most interesting and significant chapters of local history. The company throughout its history has pursued a liberal policy, and its management has been in wise and considerate hands. To this, no less than to the valuable franchises it holds, its great and steadily increasing prosperity is to be attributed.

**Everett & Post.**—Pig Lead, Spelter, and Ingot Copper; 24 North Third street (Republican Building), St. Louis, Mo., and 205 La Salle street, Chicago, Ill.—This firm is composed of Richard Everett and Henry R. Post, and was established in 1878, succeeding to the business of the old firm of O. E. Schmidt & Co., of New York. Mr. Everett represents the firm at St. Louis, and Mr. Post at Chicago. They have also an office in New York, and direct representation in Boston, Philadelphia and other Eastern cities. Their business is confined to the handling of the leading brands of Pig Lead, Spelter (Zinc) and Copper. They are the sole agents for the celebrated "M. & S." brand of Lead, and for the "Cherokee," "Rich Hill" and "Collinsville" brands of Spelter. They are the largest handlers of this metal in the United States, as they directly represent the largest producers. They are also the agents for the "B. & H." brand of Ingot Copper, manufactured by the Block & Hartman Copper Co., of Belleville, Ill. The facilities of this house for supplying consumers in large quantities are unsurpassed.

**Lambert Pharmacal Company.**—J. W. Lambert, President; Manufacturing Chemists; Pharmaceutical Specialties Exclusively for Physicians; 116 Olive street.—The Lambert Pharmacal Co., a corporation of manufacturing chemists, formed in 1880 for the manufacture of medical specialties exclusively for the use of physicians, occupies the four-story building with a frontage of 25 feet by a depth of 60 feet at 116 Olive street. The laboratory of the company gives constant employment to twelve skilled and experienced hands, and the specialties manufactured by them, on account of their excellence, uniformity and purity are known, approved and used in practice by the medical profession in all parts of the country, and have created business relations with every drug jobber in the United States. These pharmaceutical products are sold by the company only to wholesale druggists in gross lots, and in turn by them to the retail pharmacist upon the prescription of the physician. The use of these specialties by almost the entire medical profession for over six years, forms the most emphatic indorsement of their scientific merit, and the wide range of the patronage of the company evidences the high repute of its products and the accurac of its business methods.

**Thomas Coffin & Company, Limited.**—Wm. S. Dixon, President; Geo. W. Allen, Vice-President; H. L. Dixon, Secretary and Treasurer; Manufacturers of Fire Brick, etc.; Office and Works, Douglass and Cornelia streets, Wabash Railroad.—This prominent manufacturing corporation was originally organized in 1864 at Pittsburgh, Pa., this branch establishment in this city dating from 1883. They manufacture fire brick, glass makers' pots, furnaces, and all kinds of clay material. Their factory at Douglass and Cornelia streets on the Wabash Railroad is a three-story building, 200x160 feet in dimensions, and is completely equipped with all the necessary machinery and plant required by the business. They also have at Gra iot Station, on the St. Louis and San Francisco Railroad, a wash house, etc., for preparing pot clay for their uses. At their factory they employ a force of ninety men, and their large trade extends to all parts of the East, West and South. They sell fire brick and clay to a large number of rolling mills, smelting furnaces, etc., and glass makers' pots to a large number of glass makers. The product of these works is justly celebrated for its superior quality, and the facilities of the company for manufacture, handling and shipment are unsurpassed.

**R. L. Rosebrough Sons.**—Marble and Granite Works; 1926 to 1932 Olive street, and Pine and Twentieth streets.—This is the largest house in its line in St. Louis, and has been built up to its present prosperity by thoroughness in every detail of its management, superior workmanship in its product, and fairness in its

dealings. It was originally established in 1858, by the late R. L. Rosebrough and his son, J. W. Rosebrough, in a little one story shop, 35x15 feet, on Broadway. Steadily the business grew and thrived as a result of their industry. Since the death of Mr. R. L. Rosebrough in 1866, the business has been continued by Mr. J. W. Rosebrough and his brothers, who have been trained to the business and educated in all its details. The firm occupy as works and salesrooms a massive and elegant building of great convenience and architectural beauty, covering an area of 73x109 feet. The force employed numbers fifty, and includes artistic designers, draughtsmen and skilled workmen. The work turned out is done in the highest style of art, the materials used being the finest Italian and American marble, and domestic and Westerly granite, for which latter they are exclusive agents; and their whole attention being paid to cemetery work, which is made in all styles from the simplest headstone to the most elaborate monument or mausoleum. Many of the finest achievements of memorial art that are to be found at Bellefontaine, Calvary and other local cemeteries are the product of these works, and the house also constantly receives orders from other parts of Missouri, from Kansas, Illinois, the South and Mexico, for their superior and beautiful work. Fine designs, perfection of workmanship, and prompt and accurate filling of orders have combined to secure for this house its prominent standing and enduring success.

**The Hartford Silver Plate Company.**—C. P. Lindley, Western Manager; corner of Locust and Eighth streets.—The only house in the city or west of Chicago, dealing exclusively in silver and silver plate goods, is that conducted by Mr. C. P. Lindley, at the corner of Locust and Eighth streets. He represents The Hartford Silver Plate Co., which has its headquarters and factory at Hartford, Conn., with branches at New York, Philadelphia, Chicago and St. Louis, the two latter being in charge of Mr. Lindley. This company manufactures hollow ware, tea services, urns, epergnes, ice pitchers, cruets, fruit and cake baskets, etc., in the richest and most artistic designs, and of the highest grade of quadruple plate. He also represents The Holmes and Edwards Silver Co., of Bridgeport, Conn., the celebrated manufacturers of flat goods, such as spoons, forks, etc., and which are of the highest quality made. This company is also manufacturing spoons, forks, ladles, knives, etc., of "✥ Mexican Silver 67," a new metal. These goods, which are sold at low prices, are superior to sterling silver or plated ware in point of non-tarnishing or resistance to atmospheric influences, and equal to solid silver for durability. Goods made of Mexican Silver can be kept clean with any silver polish, as there is no plate to wear off, being solid metal. This St. Louis branch, which occupies the main floor and basement, 30x100 feet, at the northeast corner of Locust and Eighth streets, was established in June, 1886, and has already built up a large and steadily increasing trade throughout the entire West and South. Mr. Lindley, who has the supervision of this branch, is one of the oldest commercial travelers in the country, a gentleman of superior business attainments and highly esteemed in commercial circles.

**Chas. Schmidt Toy and Notion Company.**—Chas. Schmidt, President; Oscar Aberer, Vice-President; Edw. Schieferdecker, Treasurer; Importers and Jobbers; 713 and 715 Washington avenue.—This corporation succeeded the old house of L. and C. Speck & Co., two years ago. They occupy the three upper stories, 50x100 feet, of the premises at 713 and 715 Washington avenue, where they carry a large and completely diversified stock of toys and fancy goods of their own importation, such as accordeons, guitars, harmonicas, base balls, baskets, canes, clocks, croquets, druggists' sundries, fishing tackle, fans, Japanese lanterns, marbles, perfumeries, playing cards, pocket books, ladies' satchels, slates, stationery, soaps, spectacles, toilet articles, violins, wagons, and innumerable other notions. They have a full force of clerks and assistants and six traveling salesmen, who represent them in a vast trade territory reaching east to Indiana, north to the Lakes, south to the Gulf, and west to the Pacific Ocean. Their large trade is the result of the uniform superiority of their goods, the low price at which they sell them, and the liberal methods of business by which they give satisfaction to every customer in their transactions with them.

**Liggett & Myers Tobacco Company.**—John E. Liggett, President; George S. Myers, Vice-President; Moses C. Wetmore, Secretary: Benjamin F. Stevens, Superintendent; Manufacturers of Plug Chewing Tobacco; Thirteenth and St. Charles streets.—The magnitude of the manufacturing operations of this company entitles it to distinguished mention in a work detailing the results of productive energy in St. Louis. The business was established about fifty years ago, by the grandfather of the present President of the company, and the firm went through a number of changes in its style prior to the formation of the firm of Liggett & Myers in 1873, followed by the incorporation of the present company in 1878. The company is now the largest manufacturer of plug chewing tobacco in the United States, and its brands are celebrated throughout the country; the principal one of them, the famous "Star" tobacco, commanding a larger sale than any other manufactured. The three large six-story buildings occupied for manufacturing purposes by the company are elegant in exterior, and have the finest equipment for tobacco manufacture in the world. They cover over half a block and give employment to one thousand people. The trade of the company extends to all parts of the Union, requiring the constant employment of twenty-five traveling salesmen. An apt illustration of the growth of the business is given by the figures of their sales, which in 1885, amounted to 13,090,450 lbs., and in 1886, to 16,150,730 lbs., an increase of 3,060,280 lbs. The government report for the first three months of 1887 shows the sales of the four leading manufacturers of the country for that period to have been, in pounds, as follows:

Liggett & Myers Tobacco Co., St. Louis............................................................4,132,915
Pierre Lorillard & Co., Jersey City................................................................3,661,983
B. J. Sorge, Middletown, Ohio....................................................................2,978,000
Drummond Tobacco Co., St. Louis..............................................................2,219,116

The increase in the output of the Liggett & Myers Tobacco Co. for the first quarter of 1887, over the corresponding period in 1886, was 596,519 lbs. From January 1, to May 1, 1887, the company sold 5,568,743 lbs. Of the mammoth product of the company, about 70 per cent. is of the "Star" brand. These figures show indubitably the leadership of the company in this industry, and are gratifying as an example of the advanced position of St. Louis among the great manufacturing cities of the country.

**Charles A. Drach & Co.**—Electrotypers and Stereotypers; "Globe-Democrat" Building, Corner of Fourth and Pine streets.—In no department of art industry have there been such vast strides made in the past two decades as in electrotyping and stereotyping. In this branch of business enterprises St. Louis ranks second to no city on the continent, and no firm in the country can produce better work in the line than that of Chas. A. Drach & Co , who are located in the "Globe-Democrat" building. The business was established in 1867 by the firm of Strausberger & Drach, who conducted it until March 1, 1882, since which Mr. Drach has carried on the business alone under the present firm style. Mr. Drach is a thoroughly practical and experienced man in this line, having been engaged at the trade for ten years at Cincinnati and four in Chicago before coming to St. Louis twenty years ago. His premises are equipped with all the necessary plant and machinery, and he employs twenty-five skilled and experienced workmen. In addition to his heavy city trade he turns out a large amount of work for Evansville, Ind.; Quincy, Carrollton, Edwardsville, Belleville and Chicago, Ill.; Sedalia and Kansas City, Mo.; Topeka and Leavenworth, Kas.; Fort Worth, Greenville and other Texas points; Los Angeles, Cal., and a large number of other cities and towns in the West and South. This large patronage has been earned and retained by the superior and satisfactory work turned out at this establishment.

**Wm. Schotten & Co.**—Importers, Manufacturers, and Wholesale Dealers in Teas, Coffees, Spices and Grocers' Sundries; 111, 113 South Second street.—This business was established in 1847, by Mr. Wm. Schotten, father of the present proprietors, who are Messrs. Hubertus and Julius Schotten. It has grown to great prominence, and is now the largest house in the line in the West. They secure their supplies (which are almost all foreign goods) direct from the producing country. Having the most direct foreign correspondence, they carry always the largest and finest, as well as the best assorted stock of coffees, spices, etc., carried in the West. Their territory comprises the States of Illinois, Missouri, Kansas, Arkansas, Kentucky, Tennessee, New Mexico, Iowa, Nebraska and Colorado. Both of the members of the firm are young and enterprising merchants, trained from boyhood to a thorough knowledge of all the minutest details of the business. Mr. Hubertus Schotten is the general manager; Mr. Julius Schotten has charge of the financial department. The premises occupied by them are a four-story and basement building, 50x165 feet, at 111 and 113 South Second street; in addition to which, they have a large three-story warehouse, 60x150 feet, at 748 and 750 South Second street. Besides these, they have another large warehouse located in the rear of 212 and 214 Walnut street, across the alley from their headquarter premises. The accuracy of their business methods, and the unsurpassed facilities they enjoy, have resulted in a steady growth of the volume of their business, and the retention by the house of the honorable standing it has enjoyed throughout forty years of its prosperous business history. The manufacturing department is of quite large proportions, and is equipped in the most approved manner. Their capacity for roasting coffees equals 500 bags per day. All kinds of mills and machinery are employed in the milling room, where spices, mustard, baking powders, etc., are manufactured in the most scientific manner. Their goods are known to the trade as standard first-class goods.

**D. R. Francis & Bro. Commission Company.**—D. R. Francis, President; S. R. Francis, Vice-President; W. G. Boyd, Treasurer; Rooms 18 to 21 Gay Building, Opposite the Chamber of Commerce.—This incorporation was formed about two years ago, succeeding the firm of D. R. Francis & Bro. The business was originally established by Mr. D. R. Francis in 1877, his brother, Mr. S. R. Francis, becoming a member of the firm four years later. This company is known as one of the largest houses in its line in the country, doing a heavy option and commission business here and in Chicago, New York, Toledo and other markets. It has a branch at New Orleans conducted under the name of The Gomila-Francis Mercantile Co., of which D. R. Francis is President; Breedlove Smith, Vice-President; S. R. Francis, Treasurer; and W. P. Kennett, Secretary. At this branch they operate a large floating elevator and do a heavy grain exporting business. Mr. D. R. Francis, the President of this company, is the Mayor of the city of St. Louis, elected in 1885 for the term expiring in April, 1889. He began his business career in this city as a clerk with Shryock & Rowland at the age of nineteen. From this modest start he built his fortunes by industry and enterprise until he attained a prominent figure in the business world, identified with every movement looking to the improvement of the business interests of the city, and becoming successively Vice-President and President of the Merchants' Exchange, prior to his election to the chief magistracy, which he conducts with a strict regard to the good government and promotion of the material interests of the city. He is also President of the Union Elevator Co., and connected with a number of other important financial and commercial institutions. Mr. S. R. Francis, Vice-President of this company, is also a director of the Merchants' Exchange.

The Union Elevator Company was formed in 1880 and incorporated soon after. Its officers are D. R. Francis, President; L. O. Goddard (Chicago), Vice-President; H. W. Weiss (Chicago), Secretary and Treasurer; and B. L. Slack, Assistant Secretary and Treasurer. The office of the company is at No. 51 Gay Building, corner of Pine and Third streets, and its elevator, located at East St. Louis, is one of the largest in the Union. It was erected in July, 1881, and in 1882 its capacity was doubled, and is now 1,500,000 bushels. A force of thirty men is employed at this elevator, in which, at this writing, there is stored 1,200,000 bushels of grain.

**The Neath Gold Mining Company.**—James C. Moore, President; H. B. Miltenberg, Treasurer; John W. Donaldson, Secretary; Office of Donaldson & Co., Corner of Olive and Third streets.—The Neath Gold Mine is situated in Clear Creek County, Colorado, in Union Mining District. It is held under United States patents, and is 3,000 feet in length by 150 feet in width. There is now about 1,200 feet of shafts and drifts upon the property; and suitable steam hoisting machinery to work the mine for the next two years is on the ground. It is a gold mine and known as a true fissure vein, having been so pronounced by Vivian, Chauvenet, Pomeroy and Foster, all members of the Mining and Engineering Institute. Mr. John M. Dumont, whose property it was, retains a large interest in the company and is also retained as manager by special contract with the new company. Mr. Dumont is one of the oldest mining engineers in Colorado. His success in opening the Hukill and the Freeland mines, both now dividend-paying mines and which have proved of great benefit to the State, is expected to follow him in the future developments of the Neath. The Colorado Central Railroad passes within one-half mile of the mine. The climate, mining supplies, supplies for labor and labor itself and the great ore market at Denver, forty miles from the mine, are conditions favorable to this property which are unsurpassed by any gold mine in any camp in Colorado. Much care has been taken by the President, Mr. J. C. Moore, of the Merchants' National Bank, in examining the titles. He has personally attended to every detail and it is presumed that he has left nothing undone to protect the interests of his associates in the purchase of this property. The directors of the company are Messrs. A. F. Shapleigh, of the Shapleigh-Cautwell Hardware Co ; Ex-Judge Charles Speck, retired merchant; James C. Moore, Cashier Merchants' National Bank; John Scudder; John W. Donaldson, of Donaldson & Co., Bankers; and John M. Dumont.

**Rice, Stix & Co.**—Jobbers and Wholesale Dealers in Dry Goods, Notions, Etc.; Southeast Corner of Broadway and St. Charles street.—Among the prominent and representative business houses of St. Louis none holds a higher place than

that of Rice, Stix & Co. This firm was originally established at Memphis, Tenn., where it acquired a prominent position as one of the largest and most prosperous of the great mercantile houses of the South, but the field proved too restricted for the firm, and in 1879 they removed to St. Louis, at once advancing to the front rank and compelling recognition as one of the greatest commercial establishments of this city or the West. The individual members of the firm are Messrs. Henry and Jonathan Rice. William Stix, and David and B. Eiseman, all merchants of thorough training and experience. The premises occupied by the firm comprise a spacious five-story and basement building at the southeast corner of Broadway and St. Charles street, shown in the accompanying illustration. Here are stored in full and complete assortments vast stocks of every description of dry goods of foreign and domestic manufacture and notions of every kind. Staple goods are here in vast supply, and all the novelties in fabrics and designs are found in profusion. The trade of the house includes in the scope of its territory the great West and South in its entirety, embracing the States of Missouri, Illinois, Kansas, Iowa, Nebraska, New Mexico, Texas, Arkansas, Indian Territory, Tennessee, Louisiana, Mississippi, etc. The force of clerks and assistants employed in the house reaches into the hundreds, while a large staff of shrewd, pushing and energetic traveling salesmen attend to its interests on the road. Vast as the business is, its operations are conducted with a perfect system in every detail, ensuring accuracy and promptness in filling every order and perfect satisfaction in the relations of the house with its customers. Alive to the wants and anticipating the demands of the trade, with a course marked no less by good judgment and business sagacity than by energy and enterprise, the steady expansion of the trade of the house is as natural as it is gratifying. The success the firm have achieved is the well-earned reward of close application to business, careful buying and selection of goods, and honorable methods in all its transactions.

**Schulenburg & Boeckeler Lumber Company.**—A. Boeckeler, President; F. L. Hospes, Vice-President; Chas. W. Behrens, Secretary; L. C. Hirschberg, Treasurer; Main Office, St. Louis avenue and Hall street.—This is one of the oldest manufacturing concerns in its line in this city or the West, having been established in 1844 by the firm of Schulenburg & Boeckeler. The present corporation was organized in 1880, and does a very large business, about half of their sales being in the city, and the remainder in Missouri, Kansas and Southern Illinois. Their planing mill at the corner of Tenth and Mullanphy streets gives employment to sixty men. Their gang saw mills at St. Louis avenue and river employs one hundred and twenty-five men; and they also have a gang saw mill at Stillwater, Minn., giving employment to one hundred and seventy-five men. In this city they have twenty clerks and salesmen, twenty men drawing lumber from the river, and one hundred and fifty men assorting, piling and measuring lumber. They own three steamboats, employing seventy-five men, have ten teams of their own in the city and hire about fifty others. In their busy season they employ many more men than are above enumerated, sometimes nearly doubling their force. All their mills are equipped with the most modern machinery and every appliance for facilitating their manufacturing operations. They have immense yards, adjoining their gang saw mill in this city, which front on the river from North Market to Harrison streets. They carry enormous stocks, chiefly of Northern and Southern pine, but embracing every kind of rough and dressed lumber, shingles, lath, cedar posts, sash, doors, blinds, etc. President Boeckeler is one of the founders of the business, and to his energy and enterprise is largely due the steady growth of the business from small beginnings to its present mammoth proportions. He is a director of the German Savings Institution and otherwise identified among the leading and substantial business men of the city. Vice-President Hospes has charge of the company's business at Stillwater, Minn. Secretary Behrens is President of the St. Louis Manufacturing Co., an extensive sash, door and blind manufacturing concern. The Schulenburg & Boeckeler Lumber Co. has acquired a foremost position and the business, for the forty-three years of its honorable history, has always been conducted on accurate and reliable principles.

**Geo. Taylor & Co.**—Cotton Factors and General Commission Merchants; 116 Walnut street.—This firm was established seven years ago, and has long held a position among the leading houses in their line. They occupy a fine store, five stories in height, and 25x125 feet in area, and do a very large business. They receive consignments of cotton from all the States in which the staple is produced, but especially from Arkansas, and sell in the city. They also act as general commission merchants, and handle wool, hides, and other lines when consigned. Mr. Taylor is thoroughly experienced in the line, and his close acquaintance with the cotton market enables his firm to offer special inducements to shippers and producers. The house pays the closest and most faithful attention to every consignment, and by uniform fair dealing and vigilance in the interests of their customers, have acquired the confidence of, and given the utmost satisfaction to those for whom they have performed commission services, and have a large and steadily increasing patronage. The prominence of Mr. Taylor in the cotton trade of the city, is attested by the fact, that he is President, for the present year, of the St. Louis Cotton Exchange, of which he has long been a leading and influential member.

**The Pauly Jail Building and Manufacturing Company.**—P. J. Pauly, President; John Pauly, Vice-President; James J. Ligon, Secretary; Office and Works, 2215 De Kalb street.—The old and well-known firm of P. J. Pauly & Bro. was established in 1856, and was succeeded by the present company in 1885, when the business was incorporated under the State laws of Missouri. The extensive works of this company are located in the southern portion of the city and occupy a big frontage on De Kalb street, extending through the block to Second street. An average force of about one hundred men are employed. This establishment is the only one in the United States that makes a specialty of building patent steel-clad cells, and the steel-clad saw and file-proof cells of the Pauly system have been approved as the best in use, by time and experience. The company does a very large business in all the South, the West, Northwest and Middle States, and have executed hundreds of contracts for the erection of new, and the reconstruction of old jails in the past few years. Specimens of this company's work are to be seen in all sections of the country. The officers are all gentlemen of great experience. Mr. P. J. Pauly, the senior principal and President, has for nearly fifty years resided in St. Louis and it was here that he learned his trade. The Vice-President, Mr. John Pauly, has also been all his life engaged in this business, and Secretary Ligon has been in the service of the Paulys for many years, and is well versed in all details of the business. Both P. J. and John Pauly have occupied positions of public trust, Mr. P. J. Pauly in the Legislature and Mr. John Pauly in the City Council.

## THE INDUSTRIES OF ST. LOUIS.

**Evens & Howard.**—Manufacturers of Fire Brick, Gas Retorts, Sewer Pipe and other Fire Clay Goods.—This important manufacturing plant was established in 1856, when it gave employment to about twenty persons. By systematic, reliable and accurate methods in management, together with the high standard adopted and followed in the manufacture of its products, it has steadily increased, until these works are the largest in their line in the United States, and give employment at present to a large number of persons.

Of the first important materials in all successful metallurgical and manufacturing operations, a substantial fire-resisting material is one of the most necessary.

They have developed at their works a bed of the finest quality of fire clay, so that their product, even the raw clay, has found a market in Boston, Philadelphia, Pittsburg, St. Paul, New Orleans, California, Mexico, and territory nearer at home. Particularly is their Missouri fire clay known to almost every glass manufacturer in the country.

The product of no single fire clay industry is as well distributed as that from the locality of this plant. Their works, located at Howard Station, Missouri Pacific and St. Louis and San Francisco Railroads, are equipped with the best machinery, housed in substantial brick buildings, having switch tracks into the yards, so that

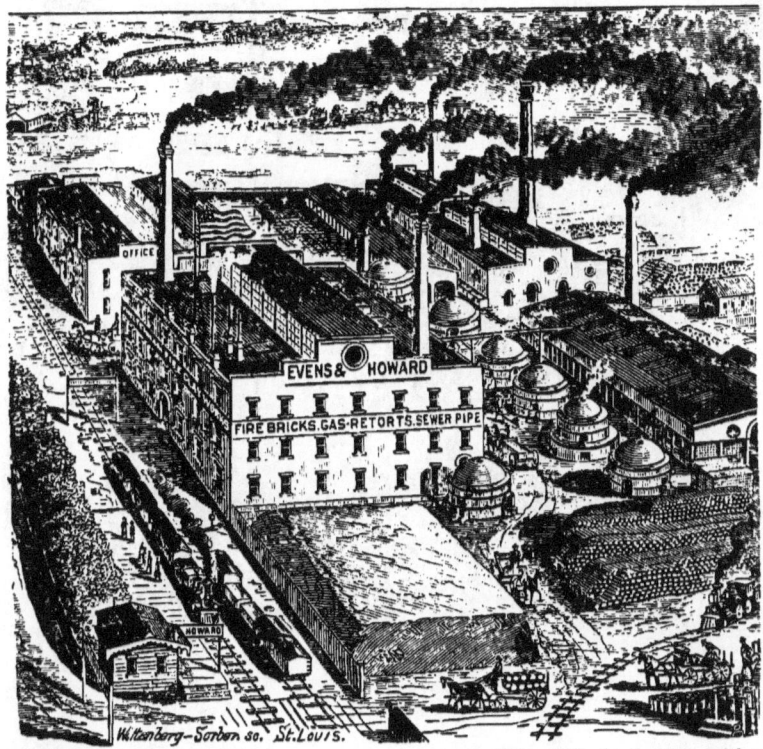

goods are carefully loaded into cars that go through to their destination without rehandling.

Evens & Howard's Gas Retorts have been sold in Portland, Me., Philadelphia, St. Paul, New Orleans, Denver and the Pacific Coast, and their lining for blast furnaces, at Green Bay, Mich., Alabama and California. Their Bessemer Tuyeres to Troy and Pittsburg, and their brick to almost every other city and section of this country, and to Old Mexico, for lining all kinds of furnaces; all shapes and sizes are made to suit the various plans.

Independent of the furnace lining industry, but made partially of the same

F. MEYROSE & CO.—See opposite page.

material, is the manufacture of clay pipes for drainage, which this factory has developed. They make them in sizes 3 to 21 inches inside diameter, in lengths of 2 feet each and in quantities of one mile per day.

They follow not only the ancient occupation of the Babylonians, in making brick, but also of the Aztecs and Arabians, in making clay pipes.

Recognizing the importance of complete drainage to the health and prosperity of any community, this company has perfected the manufacture of clay drainage pipes, for cities and farms, and culverts for large flow of water, so that this product, like their fire clay product, is known all over the West, even as far as San Diego, Cal.; in St. Paul and New Orleans, large quantities are used.

**Western Railroad Lamp and Lantern Manufactory.**—F. Meyrose & Co., Proprietors; 731, 733 and 735 South Fourth street.—One of the largest and most important industrial establishments of the city, engaged in a special line of manufacture, is that of F. Meyrose & Co., which, under the well known name of the Western Railroad Lamp and Lantern Manufactory, occupies a four story and basement building, 60x100 feet, at 731 to 735 South Fourth street, to which an extension, 30x100 feet, is now being added. The business was originally established in a modest way, in 1852. From small beginnings it has grown and prospered until it has no superior, either in the merit of the goods manufactured, in its line, or in the volume of its sales of lamps and lanterns. The factory is fitted up with the most modern and improved machinery and appliances adapted to the business, to speedily and promptly meet the large and growing demand for their goods throughout the country, by the jobbing hardware and crockery trades. At the manufactory, are manufactured the full line of the celebrated and well known Tubular Lantern and Lamp goods, railroad, lake and river, and police lanterns, street lamps, student lamps, Diamond M electric lamps of 60 candle power, barn, station and kitchen lamps, conductor lanterns, etc. All are of the very best workmanship, and free of infringement of the patents of any other maker, nearly all being the invention of and patented by Mr. F. Meyrose. The trade of the house extends to every jobbing part of the Union, Canada and Mexico, and are shipped, through New York jobbers, to all parts of Europe. A staff of traveling salesmen are engaged and continually on the route to represent the house to the jobbing trades. The vast proportions which its trade has assumed, are the legitimate result of honest goods and enterprise, business tact and energy.

**B. H. Brownell.**—Tailor and Importer; 716 Olive street.—This leading tailoring establishment has for sixteen years held the highest place in the esteem of the gentlemen of St. Louis. Mr. Brownell is a direct importer of the finest foreign fabrics. He carries the largest, finest and most complete stock of fine woolens in the West, and employs only the most artistic cutters, and most skilled and experienced workmen. In addition to a heavy high class city trade Mr. Brownell has an extensive order business in all parts of the West and South, the perfect fit and superior workmanship and finish of his garments having secured for him a wide spread and unexcelled reputation. His elegant store is the recognized headquarters of correct taste in dress matters, and the uniform satisfaction given by the products of his establishment has secured for him a patronage which increases from year to year, and a prosperity which is the well earned result of superior merit. Mr. Brownell makes a specialty of wedding outfits.

**John Byrne, Jr., & Co.**—Real Estate Agents; 618 Chestnut street.—Mr. John Byrne, Jr., is the oldest real estate operator in the city, having established this business in 1840. His partner, Dr. F. L. Haydel, has been associated with him since 1864 and is now the active member of the firm, as Mr. Byrne does not now give his personal supervision to the business of which he has been the head throughout its honorable and prosperous career of forty-seven years. The firm have a very large rent roll, embracing some of the most desirable residence and business property of the city, and have constantly on hand and for sale a large and superior list of improved and unimproved city property. They carry on all departments of a legitimate real estate business, buy and sell property, negotiate loans, etc. Their established reputation has secured for them the care and management of a large number of valuable estates, and in all its branches their business is thriving and prosperous, their long and intimate acquaintance with real estate movements in the city having given them a close and accurate knowledge of values. No firm excels them in the extent of yearly transactions and they still maintain their place among the leading real estate concerns of St. Louis.

## THE INDUSTRIES OF ST. LOUIS.

**John J. Ganahl Lumber Company.**—John J. Ganahl, President; Fidel Ganahl, Vice-President; Adolph A. Nuelle, Secretary; Dealers in Pine, Poplar, Cedar and Hardwood Lumber.—This business was established in 1863 under the firm name of Fleitz & Ganahl, and has in its development kept pace with the growth and progress of St. Louis. There are but few business men, in the city, better known, or that hold a higher place in the estimation of their fellow citizens than Mr. Ganahl. He is recognized as a shrewd, far-seeing merchant, whose judgment and estimate of the city's future has been amply repaid, and endorsed by the great expansion of his business, which was so large that it was found necessary to form a company, and in 1881 the business was incorporated under the name of the John J. Ganahl Lumber Co., with a paid up capital of $100,000. Besides a large and well assorted stock of all kinds of white pine lumber, which the company mostly receives by raft from the mills in Wisconsin, they make a specialty of yellow pine timbers, joist and finishing lumber, and in connection with other hardwoods they deal largely in poplar, cypress, and even California redwood. Their sash, door, blind and moulding business is very extensive and they keep a large stock constantly on hand, so that they are prepared to furnish everything in their line for building purposes. The principal office of this company has been removed to their new and elegantly finished office on the northwest corner of Second street and Park avenue, which can easily be reached by taking green cars on the Fourth street line going south.

**Fruin-Bambrick Construction Company.**—W. H. Swift, President; J. Fruin, Vice-President; P. Bambrick, Secretary; Contractors, Builders of Railroads, Water Works, etc.; 805 Pine street.—This immense business was established in 1872, by the firm of Fruin & Co., under which style it was conducted until about three years ago, when in order to facilitate the operations of their steadily expanding business, the present corporation was organized, uniting the firms of Fruin & Co., and Bambrick, Monaghan & Co. The company own and operate the Benton, Grand avenue, Chouteau avenue, Clifton Heights and Rock Springs quarries, and are extensively engaged as general contractors and builders of railroads, water works, etc. They are among the most extensive employers of labor in the West, having constantly in their employ, according to the season, from 1000 to 2000 men. They own and work 150 teams, and employ others by the hundreds. As an indication of the vast scale upon which their operations are conducted, it may be stated, that although the strikes of last year retarded their business considerably, causing them to lose two months, they paid out for wages during the year the enormous sum of $700,000. They have ample resources, and facilities for carrying on their business which are not surpassed by any firm or corporation in the country, and are prepared to contract for works of any magnitude upon the most advantageous terms. President Swift, of this company, was for many years clerk of the City Council, and Messrs. Fruin and Bambrick, the other principals in the company, have both been prominent in public affairs, having large experience in public works, and are recognized as substantial and leading business men. The affairs of the company are conducted with marked efficiency, and with a perfect and accurate system appropriate to its important position among the great business corporations of the city.

**Martin Collins.**—Insurance; 210 and 212 Olive street.—Mr. Collins has been prominent in the insurance circles of St. Louis for more than twenty-five years, and is thoroughly experienced and efficient in all the details of the business. He represents only reliable fire and marine insurance corporations of large capital and resources, and with established reputations as prompt payers of losses, including the Fire Association of Philadelphia, organized in 1817, and which wrote Missouri risks in 1886 to the amount of $4,568,415; the Rhode Island Underwriters Association, of Providence, which took fire risks in Missouri last year amounting to $1,933,538; and other companies with Missouri risks in 1886, as follows: New Hampshire Fire Insurance Co., $2,090,579; American Fire Insurance Co., New York, $949,051; Lancashire Insurance Co., Manchester, England, $1,887,556; Atlantic Fire and Marine Insurance Co., Providence, R. I., $404,622; and the Commercial Fire Insurance Co., of California, $1,216,627. Mr. Collins occupies handsome offices and does a large business, numbering among those who place their insurance through his agency, many of the leading property owners of the city. He is highly esteemed, not only in business circles, but also in the other relations of life. He is especially prominent in masonry, having been a member of the Missouri Grand Lodge for years, and being President of the Board of Masonic Relief of St. Louis, and President of the General Masonic Relief Association of the United States and Canada.

**E. F. W. Meier.**—China, Glass, Queensware, etc; 513 North Main street.— In 1857, the firm of Westermann & Meier was formed and occupied a store on Broadway, removing in 1858, to 513 North Main street, where the business was carried on by the firm until its dissolution in July, 1880, and has since been continued by Mr. E. F. W. Meier, at the old stand, a commodious six-story building, 25x150 feet. He also occupies for warehouse purposes, the large five-story building with a frontage of 35 feet, at 931 North Main street, by a depth of 125 feet. Mr. Meier, is a direct importer and wholesale dealer in china, glass, queensware, lamp goods, etc. In granite goods, he handles only the manufacture of the world-famous and unsurpassable "Royal Alfred" pottery of Alfred Meakin, Tunstall, Staffordshire, England, which he imports in the white or glaze, and which he has decorated here when desired by his patrons. He also deals largely in French, English and American china and glassware, lamps and lamp goods. He maintains the most favorable relations with foreign and domestic manufacturers, and is enabled to offer unsurpassed inducements to the trade. His business is very large and extends throughout the States of Missouri, Illinois, Nebraska, and the entire Northwest, West, Southwest and South; nine experienced and energetic traveling men being employed to represent the house on the road. The house has for many years held a high place in the esteem and confidence of the trade, by the superior merit of its goods, and the perfect system and probity of its business methods; and its patronage still exhibits a steady growth, its fall trade of 1886 having been especially immense in its proportions, and that of the entire year eminently satisfactory. Thirty years of an honorable and successful business career still finds the house full of vigor and enterprise, with the added advantages of ripe experience and a highly valuable business connection.

**S. W. Cobb & Co.**—Commission Merchants; 317 and 319 Chamber of Commerce.—There is not a firm in this city, devoted to the grain commission business, that is better known than that of S. W. Cobb & Co. The business was established in 1870 by Mr. S. W. Cobb, who is the sole proprietor and has never had a partner connected with him. At the inception of his business career his capital consisted of only a few hundred dollars, but through his patient industry and his untiring perseverance and broad and liberal methods, the volume of his trade has so expanded that a large capital is now required to carry on the extensive business which he has built. He is one of the leading operators of the Merchants' Exchange and one of the largest grain exporters in the West. S. W. Cobb was born in Southampton County, Va., 1838, and served throughout the war as an artillery officer in the army of Northern Virginia. He came to St. Louis in 1867, and obtained employment in a grain house. After three years' experience he established himself in business and has won an honorable record that may well cause him pride. He has never been in financial distress, nor has his credit been questioned during his career. The City of St. Louis possesses few men who equal in public spirit Mr. Cobb. He is foremost in any and all enterprises calculated for the municipal or commercial advancement of the city. He was nominated by the members of the Merchants' Exchange, and unanimously elected as President of that body, which position he held during the year 1886. His administration was one of the best in the history of that organization and he retired with the regrets of all that the custom of the Exchange prevented the re-election of its President. Mr. Cobb is the President of the new Merchants' Bridge Co., and was one of the originators of that enterprise which, with his associates, he is now pushing with that zeal and energy which must finally be crowned with success. The new bridge, so much needed, cannot be built without adequate terminal facilities. A bill before the Municipal Assembly, asking terminal facilities for the bridge and new railroads projected and in course of construction, as well as roads seeking ingress, is being fought by property owners along the route. While the projectors of this enterprise feel that the prosperity and commercial life of the city depend in a great measure upon the granting of this franchise, the objectors fear that their property will be depreciated in value by the laying of the connecting tracks. It is to be hoped that the difficulties may be amicably settled and that the growth and prosperity of the city may not be impeded by a local fight which alienates friends and clogs the wheels of commerce at the expense of the city.

**St. Louis Bank Note Company.**—C. C. Cheney, President; F. J. Pope, Treasurer; Engraving, Printing, Steel Plate and Lithography; 214 and 216 Chestnut street.—Among the many establishments which add to the celebrity of St. Louis as a center for the finest work in the artistic lines of industry, none is deserving of more prominent mention than the St. Louis Bank Note Company, which occupies a spacious five-story building at 214 and 216 Chestnut street. These premises are fully equipped with the most modern and improved machinery and plant for the successful prosecution of the company's business. A force of highly skilled workmen are employed, and experienced and energetic traveling men represent the company on the road. The company executes fine steel plate engraving, lithographing and every description of state, county, city, mining, railroad and other bonds, checks, drafts, headings, etc. They do a large amount of work for banks, municipalities, mining companies and other stock corporations as well as for commercial and manufacturing houses, and their patronage extends not only to every part of the Union, but also to Canada, Mexico and England. The great reputation evidenced by this wide-spread business has been fairly earned by the merit of the company's work, which is of one grade only, and that the finest known to the art; their designs being distinguished by beauty and appropriateness and the execution and finish perfect beyond criticism. Since the incorporation of the company in 1875, it has experienced a steady and healthy growth in its business, and has now attained a great prosperity as a result of superior work and intelligent and sagacious business management.

**St. Louis Bridge and Iron Company.**—H. W. Sebastien, Manager; R. L. Miller, R. H. Phillips, W. E. Stearns, Civil Engineers; Bridge Builders and Contractors; 16 North Fourth street, Rooms 9 and 11.—St. Louis is the headquarters of a number of large contracting firms and companies by whom works of great public importance and magnitude are conducted. Prominent among these is the St. Louis Bridge and Iron Co., which has its offices at 16 North Fourth street, rooms 9 and 11. This business was originally established as H. W. Sebastien & Co. in 1875, changing to its present style in 1883. This company does a very large business as bridge builders and contractors, making a specialty of wrought iron, combination and wooden railroad and highway bridges. They operate principally in the States of Missouri, Illinois, Kansas, Indiana, Iowa and Tennessee, and some idea of the magnitude of their works may be given by stating the fact that in 1886 they built highway bridges costing $100,000 and began work on a railroad contract for bridge building amounting to $125,000. In addition to this they have now in course of construction about a dozen bridges in and around the State of Missouri. The company has a large warehouse on Biddle street, between Seventh and Eighth streets, which it uses for storage of its plant and machinery, saw mills, pile drivers, etc. The company has unsurpassed facilities for work in its line, which it executes with a completeness which insures satisfaction and is prepared at any time to furnish plans, strain sheets and estimates on application. Mr. Sebastien, the company's manager, is a thoroughly practical and experienced man at the business, and under his management the works are conducted with uniform success. On January 1st, 1887, the company opened a branch office at Leavenworth, Kansas, with W. E. Stearns, C. E., in charge of the office, to attend to the affairs of the company in Western territory, Kansas, Nebraska, Colorado, Minnesota, etc.

**Walter A. Wood Mowing and Reaping Machine Company.**—Walter A. Wood, President and General Superintendent; William S. Nicholls, Vice-President; Willard Gay, Treasurer; Charles M. Coulter, Secretary; Danforth Geer, Assistant Secretary; J. M. Rosebrooks, Superintendent of Construction; F. W. Drury, General Southwestern Manager; 943 North Second street.—Nothing so emphasizes the march of progress in the Nineteenth Century as the great strides taken in agriculture and the invention of agricultural machines. Leading in the line of useful invention in harvesting machines is Mr. Walter A. Wood who, in 1853, established the business which, under the style of the Walter A. Wood Mowing and Reaping Machine Company, incorporated in 1866, now operates the largest works of their kind in the world, employing two thousand skilled and experienced workmen, manufacturing over fifty thousand machines per annum, and occupying at Hoosick Falls, N. Y., for its workshops, store-houses and lumber yards, eighty-five acres of land, each part connected with the other by the company's own standard-gauge railroad tracks, seven miles in length, and employing two powerful locomotives of its own for transportation and switching. These machines have been awarded the highest prizes at the leading international expositions, and Mr. Wood has received from Napoleon III, Emperor of the French, the decoration of the cross of Chevalier of the Legion of Honor, from the French Republic the cross of Officer of the Legion of Honor, and from the Emperor of Austria the Knights' cross of the Imperial Order of Francis Joseph. The mowers, reapers and self-binding harvesters made by this company are in great demand all over the world, and it has branch houses at New York, St. Louis, Chicago, San Francisco, Minneapolis, Portland, Oregon; London, Eng.; Paris, France; Buenos Ayres and Valparaiso, South America; Capetown, South Africa; Christchurch, New Zealand; and Brisbane, Melbourne, Sydney and Adelaide, Australia. The St. Louis branch was formerly under the direction of J. E. Hayner & Co. as general agents, but since the dissolution of that firm has been in charge of Mr. F. W. Drury as general Southwestern manager, and in whose hands the business of the company has faithful and watchful care in the territory embracing all the Western, Southwestern and Southern States. The premises, 943 North Second street, occupied by the St. Louis branch office, consist of a four-story building, 40x185 feet, and a warehouse, corner of Main and Ashley streets, 130x185 feet. Twenty assistants are employed in the house while twenty active commercial travelers represent the company in the territory allotted to this branch, and in which a very large and annually growing business is done in the sale of the "Wood" machines.

**St. Louis Moulding and Frame Factory.**—J. R. Webber & Company, Proprietors; 2000, 2002 and 2004 North Broadway.—This important manufacturing business was inaugurated in 1881 by Mr. J. R. Webber, who still remains the sole

proprietor, and by close attention to all its details has achieved the success accorded to well-directed industry and enterprise. The factory is a three-story building with a frontage of 60 feet by a depth of 180 feet, and is completely equipped with all the most improved modern machinery adapted to the requirements of the business, and every convenience and facility for the handling and shipment of material and manufactured product. At the factory a force of forty employes are busily engaged in the manufacture of picture mouldings, frames and looking glasses, the works having a capacity for the production of 10,000 feet of mouldings and 1,000 picture frames per day. The goods manufactured at this factory have a wide-spread reputation for superior excellence, and J. R. Webber & Co. have a large business extending all over the United States, Canada and Mexico, but principally in the States and Territories of the South and West. In addition to the products of their own manufacture they are dealers in pictures, chromos, oil paintings, engravings, combination and plush frames, mats, and everything pertaining to the picture frame trade.

**B. Thalmann.**—St. Louis Printing Ink Works; Office, 210 Olive street; Factory, 2117 to 2121 Singleton street.—Mr. B. Thalmann established his St. Louis Printing Ink Works in 1869, and has seen his enterprise steadily grow until it ranks among the leading factories of its kind in the country. His office is at 210 Olive street, and his spacious factory, 100x105 feet in dimensions, is at 2117 to 2121 Singleton street, but so extensive has his business become that he finds even these large premises inadequate, and is preparing to build additional manufacturing premises to supply an increased demand for his goods which is severely taxing his capacity for production. The works on Singleton street are equipped with a 45 horse-power engine, eight mills and all the latest improved machinery. Mr. Thalmann employs none but the most skilled labor, and carries on all the processes of printing ink manufacture, buying nothing but the raw oils and colors. Everything else is produced in the factory; he has his own black room, makes his own lamp black, and manufactures lithographic, steel plate, book, job, news and all kinds of printing inks, black and colored, of highest grade. His patronage steadily increases from year to year and is very large, including, besides a heavy city business, a large trade in the States of Missouri, Arkansas, Texas, Louisiana, Alabama, Tennessee, Illinois, Kansas, Colorado, Wyoming, Nebraska, Iowa, Minnesota and Wisconsin. This immense trade has been secured and retained by manufacturing superior goods and keeping them up to a uniform grade of merit, and by strictly attending to every detail of the business and applying correct principles to all his transactions. The ink used in this book is from Mr. Thalmann's factory.

**F. B. Chamberlain Commission Company.**—Commission Merchants, etc.; 300 and 302 North Main street.—A house that has enjoyed a successful business career of nearly forty years can justly claim that its methods are meritorious. Of such a character is the house known as the F. B. Chamberlain Commission Co., founded in 1848 by Mr. F. B. Chamberlain, who is still at its head, the other member of the firm being Mr. W. F. Chamberlain. The spacious premises occupied by the firm front 40 feet on North Main Street, running back 130 feet to North Commercial street. The firm does a large commission business in flour and grass seeds, and manufactures Chamberlain's celebrated Self-Raising Buckwheat Flour of the "Ready For Use" brand, an article of great merit and which has established a high reputation with the trade and consumers. The trade in this article is steadily growing, and a large number of carloads of the product have been sold the past year. In addition to this branch of the business they are agents for King's Great Western Powder Company, whose rifle and blasting powder is conceded to be of the best quality. The high standing of the F. B. Chamberlain Commission Co., acquired many years ago, is steadily maintained by a course of enterprising and honorable business dealing, and the trade of the firm is very large, both in the city and the states surrounding it and tributary to its market, and continues to increase from year to year.

**Catlin Tobacco Company.**—Manufacturers; corner of Chestnut and Thirteenth streets.—The Catlin Tobacco Company are the largest manufacturers of fine cut chewing and smoking tobacco in the United States. They occupy their own six story building, fronting 225 feet on Chestnut street, corner of Thirteenth, and are the originators and exclusive owners of the celebrated brands of "Golden Thread Fine Cut" and "Meerschaum" and "O. S." Smoking Tobaccos, which have stood the tests of the most critical chewers and smokers for thirty-nine years.

**St. Louis Glass Works.**—J. K. Cummings, President; Charles Bauman, Secretary; 2301 to 2315 North Broadway.—This is the oldest glass factory in the city, having been established in 1847 by Capt. J. B. Eads, who has since attained a world-wide celebrity as one of the greatest engineers of the age. The works passed through many changes of ownership until Mr. Cummings, who had been clerk for the old company, and Mr. Bagot, foreman of the works, formed the firm of Bagot & Cummings in 1861. Mr. Bagot died in 1870, and Mr. Cummings continued the business alone until March, 1886, when the present company was incorporated, Mr. Cummings becoming its President. The works, which give employment to a force of eighty employees, cover two-thirds of a block, and are fitted up with all the necessary machinery and plant for the manufacture of fine flint druggists' prescription bottles, flasks, etc., to which department of glassmaking the company confines itself exclusively. They have a large trade in the city and the territory of which it forms the business center, the goods made by them having an established reputation for superior excellence. Mr. Cummings, the President of the company, and to whose efficient management the prosperity of the works is mainly due, is well-known in commercial circles as a gentleman of superior business attainments. He is also a prominent figure in the politics of the city, and has served as a respected and prominent member of the City Council.

**Philibert & Johanning Manufacturing Company.**—J. H. Kaiser, President; Herman Kunz, Secretary and Treasurer; Manufacturers of Sash, Doors, Blinds, Etc.; Office and Factory, 1502 Market street.—This large and important manufacturing concern was established in 1837 by Mr. Benjamin J. Philibert, now deceased. In 1874 the firm became Philibert & Johanning, which was succeeded in 1882 by the present corporation. The company do an extensive business as manufacturers of sash, doors, blinds, frames, glazed windows, mouldings, stair railing, balusters, newel posts, lumber, lath and shingles, and dealers in all kinds of building material. They occupy as office and factory a spacious and handsome three-story

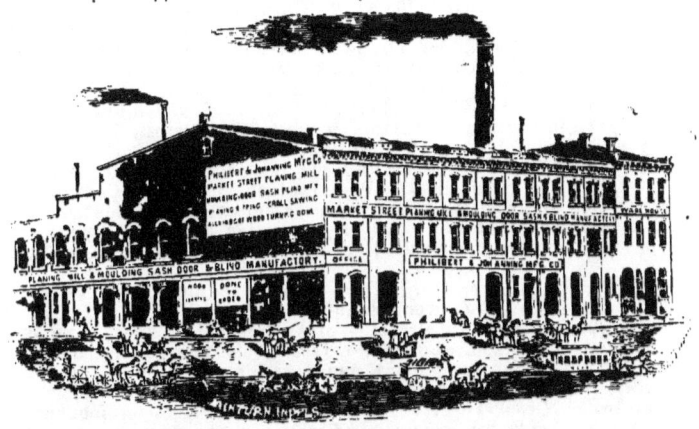

brick building, 225x140 feet, supplied with machinery of the most modern and improved make, and all the necessary plant and equipments for planing mill, scroll sawing and wood-turning purposes. They also have a branch office and salesroom at 115 and 117 Olive street, and large yards at Seventeenth and Market streets and at Eighteenth and Walnut streets. They employ one hundred and thirty men and five wagons, and have first-class facilities for manufacture, handling and shipment. They have a large trade, extending all over the West and South and have a widespread and merited reputation for the superiority of their manufacture, their promptness in filling orders, and the fair and honorable methods which have ever characterized the business conduct of this house throughout the half century of its successful and honorable history.

**Barnhart Mercantile Company.**—William R. Barnhart, President; C. L. Barnhart, Vice-President and Treasurer; H. P. Miller, Secretary; Wholesale Dealers in Fancy Groceries, Foreign and Domestic Fruits, etc.; 413 North Second street.—The large establishment conducted by the Barnhart Mercantile Co. was founded in 1877 by Mr. William R. Barnhart, and was incorporated under its present name in 1883. The premises occupied by the company consist of a commodious five-story building, 40x150 feet, comprising No. 413 North Second street. They do a very large wholesale business in fancy groceries, of every description, to which branch of their trade they devote special attention, and are also large jobbers in foreign and domestic fruits, nuts and canned goods, making specialties of oranges, lemons, cranberries, peanuts, pecans, etc. They do an extensive business sending foreign nuts, cranberries, etc., to California, from whence they bring fruit; send nuts, sauer kraut, etc., to New Orleans, and do a large trade east to Indianapolis, and all west to California, and in all the territory north and south between these two points, enjoying a specially large patronage in the States of Missouri, Iowa, Minnesota and Kansas. The company employs five experienced traveling men to represent their business on the road, and have twenty competent assistants employed in their store. They have a complete plant of the most modern machinery and appliances for hand-picking and cleaning peanuts, which they handle in immense quantities. Few people have any adequate conception of the importance of the trade in peanuts, which are as staple as coffee, and an article of commerce in which transactions of great magnitude are carried on, and from which St. Louis receives much profit. The history of the house has been one of steady and continuous growth, and it has had a large share in the prosperity resulting from the general revival of business in 1886, while its outlook for the future is bright and promising. With every facility for advantageous transactions in its line of trade, and a high reputation for the uniform superiority of its goods, the spirit of fairness and liberality by which its dealings are ever characterized, and the absolute correctness of its business methods, this house enjoys, in an eminent degree, the esteem and confidence of the trade, and that high standing and assured success which legitimately results from manifest merit.

**Joe J. Mullally.**—Broker; 109 North Third street.—Mr. Mullally, who carries on a prosperous business as a broker, at 109 North Third street, has only been established here since March, 1886, but he has already attained a prominent position in the commercial and financial circles of the city. Receiving the solid foundation of a liberal collegiate education in this city, his first venture into commercial life was in the grain business at Williamsburg, Kansas, which he built up to a successful development, and in which he still retains a substantial interest. Since his removal to this city, he has carried on the business of a broker in bonds, stocks and every description of reliable investment securities, making a specialty of the better class of mining stocks, for the buying and selling of which his facilities are unsurpassed. By close attention to the details of every transaction entrusted to his care and management, he has established an excellent reputation as a reliable medium for the investor in stocks, and has acquired a large and valuable business connection.

**Branch-Crookes Saw Company.**—Joseph W. Branch, President; R. L. Fosburgh, Secretary and Treasurer; Manufacturers of all kinds of Saws, Planing Knives, etc.; 522 North Third street; Works, 3000 to 3018 North Broadway.—In 1849, Mr. Joseph W. Branch, who had previously been engaged in the manufacture of saws in New York City, came to St. Louis and bought out the St. Louis Saw Works, which had been recently established by the firm of Childs, Pratt & Co. The firm of Branch, Crookes & Frost was then established and continued the business until 1857, when the style was changed to Branch, Crookes & Co., which was maintained until the incorporation of the present company, the founder of the house becoming its President, and Mr. R. L. Fosburgh, who had been a member of the firm of Branch, Crookes & Co. since 1874, becoming Secretary. From its inception, the history of this house, now in its 38th year, has been one of steady, constant and honorable growth, the articles of its production having attained a merited celebrity with manufacturers of lumber in all the regions in which those industries are carried on, and having a very large sale in the States of Michigan, Minnesota, California, Oregon, Florida, Texas, Arkansas, Washington Territory, and all timbered regions. The office and salesrooms of the company are located at 522 North Third street, and its works at 3000 to 3018 North Broadway cover nearly an entire block, running through to the Wabash, St. Louis and Pacific railroad. These works give employment to a force of one hundred skilled workmen, in addition to which the company has five traveling salesmen constantly on the road. The company manufactures circular saws adapted to every use to which they can be put, ice saws, drag saws, cross-cut saws, patent cross-cut saw handles, felloe web saws, turning web saws, scroll saws, veneering saws, butchers' saws, band saws, etc., saw gummers, swages, mandrels, cant hooks, saw files, patent post-hole augers, planing machine knives, etc., and handles rubber and leather belting, grindstones, etc. Its stock embraces everything adapted to the use of lumbermen and saw-mills, planing mills, etc., and cannot be surpassed for quality, while its business methods have earned for it the approval and the confidence of the trade throughout the country.

**I. B. Rosenthal & Company.**—Importers, Manufacturers and Jobbers of Millinery Goods; Northeast Corner of Washington avenue and Broadway.—The firm of I. B. Rosenthal & Co., composed of Messrs. I. B., M. B., and Sig. Rosenthal and S. R. Lipsis, established in 1876 its business in this city, and have also a house in New York. They manufacture pattern hats here, employing a force of fifty girls, and are large importers and jobbers of ribbons, silks, feathers, flowers, velvets, straw goods, trimmings and everything pertaining to the millinery line, of which they carry a heavy and thoroughly assorted stock. From their two houses they have a trade which extends to every part of the Union, and from their house here have eleven salesmen as traveling representatives of the firm. They have superior facilities for the transaction of their business, occupying a spacious five-story building, 50x120 feet, and manage their affairs with a perfect and accurate system, upon enterprising and liberal methods. At their New York house they manufacture ostrich feathers, in which specialty they have no superior in the country. The St. Louis house is the headquarters of the firm, whose members are all well-known in business circles. Mr. I. B. Rosenthal, the senior partner, is a director in the Fifth National Bank.

**A. E. Faust.**— Wholesale and Retail Dealer in Fresh Oysters, Sea Fish, Celery, and Other Foreign and Domestic Delicacies; Corner Broadway and Elm street.— As an importer and large dealer in high-class foreign and domestic delicacies, Mr. Faust has held the most prominent position in St. Louis for the past fifteen years. He is the proprietor of the most fashionable saloon and restaurant in the city—the famous Fulton Market and Exposition Restaurant. He employs from seventy-five to one hundred hands at the Broadway establishment, twenty-five on the terrace over the same, and from sixty to seventy-five at the Exposition Restaurant. He is the proprietor of "Faust's Own" brand of fresh oysters, of which, in his spacious and completely equipped packing rooms under the Fulton Market, he puts up 7,000 cans per day in the season. He has recently secured a renewal of the lease of the Broadway establishment, adjoining the Southern Hotel, for fourteen years, and purposes erecting a fine building at that location, in furtherance of which object he is now making a European tour. The new premises will have all the latest improvements of similar first-class establishments of European and Atlantic cities. Among the delicacies dealt in by Mr. Faust in addition to oysters, sea fish and celery, are all kinds of imported cheese, fine bottle goods, such as pickled oysters, capers, pickles, olive oil, salad dressings, sauces, soys, mangoes, anchovy and shrimp pastes, catsups, curry powders, prepared mustards, gumbo file, canned goods such as turtle meat, soups, pate de fois gras, chili con carne, boned chicken and turkey, deviled ham, crab butter, chowder, boneless pigs' feet, salmon, lobster, sardines, sprotten, tuny fish, shrimps, caviar, eels, truffles, asparagus, peas, mushrooms, figs, artichokes, okra, etc., fruits in glass, olives, sausages, Westphalia ham, Findon haddock, and all kinds of delicacies, fresh fish in great variety, frogs, crabs, terrapins, and all game in season. This great Fulton Market is the only establishment of its kind west of New York, and enjoys a large family trade. Seven wagons are required for city delivery, and the establishment is the popular resort of the city. Mr. George J. Hagaman, who has been with Mr. Faust for over eight years, is his general manager and buyer. He is thoroughly experienced in the business, is widely and favorably known, and has greatly aided in bringing about the steady increase which is yearly experienced in Mr. Faust's successful business.

**Gerber & Signaigo.**—Fruit and General Commission Merchants; 816 North Third street.—The business now conducted by the firm, of Gerber & Signaigo, of which Messrs. Charles Gerber and D. J. Signaigo are the members, was originally established over twenty-five years ago by Mr. Valentine Gerber, the firm afterward becoming Gerber, Signaigo & Bro., and later adopting its present style. Occupying a commodious five-story building, 25x100 feet, the firm has every facility and convenience for the transaction of its large and constantly increasing business, and the house is headquarters for Florida oranges and deals extensively in every description of foreign and domestic fruits, making fine tropical varieties a leading specialty, and also handle all kinds of small fruits. The house has a large city trade and also enjoys an extensive patronage covering the States of Missouri, Nebraska, Iowa, Illinois, Arkansas, Kentucky, Indiana, Texas and Kansas. In the business history of this house, covering a period of a quarter of a century, it has ever held a high place in the esteem and confidence of the trade by the entire reliability of its dealings and the freshness and superiority of its goods.

**The Mechanics' Bank.**—D. K. Ferguson, President; R. R. Hutchinson, Cashier; corner of Fourth and Pine streets.—The incorporation of the Mechanics' Bank was effected early in 1857. The bank was opened for business in November, 1857, Joseph Charless being the first President, to whom succeeded in order, J. W. Wills, Oliver Garrison and, in 1879, D. K. Ferguson, the present incumbent. J. W. Wills was the first cashier, and he was followed in succession by Charles Everts, George T. Hulse, and R. R. Hutchinson, the latter taking his position in 1879, and still retaining it. The financial history of this bank has been one of steady and healthy growth. It has always held a prominent position among the financial institutions of the city, and is justly regarded as one of the strongest and best conducted. The statement of its financial condition published at the beginning of the current year makes a healthy showing. The capital stock was $600,000; surplus, $217,872.14; while its resources amounted to a total of $3,219,808.36. The affairs of the bank have thrived in an especially satisfactory manner, fully participating in the business revival of 1886, which was the most prosperous year in its history, and the present year giving promise of a business equalling, if not excelling, its predecessor in satisfactory results. The present directors of the bank are O. Garrison, D. K. Ferguson, E. N. Leeds, John N. Booth, D. R. Garrison, Ben B. Graham, W. L. Wickham, J. T. Drummond, Ezra H. Linley, George M. Flanagan, Theo. F. Meyer, Wm. Somerville and R. R. Hutchinson.

**Pacific Oil Company.**—O. L. Mersman, President and Treasurer; B. F. Parmalee, Secretary; Producers and Manufacturers of Lubricating, Valve and Railway Oils; 207 North Third street.—The Pacific Oil Company has been well known for some twelve or fifteen years, although the incorporation only dates from 1885, prior to which other interests were purchased by Mr. Mersman, now President of the company. The company have a large factory on Sixteenth and Poplar streets, on the Missouri Pacific Railroad, with the best machinery for compounding fine oils, and employing a large force of skilled workmen. The business of the house is very large, extending over the States of Missouri, Illinois, Louisiana, Florida, Alabama, Georgia, Tennessee, Texas, etc., and the Republic of Mexico, and Canada. They sell largely to railroads, having over thirty large railroads on their books, supplying some by yearly contracts, and some from month to month; also to coal mines, brewers, car works, foundries, large factories, plantations and all who use lubricants. The company's special brands, "Paris Valve Oil" and "Kohinoor Car Grease," are in great demand, because of their superior excellence and effectiveness. The company has an agency at Fort Scott, Kansas, and have recently established one at St. Paul, Minn. Twelve active and energetic travelers represent the company on the road; and the great superiority of its goods, and the perfect system and reliability of the business methods by which it is managed, have secured for it a high reputation and assured success. Mr. Mersman, the President, is highly esteemed as a business man of superior attainments, and Mr. Parmalee, the Secretary, has been well and favorably known to the oil trade for the past twenty years.

**The Heisler Electric Light Company.**—Charles Heisler, President; Manufacturers and Patentees of Arc and Incandescent Dynamo Machines and Lamps, also of Heisler Electric Bells, Burglar Alarms, Annunciators, etc.; also American Carbon Co., Manufacturers of Carbons for Electric Lights; also St. Louis Illuminating Company; St. Louis Offices and Works, 809 to 817 South Seventh street.—The history and career of the inventive genius, and founder of these enterprises is a remarkable one, and furnishes abundant illustration of what can be accomplished by brains, pluck and enterprise. Mr. Charles Heisler, President of the company whose title heads this paragraph, and managing director of the others which are the result of his wonderful powers of invention, began his career in St. Louis in 1870, and has since done more to devise and render electric lighting practical and popular than

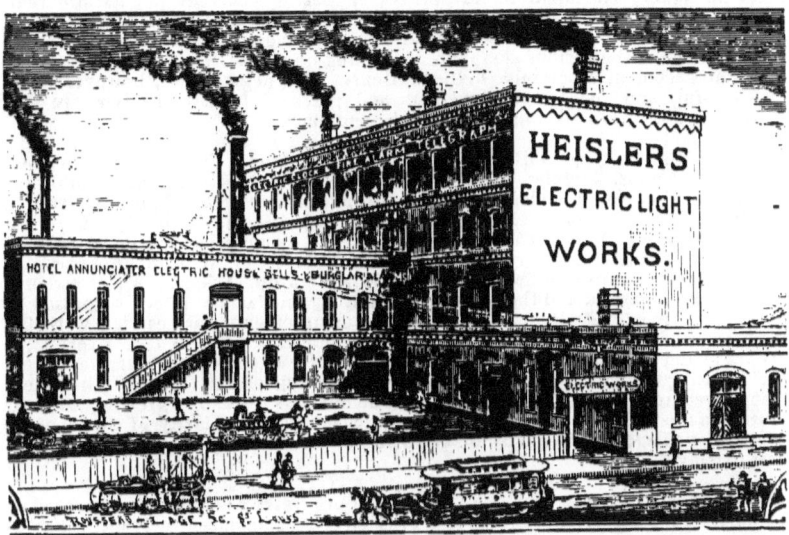

any man living. He is a German, possessed of thorough education, and is a mechanical engineer and electrician of world wide celebrity. He established himself here in the business of manufacturing hotel annunciators, house bells, burglar alarms, etc., which was a very successful enterprise from the first. When his business had become thoroughly established, and had reached important proportions, he formed the Heisler Electric Bell and Burglar Alarm Co. The apparatus manufactured by this company are of a very superior order and they are in general use everywhere. There are many thousands of them in use, and they are so perfect that no readjustment or attention is required after once put up. Notwithstanding the great and immediate success with which Mr. Heisler met in this line, his whole desire was to arrange and perfect a system of electric lighting, and much of his time was devoted to the accomplishment of this object. He at last succeeded in this as in all other things, and the value of his discoveries and patents were early demonstrated in St. Louis and other Western cities. So great was the success of his system, and so perfect the results that in 1882 the Heisler Electric Light Co. was incorporated, with a paid up capital of $200,000, which has been most successful in the development and application of electric light for general illumination. The company now exclusively manufactures complete systems of incandescent lights, used for street and outdoor illumination as well as for all indoor purposes. The Heisler system is used in many of the cities of the country, and has proven highly satisfactory wherever introduced, and is making steady progress all over this country. It is at the present time the only successful long distance incandescent system. The character and high business standing of the patrons of this system indicate that it is its destiny to assume the most gigantic proportions as a general illuminator and competitor of gas. We mention chiefly the Brush Electric Light Companies of Salt Lake City and Ogden City, Utah, and of Norfolk, Va.; the Thompson & Houston Companies of Leavenworth (Coal Co.) and Ottawa, Kansas, and of Cleveland, Ohio; besides a number of new and prosperous plants in nearly all the States. Another important industry of which this wonderful mind is the directing spirit is the American Carbon Co. This company manufactures the carbon points for electric light, and its carbons are pronounced to be the very best that are made. The product goes to all parts of the country, and three-fourths of it is shipped to New York city. Still another result and outgrowth of Charles Heisler's brain is the St. Louis Illuminating Co., a company organized for the purpose of supplying electric light from central stations. This system, devised by Mr. Heisler, can be transmitted, over a moderate sized wire, to any distance from the central station. It is said light can be transmitted thirty miles under this plan. The manifold advantages of these systems are at once apparent, and testimonials from all sections are embraced in the catalogue of the company. It is but recently that an Eastern syndicate, representing millions of capital, endeavored to purchase the various companies operating under Mr. Heisler's systems, and direct and control absolutely his inventions. The negotiations, however, were unsuccessful, and the system invented and patented by Mr. Heisler are still St. Louis enterprises and controlled by this gentleman.

**L. Moller & Co.**—Builders of First Class Carriages, Rockaways, Barouches. Surreys, Phaetons, Buggies, etc.; 604 Market street.—This is an old established business, having been founded by the late Nathan Card in 1849. Upon his death in September 1886, Mr. Louis Moller, who had been associated with Mr. Card for eleven years as foreman and salesman, bought the business, and associating with himself Mr. Frank Moller, Jr., established the present firm. The premises occupied by them are four stories in height and 30x130 feet in dimensions. About twenty-five men are employed and the work turned out by the factory is not surpassed by any in the city or elsewhere. A specialty is made of first-class carriages, rockaways, barouches, surreys, phaetons, buggies, etc., and the firm have a very large city trade and a generous share of the best country business, the character of the work inviting the patronage of people of wealth and good taste. Only skilled labor is employed and the best materials used. The business is steadily growing, and the house sustains the reputation it has long held for the superiority of the vehicles built at their factory. They also make a specialty of painting and repairing of first-class carriages.

**F. W. Humphrey & Co.**—The live and progressive clothing firm located on the northeast corner of Broadway and Pine street, commenced mercantile operations on the 20th of September, 1873, the day so well remembered in financial circles by the failure of Jay Cooke in New York, and the subsequent great panic that paralyzed the monetary system of the whole country for the time being. The young firm of F. W. H. & Co., however, came here to raise a panic on their own account—their straight-forward, iron-clad, one-priced system of business created havoc in the ranks of their then competitors, who used to do that kind of "wildcat" business which caused a certain amount of odium to attach itself to the clothing trade. All that is changed now, and the enterprising firm of F. W. H. & Co. are justly entitled to the laurels they won as the pioneers of a clean and wholesome clothing business, an institution that was unknown anterior to their establishment here. The store room that they first occupied was only one fifth of their present space and even now every hole and corner is crowded with the choicest and most reliable articles called for in their four main departments. viz: Male attire—Juvenile attire—Hats—and Furnishings, and their cry is still room, room, more room.

**Wrought Iron Range Company.**—L. L. Culver, President; R. H. Stockton, Vice-President; W. W. Culver, Secretary; Manufacturers of Ranges and Furnaces; Nineteenth street and Washington avenue.—This corporation was formed and incorporated in 1881, with a paid up capital of $500,000. The premises occupied by the company comprise a spacious four-story building fronting 100 feet on Washington avenue, and running back 150 feet on Nineteenth street. Here a force of two hundred workmen are employed, and outside of this force the company uses the product of over one thousand molders and annealers, and buy annually two hundred and fifty thousand pounds of the best wrought iron that is made and two hundred thousand pounds of sheet steel. The company have long been celebrated as the manufacturers of the "Home Comfort" wrought iron ranges and wrought steel furnaces, which are acknowledged to be the best in use. The merit of their manufacture has obtained for the company a large trade which extends to every part of the country. Their works are equipped with a complete plant and every facility and convenience for the successful prosecution of their manufacturing operations. The business has steadily grown from its inception, and the ample means and efficient management of the company have enabled it to distance all competitors and achieve a success commensurate with the superiority of their product.

**Crescent Furniture and Lumber Company.**—W. B. Duncan, President; A. H. Kayser, Secretary and Treasurer; Manufacturers of Kitchen Safes, Tables, Wardrobes, Etc.; 1620 to 1628 North Tenth street.—This corporation, which was formed in 1884, occupies spacious four-story premises, 100x150 feet, which are completely fitted with all the most modern and improved machinery adapted to

the requirements of the business. A force of one hundred skilled and experienced workmen are employed, and the firm manufacture kitchen safes, tables, washstands, beds, suits and wardrobes and deal in poplar lumber, of which they carry a large stock in all useful lengths and dimensions. Confining their manufacture to the specialties above mentioned, the firm has acquired a prominent standing in the trade for the superiority of its workmanship, and the products of its factory are in great demand in a territory embracing the States of Missouri, Illinois, Kansas, Iowa, Nebraska, Minnesota, Colorado, Arkansas, Texas and the entire West and South. The business has steadily increased from its inception, and the company enjoys unequaled facilities for carrying on its line of manufacture. It is managed on systematic business principles and with a practical supervision of every detail by which the goods made are kept up to the high standard, as a result of which the success of the company has been achieved.

**James A. Smith & Sons Ice and Fuel Company.**—James A. Smith, President; Stephen L. Smith, Vice-President; James A. Smith, Jr., Secretary; Wholesale and Retail Dealers in Ice and Fuel; Office, Seventh and Franklin avenue.—The advantage of water transportation to the South, as well as extensive railroad facilities, has caused St. Louis to become an important depot of supply in the ice trade with Western and Southern cities. Every season many thousands of tons of ice are cut from the river at this point and stored for the summer's requirements. One of the largest, as well as the oldest and one of the most prominent, firms engaged in the ice trade in St. Louis, is that of James A. Smith & Sons, which was incorporated in 1884 as the James A. Smith & Sons Ice and Fuel Co., with a paid up capital of $150,000. The business of this company is very extensive, and has kept pace with the growth of the city. The business was founded in 1854 by Mr. James A. Smith, who has continued in it since that early day, and has by untiring energy and enterprising business capacity expanded it until to-day it is the largest concern of its kind in the West. President Smith has had his sons associated with him in the business for several years, and the business instinct and qualifications so largely possessed by the elder are inherited by the sons, who, since their admission into the firm, have developed extraordinary business aptitude, and have given to the business of the house an additional impetus that has resulted in largely increased trade. President Smith and his sons, Stephen L., James A., Jr., and Arthur F., the latter in charge of the storage houses at Litchfield, own all of the stock, except $1,000 that is held by one of the foremen. The company has storage for ice at Deep Lake, Indian Lake, Minnesota; Milan, Rock Island Co.; Sears Mill, Rock River; Litchfield Reservoir; Southeastern Depot, East St. Louis, Smith's Bay, Arsenal Island, Illinois; and at Seventh and Franklin avenue, and Second and North Market streets in St. Louis. Besides the storage houses in this city, the company have depots for the sale of ice at 817 North Seventh street, and Second and North Market streets. It also has a branch office at the railroad ice switch, on Clark avenue and Eighteenth street. The capacity of this company is about 120,000 tons, which are handled annually. Ice is shipped to all points South and also to Missouri and Missouri River points. The company has machinery and all of the latest appliances for the cutting of ice. Mr. Stephen L. Smith is the inventor of an ice planer and groover, a stationary knife, on the elevator which planes the frozen snow from the surface of the ice, and grooves the cakes in such a way that they can be easily removed from the storage houses without breaking. The appliance has attracted wide attention. King's Lake in Lincoln County, Mo., is owned by the company, and over $8,000 has been expended in erecting railroad switches to it. Vast quantities of pure ice are cut from the lake every season.

**Mississippi Glass Company.**—Edward Walsh, Jr., President. St. Louis; E. W. Humphreys, Vice-President. New York: Manufacturers of Rough and Ribbed Plate Glass; Main and Angelica streets.—That Missouri furnishes in an unequaled degree the natural facilities in the way of materials is an admitted geological fact, and this has caused several enterprises in the line of glass making to be established here. The Mississippi Glass Company, however, occupies a field peculiarly its own, being one of the only two concerns in the country that manufactures rough and ribbed plate glass, crown disc and cathedral and patent ondoyant glass, the latter taking the lead of all for church and house decorative purposes. The other factory is in Massachusetts, but lacks the advantages of material and eligible location possessed by the St. Louis establishment. The grounds cover over three acres, upon which are two factories, 100x150 feet each; several large warehouses, some of which have been recently erected, and a handsome suite of offices lately built by the company. A large force of workmen, about two hundred and fifty in number, are constantly employed, and the annual business amounts to over $500,000 yearly, the trade of the company extending from the Atlantic to the Pacific and from the Canadian border to the Gulf of Mexico. The product of these factories is not excelled in quality by that of any similar establishment in the world. The business, from the incorporation of the company in 1870 to the present, has steadily grown, and the management of the company's affairs, under the direction of Mr. Edward Walsh, Jr., the President of the company, has been characterized by energy and enterprise, and has been attended by great prosperity. Mr. E. W. Humphreys, the Vice-President, resides in New York, and has charge of the Eastern business of the company.

**A. Frankenthal & Brother.**—Manufacturers and Dealers in Men's Furnishing Goods; 409 North Broadway.—One of the largest firms in St. Louis engaged in the manufacture of gentlemen's furnishing goods is that of A. Frankenthal and Bro., who entered into business in 1863. The firm was located in the building at No. 18 North Main street for many years, but the establishment becoming insufficient to accommodate the large business which had been built up by the firm, a change of location was imperative. In 1878, Mr. Frankenthal, realizing the fact that the natural tendency of the jobbing trade was toward locations farther west, secured the convenient and desirable building at 409 North Broadway, and removed during that year to the new store. It is a five-story and basement structure, built of stone and iron. It is equipped with elevators and steam apparatus, and is in every way well adapted to the requirements of the firm. All of the floors are filled with a large and well assorted stock, and the adjoining building, No. 407, is used for the storage of reserve stock. An insurance of $270,000 is carried on the stock, which never runs below $300,000. The annual business of the house is close to $750,000, and the trade is located in Missouri, Illinois, Kansas, Arkansas, Louisiana, Texas, Indian Territory, Colorado, Nebraska, Iowa, and nearly all sections of the West and Southwest. The firm manufacture largely its own goods, but not all by any means. They have factories located at 717 and 719 North Third street, and give employment steadily to about one hundred and twenty hands. They are one of the solid and representative jobbing firms of St. Louis.

**A. Cafferata, Sons & Co.**—Importers and Wholesale Dealers in Tropical Fruits, Florida and California Oranges, etc.; 714 North Fourth street.—This leading firm of importers and wholesale dealers in tropical fruits is now composed of Messrs. A. J. Cafferata, L. D. Cassenelli, F. I. Cafferata and Charles DeVoto. The establishment is the oldest of its kind in St. Louis, having been founded in 1854 by Mr. A. Cafferata, who remained at the head of the house until his death in 1881, and to

## THE INDUSTRIES OF ST. LOUIS. 99

whose far-seeing sagacity is due the early growth of a house acknowledged as a leading one in its line, and now occupying the spacious four-story building, 25x125 feet, at 714 North Fourth street. The firm deals largely in Florida oranges, California grapes, oranges, pears and other fruits, tropical fruits, nuts, dates, figs, raisins, imported macaroni, vermicelli, olive oil, etc., making a specialty, in their season, of Florida and California oranges. They are the agents of The Cresent Orange Grove Co., of Citra, Marion County, Florida, whose groves are celebrated for the superiority of their product. They import bananas direct from Honduras and Aspinwall, and maintain the most favorable relations with shippers and producers of fruit in all the countries from whence their stock is derived, giving them facilities which enable them to offer special inducements, both in price and quality, to the trade. They have a very heavy city trade, as well as a large patronage in the States of Missouri, Iowa, Illinois, Kansas, Arkansas, Texas, Nebraska, Indian Territory, Louisiana, Mississippi, etc. The house has always borne an excellent reputation for correct dealings and stands prominent in the esteem and confidence of the trade.

**Wm. Koenig & Co.**—Reapers, Mowers, Binders, Threshers and Canton Engines; 120 and 122 South Eighth street.—This well-known and substantial house was established in 1858 as John Garnett & Co., changing later to Blunden, Koenig & Co., then to Koenig & Bauer, and about 1867 to its present style, and is now conducted by Mr. Koenig as sole proprietor. He represents Aultman, Miller & Co., of Akron, Ohio, manufacturers of the most complete line of grass and

grain cutting machines made by any one house, including the Buckeye Folding Binder, Buckeye Down Binder, New Buckeye Light Mower, New Buckeye Mower to Combine, New Buckeye Table Rake, New Buckeye Dropper, and Akron Mower. These machines have long been acknowledged to be unsurpassed by any manufactured and are standard articles of farm machinery. Wm. Koenig & Co. also represent C. Aultman & Co., of Canton, Ohio, manufacturers of portable engines and threshing machinery, including Miller's New Model Vibrating Thresher; the Canton Monitor Plain and Traction Farm Engine; the Star Portable and Traction Engine; the Phœnix Straw-Burning Portable and Traction Engine; the Monitor Semi-Portable Engine; and the Cary and Improved Dingee-Woodbury Horse Powers, all leading machines which have met with the widest approval and proved their superiority by the test of practical use. Mr. Koenig has handled these lines of machinery for twenty-six years, and has had great success with them, doing a large business throughout this section, employing six traveling salesmen and having about one hundred and forty sub-agents in the district. He occupies spacious four-story premises, 60x130 feet, and carries a complete stock of the machines above enumerated. Mr. Koenig is one of the best known and most highly respected business men in the city, and is regarded with confidence by the community. He is, and has been for a number of years, chairman of the Ways and Means Committee of the School Board; is Vice-President of the St. Louis Mutual Building Association, director of the German Savings Institution, and otherwise prominently identified with many important business enterprises. His great success is the legitimate result of close attention to business and integrity in all the relations of life.

**The Hydraulic Press Brick Company.**—E. C. Sterling, President; J. H. Clark, Vice-President; H. W. Eliot, Secretary and Treasurer; Louis Chauvenet, Assistant Secretary; W. N. Graves, Superintendent; Office, Turner Building, 304 North Eighth street.—This business was established in 1866 by Mr. E. C. Sterling.

now President of the company, which was incorporated in 1868 with a capital stock of $600,000. It soon took a foremost position in this line of industry and is recognized as the largest manufacturing concern in its line in the United States. The works are run to their full capacity, which is 60,0 0,000 common brick and 10,000,000 pressed front brick per annum. These works are located as follows: Yard No. 1 Grand and Chouteau avenues; Yard No. 2, King's Highway and Pacific Railway; Yard No. 3, Cheltenham; Yard No. 4, Wabash Railway and Manchester road, and Yard No. 5, King's Highway and San Francisco Railway. The company has telephone connection with all yards and 4,500 feet of private switches, connecting with three railroads and through the Union Depot with all railroads in the country. In addition to these works and facilities the company control the Union Press Brick Works and handles their entire output, amounting to about 30,000,000 brick per annum. Of this company E. C. Sterling is President and G. W. Simpkins Secretary. The Hydraulic Press Brick Co. is noted for the great superiority of its manufacture. From five hundred to seven hundred men are employed, according to the season, and the company enjoys a trade not equalled by any other brick manufacturing concern. Its common brick is mostly sold in St. Louis and the country immediately surrounding it, but its pressed, molded and ornamental bricks, manufactured by its own process, have a much wider market, extending northward into Canada and south to the Gulf of Mexico. Chicago is a very large customer, the greater part of the pressed brick used in the fine buildings there being supplied from these works, and the company maintains a branch office in that city. Every city of the West, Northwest and South draws upon this company for these fine brick. The front brick manufactured by this company are of perfect shape, good color and great strength. No artificial colors are used, the bricks are less troubled with whitewash than any bricks in the country, and are homogeneous and can be carved as easily as stone. About one hundred different styles are kept in stock, all of the finest quality. The great success of the company is a proof that superior goods and accurate methods are the roads to prosperity in business.

**Schwab Clothing Company.**—Isaac Schwab, President; Max Schwab, Secretary; Manufacturers of Clothing, 803 Washington avenue.—This house was established in 1865, and has enjoyed a successful career and a steadily expanding business. In 1883 the present corporation was formed, and it now occupies a spacious seven-story building, 30x125 feet in dimensions. The company keeps from twenty-five to thirty skilled and experienced cutters constantly employed and send their work out to shops which they control and supply with capital and work, and in which from five hundred to six hundred workmen are employed on work for the company. The stock carried by the house is large and complete, and embraces everything in the line of clothing in heavy supply. Eight traveling salesmen represent the house and the company's trade extends to the States of Missouri, Illinois, Kansas, Nebraska, Iowa, Colorado, Texas, Arkansas, Louisiana, Mississippi, Tennessee and the entire South and Southwest. The house has a leading position in the trade and is justly esteemed as one of the most thriving, fair and liberal in the West.

**Druhe Hardwood Lumber Company.**—William Druhe, President; William Kroeger, Vice-President; John Druhe, Secretary; Wholesale Dealers in Hardwood Lumber: Office, Tenth street and Clark avenue.—It is more than twenty years since this business was originally established by Mr. William Druhe, who still remains at its head as the honored President of the Druhe Hardwood Lumber Co., incorporated in 1880. The company have mills in Arkansas and Indian Territory, completely fitted with every description of machinery and first-class plants for the conduct of the business, and employing about one hundred men. In this city they have a large warehouse for fine stock, which, with the adjoining yards, covers about a block, and employ twenty men and eight teams in the handling of their immense stock, comprising walnut, cherry, poplar, ash, hickory, oak, gum, California redwood, and quarter sawed oak and mahogany. They make a specialty of walnut, in which their stock is not excelled in amount or quality by any concern in the West. They do a large city trade and also ship to all points in the North, East and West. They have unsurpassed facilities for the handling and shipment of lumber and maintain the excellent reputation which they have enjoyed for twenty years by adherence to the accurate and reliable principles by which their immense business has been built up to its present proportions. They are prepared to fill all orders in a prompt and satisfactory manner.

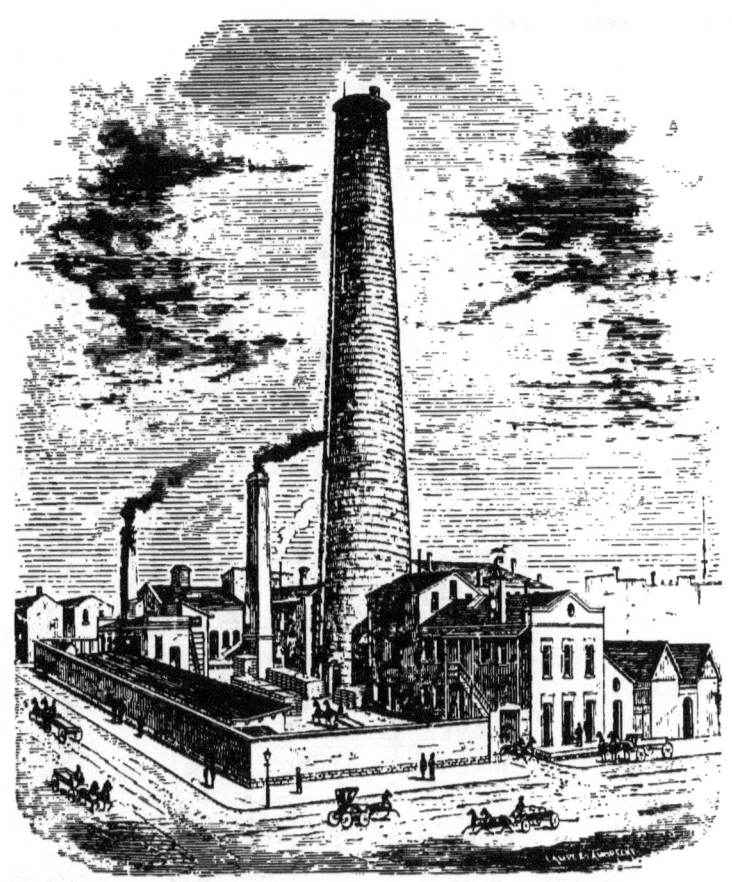

**St. Louis Shot Tower Company.**—G. W. Chadbourne, President; J. W. McLanahan, Secretary; Manufacturers of Shot and Bar Lead; Works, 1405 Lewis street; Office, 100 North Main street.—One of the striking monuments of the city's industry is the tall tower, 186 feet high, of the St. Louis Shot Tower Company, manufacturers of shot and bar lead and dealers in pig lead. Upon this page is presented a view of the tower and the works of the company, which cover one-fourth of a block on Lewis street. The diameter of the tower is thirty-one feet at the base and seventeen feet at the top, and its casting floor is 176 feet from the water tank. The tower is built of hard burnt brick and thoroughly substantial, and its capacity is twenty-five tons per day. The works are completely equipped with the most modern and improved machinery and give employment to about thirty-five skilled workmen. The office is located at 100 North Main street. The business was established in 1846 and incorporated in 1857. Prior to the incorporation it was conducted by the firm of Kennett, Simmonds & Co., although it was always known as the St. Louis Shot Tower Co. The president of the existing company, from its incorporation, Mr. G. W. Chadbourne, has had forty-seven years' experience in the business of shot manufacture, and under his able management the business of the company has been a great financial success. The proximity of this city to the mines gives the company great advantage over the manufacturers of other cities, and the uniform merit of its product has secured for it a large trade in shot, and in bar and pig lead over the entire scope of the West and South from Minnesota to the Gulf of Mexico.

HAYDOCK BROS.' NEW FACTORY.—See opposite page.

**Haydock Brothers.**—Wholesale Carriage Manufacturers: Northwest Corner of Chouteau Avenue and Third street.—The prominence of St. Louis as a center for the manufacture and distribution of carriages has been adverted to in a former portion of this work, and is a gratifying fact in the business development of the city. In this line of productive industry no firm stands more prominent before the public than that of Haydock Brothers, whose establishment here is the largest of its kind west of the Mississippi River, and has an important standing among the leading factories in the United States. The business was commenced in St. Louis in 1878 by Haydock Brothers, who had for many years previously been engaged in the same business in Cincinnati. In 1883 Mr. D. W. Haydock withdrew from the firm, and since then the business has been conducted by Mr. Wm. T. Haydock, under the old firm name. The factory covers the entire block on Third street, from Chouteau avenue to Lombard street, a distance of 300 feet, and has a frontage of 150 feet on each of the latter thoroughfares. In addition to the main factory the premises include an adjoining building on Chouteau avenue. Mr. Haydock has also recently leased the old warehouse building, occupying the block between Broadway and Sixth street on Chouteau, which he utilizes for storage of material, etc., and which is a large and commodious two-story building. The factory premises have a most complete plant, including all the most modern and improved machinery, and every device and accessory calculated to aid or expedite the vast manufacturing operations of the firm. This mammoth enterprise gives steady employment to a force averaging about four hundred hands, and manufactures about 10,000 vehicles annually. The work turned out at this establishment has a widespread reputation for its superior quality, the excellence of the material used and the completeness of workmanship and beauty of finish which is characteristic of every vehicle built at this factory. The vehicles manufactured by this house include piano-box, drop front, coal box, Brewster side-bar and Timken side-bar buggies, Dexter spring "Fairy Queen" buggies, Haydock's Perfect side-spring, side-bar buggy, "Royal" triple spring buggy, "Concord" and "Texas" side-spring buggies, Gorham buggies, side-bar road wagons, two and three-spring phaetons, platform spring phaetons, Dexter spring "Fairy Queen" phaetons, basket phaetons, three-spring jump seats, Timken side-bar jump seats, three-spring "Eureka" slide seats, Timken side-bar jump seat surreys, extension tops, park wagons of every kind, office wagons, farmers' carriages, delivery wagons, combination spring wagons, buckboards and everything in the line of a light vehicle. The business done by this house is very large, and covers a vast territory extending east as far as New York, and north, south and west to every State and Territory of those regions. Besides his extensive interests in this city, Mr. William T. Haydock still retains valuable business connections in Cincinnati, and is the President of the T. T. Haydock Carriage Company, of that city. The rapid expansion of the business of Haydock Bros. has rendered their Chouteau avenue premises, already described, and in which the business is conducted, entirely inadequate to the requirements of the firm, and made the procurement of more spacious quarters an absolute necessity. The firm, in order to meet this want have, in addition to their present factory, now under process of erection, and a part of which is already completed, a factory on Papin street, extending from Thirteenth to Fourteenth streets, six stories in height, and having a frontage on Papin street of 325 feet by 85 feet on Fourteenth street and 135 feet on Thirteenth street. The area of the floors of this vast structure will foot up a total of 202,200 square feet, and the building will be, when completed, the largest carriage factory in the world, and will have a capacity for the manufacture of one hundred vehicles per day. The architecture of this edifice is shown by the illustration facing this account. It will be a worthy home for this great and enterprising carriage house, enlarging its facilities and befitting the high and prominent standing the firm has for so many years enjoyed as the merited result of superior workmanship, reliable business methods, and promptness in filling orders. It will be replete with all the best appliances, and every convenience and facility for carriage manufacture, being designed and arranged specially for the business, and containing every improvement that experience has suggested or ingenuity can devise. Not only in the processes of manufacture, but also in arrangements for handling and shipment, the building will be the most complete in the country. With this increased capacity will doubtless come a still more expanded trade. The great prosperity enjoyed by this house is an evidence of the energy and enterprise of its proprietor, the close attention paid by him to every department of the business, and his accurate knowledge of all its details. He is a man of superior business attainments, and has demonstrated his ability by the success he has achieved.

**J. B. Legg.**—Architect; Southeast corner of Broadway and Olive street.— Upon no other profession does the present and future reputation of a city depend to  such a degree as upon that of the architect. We base our estimate of past ages and peoples largely upon the structures they have left as indices of their place in the history of civilization, and our judgment of the cities of to-day is influenced, to a considerable extent, by the edifices which indicate the progress of architectural taste. Of a leading prominence among the best architects of this city and the West, is Mr. J. B. Legg, who has been continuously engaged in the practice of his profession for over seventeen years. That great triumph of architectural art, the St. Louis Exposition and Music Hall building, was built from his designs. Many others of the most prominent buildings in this city attest the skill of Mr. Legg. His efficient work is not, however, confined exclusively, or even principally, to this city. He maintains branch offices at Wichita, Kas.; Springfield, Mo.; Mexico, Mo., and Fort Smith, Ark., and has a large and steadily growing business throughout the States of Iowa, Texas, Tennessee, Mississippi, Missouri, Illinois, Kansas, Arkansas, Florida, Indiana, California and other States and Territories. He designed and superintended the building of the Illinois State Institution for the Blind, at Jacksonville; the Eighth Street Church at Little Rock, Ark., court houses at Carlyle, Ill. and Ste. Genevieve, Mo.; opera houses at Neosho, Mo., and Fort Smith, Ark.; the Ashy Block at Helena, Mont.; Comstock & Avery's building at Peoria, Ills., and other buildings of prominence in all parts of the West and South. There are now in course of construction from his designs, many fine residences in this city, $200,000 worth of buildings at Wichita, Kas., and many structures at a number of other places. He is prepared to contract for furnishing plans and supervising the construction of buildings in the most perfect style of the art of which he is an acknowledged master.

**Kohn & Co.**—Bankers and Brokers; 319 North Third street.—This business was established in 1874, by Messrs. D. Kohn, William M. Kohn and E. Popper, and has enjoyed a large and steadily increasing business from that time to the present. The offices of the firm are eligibly located at 319 North Third street, in the heart of the business center, and they are members of the New York Stock Exchange, the Chicago Board of Trade and the St. Louis Merchants' Exchange. They deal in New York stocks, and every description of bonds, stocks and securities, grain, etc. They also deal in the better class of mining stocks, handling exclusively "Granite," "Small Hopes" and "Hope" stocks, in which they are making money for their customers, but do not handle smaller and unreliable stocks. The standing of the house is very high, and its facilities for placing investments profitably and safely are unsurpassed.

**J. S. Merrell Drug Company.**—C. P. Wallbridge, President; H. S. Merrell, Vice-President; Ed. Bindschadler, Secretary and Treasurer; Wholesale Dealers in Drugs, Druggists' Sundries, Medicines, etc.; 620 Washington avenue.— This is the oldest wholesale drug house in the city, having been established in 1853 by Dr. Jacob S. Merrell, who had previously been engaged in the same line in Cincinnati for eight years. He gave his entire attention to the development of this business from its establishment to the time of his death, and built it up to a commanding position among the leading houses of the Western country. The present corporation was formed in 1885, and occupies the spacious five-story building with a frontage of 28 feet at 620 Washington avenue, and running back 155 feet to a similar frontage at 621 St. Charles street; in addition to which the company has a laboratory at 713 St. Charles street, in charge of Mr. H. S. Merrell, Vice-President, who personally superintends every detail of the manufacture. The company does an immense business as wholesale dealers in drugs, druggists' sundries, medicines, paints and oils, shop furniture, surgical instruments, etc., which they sell to dealers in Illinois, Missouri, Arkansas, Texas, Kentucky, Tennessee, Iowa, Kansas, Nebraska and the entire West and South; in which extensive trade territory a staff of thirteen traveling salesmen represent the house. The laboratory products of the house include a complete list of staple fluid extracts, medicinal elixirs, powders, plasters, syrups, ointments, etc. A specialty of the house is the compounding of Merrell's Family Medicines, first-class articles indorsed by physicians, and of acknowledged efficacy, including Merrell's Female Tonic, Merrell's Penetrating Oil, Merrell's Cough Balsam, Merrell's Liver Pills, Merrell's Medicated Cordial and twelve or fifteen other preparations, all of which are in great demand and sold by the house to the leading wholesale druggists of the country, and through them to the trade. A force of thirty clerks and assistants are employed, and the house still maintains the high-class reputation which has attached to it for more than a third of a century of honorable and prosperous existence.

**Benj. Kimball.**—Licensed Broker for the Assured; 208 Olive street.—Mr. Benj. Kimball has been for some twenty-five years prominently identified with the insurance business in this city. At the outset he represented several companies, but five years ago, realizing the fact that while every insurance company has its agents endeavoring to secure risks and the premiums incident thereto, the property owner is, as a general thing, left to work out, in fear and trembling, the problem as to the safety of his investment in insurance for himself, Mr. Kimball established himself in business as a broker for the assured only, thus affording to property owners a means by which large lines of insurance for big houses can be looked after, relieving them of all care on the subject, and effecting a material saving in premiums, insuring much cheaper than they can do it themselves. In this business, Mr. Kimball has thrived and prospered, his clientele embracing hundreds of the largest manufacturing and commercial houses, street railway companies, hotels, real estate owners and agents, etc., in the city. He represents no companies and writes no policies, but guards his patrons against doubtful, shaky, or litigious companies. He is the only broker in his line in the city and his services are appreciated by his patrons, who have always found the insurance placed by him satisfactory in every particular.

**P. C. Murphy.**—Manufacturer and Wholesale and Retail Dealer in Trunks and Traveling Goods; 504 and 506 North Third street.—Mr. P. C. Murphy has earned, by his industry and enterprise, the right to be ranked among the most successful of the manufacturers of the city. Starting in business in a comparatively small and modest way, his enterprise grew under his good management to its present proportions, now employing the services of one hundred workmen. He occupies as wholesale store and offices, the five-story building, 30x170 feet, at 504 and 506 North Third street, with a warehouse in the rear, fronting on Vine street, five stories high and 35x120 feet in dimensions. These premises were erected by Mr. Murphy expressly for the purposes of his business, and are fitted up with every facility and convenience for carrying on his operations in a successful manner. He also occupies a large retail store at 319 North Fourth street. The trade of the house is heavy in the city, and in the entire Southern, Southwestern and Western country. Mr. Murphy's business has steadily grown from its inception and he has prospered greatly. The large building occupied by the St. Louis Type Foundry, at the corner of Third and Vine streets, was erected and is owned by him, and he has accumulated other profits from the business in which he has been successful by the merit of his goods and the reliability of his methods.

**J. H. Wear, Boogher & Company.**—Importers and Jobbers of Dry Goods, etc.; Southwest corner of Sixth and St. Charles streets —This firm, which is properly classed as one of the greatest dry goods jobbing houses of the Mississippi Valley, is composed of Messrs. J. H. Wear, Jesse L. Boogher, John P. Boogher and Murray Carleton. The business was established in 1863, by Mr Wear, who associated with him Mr. John W. Hickman, under the firm name of Wear and Hickman. In 1867, Mr. Hickman withdrew, and the business was continued under the firm name of J. H. Wear & Co., later changing to its present style of J. H. Wear, Boogher & Co. Messrs. Jesse L. Boogher and John P. Boogher have been in business since 1854, and prior to their association with Mr. Wear were with the old dry goods house of Henry Bell & Son. Mr. Murray Carleton, the other member of the firm, is also a gentleman of experience and a high order of business attainments. When the business was inaugurated, in 1863, it was at a store at the corner of Main and Chestnut streets The rapid expansion of the business from time to time compelled other

removals until the firm finally located in the spacious five-story and basement structure, 100x124 feet, at the corner of Sixth and St. Charles streets, and which is equipped with every facility and convenience for the efficient prosecution of the business. A force of about one hundred clerks and assistants are employed about this building, while an efficient force of traveling salesmen represent the house in a trade territory which it fully occupies, and which covers the States of Missouri, Illinois, Indiana, Kentucky, Tennessee, Mississippi, Louisiana, Texas, Arkansas, Kansas, Nebraska, Iowa, Colorado and the Territories. The stock carried by the house is a very heavy one, and embraces everything in the line of dry goods, and its trade is of immense proportions, being the result of the steady growth of twenty-four years of sagacious, far-sighted, fair and liberal methods of dealing. The great success achieved by this house is the legitimate outgrowth of its long and honorable history, in which close attention to every detail, good judgment in guiding its destinies, honest goods and accuracy in its dealings have been the moving causes of the prosperity it now enjoys. Mr. Joseph H. Holliday was connected with this house as a partner in the firm of J. H. Wear & Co., and also for 1884 and 1885 in the present firm, and had charge of the credits until December 24, 1885, when he died, lamented by the entire business community, and by the customers and friends of the firm throughout the country.

**A. F. Shapleigh & Cantwell Hardware Company.**—A. F. Shapleigh, President; John Cantwell, Vice-President; Frank Shapleigh, Second Vice-President; Alfred Lee, Secretary and Treasurer; 519 and 521 North Main street.—As a hardware market St. Louis stands first and foremost among the Western cities, and the jobbing trade in hardware done in St. Louis exceeds in volume that of either New York, Philadelphia or any other Eastern city. One of the reasons for this is the vast extent of the territory tributary to this city as a market of supply. The oldest hardware concern in the West is that of the A. F. Shapleigh & Cantwell Hardware Company, which has been actively engaged in business on Main street for the past forty-four years. This house was established in 1843 as Rogers, Field & Co., the business being conducted on Main street, between Washington and Christy avenues. In 1845 the firm was changed to Rogers, Shapleigh & Co., and in 1847 to Shapleigh, Day & Co. and removed to 414 North Main street, in the year 1851. Again, in 1863, the style was changed to A. F. Shapleigh & Co., and finally, in July, 1880, the present concern was established as the A. F. Shapleigh & Cantwell Hardware Co., Nos. 414, 416, 418, 420 and 422 North Main street. Canvassing at first, in 1843, a small number of states, this house has steadily added to and increased its territory until now, with thirty traveling salesmen, they are represented as far north as the British Possessions and are only limited on the west by the Pacific Ocean and south by the Gulf of Mexico. The A. F. Shapleigh & Cantwell Hardware Co. are pioneers in the far west trade, and to-day cover more actual territory than any jobber of hardware in the world. Their business is extensively distributed over Missouri, Illinois, Iowa, Kansas, Nebraska, Arkansas, Texas, Mississippi, Tennessee, Arizona, Colorado, California, Dakota, Idaho, Indiana, Kentucky, Old and New Mexico, Indian Territory, Minnesota, Montana, Nevada, Oregon, Utah, Louisiana and Wyoming; their sales reaching several millions annually and constantly increasing. This company are proprietors of the celebrated "Diamond Edge" brand of edge tools, such as axes, hatchets, cutlery, saws, etc., and by furnishing only the very best articles in this line that skill can make and money buy, have introduced them in nearly every village and city in the West and South. While dealing heavily in staple hardware, they carry a particularly large and handsome line of builders', carpenters' and miners' goods of the best makes and latest styles and patterns, which they sell at manufacturers' prices, freight added. One of the features of the business is their cutlery department, in which their stock is enormous, comprising several thousand different patterns of pocket and table cutlery of both foreign and domestic makes. On December 11, 1886, the firm had the misfortune to lose by fire their entire stock of hardware, invoicing $500,000. The fire occurred about 2 o'clock in the afternoon, and while still a mass of smoking ruins the company secured the elegant stores at 519 and 521 North Main street and announced themselves "ready for business." A complete stock of all kinds was at once ordered out, and to-day the new houses are well filled with fresh, new goods of the very latest designs. The new premises are of stone, five stories, 60x160 feet, well lighted, strong and substantial and, together with the company's several warehouses, will contain as large and fine a stock of hardware as can be found in the country. The house has spent several thousand dollars in fitting up these premises, and are now prepared to welcome their friends and attend to the wants of their customers as before their great calamity. All the old force of salesmen and employes have been retained, and although at first hampered, immediately after the fire, the company filled every order sent them direct, a record scarcely approached in the history of the hardware trade.

**H. A. Redfield & Co.**—Commission Merchants and Dealers in Provisions; 320 North Second street.—The house of H. A. Redfield & Co. has been successfully engaged in business as commission merchants and dealers in provisions ever since its establishment in 1870. The premises occupied by the firm are conveniently and centrally located at 320 North Second street with every facility for the successful prosecution of the business. They deal largely in provisions of all kinds, (dried beef, hams, etc.,) and as commission merchants buy and sell provisions, grain, produce and everything in their line. Their patronage is very large and widely extended, including in the scope of its operations Arkansas, Tennessee, Mississippi, Kentucky, Louisiana, Missouri, Illinois, and the entire South, Southwest and Southeast. In the many years of the busy and honorable career of this house it has planted itself firmly in the esteem and confidence of producers and shippers by its close and earnest attention to every detail, and the high plane upon which its business is conducted.

**The St. Louis Manufacturing Company.**—Chas. W. Behrens, President; John H. Douglass, Vice-President; J. G. Chapman, Treasurer; Henry Meyer, Secretary; A. Boetticher, Manager; F. Lohse, Superintendent; Manufacturers of Sash, Doors, Blinds. etc.; Northwest Corner of Tenth and Mullanphy streets.—This

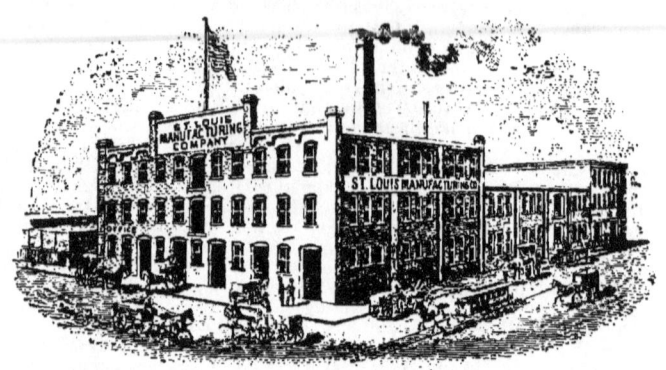

business was originally established by the Mullanphy Planing Mill Co., which was succeeded by the present corporation in 1883. They occupy as works the spacious building, partly of three stories and partly of two, with a frontage of 125 feet on Mullanphy street by a depth of 200 feet on Tenth street. This factory is fully and completely equipped with all the latest improved machinery and plant adapted to the requirements of the business, and gives employment to one hundred and twenty-five men. The company manufacture sash, doors, blinds, mouldings, brackets, door and window frames, etc., and do a very large business in the city and the surrounding country in the States of Missouri and Illinois. The stockholders in the company are all prominent lumbermen. President Behrens is Secretary of the Schulenburg & Boeckeler Lumber Co.; Mr. Douglass, the Vice-President, is Treasurer of the Knapp-Stout Lumber Co.; Mr. Chapman, the Treasurer, is also Treasurer of the Eau Claire Lumber Co., and Mr. Meyer is of the John Meyer Lumber Co. The business done by the company is the largest in its line in the city. It has unsurpassed facilities for the prosecution of the business and enjoys a high place in the confidence of the trade.

**C. D. Comfort.**—Manufacturer of Hosiery, Overalls, etc; 100 and 102 South Eighth street.—Mr. Comfort embarked in the ice business when a very young man, some eleven or twelve years ago. In 1883 he became a member of the large dry goods firm of Dodd, Brown & Co., and secured an act of incorporation for his ice business, which is still successfully carried on. In June, 1885, upon the retirement of Mr. Dodd and the change of the firm to Brown, Daughaday & Co., Mr. Comfort also retired from membership, accepting a clerical position with the new firm, which he held until the beginning of the present year, when he purchased from them his present manufacturing business, which they had been running for several years. The factory occupies two stories and basement, 60x160 feet, has eighty knitting machines and all the latest and most approved plant adapted to the business, and gives employment to one hundred and seventy-five hands. The business is about equally divided between the manufacture of woolen hosiery and of overalls, according to the season, and the product of the factory finds a ready market, city jobbers taking all it can make. Mr. Comfort, who is about thirty years of age, is the founder, president and almost sole proprietor of the Comfort Ice Co., and president, with a controlling interest, of the Comfort-Henry Ice Co., the former being the wholesale and the latter the retail branch, and has about $30,000 invested in that business. Their ice office is at 913 North Seventh street and their warehouse has a storage capacity of over 25,000 tons. They employ fifteen men, run thirteen ice wagons and sell chiefly in the city and surrounding country. Mr. Comfort is a gentleman of superior business qualifications, and greatly esteemed in all the relations of life. He was nominated at the Republican City Convention held March 25, for the City Council and was elected by the people April 5. He is justly regarded as a representative and worthy citizen.

**Ludlow-Saylor Wire Company.**—R. C. Ludlow, President; C. L. Dean, Vice-President and Treasurer; William E. Griffiths, Secretary; William C. Ludwig, Superintendent: Manufacturers of and Dealers in Wire and Wire Goods; 116 South Fourth street.—This establishment is one of the largest, in its line, of any in America. The house is an old one, and was established in 1856 by Mr. R. C. Ludlow, president of the present company, and under his able and experienced direction has reached its present supremacy. In 1875 the business of the firm had assumed such massive proportions that for better convenience it was incorporated, and now is in possession of a trade that extends from the Gulf of Mexico to the Northern lakes and from the Ohio River to the Pacific Coast. So enormous is the volume of its trade West and South, that the house has almost a monopoly in such specialties as wire cloth, wire rope, fences, screens, etc. The immense establishment occupied by the company is six stories in height, and is filled from the basement to the roof with a mammoth and well assorted stock of wire goods. The company issue an elegantly bound catalogue, containing illustrations and price lists of their goods, that is itself a work of art. The house, owing to its long and successful existence, is well and favorably known, and amply prepared with its abundant capital and resources to meet all the demands of trade. Mr. R. C. Ludlow, the president, is an old and prominent resident of the city, interested deeply in its progress and respected by the entire business community.

**Hunter Brothers.**—Flour, Grain and Feed—Shipping and Commission; 407 Chamber of Commerce.—This business was established thirteen years ago. The firm now consists of Messrs. John A. Hunter and E. O. Hunter. Mr. John A. Hunter has been a member of the firm about eight years. Mr W. W. Hunter, one of the founders of the firm, is now in the same business in Chicago, and his place in the St. Louis house was taken by Mr. E. O. Hunter. The firm has its office at 407 Chamber of Commerce, and handles on commission and personal account, flour, grain and feed in car-load and round lots, making a specialty of mill feed. They do a very large and constantly growing trade, and ship to all Eastern points by rail and South by rail and water. They have unexcelled facilities for the handling and transportation of the products in which they deal, and their reliable and systematic methods of business have secured for them a high reputation and merited prosperity.

**The Mercantile Agency.**—R. G. Dun & Co., Proprietors; C. B. Smith, St. Louis Manager; Gay Building, Pine and Third streets.—This agency, the operations and reputation of which are world wide, was founded in 1841 by Judge Lewis Tappan in the city of New York. Since that time it has been carried on uninterruptedly by his successors, under the styles of Lewis Tappan & Co., Tappan & Douglas, B. Douglas & Co., Dun, Boyd & Co., Dun, Barlow & Co., and R. G. Dun & Co., and in Canada as Dun, Wiman & Co. It has never been incorporated, and the only changes that have occurred in the firm have been caused by the death or retirement of partners. The purpose of the agency is to furnish to its subscribers, for business purposes, information as to the standing of merchants, manufacturers, bankers, etc., and the agency expends millions annually in the effort to gather its vast stores of information, and to make its reports accurate. The St. Louis branch of the agency is located in the Gay Building, corner of Pine and Third streets. It is under the management of Mr. C. B. Smith and has a force of seventy-five employes; and in addition to its other facilities has a private printing and publishing department. The St. Louis branch, like all others maintained by this company, has a well appointed collection department attached to it.

**St. Louis Type Foundry.**—William Bright, President; James G. Payver, Vice-President; C. S. Kauffman, Secretary and Treasurer; Type Founders, Printing Machine Works and Wholesale Paper Warehouse; Third and Vine streets.—The old established St. Louis Type Foundry has a foremost place among the leading manufacturing houses of the city. Founded in 1840 by Augustus P. Ladew, the firm afterward became Ladew, Peers & Co., who were succeeded by the gentlemen who are officers of the present company in 1860. One year after the reorganization, by special act of the legislature of 1861, the company was incorporated for twenty-five years, and in 1886, its charter having expired, was reincorporated for a term of fifty years. For store, office, type foundry, electrotype and stereotype departments, it occupies the spacious and substantial building, 60x140 feet, at the corner of Third and Vine streets, and in addition owns and occupies a four-story building, 80x160 feet, at the corner of Broadway and Poplar street, as a factory for the manufacture of printing presses, paper cutters, type cases, cabinets, and printers' woodwork of every description. The outfit of machinery and equipments for the prosecution of the vast manufacturing operations carried on at the foundry and works is complete in every particular and embraces all the latest and best inventions adapted to these lines of industry, and the employes of the company number over one hundred. It manufactures and deals in all kinds of printing types, including besides all standard faces a vast number of new, fancy and unique designs in type faces prepared to meet the demands of artistic job-rooms; cuts, rules, dashes, circles, ovals, leads, slugs, metal and wood furniture; printing presses, hand and power; paper, card, lead and rule cutters; mitering machines, chases, galleys, shooting sticks, galley racks, composing sticks, type cabinets, cases, stands, imposing stones, etc. It also manufactures the celebrated Mustang nailer, of which it owns the patent, and which commands a very large sale in this country and Canada, and is acknowledged to be the best, cheapest and simplest of all mitering contrivances. It also manufactures the Clipper, Daisy, Boss and Climax paper cutters, and deals in all kinds of printing paper, news, book and writing; cards, card boards, chromo, advertising and visiting cards, wedding stationery; news, book and job inks, bronzes, rollers and roller composition, and everything used by printers and bookbinders. The business of this house is of immense proportions, covering all the States of the West, South and Southwest, and also extending into Canada and Mexico. It is the largest establishment of its kind in this section and in facilities, quality of goods and extent of trade is unsurpassed in the country. The original reorganizers of this house in 1859 are still members of it, and under their efficient management it has achieved great success, and worthily gained, by its accuracy of methods, the proud name of "The Old Reliable."

**Stamm Brothers.**—Wholesale Bottles and Bottlers' Supplies; Also Proprietors of Eclipse Bottling Company, Manufacturers of the Celebrated Eclipse Tonic Beer and Ginger Ale; 828 and 830 South Seventh street.—This business was established about twenty years ago by the father of the present proprietors, Messrs. E. W. and George C. Stamm, by whom they were given a practical training in the business and all its details, which has enabled them to bring it to its present pronounced and gratifying success. They were for years at 729 South Seventh street, but the great growth of the business rendered those premises inadequate, and caused them to erect the handsome brick building now occupied by them, with a frontage of 50 feet on South Seventh street by a depth of 130 feet, and especially designed for the purposes of their business. This building is fitted with all the machinery and appliances adapted to the requirements of the business. They deal wholesale in bottles of every kind and every description of bottlers' supplies, of which their stock is large and not excelled in completeness of assortment by any in the country. In this line they have a large trade in nearly all the States of the Union and an especially large one in Texas. They are also proprietors of the Eclipse Bottling Co., and have a heavy city trade in the Eclipse Tonic Beer. They also have a very large trade in ginger ale, which they make on a mammoth scale and of quality not excelled by any house in the country. This superior article is in heavy demand in New Orleans and throughout the South, and its reputation is securing for it a rapidly expanding trade. They are also agents and bottlers of the "Standard Nerve Food," of which Messrs. Beach & Claridge, of Boston, Mass., are the proprietors. The perfect system with which they conduct their business, the prompt and satisfactory manner in which they fill all orders, and the accuracy and reliability of their business methods have given this firm a prominent standing which they have maintained for many years.

**Starr Safe Company.**—J. J. Starr, President; Charles W. Riegel, Secretary; Safes, Locks, etc.; 408 and 410 North Third street—This business was established in 1868, by Mr. J. J. Starr, who successfully conducted it until the formation of the present company in 1886. The company occupies commodious premises at 408 and 410 North Third street, and have a large and constantly increasing trade in the South and Southwest. They deal only in the safes, bank locks, vault works, etc., made by the Hall Safe and Lock Co., of Cincinnati, which company invents, patents and manufactures all its own locks. The safes manufactured by the Hall Company stand second to none in workmanship, security or finish; and Mr. Starr has, for the nineteen years in which he has been engaged in the business in the same premises occupied by the company of which he is President, maintained a high reputation for the correctness and reliability by which his dealings have ever been characterized.

**The Covenant Mutual Life Insurance Company.**—E. Wilkerson, President; A. F. Shapleigh, Vice-President; Chas. E. Pilling, Assistant Secretary; H. H. Mudd, M. D., Medical Director; Geo. H. Shields, Attorney; 712 Pine street.—The record of thirty-four years of honorable and active business enjoyed by this company is without reproach. The company, which was organized February 24, 1853, is the oldest in the West, and has been solvent throughout its existence, successfully passing through crises that have proven too severe for less substantial institutions, promptly paying all losses, and throughout its long business career contesting the payment of one policy only. It issues policies upon all plans of life and endowment assurance that have been approved by the test of experience, and these policies are free from restriction as to travel, residence or occupation. After the payment of two annual premiums the policies are non-forfeiting, the conditions being clearly expressed. The policy is a plain, simple contract, easily understood and without confusing phraseology. The State Superintendent of Insurance of Missouri places the following official certificate on all policies issued by the company. "This policy is registered and secured by pledge of bonds or deeds of trust on real estate deposited with this department." The Covenant Mutual is the only company that makes deposit with this State covering its entire liabilities to its policy-holders. At the beginning of the present year the assets of the company amounted to $397,601.50 and its net surplus over all liabilities to $48,495.01. The President of the company, Mr. Wilkerson, is a thoroughly experienced life assurance underwriter and gives his personal attention to the company's business. The board of trustees embraces a number of the most prominent and substantial citizens, including Messrs. A. F. Shapleigh, Geo. H. Shields, Hon. Nathan Cole, Wm. H. Woodward, E. Wilkerson, Chas. A. McNair, Given Campbell, Wm. C. Orr, Marcus A. Wolff, Wm. Brown, Hermann Eisenhardt and Joseph N. Evans.

**F. A. Kauffmann.**—Manufacturer of Vinegar and Sauer Kraut, and Wholesale Dealer in Ohio and New York Country Cider: 21 South Main street.—The vinegar manufactured by this establishment has a first-class reputation in St. Louis and the surrounding country, and the demand for it has been so great that the capacity of the factory has recently been doubled. The proprietor, Mr. F. A. Kauffmann, began business five years ago, and having the knowledge and experience so necessary to success, has enjoyed a prosperous and lucrative trade, and increased his factory far beyond its original capacity. In addition to the manufacture of vinegar he puts up large quantities of sauer kraut and pickles. He is also the wholesale agent for St. Louis and neighboring cities, of Oliver Bros.' cider, Lockport, N. Y. The bulk of Mr. Kauffmann's extensive trade is confined to the city and surrounding towns.

**Sheridan & Ryan.**—Wholesale Dealers in Hay, Grain and Millstuff; 104, 105 and 106 South Levee.—The immense Southern trade enjoyed by this firm is the result of the pre-eminent business qualifications of R. B. Sheridan and F. H. Ryan, who are the members. Both gentlemen are thorough, wide-awake merchants, ripe in experience and fully acquainted with the trade which they handle. The co-partnership was formed about five years ago, and has been a notably successful one. Hay, grain and millstuff are handled by the house in large quantities, and the annual volume of business is phenomenally large. The warehouse occupied is situated on the levee, and the firm are in possession of unexcelled shipping facilities, both by rail and water. The business connections of this firm are extensive and first class.

**Scherpe & Koken.**—Enterprise Architectural Iron Works and Foundry; South Eighth street and Park avenue.—This firm was established in 1880 by Messrs. John F. Scherpe and William T. Koken, by whom the business is still conducted.

From the inception of their enterprise to the present time they have enjoyed a steadily increasing business, so much so that their two-story works, 150 x 150 feet in dimensions, have proved inadequate to their needs, and they have recently added to them by the erection of another building adjoining, covering an area of 60x300 feet, and considerably augmenting their manufacturing facilities. These premises are fully equipped with all the latest and most approved machinery and appliances, and give employment to a force of one hundred and fifty men. The firm manufacture all kinds of iron work for building purposes, including store fronts, girders, lintels, caps and sills, jail and vault work, railings, shutters, etc. They also manufacture, as a specialty, all kinds of Patent Illuminating Tiles (Hyatt's and Concrete) for sidewalk areas, skylights and floor lights. They have a large trade in the States of Texas, Arkansas, Kentucky, Illinois, Iowa, Missouri, Nebraska, Kansas, Colorado and all the Territories, as well as a heavy city business. They have an excellent reputation for the quality of their work, and the promptness and reliability by which all their business dealings are characterized. Scherpe & Koken have recently published a magnificent illustrated catalogue which they mail to architects and builders, free on application.

**H. McK. Wilson & Co.**—Improved Apparatus and Supplies for Cheese Factories, Creameries and Dairies; 112 North Second street.—In the line of dairy, cheese factory and creamery supplies the house of H. McK. Wilson & Co. holds a deserved prominence. This firm, the members of which are Messrs. Henry McK. Wilson and Joseph W. Sheppard, was established in April, 1885. They deal in everything in their line: engines, boilers, cheese apparatus, butter workers and printers, testers, scales, rennet, churns, vats, etc. A specialty of the firm is the Backstrom Cream Separator, for factory use, which takes out all the cream, preserves the butter globules intact, and is the best, cheapest, simplest and safest cream separator ever offered to the public. Of this celebrated separator H. McK. Wilson & Co. are the exclusive Western agents, as they are also of the Hand Separator for family use. The stock of the firm is complete with a full assortment, in large quantities, of everything in the line of dairy, creamery and cheese factory supplies, and they occupy as office and salesrooms the three-story building 25x100 feet, at 112 North Second street, with rear wareroom, two floors, 25x60 feet. In addition to this they have a branch house at 19 Wabash avenue, Chicago, to facilitate their trade in the Northwest. From the main house in St. Louis the trade of the firm is very large in Southern Illinois, Missouri, Kansas, the Southwest and all the Southern States. The unsurpassed facilities of the house, the great merit of its goods, and the fairness and liberality of its methods have given it a high standing and merited success.

**Cole & Glass.**—Star Moulding, Turning and Planing Mill; Office and Factory, Southeast Corner Market and Sixteenth streets.—This firm, of which Messrs. Nelson Cole and Stephen Glass are the individual members, was established in 1868 and has ever since held a merited prominence among the manufacturing concerns of the city. Their fine three-story brick mill, which fronts 130 feet on Market street and 130 feet on Sixteenth street, is completely equipped with all the latest and most improved plant and machinery adapted to the requirements of the business and gives employment to a force of sixty workmen. The firm manufacture and deal in sash, doors, blinds, door and window frames, mouldings and finish of all kinds, planed and rough lumber, etc., and do job turning in stair rails, balusters, plain and fancy newel posts and stair work of every description. The firm is noted for the superior merit of its goods and workmanship and does a large business, not only in the city, but also in all the States of the South and West. The firm has a high standing in the trade, both members of it being thorough and experienced business men and old and respected citizens. Mr. Cole is a Union veteran, and formerly commander of the Department of the Missouri, Grand Army of the Republic. He was nominated for the short term in the City Council by acclamation by the Republican City Convention which was held April 24th last, and was elected by the people to that position.

**Speer, Jones & Co.**—Manufacturers of Machinery Oils, Greases, etc.; 708 and 710 North Main street.—No industry is of more importance to the manufacturing interests than that having for its object the supplying of machinery oils and other lubricants. A leading firm engaged in this branch of business is that of Speer, Jones & Co., occupying four spacious floors, 40x120 feet, at 708 and 710 North Main street. This business was originally established by the firm of Selden & Speer, afterward becoming A. A. Speer & Co., and then the present style, the members of the house now being being Messrs. A. A. Speer and George P. Jones. They manufacture fine machinery, engine, cylinder and other lubricating oils, all of which are designated by their trade-mark, "Peerless;" also lubricating greases. They deal in coal oil, gasoline, naphtha, etc., and do a large business in all the lines in which they are engaged, the acknowledged superiority of their goods having earned for them a high reputation with consumers and the trade. They have a branch at Kansas City which also does an extensive business. These goods are sold all over the South, West, Northwest and Southwest, giving the satisfaction only accorded to merit, and the firm is not surpassed in its line by any house in this city or the West.

**Chas. Dauernheim.**—Paper Hangings, Window Shades, Weather Strips, Wire Screens, etc.; 214 North Broadway.—Mr. Chas. Dauernheim has been established in business for the past twelve years. He makes a specialty of high class decorations of fine interiors, carrying a large and completely assorted stock of imported and domestic manufacture, Lincrusta Walton, and all novelties in his line including Japanese and other rare foreign papers. He employs a force of twenty-five skilled and experienced workmen, and occupies spacious premises, 25x130 feet, at 214 Broadway, and has a branch house at 3331 Olive street. Mr. Dauernheim has had a successful career and a steadily increasing patronage from the inception of the business to the present time. This prosperity is the legitimate result of the superiority of his goods, the excellence of his workmanship and the promptness and reliability with which he attends to every detail of his business and the satisfactory manner in which he fills every order.

**John F. Fallon.**—Carriage Builder; 1108 to 1116 St. Charles street.—This old established and prominent carriage building establishment was founded in 1845, by Mr. Wesley Fallon, who died in 1876, when his nephew, Mr. John F. Fallon, took charge of it and managed the business for his uncle's widow until three years ago, when he acquired it for himself. He formerly occupied the building at the corner of Tenth and St. Charles streets, which he still owns, but in which Mr. D. W. Haydock, carriage manufacturer, is now located, Mr. Fallon now occupying the three story building, 100x150 feet, located at 1108 to 1112 St. Charles street. Forty of the most skilled mechanics are employed by Mr. Fallon, and he does a large business, chiefly on city orders, although he sends work as far as California. He makes a specialty of high class work, and builds only the finest buggies and carriages, identical with those manufactured by the Brewsters, of New York, whom he represents in St. Louis, and who are now using and advertising the drop perch invented by Mr. Fallon on their buggies, etc. This is an invention by which the perches are placed under the fifth wheels, instead of over them, giving greater strength, and it has swept all prizes wherever it has entered into competition. Mr. Fallon owes his large success and steadily increasing business to his superior work and close supervision of all its details.

**A. Geisel.**—Manufacturer of Tinware of all Descriptions, and Wholesale Dealer in Tin Plate and Metals; 1720 and 1722 South Broadway.—This establishment was founded in 1852 by Mr. A. Geisel, then a young man starting his career in life with a complete knowledge of his trade, brains and energy as his sole capital, three useful possessions that when well handled are better than money. The result is well illustrated in the success of Mr. Geisel, whose establishment is now one of the largest in the West, and has a trade measured only by the length and breadth of the Mississippi Valley. Articles from this house are shipped to Kansas, Nebraska, Colorado, the Territories, Minnesota, Illinois, Iowa, Arkansas, Texas, Louisiana and the Southern States generally, the trade even extending to the competing cities of Chicago and Cincinnati. The extensive facilities of the establishment permits the manufacture of tinware and tin cans of every description. The specialties, in the manufacture of which the house is largely engaged, are pieced and japanned ware and gasoline and gas ovens, gasoline trimmings and stove trimmings. Ninety-six hands are now employed. Mr. A. Geisel, the proprietor, is a prominent and esteemed citizen who is possessed of large financial interests in various institutions.

**Heller & Hoffman.**—Manufacturers of Chairs; Corner of Eighth and Howard streets.—The manufactories and buildings of this concern spread out on three corners of the junction of the two streets, Eighth and Howard, and cover a large area of ground. The firm of Heller and Hoffman was established in 1855, and the

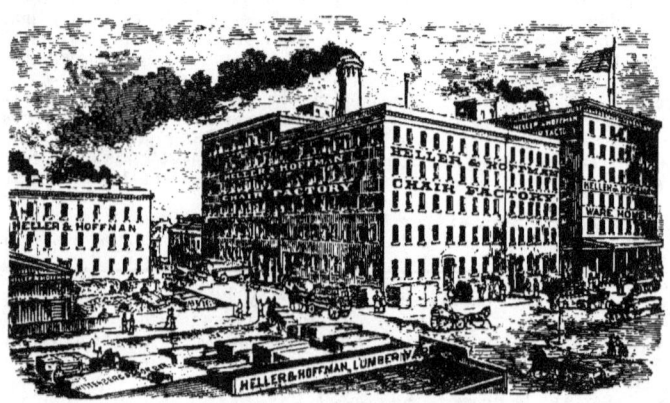

business of the firm is now as large, if not larger than that of any similar concern in the country. An idea of the extent of the vast interests of this firm can best be conveyed by the accompanying illustration of their premises. About two hundred employes are engaged constantly at work in the manufacture of chairs. The product is distributed all over the United States, but the bulk of the trade is from the Western and Southern States. The gentlemen who form this well known firm, Messrs. Michael Heller and Sebastian Hoffman, have attained the highest standing in business and financial circles, and Judge Heller has occupied several positions which he filled with distinguished ability, and to the best interests of his constituents and fellow citizens. The remarkable business qualifications possessed by both of these gentlemen is witnessed in the progress and development of their business. In private life, as well as in the busy marts of trade, they are recognized as valued citizens.

**Capitain & Steinmann.**—Architects; 814 and 816 Chestnut street.—In May, 1886, Messrs. F. J. Capitain and H. Steinmann, both celebrated and experienced architects, entered into partnership and are now pursuing the practice of their profession under the firm name of Capitain & Steinmann. They are graduates of the Royal Academies of Fine Arts of Munich and Stuttgart; have been continuously engaged for nineteen years in active business and have a thorough knowledge of everything pertaining to their art. Among the prominent buildings in this city for which these gentlemen have furnished designs and specifications, are the New Laclede Hotel, the Monastery of St. Alphonsus Church, the Boatmen's Bank, the Merchants' Grain Elevator, the residence of Mr. W. G. McRee, Cabanne Place, and scores of other residences and business structures, in which art has been combined with strength, utility and economy in a manner indicating the thoroughness of the architects. As a consequence of their great skill Messrs. Capitain & Steinmann have a large and steadily increasing patronage. Any business entrusted to their care will be executed in an efficient and entirely satisfactory manner.

**Fehlig Bros. Box Manufacturing Company.**—Southern Box Factory; Theodore Fehlig, President; Frank Fehlig, Secretary; 1913 to 1923 Wash street.— The "Southern Box Factory," under which name this prosperous establishment is popularly known, was started in 1870 by Messrs. Theodore and Frank Fehlig under the style of Fehlig & Bro. The business enjoyed a steadily increasing and permanent growth from its inception and in January of the present year, in order to facilitate its operations, was incorporated under the present style. The factory, which is a three-story building, 180x150 feet in dimensions, is completely equipped with all the requisite machinery and plant for carrying on the operations of the business, and gives employment to a force of forty men. Every description of boxes are manufactured and the company enjoys a large trade with the manufacturing and shipping firms and corporations of the city. They make a specialty of soda water and beer boxes, supplying the whole city with soda water boxes, with one or two exceptions. They do more printing on boxes than any other firm. The boxes made at this factory are justly celebrated for their superior quality and their durability, and the prosperity enjoyed by the company is the result of this merit, and their fair and accurate dealings with their customers.

**W. H. Cook & Co.**—Brokers in Cotton, Coffee, Grain and Provisions; 311 Pine street.—This business was established in 1874 as the firm of Ewing Hill & Co., of which Messrs. Ewing Hill and W. H. Cook were the individual members. In the early part of the present year Mr. Hill withdrew and Mr. Cook, with whom Mr. J. K. Montgomery is associated, continued the business, assuming the present style. The firm operate very largely on the Exchange in this city, and also very extensively in the New Orleans, Chicago, New York, Liverpool and other leading markets, and have a very heavy and steadily growing patronage in every branch of the business. This large business results from the superior facilities for advantageous dealing possessed by the firm, their close attention to the details of every transaction placed in their hands, and the accurate system upon which their business is conducted. Both members of the firm have superior business attainments, and are well known and successful, enjoying the confidence of the commercial community. Together they form a firm to whom commissions may be entrusted with an assurance that they will be executed in the most satisfactory manner.

**Metropolitan Life Insurance Company.**—James S. Holmes, Superintendent Northern District Industrial Branch; Rooms 503, 504 and 505 Law Building, Northeast corner of Broadway and Chestnut street; John H. Higginbotham, Superintendent Southern District Industrial Branch; Rooms 511 and 512 Temple Building.—The Metropolitan Life Insurance Company, of New York, was incorporated in 1868, and is one of the strongest insurance corporations of the country. It had resources amounting to $3,705,970.61 at the beginning of the present year, and surplus security to policy holders amounting to $1,043,023.03. A leading feature of its business is its plan of industrial insurance, by which lives can be insured by the payment of small weekly sums of from five to sixty cents, thus offering the cheapest safe insurance ever provided. This plan embraces infant as well as adult lives, and is especially adapted to persons of moderate means. The St. Louis agency of the company was established in 1882, its industrial branch in this city being divided into two districts, the company having 40,000 policy holders in the city. Mr. James S. Holmes has been in charge of the Northern District as Superintendent since May, 1886; and the Southern Branch is under the direction, as superintendent, of Mr. John H. Higginbotham, who formerly represented the company for one year at Harrisburg, Pa.; two years at Rochester, N. Y., and one year at Cincinnati. Both are active and efficient representatives of the company, and courteous gentlemen who are popular with the policy-holders. Persons desiring insurance which combines economy with safety cannot do better than to see what these gentlemen have to offer for their consideration.

**Bethesda Mineral Water.**—Charles Moss & Co., Agents; 119 North Second street.—The water that we drink has become an interesting subject, and the fact, that many of the contagious diseases and epidemics are assisted in their progress by means of the impure condition of the water that is so largely drank in all cities and towns, has been acknowledged by thinking scientific men who have sought to remedy these evils as far as possible. A careful analysis of the well water of cities and towns has shown the presence of chlorine and other deleterious substances, and also organic matter in hurtful quantities. Hydrant water, in all of our large cities, is more or less contaminated and is seldom pure. Even St. Louis, which boasts of the purity of its water supply, suffers at times with an unwholesome fluid, as a casual examination of the sediment from a bucket of water, that has been allowed to settle, will readily disclose. It is, however, unnecessary for the people of St. Louis to drink water that is impure, as the famous Bethesda Mineral Water can be had in abundance. The agency for St. Louis and vicinity of this famous water is with Charles Moss & Co., the wholesale grocers at 119 North Second street. Bethesda Mineral Water, aside from its medicinal qualities, takes high rank as a table water, and it has been pronounced absolutely free from impurities by the most eminent chemists of America. The purity of Bethesda water has long been known and it has attained a world-wide reputation. It is so delicately proportioned in mineral qualities by nature, as to make it agreeable and wholesome in health, and curative in disease. The Bethesda Springs at Waukesha, Wis. were discovered in 1868, and since that time thousands of people have used their waters. No other water at Waukesha possesses the purity and properties of the Bethesda, and consumers should not be deceived and imagine that any water that comes from Waukesha is the Bethesda. The medical fraternity of both continents have pronounced in favor of Bethesda as a curative, and also as a table water. It is prescribed by eminent physicians in cases of diabetes, Bright's disease, dyspepsia, indigestion, kidney troubles of all kinds, and similar complaints. Bethesda water loses none of its virtues or forces by being bottled and transported. It has the same effect after it has been bottled or barreled for months as when taken fresh from the springs. An extensive demand has sprung up all over the country for this wonderful water, and with many it has superseded all others for table use. Among the distinguished men who endorse in the highest terms its purity and wholesome qualities as a table water are, U. S. Senator Sawyer, of Wisconsin; Hon. J. Warren Keiffer, of Ohio, ex-Speaker of the U. S. House of Representatives; ex-Gov. Foster, of Ohio; the late Chief Justice, Salmon P. Chase; ex-Secretary of the Treasury, Windom; Gov. Rusk, of Wisconsin; Bishop Fuller, of Canada; Gen. Phil. Sheridan, of the U. S. Army and many others equally prominent. Thousands of people in St. Louis and vicinity use the water, and Charles Moss & Co. have a large demand, which is rapidly increasing, for this pure, life-giving water.

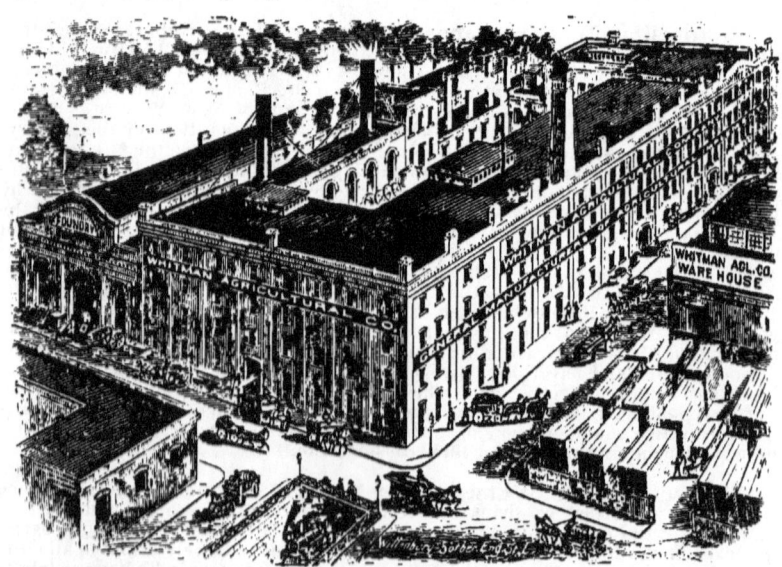

**Whitman Agricultural Company.**—Chas. E. Whitman, President; N. W. Perkins, Treasurer; H. L. Whitman. Secretary; Manufacturers of Hay Presses, Agricultural Implements, etc.; Clark avenue and Eighth street.—Among the large manufacturing concerns of the city, none enjoys a higher standing or more wide-spread reputation and patronage than the Whitman Agricultural Co. The business was established about twenty years ago, by Mr. Charles E. Whitman, who still remains at its head as President of the company, which was incorporated in 1880. The works, three stories in height, occupy an area of 300 feet on Eighth street, by 150 feet on Clark avenue, also large buildings running through to Ninth street. These premises are completely fitted with machinery of the most modern and improved design, and all the necessary appliances for the successful prosecution of all the manufacturing details of the business. A force ranging from 200 to 300 men is employed, and the company manufacture hay presses, lever horse powers in all sizes, railway or tread presses, sawing machines, road scrapers, corn shellers, seed sowers, feed cutters, cultivators, barrows, cider and wine mills, garden, coal, wood, brick and mortar barrows, railway and warehouse supplies, hose reels, lard and wine presses, well boring machines, dump cars, iron and pork trucks, dry goods wagons, warehouse trucks and wagons, baggage barrows, field and garden rollers, etc. The trade of the company extends to every part of the Union, Canada, Mexico and South America, and in many of the articles of their manufacture to Europe. The company takes special pride in the superior workmanship of its goods, and the Whitman Hay Press has taken the honors wherever it has been exhibited in competition with those of other makers. It took the first prize in 1880, 1881 and 1882, the gold medal in 1883, and silver medal in 1885, at the New York State fairs; the silver medal at Denver in 1884 and the first prize at the New Orleans World's Fair in 1885. During the year 1886, it took first prizes at Dallas, Texas State Fair; Buenos Ayres; first prize, gold medal, New England Fair at Bangor, Me.; Nebraska State Fair, Maine State Fair, and at the Northern, Central and South American Exposition at New Orleans. A new railway power, with governor or speed regulator, has been placed upon the market the past season, which is pronounced by all who have seen it to be superior to anything yet invented. The company has unsurpassed facilities for carrying on all the details of the business, is managed with marked efficiency, and is prepared to fill all orders in the most prompt and satisfactory manner.

**M. A. Wolff & Co.**—Real Estate Agents; 105 North Eighth street.—This is one of the oldest and most favorably known real estate firms of the city, and was established in 1859 by Mr. Marcus A. Wolff, who has been prominently identified with real estate matters for many years. The firm gives its special attention to the care of estates and the collection of rents, and no firm in the city transacts as large a business in this line as M. A. Wolff & Co. Legal papers of all kinds pertaining to real estate are carefully drawn and prepared by the firm, and the interests of clients are carefully attended to. Among the prominent estates now in the care of this firm are those of Ex-Mayor Luther M. Kennett, Albert Todd, Dr. Henry Van Studdiford, Robert A. Gordon, one of the Lindell heirs, and others. Mr. Marcus A. Wolff is one of the most prominent residents of the city, and has by his public spirit and brilliant business course, done much for the prosperity and advancement of the city. He is actively and prominently connected with many different enterprises. He was one of the original stockholders of the Boatman's Saving Institution, and is interested in the Second National Bank, East St. Louis Elevator Co., Hope Mutual Insurance Co., St. Louis Distillery Co., St. Louis Transfer Railway Co., and the South St. Louis Street Railway Co. He was, last year, President of the St. Louis Real Estate Exchange.

**John R. Triplett.**—Insurance Agency; 118 North Third street.—Mr. Triplett holds a prominent position in the insurance circles of the city, having been successfully engaged in the business for about fifteen years. He is now, and has been for many years past, the Vice-President of the St. Louis Board of Fire Underwriters. The list of companies represented by him is a substantial one and made up of corporations of ample capital and resources, all of which are of firmly established reputation for the prompt payment of all losses and just dealing with their policy-holders. The list includes the Williamsburg City Fire Insurance Co., of New York; the Pacific Fire Insurance Co., of New York; the New York Bowery Fire Insurance Co.; the Mechanics' Fire Insurance Co., of New York; the Fireman's Fund of California, San Francisco; the People's Fire Insurance Co., of New York; the Mercantile Fire Insurance Co., of New York, and the Virginia Fire and Marine Insurance Co., of Virginia. Many of the leading business and residence buildings of the city are insured in these companies through Mr. Triplett's Insurance Agency, and his dealings with policy-holders, throughout his long and honorable connection with the business, have always been of the most satisfactory character.

**Waters-Pierce Oil Company.**—W. H. Waters, President; H. C. Pierce, Vice-President; C. M. Adams, Secretary; Lubricating and Illuminating Oils; Works cover ground between Gratiot and Austin, Twelfth and Fourteenth streets; Office, 600 North Fourth street.—This important and prosperous corporation is the largest in its line west of the Mississippi River. The extensive works of the company in this city are connected with their works in East St. Louis by a pipe line, by which the oil is conveyed underneath the river. They have every facility for the handling and shipment of oil, including a large number of tank cars, by which their oil is conveyed to every town reached by railroad and water in Arkansas, Missouri, Indian Territory, Texas, Louisiana and Mexico, in each of which towns they have

branches or agencies. They control all of the petroleum business of Mexico, owning and operating an oil refinery in the City of Mexico, and supplying the entire country from there. In illuminating oils their specialty is "Eupion Oil," which for the purity and brilliancy of its light is not surpassed by any oil produced. They also deal largely in lubricating oils of superior quality, which they supply to railroads, manufacturing establishments, etc. The works have been established for thirty years, having been founded in 1857 by John R. Finlay as the St. Louis Coal Oil Works. The process used was the Scotch method of extracting oil from shale, the coal for the purpose being brought from Kentucky. After the petroleum industry had begun to develope, crude oil was brought to the works by river routes and the works were turned into a petroleum refinery. In 1869, H. C. Pierce & Co. succeeded to the business, and introduced the plan of cylindrical tank cars for transporting the crude petroleum from the oil regions. This firm afterward became Waters, Pierce & Co., and in 1878 the present corporation was organized. Its career has been one of continuous and steadily expanding success. With ample resources, and the introduction of superior methods of handling, the product has been maintained at the highest standard of quality, and being shipped in car load lots to all points covered by the company's territory, and delivered from depots in quantities to suit the trade, prices have been kept low and the consumer benefited by the admirable system adopted by the company.

**The Liverpool and London and Globe Insurance Company.**—Archie Robinson, Resident Agent; Northwest Corner of Third and Chestnut streets, Chamber of Commerce Building.—This mammoth corporation was established in 1836, entered the United States in 1851, and is the largest fire insurance company in the world. Its total assets amount to nearly $35,000,000, of which $6,000,000 is in the United States. The company has a world-wide reputation for the promptness with which it meets its obligations and pays valid losses in cash, without deduction of interest. At Chicago, in 1871, the company paid $3,239,091, and in the year following at Boston, $1,429,729, without touching the United States assets. The company has heretofore pursued a conservative policy in St. Louis, owing to the insufficient water facilities, but the recent improvement in this respect will enable it to increase its lines and accept additional first-class risks. The St. Louis agency was established in 1862, and Mr. Archie Robinson, the resident agent, has managed its affairs nearly all the time since that date in an efficient manner, giving entire satisfaction to the company and its local policy-holders.

**Brownell & Wight Car Company.**—F. B. Brownell, President; A. S. Partridge, Secretary; Manufacturers of Street Cars; 2300 Broadway.—This business was originally established in 1858, the present company being incorporated in 1875. The works cover half of two blocks at 2300 Broadway, and are fully and completely equipped with all the necessary machinery, plant and appliances for facilitating the efficient prosecution of the business. Employment is given to a force ranging from one hundred and fifty to two hundred workmen. The company manufactures street cars and has established an unsurpassed reputation for the superior workmanship, finish and perfect mechanism of its cars, of which it turns out from three hundred to four hundred per annum. Only skilled labor is employed and the best materials used in construction, and the careful supervision given to every detail of the business has resulted in a large trade extending into every portion of the Union, Mexico and the Dominion of Canada.

**P. F. Keleher & Co.**—Stock and Bond Brokers: 317 Olive street.—A prominent firm engaged in business as stock and bond brokers is that of P. F. Keleher & Co., with an office located at 317 Olive street, and which was established in 1871. They buy and sell bonds of the United States, and of the several states, counties, and municipalities; railroad, insurance, telegraph, mining, banking and commercial stocks, notes and all investment securities; negotiate secure loans upon the most advantageous terms, deal in exchange on the principal European cities, and transact all business in the line. They deal extensively in this city, as well as in New York, San Francisco, Philadelphia, Boston and Chicago, and all leading markets of the country. The house is of prominent standing and good repute, and possesses unsurpassed facilities for the prompt and efficient execution of every order placed in its hands.

**Redmond Cleary & Co.**—Commission Merchants; Chamber of Commerce.—One of the largest as well as among the oldest commission houses operating in this market is that of Redmond Cleary & Co., the offices of which are eligibly located on the main floor of the Chamber of Commerce, and which has extensive warehouses at 26 South Commercial street. The house was originally established in 1865 as Cleary & Taylor, which firm was dissolved some years since, leaving Mr. Cleary sole proprietor of the business, which amounts to between $7,000,000 and $8,000,000 annually. He does a general commission business in all lines in their season, making a specialty at present of grain and hay, which he receives in lots of five thousand bushels and upward from Missouri, Illinois, Kansas, Iowa and Nebraska, and sells on 'Change. For twenty-two years, Mr. Cleary has been identified with the largest operations on the floor of the Exchange, and the uniformly satisfactory manner in which he has protected the interests of producers and shippers for whom he has transacted commission services has secured for him the large and important business he now controls and an unrivaled reputation as one of the most active and judicious commission merchants of the city.

**Rohan Bros. Boiler Manufacturing Company.**—Michael Rohan, President; Philip Rohan, Secretary and Treasurer; John Rohan, Vice-President and Superintendent; Manufacturers of all kinds of Steam Boilers and Sheet Iron Work; 1100 to 1120 Collins street.—Of special prominence in the important line of boiler

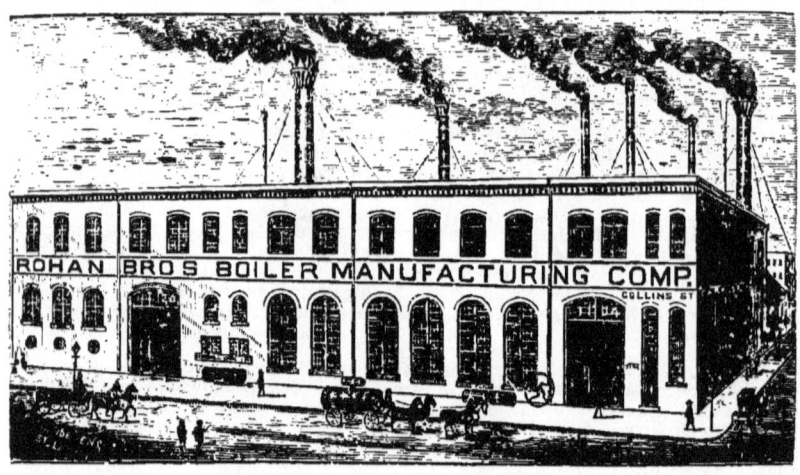

manufacture, is the factory at 1100 to 1120 Collins street, of the Rohan Bros. Boiler Manufacturing Co. The business was established by Ellison & Rohan in 1866, became Rohan Bros. in 1874, and was incorporated under its present style in 1881. The works front 225 feet on Collins street, 110 feet on Carr street and 110 feet on Second street, and the company, which owns the greater part of this large and valuable property, is negotiating with the Mullanphy Board for the purchase of the remainder. The premises are fitted up with machinery and plant unsurpassed by any house in the country, including a 35-ton Sampson punch and shears, and employing one hundred and seventy-five skilled mechanics. The work is done by contract, the manufacture of boilers being the specialty of the company, but they also make to order any kind of wrought iron work for steam or heating purposes. The house has for many years held a foremost position in its line, attained by the uniform excellence of its workmanship, and its trade is very large, not only in the city, but also throughout the entire States of Missouri, Southern Illinois, Western Kentucky, Tennessee, Mississippi, Louisiana, Arkansas, Texas, Colorado, etc.; and also in Mexico. As an apt illustration of the merits of their work, it may be stated that at the time of the anticipated troubles between Russia and China, the Russian government concluded to place steamers on the River Amoor, and sent a commissioner to this country to look around. He placed his orders in St. Louis, and this house supplied the boiler work for the whole line of fourteen steamers. The house is first-class in every respect, and enjoys a success which has been fairly earned.'

**Blakely, Sanders & Co.**—Commission Merchants for the Sale or Forwarding of all kinds of Live Stock: Offices, 5 National Stock Yards, East St. Louis, and 5 and 6 Union Stock Yards, St. Louis.—This firm, composed of Messrs. John W. Blakely, James T. Sanders and R. H. Mann, was formed about fifteen years ago, and holds a prominent position among the leading live stock firms of this market, operating largely in both the Union and National Stock Yards. They give their personal attention to all stock consigned to them at either yards, and do a very large business, the firm having for many years maintained the most favorable relations with shippers, to whom they have commended themselves by the faithful manner in which they execute every commission entrusted to them. All the members of the firm are practical and experienced men in the business. Mr. Blakely attends to consignments of hogs and sheep to the Union Stock Yards; Mr. Mann takes the same department at the National Stock Yards and Mr. Sanders is the cattle man of the firm at the Union Stock Yards.

**Domestic Sewing Machine Company.**—E. L. Green, Manager; 906 Olive street.—The St. Louis branch of the Domestic Sewing Machine Company was established in 1880 in order to better accommodate its growing business in the States of Missouri, Arkansas, Louisiana, Texas, Mississippi, Kentucky, Tennessee and Southern Illinois. The branch has prospered greatly under the efficient management of Mr. E. L. Green, to whose zeal and energy, combined with the superior merit of the machines manufactured by the company, the great increase in its business in the territory controlled from St. Louis is due. The Domestic machines are unsurpassed in their general adaptability to the purposes of the family. They are simple in mechanism, easy to learn, made of the best material with the finest workmanship, are light running and almost noiseless, and combine in the highest degree utility and elegance. The offices occupied by the company are elegantly equipped and a large force of competent and affable ladies and gentlemen are always on hand to attend to the wants of customers. Over a million of these elegant machines are in use throughout the country and they never fail to give satisfaction to the purchaser. They maintain their great popularity against all competition and are always heartily commended by those who give them a trial.

**Glaser Brothers.**—Importers and Manufacturers' Agents of Gents' Furnishing Goods and Notions; 700 and 702 Washington avenue.—This firm is composed of Messrs. Louis, Joseph and Adolph Glaser, and is one of the largest in its line in the city or the West. They occupy an elegant five-story and basement building fronting 60 feet on Washington avenue and running back 90 feet on Seventh street. They are importers and manufacturers' agents for every description of gents' furnishing goods, notions, hosiery, gloves and fancy goods of all kinds. Twenty clerks and assistants are employed in their store, while six active and wide-awake traveling salesmen represent the house in a large territory, embracing the States of Missouri, Illinois, Kansas, Arkansas, Texas, Tennessee, Mississippi, Louisiana and the West and South generally. The house has been established six years, and has obtained a reputation for the superiority of its goods, and the promptness and accuracy of its business methods, which has made it popular in the trade. The firm carry large and complete stocks, severely taxing the capacity of their building, and embracing every description of articles in their line, in the latest styles, and also including all the latest and most fashionable novelties.

**Samuel Virden & Co.**—Commission Merchants in Hay; 506 Chamber of Commerce.—For over thirty years Mr. Samuel Virden has been in the commission business and recognized as among the prominent and successful business men of the city. He formerly kept a large warehouse and dealt in all kinds of grain, hay, seeds, etc., but of late years has found that too troublesome for the profit in it, and now devotes himself exclusively to hay, which he receives from Missouri, Illinois, Kansas, Iowa, Minnesota, and other States, and sells exclusively in car load lots on track. He does a very heavy business, his long experience in his line, and knowledge of the market, together with the large business connection he has acquired in over thirty years of honorable dealing, giving him unsurpassed facilities for purchase and sale. His reliable methods have contributed largely to the success he has so long enjoyed.

**O'Connor & Harder Furnace and Range Company.**—E. J. O'Connor, President; J. H. Niederman, Secretary; Manufacturers of and Dealers in Furnaces, Stoves, Ranges and House Furnishing Goods; 1011 Olive street.—This business was established by Mr. E. J. O'Connor in 1872. He formed a co-partnership with Mr. A. Harder in 1875, from which was incorporated the O'Connor & Harder Furnace and Range Co. This firm now occupy a four story building at the above number and have the most completely equipped establishment of its kind in the country. They employ from thirty-five to fifty hands, and besides their immense city trade have also a large country trade in Illinois and Missouri. They deal largely in wrought and cast iron furnaces and ranges, and having State agencies of the celebrated Ruby, Carton, Reynolds and Barstow furnaces, enables them to meet the wants of any one needing furnaces, no matter how difficult the building may be to heat. Mr. O'Connor has made the question of heating and ventilating a life study, and only employs the most skilled mechanics. The great number of public and private buildings in which they have put furnaces in this city, as well as throughout Missouri and Illinois, establishes the fact of the standing of the firm in their line of business. Parties entrusting any work to this firm may be assured of good work and trading with a live, energetic house. Catalogues sent to any address on application.

**Brown-Desnoyers Shoe Co.**—George W. Brown, President; J. D. Desnoyers, Vice-President; R. W. Parcels, Treasurer; W. H. Jordan, Secretary; Manufacturers of Boots and Shoes; 805 Washington avenue.—This large and prosperous manufactur-

ing establishment was started in 1870 as the Bryan-Brown Shoe Co., changing to its present style in 1886, when Mr. Bryan retired, the present members having been in the former firm. The company lease the large new five-story and basement brick factory, 60x160 feet in dimensions, forming the southeast corner of Eighth and Walnut streets, and sub-let the two lower floors, occupying the remainder. This factory is completely supplied with all the requisite plant and most improved modern machinery adapted to the business. Here 325 hands are employed in the manufacture of women's, misses' and children's fine shoes exclusively. The company have another factory at Jeffersonville, Ind., where they manufacture goods for men's wear, and employ two hundred hands. Their warehouse, at 805 Washington avenue, is an elegant six-story and basement edifice, 30x160 feet in area, and is filled with a large and diversified stock of everything in their line. The company do an immense business, covering the States of Missouri, Illinois, Kentucky, Tennessee, Mississippi, Arkansas, Indian Territory, Colorado, Nebraska, Kansas, Texas and Louisiana, and have fifteen traveling salesmen to represent them in this vast trade territory. The office and warehouse are under the management of President Brown, while Mr. Desnoyers, the Vice-President, has supervision of the factory in this city. The company enjoys a first-class reputation for the quality of its goods and the reliability of its business methods.

**Fabricius Toy and Notion Company.**—Mrs. Agathe Fabricius, President; Henry H. Fabricius, Secretary and Treasurer; Importers and Dealers in Toys, Fancy Goods, Notions, etc.; 703 and 705 North Fourth street.—This business was originally established some twenty-five years ago by Mr. Henry P. Fabricius, lately deceased. The present corporation was organized in April of the present year, the capital stock of the company being $25,000. The management of the affairs of the house is now in the hands of Mr. Henry H. Fabricius, son of the founder, who has been actively connected with the business for the past eight years, and is thoroughly experienced. The company does a large wholesale business throughout Illinois and Missouri, as well as a retail business in the city, a competent force of twenty men being employed in the house, while a staff of traveling salesmen attends to the interests of the house on the road. The company deals in every description of toys, fancy goods, notions, baby carriages, willow ware, traveling bags, china goods, bird cages, albums, harmonicas, pocket cutlery and scissors, base balls, croquets, etc., and has every facility for filling all orders promptly and upon the most reasonable and satisfactory terms.

**Billingsley & Nanson Commission Company.**—R. L. Billingsley, President; J. S. Nanson, Vice-President; W. B. Anderson, Secretary; George H. Hall, Treasurer; Grain, Hay, Flour, etc.; 202 Chamber of Commerce.—This business was established in 1851 by the firm of Nanson, Dameron & Co., who were succeeded by Nanson, Bothwell & Co., followed in 1881 by Billingsley, Nanson & Co., and finally incorporated in 1884 under its present name. The offices of the company are located at 202 Chamber of Commerce, and they have also a commodious warehouse at 207 North Second street. They have elevators at seven points in Iowa and buy corn on tracks in all parts of the West. The firm buys and sells for personal account and on commission, grain, hay, flour, seeds, wool and hog products, making a specialty of corn, which they buy in large quantities and ship South. All of the officers of this company are men of large business experience and their ample means, unsurpassed facilities and thorough knowledge of the market, together with their prompt and reliable methods of dealing, have given them a high reputation with shippers and producers, and gained for them a great and steadily increasing prosperity.

**Donk Bros. & Co.**—Miners and Dealers in Bituminous and Anthracite Coal; 316 Olive street.—Donk Bros. & Co. is one of the oldest and best known coal firms in the city. For twenty-five years they have stood among the leading mine operators in the Illinois bituminous coal district. They also make a specialty of dealing in the best qualities of anthracite, the demand for which, for office and household heating purposes, has grown so much in St. Louis of late years, and as they buy only in large quantities from Pennsylvania, they are enabled to give their customers the advantage of the lowest quotations. The name of the firm is best known, however, through the fact that they have introduced and established a brand of coal for household use, known as "Donk's Domestic." Its peculiarities are that it burns freely and readily—producing the maximum of heat in the shortest time—and that it leaves nothing behind but a clean white ash, no clinker or hard cinder of any kind to clog up the grate. In fact it is nearly as clean in burning as the best anthracite, while it is, of course, much more easily ignited and kept in full combustion. In order to place this coal in the market in the most convenient shape for consumers, Donk Bros. & Co. cause it to be sorted in various sizes and grades, rigidly discarding all dust, dirt and other extraneous matter. "Donk's Domestic Egg Coal," for instance, is specially sorted by hand for use in parlor grates, ranges and stoves; "Donk's Domestic Lump Coal" is similarly prepared for general household use; "Donk's Domestic Nut Coal" is sorted into smaller sizes for small stoves, and besides these they carry immense stocks of coal for steam and general manufacturing purposes. Their yards in the southern and western parts of the city are among the most extensive in the trade, and the firm, which is composed of August F. Donk and Edmund C. Donk, have won an enviable reputation in the community for the absolute fairness of their dealings and their fidelity and promptness in fulfilling all contracts.

**Platt & Thornburgh Paint and Glass Company.**—H. S. Platt, President; W. H. Thornburgh, Vice-President; H. Boardman, Secretary; 620 Franklin avenue, corner of Seventh street.—This old and prominent house was established about thirty-five years ago by Mr. H. S. Platt, who was afterward joined by Mr. W. H. Thornburgh, the firm becoming Platt & Thornburgh, to which the present corporation succeeded in 1880. The business of the house steadily expanded, keeping pace with the growth of the city, and is now immense in its proportions, covering a territory embracing the States of Missouri, Illinois, Indiana, Kentucky, Tennessee, Arkansas, Texas, Indian Territory, New Mexico, Colorado, Kansas, Nebraska and Iowa, a staff of five active commercial travelers being employed attending to the wants of the customers in the States enumerated. The company occupies the four-story building, 25x125, at the corner of Franklin avenue and Seventh street, and also a three-story warehouse, 50x150 feet, at 816 and 818 North Seventh street. They carry very large and complete stocks of dry and mixed paints, oils, varnishes, putty, glass, brushes, and everything in the line of painters', decorators' and glaziers' stock, tools and supplies. A force of forty clerks and assistants is employed in their store and warehouse, and all the operations of the company are conducted with perfect system and order. The house has, throughout its long and honorable history, held the confidence of the trade by the uniform reliability and superiority of its goods, and the perfect fairness and accuracy by which all its dealings are actuated.

**St. Louis Coal Tar Company.**—J. Sibley White, President; G. H. Parsons, Secretary; Manufacturers of Roofing and Paving Materials, Coal Tar, etc.; Levee and Convent street.—The factory of this company is located here at St Louis, occupying convenient premises at the foot of Convent street. The concern was established in 1866, by Page, Smith, Lewis & Co., and was incorporated in 1867 as the St. Louis Coal Tar Co., Eastern capital withdrawing and being succeeded by St. Louis parties shortly afterwards. President White was engaged in the roofing business for many years previous to his arrival in St. Louis, and is thoroughly experienced in all of its requirements, and in the manufacture of coal tar products. He came to St. Louis in 1866, and has since been the able and efficient executive officer and manager of this company. Secretary Parsons is also a practical and energetic business man, and the affairs of the company are in a prosperous condition. The products made by this establishment go to all portions of the United States, and it is but recently that two heavy shipments were made to widely different points. One was several car loads of creosote to California, another, a big shipment of various products, to Baltimore, Md.

**Bemis Bro. Bag Company.**—J. M. Bemis, President; S. A. Bemis, Secretary; Manufacturers of Bags and Burlaps; Corner of Poplar and Fourth streets.—This important establishment was founded in 1858 as Bemis & Brown, to whom the firm of Bemis Bro. & Co. succeeded. In 1885, in order to more efficiently conduct their large and steadily growing business, the members of the firm incorporated under the style of Bemis Bro. Bag Co., and shortly afterward removed from their former location on Main street to the more spacious and elegant quarters now occupied by them comprising the new buildings, six stories and 60x150 feet in dimensions, at the corner of Poplar and Fourth streets, with offices adjoining, fronting on Fourth street, 60x40 feet. Besides their house here they have establishments in Boston and Minneapolis, and their trade, which extends to every part of the Union, is not excelled in volume by that of any house on the continent. They carry a large and complete stock of bags and burlaps, and are agents for the Home Cotton Mills, corner of Barton and Columbus streets, the products of which they handle. Their facilities are unsurpassed and their business methods accurate and reliable. Having maintained for nearly thirty years a foremost standing and an honorable reputation, the house merits the prosperity which has been enjoyed by it and which increases from year to year.

**O. Voelker & Co.**—Commission Merchants; 916 North Third street.—The firm of O. Voelker & Co. has been successfully engaged in the commission business since 1875. They are located at 916 North Third street, and deal on personal account, as well as on commission, in all kinds of country produce, eggs, game, poultry, etc., which they receive from all the territory tributary to the St. Louis market in large quantities and ship to all the Eastern cities. The business of the house has steadily increased from its inception to the present, and the accurate methods which have ever characterized all the transactions of the firm have secured for them an excellent standing among shippers and producers, and have resulted in the steady expansion of the trade territory of the house and merited prosperity. They possess ample facilities for the transaction of every department of their business, and execute all commissions placed in their hands in a satisfactory manner. The firm issues a pamphlet on the game laws of different States, which they will be pleased to mail to any person forwarding his address to them.

**St. Louis Dairy Co.**—T. T. Turner, President; J. F. Lee, Jr., Vice-President; Heinrich Dettmer, Ph.D., Chemist and Inspector; Charless Cabanne, Secretary and General Manager; Northwest Corner of Twelfth and Chestnut streets.—The ease with which adulteration of milk with water and otherwise can be perpetrated renders the milk sold in cities, as a general thing, unreliable. This well-known fact has caused the St. Louis Dairy Co., a corporation organized in May, 1882, to take special and extraordinary pains to preserve a uniform standard of purity and excellence in their milk and cream. To effect this result the scientific knowledge of the company's chemist and inspector, Heinrich Dettmer, Ph. D., with a corps of assistants, is called into practice. Samples of all milk received by the company are analyzed in the laboratory. Samples are afterwards taken daily by the assistant inspectors from the delivery wagons in all parts of the city and tested to prevent the drivers from adulterating the milk, and again taken from the houses of customers and tested to prevent its being tampered with by servants. The inspectors are required to go into not less than fifteen houses every day to have a paper signed by the customer asking if there is any dissatisfaction, thus controlling the assistant inspectors. When a complaint is made the matter is followed up until the blame, if any, is properly located. Only one grade of cream and one grade of milk (pure milk) is carried on the retail delivery wagons of the company. These careful safeguards against adulteration have proven a remarkable success, and the company has secured the confidence of the St. Louis public in an eminent degree, and a large patronage requiring fifteen retail wagons, one wholesale wagon, one depot wagon and the services of thirty-five employes. That the high standing enjoyed by the company is merited is sufficiently shown in the following list of prominent and substantial citizens, who compose its board of directors: T. T. Turner, R. H. Hutchinson, J. F. Lee, Jr., Dr. I. G. W. Steedman and Chas. P. Chouteau.

**Consolidated Coal Company of St. Louis.**—Chas. Ridgely, President; E. J. Crandall, General Manager; Geo. T. Cutts, Secretary; Thos. D. Price, Treasurer; Miners and Shippers of Bituminous Coal; Northeast Corner of Fourth and Chestnut streets.—This great and solid corporation was organized in September, 1886, as the consolidation of heavy mining and shipping interests in the bituminous coal industry. They own and operate a large number of mines on the Wabash, Illinois and St. Louis, Indianapolis and St. Louis, Ohio and Mississippi, Vandalia, Louisville and Nashville and Cairo Short Line railways, including the celebrated mines of Danville, Mt. Olive, Staunton, St. Bernard, Gillespie, Dorsey, Domestic, Collinsville, Abbey, Rose Hill, Green Mount, Pittsburg, Breese, Trenton, Lebanon, Giant, Richland, Marissa, White Oak, Concordia, Knecht, Reinecke, Birkner and Dutch Hollow. These mines have a capacity of 40,000 tons daily and give employment to 4,500 men. The company have large yards on Anna street, Anglerodt street, Seventeenth street and Clark avenue. They supply all the railroad lines in and around St. Louis, large manufacturers, dealers and consumers, in car load lots at reasonable rates. They ship largely to Chicago, Omaha, Council Bluffs, Jefferson City, and all points where they can compete in freight rates. For their river trade they have four steam tugs and a full line of barges, which gives them every facility for prompt and satisfactory filling of orders. The office of the company's Superintendent of River Department is on wharfboat, foot of Pine street. The company are the largest miners and shippers of coal west of Ohio, and with practically unlimited resources, able management and ability to fill the largest orders for the best quality of coal with the greatest dispatch, the foremost position in its line which it holds is assured of permanent continuance.

**J. T. Donovan & Co.**—Real Estate and Financial Agents; 513 North Sixth street.—This well-known firm is one of the leaders in the real estate business of St. Louis.—J. T. Donovan engaged in the business with his father in 1865, and upon the death of D. H. Donovan in 1871, the business was continued by his son under the firm name of J. T. Donovan & Co. The firm have been very successful; they are the confidential agents for many large owners and for capitalists who invest in real estate loans. The firm transact a general business and have an experienced corps of assistants to attend to the collecting and renting departments. Mr. Donovan is a large owner of real estate and has been an extensive dealer. His intimate knowledge of values in all sections of the city is a great advantage to their patrons, particularly those who invest in property or in real estate loans. They do a very large business in loaning money to erect improvements and in all matters are prompt and reliable.

Jos. T. Cunningham,
President,
Rochester, N. Y.

Rufus K. Dryer,
V.-Pres't and Sec'y,
Rochester, N. Y.

Chas. H. Wilkin,
Treasurer,
Rochester, N. Y.

Charles Strobridge
Resident Manag'r,
St. Louis, Mo.

The James Cunningham, Son & Co's. Carriage Works,
Rochester, N. Y.

St. Louis Branch,
1104 and 1106 Washington Ave.

**The James Cunningham, Son & Company.**—Builders of High Grade Carriages; Charles Strobridge, Resident Manager; 1104 and 1106 Washington avenue, St. Louis.—The foregoing page represents the works of this company, located at Rochester, N. Y., which cover a whole square of ground, and which were established by the late James Cunningham in 1838, and have long been recognized as the largest establishment in the world, engaged in the manufacture of high grade pleasure and family carriages.

Their productions include: Coupes, coupelets, broughams, extension broughams, landaulets, demi-landaus, 4-seat rockaways, 6-seat rockaways, 5-glass landaus, Berlin coaches, suspension landaus, drags, breaks, victorias, cabriolets, T carts, wagonettes and dog carts.

This company have large warerooms in New York, Boston, Chicago and St. Louis. Their establishment on Washington avenue in this city includes two elegant 5-story buildings, 60 by 150 feet, where are shown all the leading styles of carriages in use in this country.

It is only due to this firm to say, that they stand foremost of the carriage manufacturers of the country, and it is in no small degree to their skill, enterprise and liberality that St. Louis must attribute the fact that it stands so high as a carriage manufacturing centre, and supplies such an immense territory with vehicles of all descriptions. Not only has this firm been for many years identified with the carriage business of St. Louis, but they have made unusual and strenuous efforts to overcome all competition from other cities and to make St. Louis the distributing centre for the entire Southwest. They have used all the vast means and facilities at their disposal to this end, and it is only just that they should receive the credit for the success that has been attained.

We have stated that this company stands at the head of the carriage manufacturing concerns of the country; this is a fact; they employ a greater number of men, use a larger amount of materials and have a larger capital invested in the business than any other single firm. The management of this immense business has been of the highest order. Not a single article is allowed to be used that has not been well seasoned and in every respect of the best description; not a mechanic is employed that is not thoroughly skilled in his particular branch of the business and not a vehicle is allowed to leave their factory until it has been closely inspected and passed by a perfectly qualified examiner.

Their large capital enables them to purchase their materials at the lowest market rates, and to carry a stock of fine wood and other articles that would bankrupt an ordinary concern to handle.

It is facilities of this nature, and this first-class management, that has enabled this company to give their customers the most perfect satisfaction in every case, in both the quality of the carriage purchased and the price at which it is sold.

**Laclede Mutual Fire Insurance Company.**—R. W. Powell, President; Jos. O'Neil, Vice-President; J. C. Bury, Jr., Secretary; P. F. Dockery, Agent; Southeast Corner Third and Locust streets.—This prominent insurance corporation, which has long been recognized as one of the safest and most substantial in the city, was chartered January 14, 1861. The bulk of its business is fire insurance on the mutual plan, but the company also writes risks for cash premiums on the stock plan. The company has gained an unexcelled reputation for stability by its care in the selection of risks and its conservative management. President Powell, who has been at the head of the company from its organization to the present time, has been closely identified with business and financial enterprises in this city since 1843. He was one of the incorporators of the Citizens' Savings Bank, of which he is now a director and Vice-President, and is a large owner of valuable city real estate. Vice-President O'Neil, of this company, is the President of the Citizens' Savings Bank. Secretary Bury of this company, has filled the position with credit for a number of years. The board of directors of the company comprises the following well-known and substantial business men: R. W. Powell, Oliver Garrison, John M. Sellers, F. L. Haydel, Chas. Slevin, J. B. C. Lucas, Joseph O'Neil, Chas. H. Turner and Trumbull G. Russell. At the close of business in 1886 the resources of the company amounted to $279,448 against total liabilities of $154,195, leaving a net surplus of $125,253. It wrote risks in Missouri alone, last year, amounting to $1,379,857, its losses aggregating $4,669. The company has earned the high standing it holds by honorable methods and efficient management.

**Southern Roller Mills.**—Eugelke & Feiner, Proprietors; Manufacturers of Corn Meal, Pearl Grits and Hominy; 804 to 808 South Broadway.— These mills are the oldest and largest corn meal mills in the West, and were established long before the war, since which they have continued in successful existence, and reached to their present great capacity by the indomitable perseverance of its proprietors and the superior quality of its products. The mills have, of late years, been thoroughly rebuilt and equipped with all modern improvements, including the new roller process. The capacity is equal to 1,500 barrels per day, and the demand is great enough to require the mills to keep at their capacity the year around. Nearly all of the meal, hominy, grits, etc., manufactured by this establishment finds a market in the South and their products are a household word there. The proprietors, although for many years in business, are liberal and progressive business men, fully alive to the achievements of the times, and maintain their mills at the highest standard of excellence.

**D. W. Haydock.**—Wholesale Manufacturer of Carriages, Buggies, Surreys, Etc.; Southwest Corner of Tenth and St. Charles streets.—Mr. Haydock came to this city from Cincinnati in 1878, becoming a member of the firm of Haydock Bros. and remaining until the dissolution of that firm in 1883. He then went into business for himself at 1010 St. Charles street. In March, 1885, he was burned out and removed to his present quarters at the corner of Tenth and St. Charles streets, where he occupies a spacious four-story and basement building, 120x100 feet, fitted with all the necessary machinery and equipments for the successful prosecution of the business, and giving employment to a force of three hundred workmen, all of whom are skilled mechanics. Mr. Haydock makes a specialty of fine and standard goods. His "D. W. Haydock Patent Cart" is the best two-wheeler in the world, while the Thomas coil spring buggy, for which he is sole agent in St. Louis, is without a superior. He manufactures Brewster side-bar, Timken side-bar, piano box, drop front, coal box, and Concord spring buggies, phætons, barouches, sporting wagons, delivery wagons, jump seats, surreys, park wagons, etc., using the best materials, uniformly dished and perfectly tracking wheels, and making everything in the best style and finest finish. Mr. Haydock devotes his whole time to his business, carefully supervising every detail, with the result that his goods are in demand in every part of the Union. He completed 4,500 jobs last year, and the indications are that 10,000 will be made during the present season. At the last exposition Mr. Haydock's display, an automatic exhibition of "Mary and Her Little Lamb" attracted much attention as one of the most unique and perfect. Mr. Haydock has earned a merited success by excelling in the quality of his goods, prompt filling of orders and fairness in his dealings.

**Clarkson-Christopher Lumber Company.**—E. E. Mason, President; H. C. Christopher, Vice-President; R. M. Fry, Treasurer; Wholesale Commission Lumber Dealers; Office, Northwest Corner of Fourth and Walnut streets.—This is one of the largest and most successful concerns in its line in the city or the West, and has done a large and steadily increasing business from its inception. They deal very heavily in dressed yellow pine flooring, ceiling, siding, bridge, car and dimension timber and Tennessee yellow poplar, all of which they sell to large dealers, car works and railroad construction companies in car load lots or otherwise, delivered at any point. They maintain the most favorable relations with manufacturers and are enabled to offer unsurpassed inducements, both in price and quality, to the trade, and do a very large business not only in the city but also throughout Missouri, Illinois, Kansas and other States tributary, in a commercial sense, to St. Louis. They possess unsurpassed facilities, and enjoy the respect and confidence of the trade as a result of their prompt and satisfactory filling of orders.

**More, Jones & Co.**—Manufacturers of Car and Engine Brasses, Babbitt Metals, Solder, Bar Lead, Etc.; 1604, 1606 and 1608 North Eighth street.—St. Louis is the seat of the lead production of the United States, and one of the best known firms of this city engaged in the manufacture of Babbitt metal, lead products and railroad brasses is the above. The firm was organized about ten years ago by Messrs. Ed. A. More and Henry T. Jones, and occupy foundry buildings and offices at 1604 to 1608 North Eighth street. The main building is about 75x150 feet in its dimensions, and is provided with the best modern appliances for the work that is manufactured. Both of the proprietors are enterprising, thorough business men, with complete knowledge of the business, which they have built up through their own exertions, aided by the superior character of their output. The establishment, while a Western enterprise, managed by Western men, is favorably known to all parts of the United States. Trade comes to this firm from all sections, East, West, North and South. The enterprise of this firm, and the solid merit of its manufactures, commend it to the people of the country.

**Wilson & Toms Investment Company.**—Henry C. Wilson, President; George W. Toms, Vice-President and General Manager; Wm. F. Leonard, Secretary and Treasurer: L. M. Hall, Counsel; Farm Mortgages; Turner Building, 304 North Eighth street.—This business was established in 1869 by Messrs. Henry C. Wilson and George W. Toms, under the firm style of Wilson & Toms, and steadily grew from year to year, until in 1886, in order to facilitate its vast operations, the present company was incorporated as the Wilson & Toms Investment Company of St. Louis, with a full paid capital of $250,000. The company, which does an immense business in all parts of the country, and particularly in the West, has its headquarters in the Turner Building, in this city, and branch offices at Edinburgh, Scotland; Hartford, Conn.; Brooklyn, N. Y.; Wichita, Kan.; Pratt, Kan., and Greensburg, Kan. Their business consists exclusively of the loaning of money on farms, on mortgages, for the account of Eastern capitalists. They have an elegant suite of offices in this city, and employ, in all, about fifty agents, clerks and assistants. With ample means for the successful prosecution of the business, ripe experience and perfect system, they enjoy unequaled facilities for the making of safe and profitable investments in farm mortgages.

**G. V. Halliday & Co.**—Safes, Time Locks and Vault Doors; 219 Pine street.—This business was established in 1866 as F. Halliday & Co., to which the present firm succeeded in 1886. They are general agents for the Cincinnati Safe and Lock Company, of which Mr. Halliday is President and Treasurer. The safes, locks and vault doors sold by this house are approved by those who have used them as absolutely fire and burglar proof, and not surpassed in efficiency, workmanship or finish by any articles of a similar nature offered to the public. The business of the house is very large and covers the States of Illinois, Missouri, Arkansas, Texas, Kansas and the entire West, Northwest, Southwest and South, a good business also being done from a branch house established in New Orleans. The safes sold by this house have always withstood in absolute safety the test of fire whenever subjected to that ordeal, and maintain a high reputation in business, financial and official circles, while the correct business methods adopted in every transaction have contributed, in no small degree, to secure for the firm the prominent standing and merited success it has achieved. Mr. D. W. Sprague is the efficient St. Louis manager for the firm, and their interests here prospered under his faithful and painstaking supervision.

**John C. Tiemeyer.**—Packer of Seed Leaf and Importer of Havana Tobacco; Southeast Corner Second and Walnut streets.—Mr. Tiemeyer has been identified with the tobacco interests of St. Louis for many years, originally establishing himself in 1849 as a cigar manufacturer, in which line he continued until 1865, when he embarked in his present business. He is an extensive importer of Havana leaf and a large packer of Connecticut seed and all native tobaccos. He carries a very large and complete stock, occupying the five story building at the southeast corner of Second and Walnut streets. He maintains the most favorable relations with foreign and domestic producers and shippers, enabling him to offer to his customers superior inducements, both in quality and price. His trade is very large in the city and all the territory tributary to its market, and three experienced salesmen represent him on the road. Throughout his long business career Mr. Tiemeyer has held a high place in the confidence of the trade, and his reliable and satisfactory methods have placed his business on a most substantial and prosperous basis.

**Geo. Gog Boot and Shoe Manufacturing Company.**—Geo. Gog, President; Manufacturers of Men's and Boys' Boots and Shoes; 217 and 219 Elm street. —Mr. Gog, the founder of this business and the President of the company which bears his name, has been for thirty years prominently identified with the boot and shoe industry. He was for seventeen years in the retail business, but thirteen years ago turned his attention to manufacturing, in which he has enjoyed a signal success. Three years ago, in order to better accommodate his steadily increasing business, Mr. Gog had it incorporated under its present style. The manufactory of the company is completely equipped with all the latest and most improved machinery and appliances adapted to the requirements of the business, and gives employment to about one hundred men, in addition

to which four traveling salesmen represent the company on the road. The company manufactures every description of boots and shoes for men's and boys' wear, pegged, machine sewed, standard screw, etc., and is in high repute for the workmanship and materials of its product. The premises occupied are 50x150 feet in area, and the company's trade, in addition to a large city business, extends throughout the States of Missouri, Kansas, Arkansas and Texas.

**New Home Sewing Machine Company.**—J. B. Carpenter, General Manager; 900 Olive street.—Since the invention of Elias Howe, there have been great strides made in the improvement of the sewing machine, until perfection at last seems to have been attained in the simple, durable, perfect running and elegant "New Home" machine, of which over eight hundred thousand are now in use. It is a lock stitch machine with a cog motion and cylinder shuttle, noted for the simplicity of its mechanism and its perfect adaptability to all kinds of work, from the heaviest and plainest sewing to the most delicate work upon the finest fabrics. It is made in all styles from the plain frame and table to the most elegant cabinet. The St. Louis branch, which is under the zealous and enterprising supervision of Mr. J. B. Carpenter, as general manager, is eligibly located at the corner of Ninth and Olive streets, and does a heavy business in the city as well as in Missouri generally, Southern Illinois, Tennessee, Mississippi, Arkansas, Indian Territory, Kansas, Nebraska, Wyoming, Colorado, Utah and New Mexico. Ten thousand "New Home" machines were sold from this branch in 1886, and its business is steadily increasing. The great merits of the machines and the accurate business methods employed in the extension of their sale have made the "New Home" a prime favorite.

**John Wahl & Co.**—Commission Merchants; Southeast Corner of Main and Market streets.—This firm was established by its senior member, Mr. John Wahl, in 1860. Its active, progressive as well as prosperous business course has won the house a world-wide reputation among shippers of all classes of grain. The amount of wheat, corn, oats, barley and other small grain handled by this firm annually, runs into the million bushels and bespeaks the foremost position the same occupies among the leading commission houses. From the inception of its career to the present date, the house has confined itself to a purely legitimate commission business. Its integrity and faithful attention to the interests of its patrons, and its untiring zeal in trying to promote all that might facilitate the business interest of St. Louis has helped to make the reputation referred to. Their means of handling grain of all kinds are unsurpassed, and the careful supervision given all departments, which are many, and of varied character, by the head of the firm, Mr. John Wahl, is keenly felt in all transactions consummated by this house.

The establishment has in its employ an army of experienced men who have made their special branches a life study, and each special article handled by this firm has an able manager who personally attends to each shipment as it is received, thus assuring its owner of most satisfactory results. In their specialty of selling wheat by sample, they recognize no superior, and the marvelous quantity of this cereal annually received by them, suffices to confirm their leadership in that line. They carry, by the way, the largest stock of seamless grain bags in the city, which they furnish to their patrons on most reasonable terms. In barley they are recognized by brewers and maltsters as the largest and best house from which to purchase supplies of this article. In pig lead, they occupy a leading position, and the product is sold by them to all classes of lead buyers throughout the land, and no wise and prudent buyer closes a transaction until he has procured a quotation from this house. Messrs. Wahl & Co.'s palatial office reminds one of a bank, so elaborate is every furnishing and equipment, and at once impresses the visitor and patron with the standing, resources, energy and enterprise of the head of the firm, who so judiciously guides the helm and anchors his patrons by deeds of honesty and fair dealing.

**Citizens' Savings Bank.**—Joseph O'Neil, President; R. W. Powell, Vice-President; Thomas P. Gleeson, Cashier; 324 North Third street.—One of the prominent banking institutions of the city is the Citizens' Savings bank, which does a general banking business, receives accounts of merchants and others, issues foreign exchange, discounts approved commercial paper, makes collections, etc. It was incorporated September 28th, 1869, by Joseph O'Neil, John Ring, David Nicholson, R. W. Powell, M. H. Phelan, John Schenk and J. P. Ghio. Joseph O'Neil became President; R. W. Powell, Vice-President and John Schenk, cashier. Thomas P. Gleeson succeeded John Schenk as cashier in 1877. The capital stock of the bank is $150,000, and its present directors are Joseph O'Neil, R. W. Powell, D. W. McAllister, Wm. Dooley, Jeremiah Murphy, M. H. Phelan and Thos. P. Gleeson.

**J. Kennard & Sons' Carpet Company.**—Carpets, Curtain Goods, Oil Cloths, etc; 420 and 422 North Fourth street.—The great and representative carpet house now conducted by the J. Kennard & Sons' Carpet Co., incorporated a few years ago, was originally established by Mr. John Kennard in 1857. Prior to that time Mr. Kennard had been engaged in the same business at Lexington, Ky. To his business tact and sagacious management the steady growth of the trade and reputation of the house up to the time of his death were due. Since that event, which occurred in 1872, the management of the house has been conducted upon the same principles of strict business integrity by which the business methods of its founder were ever characterized. The premises occupied by the company comprise two five story buildings at 420 and 422 North Fourth street. 60x200 feet, having three frontages on North Fourth, St. Charles and Vine streets, and fitted up with every facility and convenience for the business. A competent force of eighty-five assistants are employed in the house, in addition to which three experienced traveling salesmen represent the company on the road. In addition to very heavy and comprehensive lines of carpets, rugs, draperies, curtain goods, oil cloths, etc., of American manufacture, the company imports, in very large quantities, the best products in these lines of the leading foreign makers. The company carries very large surplus stocks, having over five hundred retail merchants who order from them by sample, sending for the exact number of yards required by their customers; it being a plan adopted by the company to cut carpets in any required lengths, thereby saving the retail merchant the investment and insurance necessitated by the carrying of large, full lines; relieving him of the loss on old stock, remnants, etc., and enabling him to keep the latest patterns to show his customers. By correct and just dealing, continued for thirty years, this house has acquired its immense business in St. Louis and the States tributary to its market, and the leading position it holds in the confidence of the trade. Mr. Samuel M. Kennard, of this company, is the President of the St. Louis Exposition Company.

**Fraatz Toy and Notion Company.**—A. W. Fraatz, President and Treasurer; John N. Kleff, Vice-President; R. Veit, Secretary; Importers of Fancy Goods, Notions, Toys, etc.; 619 and 621 North Fourth street.—Twelve years ago, Mr. A. W. Fraatz, who had previously been engaged for eight years in the same line in Baltimore, established this business. The present company was incorporated in January of the present year, and occupies commodious and eligibly located premises at 619 and 621 North Fourth street. They are extensive importers and dealers at wholesale and retail in notions, toys, holiday goods, fancy decorated glassware, baby carriages, etc., and carry a large and finely assorted stock of all articles pertaining to their line. In addition to their heavy local business, they have a large and steadily increasing trade throughout Missouri and Kansas and in Illinois; a staff of active traveling salesmen representing the house in these States. In the departments here, a corps of twenty-one assistants is employed. Mr. Fraatz is thoroughly experienced in all the details of the business, and to his active management the company owes, in a large degree, the prosperity which it enjoys.

**P. Brockman & Co.**—General Commission Merchants; 22 South Main street.—This firm was established in 1879 by P. Brockman. The character of the business done by this house is general commission, and consignments of all kinds of produce are handled, but the great specialty is barley, and Mr. Brockman is one of the heaviest dealers in that grain in the Western country. His experience on this market, and a thorough knowledge of it at all times, makes him specially qualified to assume the responsibilities regularly entrusted him by the barley raisers of America. It is an article which enters largely into the manufacture of beer, and the extensive brewing interests of this city make this an important point in its distribution. The firm has an extensive business regularly consigned to it from Minnesota, Wisconsin, Iowa, Nebraska, California and Canada.

**H. S. Hopkins Bridge Company.**—H. S. Hopkins, President and Treasurer; J. H. Higby, Vice-President; G. H. Kahman, Secretary; General Contractors; Lucas Building, Fourth and Pine streets.—This business was established in 1868, by Mr. H. S. Hopkins, who is still at its head as President of the corporation bearing his name, and which was organized in 1883. The company have a large business as general contractors in all branches, making a specialty of the building of wrought iron, combination and wooden railway and highway bridges. They have attained an unsurpassed reputation for the reliable, prompt and satisfactory manner in which they execute every contract undertaken by them, and have built hundreds of bridges for railway corporations, counties and municipalities, in Missouri, Arkansas, Texas, Tennessee, Indiana, Illlinois, Michigan, Colorado and other States. They are, at this writing, building six spans of bridges in Texas, aggregating $125,000; a dam in Texas for $15,000; about $25,000 worth of bridges in Missouri, and other large works. They maintain warehouses wherever they have works, and employ large forces of men. They pay special attention to substructures, and every detail of work performed by them is carefully supervised to secure solid and substantial work. By this means they have maintained the excellent standing of the company and secured a business that steadily increases from year to year.

**James Cummiskey.**—Real Estate; 12 North Eighth street.—Mr. Cummiskey occupies a deservedly prominent position among the leading real estate dealers of the city. He is a native of St. Louis, and has been actively engaged in the real estate business for the past twenty-two years, during which he has acquired a close and accurate knowledge of values and an experienced judgment in regard to opportunities for advantageous investments. He does a very large business, dealing in real estate in the city, suburbs and St. Louis county, and has an extensive clientele, embracing many of the most wealthy and enterprising of the residents of the city. He negotiates loans on real estate security, and in this branch also has a large business, and makes investments, principally for local capitalists, finding plenty of capital in the city ready to enter into good investments, and therefore not soliciting Eastern business which is unsatisfactory from the time and trouble necessary in submitting propositions. Thoroughly acquainted with every branch of the business, and closely attending to all its details, Mr. Cummiskey's great success has been the legitimate result of energy united to sound judgment.

**Chester & Keller Manufacturing Co.**—E. S. Chester, President; Theo. Tamm, Vice-President; George Keller, Secretary and Treasurer; Manufacturers of Hickory Handles, Spokes, and Wagon and Buggy Woodwork; Main and Victor streets.—This establishment, which is properly classed and recognized as one of the largest and most prosperous manufacturing concerns in the city, was started in 1870 as the Woolworth Handle Works, changing to its present style four years ago, when it was reincorporated. The company do a very large and steadily expanding business. They have very large factory premises and yards in this city, at Main and Victor streets, fitted up with all the requisite machinery and plant adapted to the business, and manufacture axe, pick, sledge, hammer, hatchet and all kinds of hickory handles, also all kinds of wagon and buggy woodwork, making specialties of oak and hickory spokes. In addition to their establishment here they have branch factories at Idlewild, Mountain Glen and Carbondale, Ill. Their output is very large, the works giving employment to 250 skilled and experienced workmen, and the trade extends to all parts of the United States, except the extreme East. They have unsurpassed facilities for manufacture, fill all orders in the most prompt and reliable manner, and have an unexcelled reputation for good work and fair dealing.

**John A. Scholten.**—Artist and Photographer; 920 and 922 Olive street.—The business of Mr. Scholten has been for thirty years established in this city. There have been great improvements in the art of photography during that period, but Mr. Scholten fully kept pace with it, and himself greatly aided in its advancement. The studio is acknowledged to be one of the finest in the country, and has an immense patronage, including many of the most prominent people of the city, and visitors from all parts of the country. It has all the most modern and improved appliances of the art, and produces photographs, which in style, tone, faithfulness and finish, have no superiors in any part of the country. In 1879, the president and ex-president of the Merchants' Exchange, in consideration of his distinguished services and artistic work, presented Mr. Scholten with a gold medal as a testimonial of esteem, and he received from the St. Louis Fair Association four first-class prizes, awarded in 1866, seventeen first-class prizes awarded in 1867, and twelve first-class medals awarded in 1874. In 1881 he carried away the two first prizes at the American Institute, New York, over all exhibitors. Since the death of Mr. Scholten the founder of the business, over a year ago, its affairs have been conducted by his son, also named John A. Scholten, who takes pride in maintaining the superior quality of the work produced at this studio, to which is due the great and merited success it has enjoyed for many years.

**St. Louis Flagstone Company.**—H. L. Haydel, Cashier; S. P. McKelvey, Superintendent; Stone Sidewalks; 618 Chestnut street.—This business was established in 1882 and has been conducted with steadily increasing success from that time to the present. The company have been city contractors for paving and flagging for the past three years. They handle every description of stone and have a very large business in laying sidewalks for property owners. About a year ago, Messrs. Haydel and McKelvey bought a half interest in the firm of P. M. Bruner & Co., manufacturers of Granitoid. Up to this writing the firm have made contracts during the present year for laying over 60,000 feet of stone flagging. They possess unsurpassed facilities for carrying on work in their line, and every contract taken by them is executed in a workmanlike manner, and to the entire satisfaction of the customer. Mr. Haydel is treasurer and Mr. McKelvey secretary of the St. Louis Reclining Car Seat Co., and both are gentlemen of superior business attainments, enjoying, in a marked degree, the esteem and confidence of the business community.

**The Parker-Russell Mining & Manufacturing Company.**—G. W. Parker, President; T. G. Russell, Treasurer; R. E. Perry, Secretary; Manufacturers of Oak Hill Gas Retorts, Fire Brick, and other Fire Clay Products; City Office, 711 Pine street.—This business was established as Parker, Russell & Co. thirty years ago, and incorporated under the same name in 1866, with a capital of $100,000. Two years ago the corporation took its present style, increasing its capital to $150,000, greatly enlarging the facilities of the company, and adding a plant for making electric light carbons. Their works are located south of Tower Grove Park, where they have been mining for coal for about half a century. They manufacture electric light carbons and carbon plates, gas retorts, fire proofing, fire brick, cupola linings for blast furnaces, supplies for gas works and all other fire clay products. They have taken many premiums for the quality of their product, which is not excelled by any made here or elsewhere. Employment is given to a force of three hundred men, and the trade of the company extends to all parts of the Union, from ocean to ocean and from the Lakes to the Gulf. The company occupies a leading position in this important line of industry, and has maintained it throughout its long and honorable career by the superior merit of its product and the uniform accuracy and straightforward methods of its transactions.

**E. E. Koken.**—Successor to Koken & Boppert; Manufacturer and Dealer in Barbers' Furniture, Perfumery and Cutlery; 506 Market street.—This prominent house, well known throughout the United States, was established by Mr. E. E. Koken in 1874. In 1880 Mr. Boppert entered the house as a partner and the firm became Koken & Boppert. The latter died in 1886 and Mr. Koken is now the sole proprietor of the business. The salesroom is at 506 Market street, and the factory is located 1858 Menard street, where all of the barber furniture sold by the house is manufactured. Mr. Koken is the sole proprietor of the celebrated "Telephone Razor," which has a great popularity, and of which a great many are annually sold. The facilities of the establishment are ample and sufficient for the manufacture of chairs and other furniture of the latest approved patterns and designs, and the stock in toilet articles, perfumery, cups, brushes and all supplies, is always extensive and well assorted. The trade of the house is with every State in the Union, and although the bulk of it is among the Southern and Western States, the extreme Eastern cities are good patrons of this establishment. Mr. E. E. Koken is a capital man of business, who has established a solid reputation for his house and its goods.

**American Cotton Oil Company.**—J. H. Maxon, President; T. P. Sullivan, Secretary and Treasurer; Main, Cedar and Gratiot streets.—This large manufacturing concern was established in 1880 by J. V. Lewis & Co., to whom the present company succeeded on its incorporation in 1884. They have immense works fronting on three streets, and occupying nearly the entire block, with railroad tracks passing through their yards and giving every facility for handling and shipment. A force of seventy men are employed in the works, which are completely equipped with the latest and most improved machinery adapted to the requirements of the business. The output of the works is very large, and all finds a ready market with jobbers, etc. The meal is shipped to the East, where it is in great demand for feed. The company is under efficient management, and the oil made at the works is produced under the best processes and is of superior quality. The company occupies a prominent place among the most important manufacturing establishments of the city.

**W. J. Haynes & Co.**—Commission Merchants; Wool, Hides, Furs and General Produce; Southeast Corner Market and Commercial streets.—This house has an extensive trade and is well known to the merchants and shippers of the West and South. The house was established about ten years ago by Langenberg Bros. & Co., who are still connected with it. About a year and a half ago the business of Langenberg Bros. & Co. having grown to such large proportions, it was thought best to divide it into two departments. Since then the wool and hide trade has been carried on under the name of W. J. Haynes & Co., while the grain trade is still carried on under the old name of Langenberg Bros. & Co. The house is recognized as one of the leading establishments of its kind in the city, and does every year a very large business. Shippers of Missouri, Kansas, Colorado and Texas consign their business to this firm and find that it is handled with promptness and dispatch. Last year Messrs. Haynes & Co. received more wool from the State of Kansas than any house in St. Louis, and its annual wool trade amounts to nearly 1,000,000 pounds. The facilities of the house are unsurpassed, and it enjoys a steady growth in reputation and the volume of its business.

**Great Western Planing Mill Company.**—Henry Kotte, President; C. H. Menkhaus, Secretary; F. Feldhaus, Assistant Secretary; Manufacturers of Sash, Doors, Blinds, Mouldings, Etc.; Southwest Corner of Anna and Bismarck streets.—This business has been successfully conducted for the past fifteen years, the present corporation, however, dating from 1879. The extensive factory of the company, which is two stories in height, occupies an area of 100x200 feet, and is completely fitted up with all the latest and most improved planing, sawing and turning machinery, and employment is given to a force ranging from eighty to one hundred men. The company manufacture sash, doors, blinds, mouldings, brackets, scroll and straight sawing and turning work, and gives special attention to all orders for counters and store fixtures. They have unexcelled facilities for carrying on the business in all its branches, and have a large trade in the city and surrounding country, the product of the factory being celebrated for the superiority of its materials and workmanship. All orders are filled in a prompt and most satisfactory manner, and those dealing with this company always find their methods fair and liberal, and their transactions accurate in every respect.

**St. James Hotel.**—Thomas P. Miller, Proprietor; Corner of Broadway and Walnut street.—This well-known and popular hotel was established about sixteen years ago, and passed through various hands before it was taken by Mr. Thomas P. Miller, about eight years ago. He has managed the hotel with marked success, and made it a favorite with the traveling public and noted for its first-class accommodations with reasonable prices. Since his proprietorship, constant additions and improvements have been made, and the house, which fronts 180 feet on Broadway and 190 feet on Walnut street, has two hundred rooms, almost every one lighted and well ventilated, and forty-five of which are on the parlor floor. The construction of the house, and the location of the boiler room, kitchen, bakery and laundry in a separate building, render the hotel practically fire-proof; and all the conveniences of a first-class hotel are provided, such as steam elevators, baths, arc and incandescent electric lights, etc. The table of the hotel is provided with the best and most seasonable supplies, the vegetables, butter and milk being procured from a farm and creamery owned and operated by Mr. Miller. The location of the house is most central and convenient to the leading business establishments and the most prominent amusement resorts. The charges of the hotel are most reasonable, the rates being $2.00 and $2.50 per day. Rooms are also provided on the European plan for guests who prefer it. Mr. Miller uses every exertion to secure the comfort and convenience of his guests, and the house enjoys a merited prosperity.

**Gartside Coal Company.**—C. E. Gartside, President; Alexander Hamilton, Secretary; Illinois and Big Muddy Coal; 514 Pine street.—This corporation, established fourteen years ago, is recognized as one of the leading concerns in the coal business of the city. They handle the product of a number of mines producing a superior quality of coal, and sell from the track to dealers, manufacturers and large consumers in round lots. They make a specialty of Illinois and Big Muddy coal, but also handle anthracite. Their business, which is chiefly in the city, is very large, and their facilities for the prompt supply of superior coal in large quantities are not surpassed by those of any firm or corporation in the city, while their prices are the lowest, according to quality, in this market. Fifteen hands are employed by the company, and all orders are filled in the most satisfactory manner. President Gartside and Secretary Hamilton are thoroughly experienced in all the details of the business, and have maintained for their company an unexcelled standing among the commercial establishments of the city by the uniform fairness and reliability of their business methods.

**Alfred Shrimpton & Sons.**—Needle Manufacturers, Redditch, England; United States Office, 718 Lucas avenue; A. A. & J. W. Wright, St. Louis Representatives.—The only manufacturers of hand and sewing machine needles having their own depot and salesroom in the United States are Alfred Shrimpton & Sons, of Redditch, England. This house is about two hundred years old, descending from father to son under the same style, the eldest son of each generation bearing the same name. This St. Louis house was established seven years ago by Messrs. A. A. & J. W. Wright, who still remain in charge of it. It is the only branch maintained by the firm in the United States, and all their goods for this country are shipped direct to St. Louis, where duties and charges are paid, and from which they are distributed to the trade in every part of the Union, from New York to San Francisco and from the Lakes to the Gulf. The result has justified the judgment by which the choice of St. Louis as the best point for distribution was made, for the trade in this country has prospered greatly under the efficient, faithful and energetic management of Messrs. Wright Bros. Fifteen clerks and ten traveling salesmen are employed, and the stock carried by the house is the largest in the United States, usually amounting to from thirty-five to forty millions of needles. The needles handled are of the best quality and workmanship, and are in great demand. They are received at the St. Louis house very largely in bulk, and are put up here at the rate of from 10,000 to 12,000 packages per day. They manufacture needles of every description, and have here all the novelties in the line, such as cabinets, fancy needle cases, etc. The business has steadily increased from year to year, and the trade in the present year, so far, indicates that it will excel its predecessors in the volume of the business transacted by the house.

**James Edwards & Co.**—Stock and Bond Brokers; Room 24, 204 North Third street, Gay Building.—This leading and reliable firm of stock and bond brokers has occupied a prominent position in financial circles since its formation in 1869. They deal extensively, on personal account and as brokers, in railroad and municipal bonds of Southern and Western States, with the value of and market in which their long experience has giving them a thorough knowledge, affording them unsurpassed facilities for profitable investments. They also deal largely in mining stocks, the market for which is widening and has reached a state of stability as a consequence of the extension of railroads, the improvements in the methods of reduction of ores and in mining machinery, by which mining has been made more profitable, failures less frequent and investments more safe and advantageous. Jas. Edwards & Co. are chiefly interested, in the mining stock department of their business, in the stocks of leading gold and silver mining properties in Colorado. Mr. Edwards, himself, is a director of the St. Louis Charter Oak Consolidated Mining and Milling Co., owning and operating the valuable North Eclipse, Blagden, Effie, Charter Oak, Augusta May, Gem and Ezra White gold and silver mines in Gilpin County, Colorado. The firm also has large quantities of cheap lands in Missouri, Arkansas and Texas for sale. By close attention to business, ripe experience, and sound judgment this firm has attained a high reputation and merited success.

**H. G. Isaacs.**—Architect; Gay Building, Northeast Corner of Third and Pine streets.—For the past thirty years Mr. Isaacs has been actively engaged in the practice of his profession in St. Louis, and has achieved a reputation as a leader among the architects of the city. Much of the architectural improvement in the

## THE INDUSTRIES OF ST. LOUIS. 137

city in recent years is the result of his skill and artistic taste, and no gentleman of his profession can show better proofs of the high class of his work than Mr. Isaacs. Among the buildings lately erected upon his plans and under his direction may be mentioned the Odd Fellows' Building, now in course of erection at the southeast corner of Ninth and Olive streets, which will cost $450,000 and which is shown in an illustration on a former page. It will be eight stories high, the two lower stories to be built of Missouri red granite and the six upper stories of brick and terra cotta. It will be an office building equipped with elevators and every modern improvement. He was also the architect of the Bank of Commerce building, just completed, at the northeast corner of Broadway and Olive street, a brick and stone eight story structure for bank and office use, and the bank room of which is the finest and most elaborate in the country; and has in course of construction the Mercantile Library building at the southwest corner of Broadway and Locust street, six stories or 120 feet in height, with the first story of granite and all above of brick and terra cotta; also the M. H. Thompson building on Olive street, between Ninth and Tenth streets. He also superintended the construction of the Roe building and is preparing plans for the Mermod, Jaccard & Co. building. These are only a few of the more recent buildings designed and superintended by him. To enumerate all the fine structures which owe their beauty and their utility to his knowledge and skill would tax beyond reasonable limit the space of this volume. It is sufficient to say that a large number of the finest business and residence structures of the city are of his designing and owe their convenience and exquisite taste to the happy combination of the practical with the artistic which is characteristic of all of Mr. Isaacs' work. He is master of his art and is always kept busy. He is now preparing plans and estimates of several important structures which represent an immense outlay of money to be spent in adding new architectural triumphs to the well-earned reputation of Mr. Isaacs.

**S. Strauss & Co.**—Wholesale Millinery, Fancy Goods and Notions; Washington avenue, corner Eighth street.—In 1860 this business was established by the firm of Strauss & Lowenstein, to whom the present firm succeeded about ten years later. The principals in the house are Messrs. Simon Strauss, Adolph Samish, and Ben. J. Strauss, and the firm occupy an elegant six-story and basement building, 30x160 feet, eligibly located at the corner of Eighth street and Washington avenue, giving employment to a competent force of forty clerks and assistants, and carrying a heavy and completely assorted stock of millinery, fancy goods and notions of every description, and a specially fine line of zephyrs, Germantowns and other fine yarns. No house in the country, in its line, has a higher standing in the trade than that of S. Strauss & Co., and its business extends east to Pennsylvania, all west to the Pacific Ocean, north to the Canadian line and south to the Gulf of Mexico. In order to give efficient attention to this vast trade, the house keeps a staff of eighteen shrewd, active, and experienced travelers constantly on the road. Sustaining the most favorable relations with manufacturers, both foreign and domestic, the house enjoys unexcelled facilities for carrying on the business, and is prepared to offer the most advantageous inducements to its many customers.

**St. Louis Transfer Company.**—General Office, 20 North Third street—The St. Louis Transfer Company, established in 1857, has recently moved its general office into new and elegant quarters at 20 North Third street, where a telephone office is provided, not only with the public telephone, but also with private wires connecting its depots, offices and stables in this city with Union Depot and East St. Louis, thus enabling shippers and consignees to make all needful inquiries and communications about freight, baggage or passengers. Freights to and from all railroad lines are received and delivered at any part of the city. The freight depots are at the corner of Second and Carr streets and Second and Poplar streets; Bell Telephone No. 1107. Passengers are transferred in carriages or omnibuses to and from all railways in the city by the St. Louis Transfer Co. Its agents are on board all incoming trains and take up passengers' baggage checks before arrival at depot. Passengers will avoid delay and confusion at Union Depot, by having baggage checked at hotels and private residences directly to destination by the Transfer Company's agent. Orders can be left at any railroad ticket office in the city, and with the Transfer Company's agent at Union Depot, or at Ticket Office, 105 North Fourth street. The following named gentlemen are the officers and agents of the company: R. P. Tansey, President and Manager; S. H. Klinger, Secretary and Auditor; T. B. Thompson, Treasurer; W. F. Tufts, Superintendent; Howard Stanton, Agent.

**Glover & Finkenaur.**—Manufacturers of and Dealers in Artists' Materials, Studies, Etc.; 302 and 304 North Tenth street.—The crab and palette shown in the annexed cut is the trade mark of a prominent emporium for the sale of every description of artists' materials; that of Glover & Finkenaur, of which firm Messrs. Griff. Glover and E. Finkenaur are the individual members. They occupy an elegant store, eligibly located at 302 and 304 North Tenth street, and carry a large and completely assorted stock of paints, canvas, easels, pencils, palettes, brushes, plaques, studies and every description of artists' materials and supplies. The firm has a high reputation for the merit of its goods and the fairness of its dealings, and enjoys a trade that extends to all parts of the West, and south to Texas, and also, to some extent, to all sections of the country. A glance at their illustrated catalogue of studies and artists' materials will show that their prices are much lower than any house in the West. The business of

the firm is well managed. Mr. Finkenaur, who was formerly of the firm of Finkenaur & Sons, New York, is a thoroughly practical man. Both members fully understand their business, and to their united efforts the great prosperity of this house is due.

**St. Louis Ammonia and Chemical Company.**—Manufacturers of Fine Ammonia for Chemists' and Druggists' Use and Refrigerating Purposes; Works, Corner of Main and Convent streets, St. Louis, and Corner of Main and Keck streets, Cincinnati, Ohio; General Offices, Main and Convent streets, St. Louis.—The manufacture of ammonia has assumed much larger proportions since the general introduction of improved machinery for purposes of refrigeration. A prominent establishment engaged in this important industry is the St. Louis Ammonia and Chemical Co., which has its main office in this city and extensive works covering over half a block in both the cities of St. Louis and Cincinnati. They manufacture annually large quantities of ammonia of the finest quality, and which, on account of its unequaled purity, is all contracted for. All the most improved appliances for the manufacture of ammonia are to be found at these works, and the best processes known to science are used. They have also added to their extensive plant at Cincinnati a large addition, containing the most improved machinery for the manufacture of anhydrous liquid ammonia, whereby they will be enabled to supply the wants of the country, for not only the aqua ammonia in all strengths; but also the anhydrous liquid ammonia, of 100 per cent. liquified gas. The magnificent machinery used for the manufacture of anhydrous ammonia in these works was erected under the patents and general supervision of the De La Vergne Refrigerating Machine Co., of New York, their work in this line being second to none in this country. The business of the company is conducted by Mr. W. A. Newman, its Secretary and Treasurer here at St. Louis; and the works are under the general superintendence of Mr. W. E. Colwell, who is most thorough in all its branches, having devoted more than twenty years of his life in the business. The standing of this company is of the highest character and its uniformly accurate methods and the superior merit of its product has secured for it a large business and the confidence of the trade throughout the country.

**The American Wood Preserving Company,**—Theodore Plate, President and Treasurer; A. Schenk, Secretary; Wood Preserving by Zinc-Gypsum Process; Works and Office, Foot of Robert avenue; City Office, Rooms 52 and 53, Gay's Central Building, Northeast Corner Third and Pine streets.—This is the only establishment of its kind in the city. The company was formed in 1883, Mr. Theodore

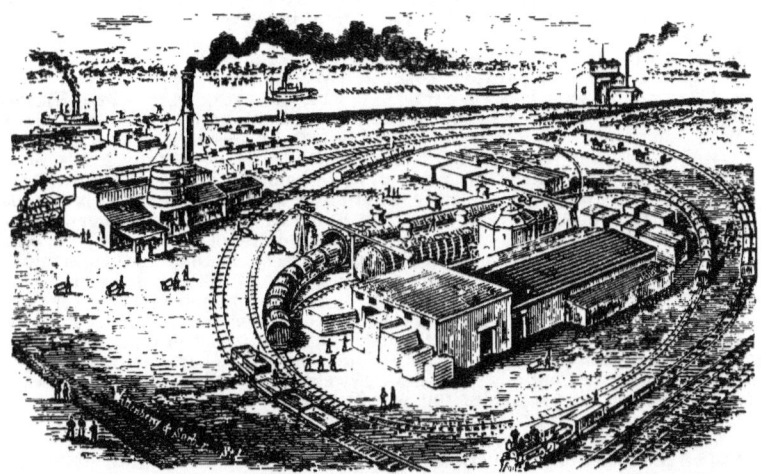

Plate becoming President and Treasurer, and Mr. A. Schenk, Secretary. Their works, at the foot of Robert avenue, in South St. Louis, cover two blocks, adjacent to the Mississippi River, with railroad tracks around and through them, affording the company unsurpassed facilities for the handling and shipment of ties and timber. The works are completely fitted up with all the improved modern machinery and appliances adapted to the business, and give employment, when running full force, to fifty men, and have a capacity for the treatment of 25,000 feet, board measure, per day. The company treats railroad ties, bridge and building timber, and all wood exposed to decay through the action of the elements, by the zinc-gypsum process, covered by letters patent for the United States, and by means of which wood is more effectually protected from the action of the elements than by any other method of treatment. It was by this process that the wooden pavements on Washington avenue and Chestnut streets in this city were treated and laid in 1884, 1885 and 1886. The business of the company has steadily grown since its formation, and its patronage now extends to every part of the country, the process having been approved and adopted by many of the leading railway systems. The company intends to put up a new cylinder for creosoting and large vats for Ryanizing. Mr. Theodore Plate, the President of the company, has for many years been prominent in St. Louis as one of its most influential and successful citizens. Coming to the city thirty-four years ago, he conducted, with marked ability and great success, a German Ladies' Seminary for twelve years. This institution grew under his sagacious management and when he had sold it to others it had quadrupled in size and importance. In April, 1862, Mr. Plate purchased the great German newspaper, the "Westliche Post," in which he was afterward joined by Dr. Emil Preetorius, Mr. Arthur Olshausen and Hon. Carl Schurz. The ownership of the paper was afterward merged into a joint stock company, of which Mr. Plate is still a member. He is also prominent in other large and important business enterprises, including, in addition to his Presidency of the American Wood Preserving Co the Inter-State Gas Co., of which he is president and chief proprietor, and the firm of John Plate & Co. composed of Mr. Theodore Plate and his son Mr. John Plate. He has large real estate interests and is a man of means generally, acquired by close industry and indomitable energy, and is entitled by reason of his high business attainments to prominent mention as one of the most representative of the successful citizens of St. Louis. The firm of John Plate & Co., mentioned above, operates electro-depositing works in connection with those of the American Wood Preserving Co. The firm was organized for the purpose of operating a new process for coating soft steel, iron and zinc with copper or brass or bronze, to take the place of copper or galvanized iron in all cornice, spout, roofing and other galvanized iron work. The firm operates two large dynamos made expressly for them and all other requisite machinery and plant for turning out 96-inch coppered soft steel plates by the hundreds per day. The product is in great demand, a market existing for all that can be manufactured, giving assurance of prosperity for this firm in this great and important industry.

**Mississippi Iron Works and Foundry.**—Pullis Brothers, Proprietors; Architectural and Ornamental Iron Work; Jail Work a Specialty; Office and Warehouse, 206 and 208 North Sixth street; Works, Seventh, Eighth and Hickory streets.—This is not only the oldest but also one of the best establishments in its line in St. Louis. The business was founded in 1839 by Messrs. Christian and T. R. Pullis, the firm afterward becoming T. R. Pullis & Sons, and finally Pullis Bros., the present firm, of which Messrs. Augustus and Thomas R. Pullis are the members. They occupy a fine double three-story building at 206 and 208 North Sixth street as warehouse and office, and their works, on Seventh, Eighth and Hickory streets, cover the greater part of an entire block. Their outfit of machinery and plant includes all the latest and most improved appliances for facilitating their manufacturing operations, and they give employment to a force of two hundred men. They manufacture iron fronts, window caps and sills, cast iron plumbers' ware, enameled grates, iron and slate mantels, jail work, bank vaults, commercial safe fronts, doors and shutters in one hundred styles, verandahs, chairs, settees and vases, ornamental iron goods, iron bedsteads, store stools, fountains and aquariums, registers and ventilators, bolts, anchors and straps, sash weights, weather vanes, zinc center pieces, enameled tiles, brass fire stands and fenders, and all kinds of cast and wrought iron work used in the erection of public and private buildings. They have an immense business in the city with builders, contractors, etc., as well as a large trade in all the States of the West, from the Lakes to the Gulf and from Indiana to the Pacific. They make a specialty of jail work, in which they have a large patronage, and all the product of their works is of the best workmanship. The house has maintained a prominent position in the industrial world throughout the period of nearly half a century of its history, and has been always noted for the promptness and reliability of its methods.

**Pennsylvania Lumber Company.**—W. S. McMullan, President; Daniel Goettel; Manufacturers and Wholesale Dealers in Yellow Pine Lumber; Room 401 Granite Block, Southwest Corner Fourth and Market streets.—This extensive business was established in 1882 by Messrs. W. S. McMullan and Daniel Goettel, both of Oil City, Pa., under the firm name of McMullan & Goettel. In 1886, in order to facilitate the extensive operations of the business, the present company was incorporated, the founders retaining control of the business and Mr. McMullan becoming President of the corporation. The company has extensive mills and drying kilns at Leeper (formerly Moss Ferry) station, in Wayne County, Missouri. They own ten miles of railroad running from the mills to their timber tracts of yellow pine of superior quality, of which they have upward of 50,000 acres. They sell in car load lots direct from the mills, and employ about two hundred hands. They have a very large business, their mills being unsurpassed by any in the State, either in capacity or equipment, and the sales being principally in the States of Illinois, Missouri, Kansas, and Nebraska. In resources and facilities for shipping and handling the company has no superior, and is prepared to fill orders in a prompt and satisfactory manner.

**Planters' Tobacco Warehouse.**—Laughlin & Blakely, Proprietors; Eleventh and Spruce streets.—This large and commodious warehouse, comprising a three story brick building 250x150 feet in dimensions, was opened for business in 1881 by Ringo, Edmunds & Ringo. They were succeeded in July, 1883, by Mr. Henry D. Laughlin, who was joined in June, 1886, by Mr. Walter J. Blakely, when the present firm was formed. The warehouse is specially adapted to the storage of tobacco, and all consignments placed in the care of Messrs. Laughlin & Blakely receive their constant care and attention. The storage charges of the firm are most reasonable and every inducement is offered to facilitate the proper inspection, sampling and care of all the tobacco placed in the warehouse. This establishment is patronized by the leading dealers and commission men who handle leaf tobacco, and the firm, by the uniform reliability and accuracy of their methods, have gained a high place in the confidence and esteem of the trade.

**Mound City Mutual Fire Insurance Company.**—Ellis N. Leeds, President; William Booth, Vice-President; Charles H. Alexander, Secretary; Wm. H. Roberts, General Agent; Southwest Corner of Sixth and Olive streets.—For over thirty years this corporation has occupied a prominent position among the most substantial insurance concerns in the West. The conduct of its affairs has always been safe and conservative, and it has earned and enjoyed, from its organization in 1855 to the present time, the confidence of the insuring public. It writes policies both upon the mutual and stock plans and issues them for terms varying from thirty days to six years. During the year of 1886 its transactions in this State amounted in mutual fire business written to $544,215 and in fire business written for cash premiums to $492,018, while its losses during the same period were only $5,919. At the close of business for 1886 it had total resources of $206,491 against accrued liabilities of $6,934. The company is known as a prompt payer of losses and its management is in every respect efficient and thorough. The following prominent and responsible citizens compose its board of directors: Ellis N. Leeds, Daniel R. Garrison, William Booth, Matthias Dougherty, Francis L. Haydel, John Maguire, Charles Hofman, Augustus Pullis and Joseph T. Donovan. The general agent of the company is William H. Roberts, well and favorably known in insurance circles.

**Maxwell & Crouch.**—Mule Market; 1414 to 1420 North Broadway.—St. Louis is admitted to be the leading mule market of the country, and among the prominent firms engaged in this line of business is that of Maxwell & Crouch, composed of Messrs. Joseph Maxwell and J. W. Crouch. The present firm was formed

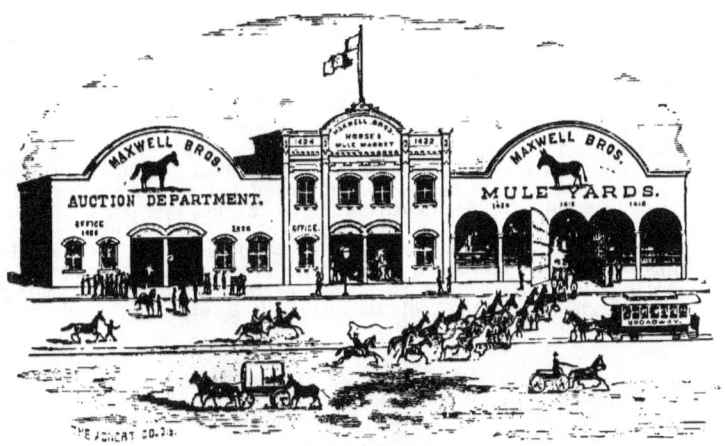

in 1885, but the members of it are experienced men in the business, Mr. Maxwell having been for many years a member of the old house of Maxwell Bros., to whose old stand the present firm succeeded, and Mr. Crouch having been a member of the firm of G. W. Crouch & Sons, prior to joining the present firm. They receive their stock from points in Missouri and Iowa, selling chiefly South, and also having a considerable trade in the East, and to buyers coming from all points. They sell chiefly in carloads and large droves, and now confine their business exclusively to mules, of which they sell, on personal account and commission, over 10,000 head per annum. Last January, they transferred their horse department to Mr. F. Sloan, still retaining an interest in that business, however. In addition to their commodious sales stables at 1414 to 1420 North Broadway, covering an area of 100x130 feet, they have large stables on the alley in the rear, and one on Thirteenth street, near Cass avenue, and for surplus stock have recently leased Isaacs' stables at 1109 and 1111 North Broadway. The firm has the largest mule trade in the city, and their transactions increase from year to year, their business for 1886 having been very large, and the season of 1887 promising a still greater and more prosperous outcome. Their close knowledge of every detail of the business and their enterprising methods and liberal dealings have given them a foremost position in their line.

**Jacob Straus Saddlery Company.**—Jacob Straus, President; Philip Costam, Vice-President; Adolph Sondheimer, Secretary and Treasurer; Wholesale Manufacturers of Saddlery, and Jobbers of Saddlery Hardware; 410 to 414 North Sixth street.—St. Louis is the greatest center in the world for the manufacture of harness and saddlery goods, and it leads all other cities in the extent and value of the annual business transacted in this line. One of the largest houses in America is that of the Jacob Straus Saddlery Co., which occupies the mammoth five-story and basement brick building 410, 412 and 414 North Sixth street. The building is one of the finest and most imposing blocks on the street and has a frontage of 60 feet with a depth of 140 feet It is entirely devoted to the offices and salesrooms of the company. The house was originally established in 1856 by Jacob Straus, the President of the present corporation, and the business was incorporated in 1884 with a capital stock of $300,000. The company employs about five hundred men, and manufacture numerous specialties, among them Straus' patent halter, Straus' all leather flexible saddle, and Straus' patent metal spring side saddle. The firm have secured first premiums in all Exposition competitions at which they have entered for prizes. The popularity of the goods of this house has made it a wide reputation, and a force of twenty traveling salesmen are in its service. Every portion of the United States and Canada is visited by the representatives of the firm and a large business is done even in the Eastern cities of New York, Boston and Philadelphia. Of late the house has sold extensively in Old Mexico. The gentlemen directing the affairs of the company are all men of long experience, and prominent residents of the city. Mr. Jacob Straus, the President, has for nearly forty years had practical experience in this line, having learned his trade, when a boy, in this city. Mr. Sondheimer has resided here for over thirty years, and was for many years in the wholesale dry goods line. Mr. Philip Costam, the Vice-President, has had a large and active business experience, and previous to his advent in St. Louis business circles was extensively engaged in general merchandising in Jefferson City, Mo.

**C. B. Carter & Co.**—Wholesale Dealers in Provisions; 112 and 114 South Commercial; 107 and 108 Front street.—This house was established in 1879 by Mr. C. B. Carter, who came here from Memphis, where he had for many years been prominently identified with the mercantile interests of that city. He is now the sole proprietor of the business, whose annual volume has become very large. The trade of the house is confined entirely to Southern points. Mr. Carter is of large experience in the provision trade, and his long Southern residence, and many years' business dealings with the people of that section, enables him to meet the requirements of Southern buyers in a prompt and satisfactory manner. He is one of the largest buyers of hog products in the St. Louis market, and is a prominent member of the Merchants' Exchange.

**M. A. Seed Dry Plate Company.**—J. B. Buss, President; A. R. Huiskamp, Secretary and Manager; M. A. Seed, Superintendent, and Henry C. Huiskamp, Keokuk, Iowa, Directors; Works at Woodland, Mo.; Office, 1202 Washington avenue. —The introduction of dry plates has effected a wonderful improvement in the art of photography by making it possible to secure a negative instantaneously. St. Louis is the principal headquarters for this line of manufacture, and among those engaged in the business no firm or corporation is more prominent than the M. A. Seed Dry Plate Company, which enjoys an unsurpassed reputation for the superior quality of its work, and has a large trade extending to every part of the Union. The works of the company, which are located at Woodland, Mo., are equipped with all the modern appliances for carrying on the business, including some that are the sole property of this company, and the "Arrow" brand of dry plates made at these works is favorably known all over the country. About one hundred and twenty-five hands are employed and four traveling salesmen represent the company on the road. The city office and salesrooms cover a space of 25x100 feet at 1202 Washington avenue, where a large stock of these famous plates are kept on hand. Mr. A. R. Huiskamp, the Secretary and Manager of this company, is a well-known business man of superior commercial attainments. The works at Woodland are under the experienced and practical superintendence of Mr. M. A. Seed, a scientific expert in the manufacture of dry plates. The business of the company increases year by year, and it enjoys the esteem and confidence of photographers and dealers in photographers supplies as a result of the prompt and accurate manner in which it fills all orders for its superior goods.

**L. M. Rumsey Manufacturing Company.**—L. M. Rumsey, President; M. Rumsey, Secretary; A. M. Wood, Treasurer; Manufacturers and Jobbers of Agricultural Implements, Pumps, Wood and Iron Working Machinery, Plumbers', Steam and Gas Fitters' Supplies. Etc.: Office, 810 North Second street.—Greatest of all the establishments of its kind in the world, the attempt to describe, within a limited space, the colossal business of the L. M. Rumsey Manufacturing Co. is an arduous undertaking, and can only result in the presentation of a brief summary. The business was established in 1860 by Messrs. L. M. & M. Rumsey, and was incorporated under its present name in 1880. The operations of the firm were large in volume at the inception of the business, but they were small compared to those of the present company after the twenty-seven years of steady increase and growth which this great business has experienced. The house now carries a stock worth $2,000,000, does an annual business of $4,000,000 and has 10,000 regular customers, all of whom are of the most solvent and responsible character. The company has works at Indianapolis, Ind., and controls the entire output of many others. Messrs. L. M. & M. Rumsey own the two large blocks bounded by Second, Morgan and Cherry streets, and the works of the company and the warehouses occupy nearly the whole of this great area, their many buildings ranging from three to five stories in height. All of these buildings are lighted by electric lights worked by dynamos owned and operated by the company. At the St. Louis works constant employment

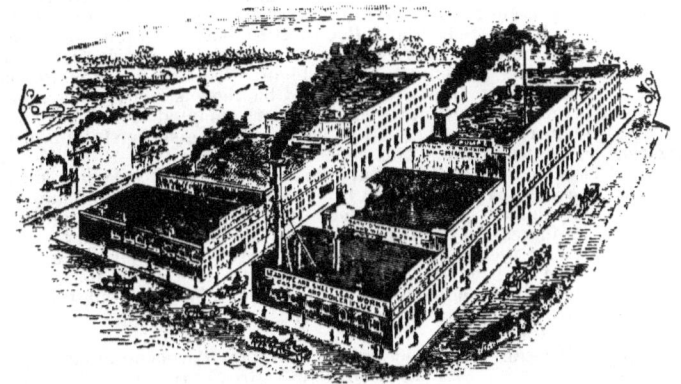

is given to a force of one hundred and fifty skilled and experienced workmen and sixteen active and energetic commercial travelers represent the house on the road. The trade of the company extends to every part of the Union, Canada, Mexico, Cuba, South America, etc. The company manufactures and carries an immense stock of every description of agricultural implements from a pitchfork to the most elaborate of modern farming machines, grist, feed, cider and cane mills in the most complete assortment, and all kinds of screw presses, broom corn machinery, etc. The company manufactures upward of one thousand different styles of pumps and supplies the world with galvanized pump chain, made by a machine invented by Mr. L. M. Rumsey, which completes and fastens about one hundred links of chain per minute. In their lead works they have heavy rollers, capable of turning out sheets of lead 8x50 feet and of any thickness from that of paper up to the heaviest in use. They keep full lines of fire engines, hose reels, trucks and all fire apparatus and firemen's supplies, hose, belting, packing, etc., and nearly everything requisite for building and equipping railroads, and manufacture and deal in all kinds of lead and iron pipes, and all fittings, tools and appliances for plumbers, gas, water and steam fitters, all kinds of iron and wood working machinery, and every description of supplies for foundries, machinists, blacksmiths, mills, wagon makers, miners and contractors. They also deal in hoisting engines, stationary and portable boilers, lathes, planers, shapers, gear cutters, files, all kinds of bells, every description of metals, etc. The catalogue might be extended indefinitely, and occupies a number of large and elegantly printed volumes issued by the company for the use of the trade, which form a library of themselves. Only a faint idea of the immensity of the business can be compressed into a short description. The company's works in this city are fitted up with the most elaborate and expensive machinery, much of it made specially for their use, and a fine 80-horse power engine is used to propel the moving mass. The company enjoyed a more than ordinarily good season during the past year, and the present one bids fair to rival even that in the volume of the transactions of the company. Their facilities are unsurpassed for the manufacture and distribution of goods in their numerous lines, their stocks complete to the most minute item, the quality of their goods unec elled by any house in the world, and their system so thorough that all the operations of this vast business empire are carried on without the slightest friction. Added to all this the fair, honorable and liberal methods of this great house and the secret of the marvelous success of this establishment is told. Built upon the sure foundation of meritorious goods, honorable conduct and just dealings. its growth has been as substantial as phenomenal, and its high standing is fixed as the triumph of industry, of energy and of the exercise of correct business principles.

**Chas. G. Stifel's Brewing Company.**—Chas. G. Stifel. President; Richard Boesewetter, Secretary and Treasurer: Chas. F. Stifel. Assistant Secretary and Treasurer; Jacob B. Schorr. Superintendent: North Fourteenth street, from Howard to Chambers streets.—Mr. Chas. G. Stifel had been connected with the brewing interest in St. Louis for some five years before he founded this business as Chas. G. Stifel's City Brewery, at the corner of Third and Cherry streets. In 1859 he removed to the present location, and in 1879 the company was organized with a capital of $200,000. Messrs. Schorr and Boesewetter, both of whom had been employes, becoming officers in the corporation at the head of which Mr. Stifel, the founder of the business, remained as President. The brewery premises cover a block on Fourteenth street, from Howard to Chambers streets, and are equipped with all the most modern and improved machinery adapted to the business, with malt houses. ice houses and every facility necessary to the successful prosecution of the operations of the company. The capacity of the brewery is 100,000 and its annual output 60,000 barrels, in the manufacture of which a force of one hundred men is employed. The beer manufactured at this establishment is in high repute, and the company does a large trade in the city, and although it does not solicit outside trade receives a steadily increasing patronage from the surrounding country. The business has prospered for the long period of nearly forty years because the beer made by Mr. Stifel has always been of good quality, and because of his thorough understanding of and close attention to business. He is a prominent and substantial citizen and connected with various financial and business enterprises.

**Petton & Kluegel.**—Manufacturers of Carriages. Barouches, Buggies, Trucks, Spring Wagons, etc.; 827, 829 and 831 South Broadway.—This firm, of which Messrs. C. H. Petton and T. J. Kluegel are the individual members, was established thirteen years ago, since which they have carried on a prosperous business. Their works on South Broadway are two stories in height, and cover an area of 80x160 feet. They employ from fifteen to twenty expert workmen, and manufacture carriages, barouches, phætons, buggies, trucks, platform, express, heavy and light spring wagons, etc. They make a specialty of superior workmanship, and have gained a very high reputation and steadily growing trade in the city and surrounding country. The practical experience of the members of the firm, the close attention paid by them to every detail of the business, and the fidelity with which they live up to all their contracts, have earned for the firm a great and merited prosperity.

**Southern White Lead Company.**—Wm. H. Gregg. President; F. W. Rockwell. Vice-President: C. W. Ferguson, Secretary: Manufacturers of White and Red Leads. Litharge. Etc.; Main and Lombard streets.—These works, which are among the largest in the United States, were established in 1865, and have ever since been recognized as one of the leading industries of St. Louis. They occupy a large area of ground on both sides of Lombard street, requiring for their accommodation a large portion of two blocks. About one hundred and fifty men are employed constantly, and the annual output is very large. The productions of this company are sold in all parts of the United States, and its trade lies with every State and Territory in the Union. There is a branch in Chicago that is nearly as large as the parent establishment. This is strictly a St. Louis institution and its officers are well-known citizens. President Gregg has been thoroughly identified with the business of the city for many years past. He is an honored and respected citizen, and is held in high esteem by the community.

**Crown Metal Perforating Company.**—J. W. Clemens, President; Wm. A. Chambers, Secretary and Treasurer; Southeast Corner Collins and Biddle streets.—This business was established about two years ago, the present company having been incorporated a few months since. They have just erected the building they occupy, which covers an area of 50x100 feet, and is specially designed for the purposes of their business. They make all their tools and plant under their own patents, and their Crown Metal Perforating Machines are the largest and most powerful in the country. With the additions now being made to their plant, they will have the largest capacity in America for the perforation of all kinds and thicknesses of sheet metals. This work they do in any style or design at the shortest notice and in a uniformly satisfactory manner. They are also builders of the Peerless Malt Kiln Dumping Floor, which is the most perfect in use for the purpose designated. The superior merit of their work has secured for them a large trade extending not only to all parts of the Union, but also to Canada on the north and Mexico on the south. The company has an unexcelled reputation and is under able and experienced management which gives assurance of a prosperous career.

**Ginocchio Brothers & Co.**—Wholesale Dealers in Foreign, California and Tropical Fruits; 713 and 715 North Third street.—The business carried on by the firm of Ginocchio Bros. & Co., of which Messrs. Domenico Ginocchio, David Ginocchio and Louis Boggiano are the members, was originally established nearly thirty years ago by the firm of A. Boggiano & Co. In 1876, the firm became Shepherd & Ginocchio, and in 1881 the present firm succeeded to the business. They occupy a fine and commodious four-story building, 60x100 feet, erected expressly for the purposes of the business, and which is located at 713 and 715 North Third street; in addition to which they have a branch house at Kansas City. They deal wholesale in foreign, California and tropical fruits, oranges, lemons, bananas, raisins, nuts, etc., and have an extensive trade in the city and in Missouri, Illinois, Kansas, Iowa, Nebraska and the entire West. They ship nuts, etc., to California and bring back fruits. The firm have unsurpassed facilities for handling goods in its line, and are held in great esteem by the trade for the uniform fairness of their dealings, the merit of their goods and their promptness in filling orders.

**St. Louis Bagging Company.**—L. Levering, President; H. R. Murray, Secretary; Manufacturers of "Phœnix" and "Globe" Jute Bagging; 119 South Fourth street.—This corporation was originally organized in 1855 as the St. Louis Bagging and Rope Co., which was changed upon the renewal of the charter to the present style. It has always been a prosperous and prominent concern, and its business has steadily grown from year to year, and it now enjoys an immense patronage in all the cotton-growing states which taxes its producing capacity. The brands of jute bagging manufactured by the company are the "Phœnix," "Globe," and "Pelican," which are prime favorites for cotton baling purposes, being the best manufactured. The company have a large factory at the corner of Twelfth and Gratiot streets fully equipped with all the latest and most improved machinery, and a complete plant for the manufacture of bagging. A force of two hundred and twenty workmen are employed, many of whom, including the superintendent, have been with the company for about thirty years, the relations of the company with their employes having always been of the most satisfactory character. In addition to their manufacturing branch the company are agents for Pittsburg "Arrow" cotton ties, and they are prepared to fill all orders for either bagging or ties in the most prompt and satisfactory manner.

**Wheeler, James & Co.**—Live Stock Commission Merchants; Union Stock Yards.—Prominent among the firms engaged in the purchase and sale of live stock on commission is that of Wheeler, James & Co., whose office is at the Union Stock Yards. All of the members of the firm are practical and thoroughly experienced in the business. Mr. Wheeler was formerly a member of the firm of Cash, Stewart & Co., dealers in live stock; Mr. James was, before the formation of the present partnership, with Dugdale & Co., and Mr. McKinnon, the other partner, had been a buyer and shipper of stock to Eastern markets for years before the formation of the firm of Wheeler, James & Co. They buy and sell and ship on order, both at the Union Stock Yards, and at the National Stock Yards in East St. Louis, all kinds of live stock. Mr. Wheeler looks after the hog department; Mr. James attends to transactions in cattle and sheep, and Mr. McKinnon has charge of the financial affairs and office business of the firm. They receive stock from all sections, and particularly from the Northwest and Southwest, and handle about five hundred car loads of stock per month. The firm is a favorite with shippers of cattle, having earned their confidence by the close attention given to all commissions placed in its hands.

**Terry & Scott.**—Real Estate and Financial Agents ; 621 Chestnut street.—This firm, which is composed of Judge John H. Terry and Samuel S. Scott, was established five years ago. Prior to the formation of the firm, Judge Terry had presided in the Land Commission Court. The firm of Terry & Scott at once advanced to a foremost position, which it has maintained, with steadily increasing prosperity, to the present time. They take charge of every description of real property, securing good tenants, collecting rents, paying taxes and having the sole charge of property when desired. They buy and sell on commission, city and suburban real estate, improved and unimproved, negotiate loans and effect mortgages in large or small sums on St. Louis property where the security is beyond question, and attend to all the details of a legitimate real estate and financial agency business. Judge Terry is executor of the large estate of Albert Todd, deceased, and the firm has charge of many other important and valuable estates, for the care and management of which their close and accurate knowledge of the business eminently fits them. They do a very large business in the investment of money for capitalists and have 1,500 tenants on their rent roll. This large business has been earned by the application of superior business attainments and fidelity to every interest intrusted to their care. No agency in the city has a higher standing than that of Terry & Scott.

**W. H. Quernheim & Bro.**—Galvanized Iron and Copper Cornices, Etc.; 1524, 1526 and 1528 North Fifteenth street.—This firm, which is composed of Messrs. W. H. and Louis Quernheim, have successfully conducted their business for the past eleven years. The premises occupied by them on North Fifteenth street, between Cass avenue and Mullanphy street, are two stories in height, and cover an area 50x125 feet. They are completely equipped with all the necessary machinery and appliances, and give employment to forty workmen. They manufacture galvanized iron and copper cornices in the most artistic designs, skylights, metal roofing, guttering, spouting, etc., including everything in the line, and in which the product of their works is not surpassed, only the best materials being used and skilled labor employed. The business of the firm is very large, including an extensive patronage from city builders, contractors, and others, and a large trade throughout Missouri, Southern Illinois, Arkansas and Texas. The firm is noted for the prompt and satisfactory manner in which it fills all orders entrusted to it.

**J. A. Harnett & Co.**—Lumber Dealers and Commission; 405 Walnut street.—The lumber interests of St. Louis are very large, and vast quantities are brought here from all portions of the timber sections. Among the many firms engaged in the lumber commission trade, which is an important line, is that of J. A. Harnett & Co., at 405 Walnut street. The firm was established in 1871, and consists of J. A. Harnett and H. C. Bagby. A very large business is transacted by the firm, who only handle consignments of lumber on commission. They receive annually a large amount of walnut, poplar and other hardwood lumber from Tennessee, Arkansas, Indiana, and other sections where it is grown, and sell the same in St. Louis, and also in the Northwestern States. The long experience of Messrs. Harnett and Bagby and their familiarity with the trade in all details enable them to act at all times advantageously for those for whom they sell.

**Regina Flour Mill Company.**—Louis Fusz, President; George H. Backer, Secretary; George Bain, Manager; Location of Mills, Main, Plum, and Poplar streets; Offices 112 and 114 South Main street.--The Regina Flour Mill Co. was organized and incorporated in 1885, with Mr. Louis Fusz, who is also President of the St. Louis Millers' Association, as the President, and George Bain as Manager. The mills which are new, having been entirely rebuilt after the fire in 1883, were formerly known as the Atlantic Mills, and were first erected about forty years ago. Among the many owners of these mills in the years that have gone, may be mentioned Henry Whitmore, Alex. H. Smith & Co., Bain & Pegram, the Atlantic Milling Co., and now the present company. The new mill- as rebuilt are large and roomy, and furnished and equipped with all of the latest improved roller and full centrifugal processes, and have a capacity of over 1000 barrels per day. All that money and ingenuity could provide or devise has combined to make these mills among the best in the world. The grades of flour manufactured by them are recognized as leading and superior brands in every market of the world. The mills are run to their capacity day and night, and the flour is sent everywhere. It is shipped on the west to California, north to St. Paul and Minneapolis, the great mill city of the United States; northeast to Montreal and Saint Johns, New Brunswick, and south to all points. A very large trade is done to Havana, the West India Islands, Rio de Janiero and Colon in Central and South America, and from Marseilles, in the South of Europe, through France, Holland, Belgium, England, Ireland and Scotland to Copenhagen on the North, all these countries taking large quantities of the flour from these mills. The gentlemen at the head of this enterprise are well known and substantial citizens who stand at the head of the mercantile and milling professions. Messrs. Fusz and Backer have been associated together for many years in the flour trade. The President, Louis Fusz, is recognized by the entire business community as one of the shrewdest merchants of the city, and his position at the head of the Millers' Association is an endorsement of the correctness of this view of his character. He is First Vice-President of the Merchants' Exchange, and one of its leading and most influential members. He is also actively identified with every movement advanced for the welfare of the city. Mr. Backer, his partner, and Secretary of the company, also occupies a high standing among the business men of the city. Mr. George Bain, the Manager, is known to nearly every man in St. Louis, and for over thirty years has been actively identified with the business interests and progress of the city. He is an honored ex-President of the Merchants' Exchange, and for seven years of the Millers' National Association, and one of the most popular men of St. Louis.

**Cherokee Brewery Company.**—F. Herold, President and Treasurer; Theo. Herold, Jr., Secretary; Jacob Loebs, Superintendent; Brewers of the Renowned "Herold's Superior Bottled Lager Beer," Ales and Porter; Brewery, Cherokee street and Iowa avenue; Branch, Southeast Corner of Sixth and Market streets.—This large and important enterprise was established by the Herold & Loebs Brewing Co. in 1867, the proprietors then being F. Herold and George Loebs. In 1883, Mr. Herold bought out his partner and the present company was formed, Mr. Herold retaining the chief interest in the company and becoming its President, and his son becoming Secretary and a stockholder, and Mr. Jacob Loebs, who also holds some stock, being Superintendent. The brewery covers an entire block and is completely equipped with all the most modern and improved machinery, propelled by a 160-horse power engine. The capacity of the brewery amounts to 3,500 barrels per month, and employment is given to fifty hands. They have two large ice machines by which their three large cellars, 45 feet under ground, are kept constantly at low temperature. They are the only manufacturers of porter in the city, and in this product, the quality of which is unsurpassed, they do a large and steadily increasing business in all parts of the West. In lager beer their principal trade is in the city, the superior quality of their manufacture having created for it a demand here which calls for their entire output. They are constantly building and adding to their plant and machinery. They use the Consolidated Bunging Co.'s apparatus in their cellars, an ingenious device which by a series of wires indicates on an indicator in the office the exact temperature of every cask. President Herold, who prior to embarking in this enterprise was a grocery merchant at Mascoutah, Illinois, has demonstrated his administrative ability and sound business judgment by the manner in which he has steadily enlarged the trade of the brewery, and with the efficient assistance of his son, the Secretary of the company, has achieved a pronounced and gratifying success.

**St. Louis National Stock Yards Company.**—Isaac H. Knox, President; Charles T. Jones, Superintendent; Yards in St. Clair County, Illinois.—In a former portion of this work the advantages of St. Louis as a market for live stock have been set forth, with statistics showing the great volume of transactions in that important industry. The most important factor in the promotion of activity in live stock at this market has been, and still is, the St. Louis National Stock Yards Co., organized in 1873. Prior to that time the natural advantages of location possessed by St. Louis were in a large measure neutralized by the lack of facilities for the receipt, handling, care or shipment of stock. As a consequence trade in this line, which would naturally, under equally advantageous conditions, have sought St. Louis as its point of distribution, was diverted to other cities better prepared with the necessary terminal facilities and stock yards conveniences. To overcome this, the great New York stock firm of Allerton, Dutcher & Moore originated the enterprise which finally culminated in the organization by Eastern capitalists, aided by a few progressive resident business men, of whom President Knox was one, of the St. Louis National Stock Yards Co., with a capital stock of $1,000,000, which their charter authorized them to increase. The original stockholders were William H. Vanderbilt, Horace F. Clark, Augustus Schell, James H. Banker, A. Boody, A. B. Baylis, Samuel F. Barger, Allerton, Dutcher & Moore, T. C. Eastman, Alexander M. White, Isaac H. Knox, John L. Macaulay, John B. Bowman and Levi Parsons. Many of these gentlemen were railroad magnates controlling the Wabash Railway, and when Mr. Jay Gould succeeded to that control he became a stockholder in the National Yards Company. The yards were located on 652 acres of land in St. Clair County, Illinois, adjoining the corporate limits of East St. Louis, and purchased at a cost of nearly $200,000; and the spacious yards were laid out under the personal supervision of Mr. Allerton. As completed the yards have ample railroad facilities, commodious yard room, stables and pens, and an unequaled system of underground sewage. One of the frame buildings is 1,122 feet long by 100 feet in width, with a holding capacity of 20,000 hogs. The cattle yards, numbering nearly three hundred, accommodate nearly 15,000 horned stock. The yards and avenues are paved with Belgian pavement, and a handsome two-story structure serves the company for its offices. At the yards, and owned by the company, is the Allerton House, a first-class hotel of 100 rooms, heated by steam and supplied with a telegraph office, billiard room and all modern improvements, which offers first-class entertainment to visiting stockmen. At these great and complete yards the bulk of the live stock transactions of this market are carried on. In 1886 the number of cars unloaded at the stock-yards tracks was 28,542. The receipts were 307,244 head of cattle, 935,995 hogs, 212,101 sheep and 16,388 horses and mules. The number of cars loaded was 13,809 and the shipments 198,346 cattle, 435,079 hogs, 174,370 sheep, and 14,705 horses and mules.

**Rösch.**—Artistic Photographer; Olive and Fifteenth streets; one block west of Exposition Building.—Although only opened in September last, this establishment has taken a leading and commanding place among the photographic studios of the West. The Messrs. Rösch are both gentlemen of long experience in the business, and have successfully introduced themselves into a liberal and extensive patronage from the society people of St. Louis and vicinity. The studio is one of the most perfectly appointed in the country, and was especially erected for Rösch. The reception rooms, parlors and operating rooms are luxuriously and magnificently furnished and adorned with rare and beautiful works of art and bric-a-brac. From the very beginning of its business this establishment has received a large and fashionable patronage which its artistic work has attracted. Many of the most prominent society people of the city have been photographed here, and its work is not excelled by any one, and is but rarely equaled. Visitors are always cordially welcome, and shown about the beautiful studio by polite attendants. It is worthy of a visit and deserving of its liberal patronage.

**Metcalf, Moore & Co.**—Live Stock Commission Merchants: Rooms 39 and 40, Kansas City Stock Yards; Rooms 12 and 14, National Stock Yards, East St. Louis, Ill—A prominent and prosperous firm, the annual transactions of which in live stock reach a large total amounting to about $5,000,000 is that of Metcalf, Moore & Co., composed of Messrs. J. Metcalf, William F. Moore, N. T. Jackman and E. J. Senseney. The business was originally established by Messrs. Metcalf & Moore in 1872, Mr. Senseney becoming a member of the firm in 1875 and Mr. Jackman in 1880. The Kansas City branch is under the management of Messrs. Moore and Jackman, while the business of the firm here is attended to by the other members, Mr. Metcalf attending to the cattle transactions, Mr. Tarlton to the hog department and Mr. Senseney to the office and financial business of the firm. Mr. Senseney is a director of the St. Louis Live Stock Exchange, of which the firm are members, and all of the partners are practical and experienced live stock merchants. They do a commission business exclusively, and enjoy, in an eminent degree, the approval of all who have transactions with them as a consequence of the faithful attention paid by them to the interests of their patrons, and the satisfactory character of their commission services.

**The Mammoth Stables and Broadway Mule Yards.**—Reilly & Wolfort, Proprietors; Offices, 1531 to 1533 North Broadway.—St. Louis is the recognized horse and mule market of the world, and more horses and mules are handled annually in this city than at any other place. One of the oldest, most extensive and best known firms engaged in this trade is that of Reilly & Wolfort, who have been engaged in business here in St. Louis for over thirty years. During the war, the firm acted as agents for the United States Government, and purchased many thousands of head of horses and mules for its uses.

During the many years of the firm's existence, it has by fair dealing and excellent business methods built up a patronage that requires for its accommodation a large extent of room. So extensive has its trade become, that the original location, 1500 to 1508 North Broadway, proved too small, and these premises are now used exclusively as mule yards. The horse stables are located about a block north, and occupy the premises at 1538 to 1544 North Broadway, while the offices are located in a magnificent brick building opposite, 1531 and 1533, which also has accommodations for several hundred head of stock. The facilities of the firm are ample to accommodate 2,000 head of stock at one time, and the annual volume of business transacted by them amounts to probably $3,000,000. Their trade reaches not only all parts of America, but also to every portion of the world, and they have a large foreign order business, and are constantly shipping horses and mules to all countries. Having acquired a reputation that is faultless, Messrs. Reilly & Wolfort enjoy the confidence and esteem of all with whom they do business.

**Booth, Barada & Co.**—Real Estate Agents: 617 Chestnut street.—Prominent among the oldest real estate firms of the city is that of Booth, Barada & Co. It was established over thirty years ago. The members of the firm are justly regarded as authorities on all matters pertaining to St. Louis real estate, and their experience in the business, and close and accurate knowledge of present and prospective values, renders the firm a most valuable medium for the transaction of any business relating to property, the purchase, sale or exchange of real estate, the placing of safe investments, the collection of rents, payment of taxes and every other matter relating to real estate or probate business. Messrs. Booth, Barada & Co. are members of the St. Louis Real Estate and Stock Exchange and have charge of many large estates. They do an extensive business in loaning money, have an enormous rent roll of store and residence property all over the city, and are uniformly busy and prosperous. They find the outlook for the present year exceedingly bright, the demand for good properties being very active. Every detail of each transaction placed in their hands is attended to with careful fidelity to the interests of their clients, and the great success of the firm is the well-earned reward of years of close application and honorable methods.

**J. L. Isaacs Wall Paper Company.**—J. L. Isaacs, President; Eugene L. Isaacs, Vice-President; J. J. Pierron, Secretary; Interior Decorations and Fresco Painting; 1210 Olive street.—This old established and prosperous business was established in 1858 by Mr J. L. Isaacs, who still remains at its head as President of the present establishment which was incorporated in 1885. This house has for many years maintained a high reputation for the most artistic and satisfactory work in its line, and a majority of the fine mansions of the city received their interior decorations from this establishment. The business is conducted in the Excelsior Building, 1210 Olive street, and occupies four stories and the finished basement, and carries the largest line of wall papers of all grades as also the most elegant stock of art decorations for interiors to be found in any establishment in the country. Lincrusta Walton, one of the modern modes of decorations, is used extensively by this house, it being indestructible and can be painted, bronzed, gilded and ornamented in a great variety of beautiful styles and colorings. It can be washed and scrubbed and will not catch and retain the dust. Another specialty of this house is their beautiful ceiling decorations, either in paper or fresco, or a combination of both. Parties contemplating repairs on their houses will do well to visit Isaacs, and while examining the elegant display of ornamental wall coverings, not to fail to see their wood carpets (or inlaid hard wood floors). They are durable, elegant, cleanly and healthful. Only the most skilled workmen are employed by this establishment, and orders are solicited and work contracted for in all sections of the country.

**Dehner-Wuerpel Mill Building Co.**—A. Dehner, President; E. Wuerpel, Secretary; Millwrights and Machinists, Builders of Complete Mills for the Manufacture of Flour and Corn Meal, and Manufacturers of General Motive Power Machinery for Mills, Storage Elevators, Breweries and Malt Houses; Makers of Power and Hand Platform Elevators, Importers of Bolting Cloth and Dealers in General Mill and Factory Supplies; 1607 to 1617 South Third street.—In referring to the manufacturing and commercial industries of St. Louis, a short history and description of these works are in order, and will possess general interest. They were established in 1877 by Dehner & Wuerpel and were incorporated in 1881, with Mr. A. Dehner as President, and E. Wuerpel, Secretary. Both gentlemen are practical mechanics, and have not only long experience, but a perfect knowledge of their business. They are endowed with liberal progressive ideas that have enabled them to keep their establishment fully abreast of the times, and given to it an extended reputation. The best mills and breweries in St. Louis and vicinity have been fitted and furnished with machinery and appliances by this company. The establishment employs about seventy-five men, and manufacture roller mills, shafting, gearing and general motive power outfits complete, mills, elevators, malt houses and white lead manufactories. They also build and erect power and hand platform elevators. The trade is general throughout the West and South, and the company's reputation for thorough, durable and economical work has attracted general attention to St. Louis as a mill furnishing center.

**Charles P. Kellogg & Co.**—Clothing and Furnishing Goods; W. P. Kennedy, Manager St. Louis Branch; 624 Washington avenue.—This great manufacturing concern has its headquarters and factory at Chicago. It was established in 1850, as King, Kellogg & Co., changing to its present style in 1868. The house has a trade extending from New York to San Francisco, and from Manitoba to Mexico. At Chicago, the firm employ 4,500 skilled hands, and run eight large cutting machines, each having a capacity of from 300 to 400 suits of clothes per day. They turn out over 1400 complete finished suits daily, carry always over $1,000,000 worth of clothing in stock, keep forty traveling men on the road, each carrying four to six trunks of samples, representing over $60,000 worth of samples constantly on the road. They have a branch similar to the St. Louis one at San Francisco. The branch here, which was established in 1878, occupies the fine four-story and basement building, 30x100 feet, forming the southeast corner of Washington avenue and Seventh street, and here they carry full lines of samples of every article of their manufacture. Mr. W. P. Kennedy, their St. Louis representative, has been with the house ever since their establishment here in 1878, and by his efficiency has helped to make this the most successful branch. From here the house sends out seven traveling salesmen. This branch controls the trade of the house in Missouri, Arkansas, Kentucky, Texas, Mississippi and the entire South. It is popular with the trade, and is prepared to fill all orders in a prompt and satisfactory manner.

## The Industries of St. Louis. 151

**Lippincott & Co.**—Manufacturers of Soda Water Apparatus, Soda and Mineral Waters, Syrups, Extracts, etc.; Northwest corner of Eighth and St. Charles streets.—The foundation of this establishment dates back to 1858, when S. S. Lippincott, the well known manufacturer, opened a branch of his great Philadelphia house in St. Louis. The business was conducted by him until 1871, when he disposed of it to Mr. B. R. Lippincott, who handled it alone until 1884, when Messrs. O. Rautenstrauch and Joseph R. Berktold were admitted, and the business has since been conducted under the firm name of Lippincott & Co. The house manufactures all kinds of soda and mineral water apparatus, also syrups, extracts, etc. Mineral waters of all kinds are handled and carbonated by the firm, who have the agency for "Silurian," a famous Waukesha mineral water. The house acts as the Western agent of Charles Lippincott & Co., Philadelphia, for the sale of their soda water apparatus and carbonating machinery, which is the oldest of its kind in the United States, having been founded early in 1832. The trade of Lippincott & Co., while mostly local, extends over Missouri and adjacent States, and the St. Louis house enjoys to a large degree the fame and reputation of the parent house, which it so deservedly merits.

**Safe Deposit and Trust Company of St. Louis.**—John R. Lionberger, President; Charles Speck, Vice-President; G. A. Hayward, Secretary; 513 Locust street.—This important corporation, which was organized in 1870, occupies the entire building at 513 Locust street, which is, in materials and construction, as thoroughly fireproof as any building in the city, and its vaults are so constructed as to afford perfect protection against fire, and are also burglar-proof. One of the vaults is fitted up with small safes, which are rented for from $7.00 to $100.00 per annum. The locks to the safes are all different, and are changed with every change of renter. Each renter holds the keys or combination to his safe and has exclusive access to it, and every possible safeguard is thrown around the deposits of every renter. The company also receive and receipt for valuables in sealed packages, securities, deeds, wills or other papers, and collects and remits the interest on securities when desired. It also executes or guarantees bonds when secured by collaterals having a quoted and market value deposited with the company. The security of valuables when deposited in the vaults of this company is absolute, and it is a great convenience to holders of bonds, retired and active merchants, manufacturers, brokers, families, mechanics, tradesmen, professional men, societies, and persons acting as trustees or holding other fiduciary positions. The advantages offered by this company are appreciated by the wealthy and the thrifty. Its management is perfect in system, and its directors are gentlemen of well known stability, including Messrs. John R. Lionberger, John N. Dyer, John Byrne, Jr., Charles Speck, J. M. Franciscus, J. G. Chapman, G. A. Hayard, A. F. Shapleigh, John Jackson, Oliver Garrison, I. G. W. Steedman, John W. Harrison and W. H. H. Pettus.

**Taussig Bros. & Co.**—Wholesale Dealers in Wool and Woolen Goods; 4 and 6 South Main street.—The wool trade of St. Louis, which has assumed great proportions may in a measure be said to be controlled by this old and well-known house. The Taussigs are among the oldest established merchants of St. Louis, and began their business career here in 1842, when the present house was established by the firm of Abeles & Taussig. For twenty years this firm continued in business together, and not only conducted a profitable and prosperous establishment, but established a reputation that has never tarnished and which is yet held in the greatest respect. In the year 1862 Taussig, Livingstone & Co. succeeded the original firm, and ten years later, in 1872, was in turn succeeded by Taussig Bros. & Co., which it still remains. In the trade the house have always occupied a strong and commanding position, and its solidity could no more be questioned than that of the Bank of England itself. The house is a large buyer and seller of wool, and have an extensive trade with the East and South. The extent of the wool trade in St. Louis amounts to over sixteen million pounds per annum, out of which gross total Taussig Bros. & Co. are credited with a large proportion. The business of this house cannot be gauged however from these statistics, as they buy and ship directly through and past St. Louis, every season, hundreds of car loads of wool which go directly East and are not included in St. Louis transactions, although they might properly be. The Taussig Brothers, Messrs. Morris and August, are identified with the commerce and prosperity of St. Louis in many other ways than that of their mercantile establishment. They are largely interested in various first-class mining enterprises, and own almost entirely the stock of several mines that are paying large dividends. They are also interested in several insurance and banking enterprises, and Mr. Morris Taussig has been a director of the Merchants' Exchange, and August is now the President of the Wool Dealers' Association.

**St. Louis & Mississippi Valley Transportation Company.**—Henry C. Haarstick, President; Austin R. Moore, Vice-President and Treasurer; Henry P. Wyman, Secretary; Office, Cotton Exchange Building, Main and Walnut streets.—This corporation which is the largest inland transportation company, on water, in the United States, was organized and incorporated in 1880, and has a full paid capital of $2,000,000. It is popularly known as "The Barge Line," and is the principal freight carrier on the Mississippi River, between here and the Gulf. At the time of the organization of this corporation in 1880, it purchased the Mississippi Valley Transportation Co., which had been in operation since 1866, and of which Henry C. Haarstick had been Vice-President and manager since 1869. Upon the purchase being consummated, Mr. Haarstick was made President of the new company, which important position he has continued to fill with distinguished ability. He is recognized as one of the best informed gentlemen on transportation matters in the country. The foresight, breadth and liberality which has always characterized his management of the affairs of this prosperous enterprise, is displayed by him in all matters with which he is connected. He was the President of the St. Louis Merchants' Exchange several years ago, and is financially interested in several local institutions. The company has in its service ten towboats and about 100 barges, 83 of which are covered grain barges. The facilities of this company for freight transportation are unequaled, and it has offices at all important points between here and New Orleans. The freight agents of the company are J. P. Burdeau, St. Louis; John A. Stevenson, New Orleans; J. W. King, Cairo; C. M. Espy, Memphis. They are experienced gentlemen, who are well-qualified for the important positions which they fill. The company during its existence has purchased the St. Louis & New Orleans Transportation Co., the American Transportation Co., and the Mound City Transportation Co. It employs in its service directly and indirectly nearly 2,500 men, on water and land.

**Drey & Kahn.**—Importers and Dealers in Plate, Window, Stained Glass, etc.; 512 and 514 St. Charles street.—This firm was established in 1867, and ranks among the largest establishments of its kind in the United States. It occupies the large five-story building at 512 and 514 St. Charles street, and extensive warehouses on North Main street, and carries the biggest stock of glass in the West: English cathedral, ornamental glass of all sizes, etc. The agency for St. Louis of De Pauw American Plate Glass Works, also for the Belcher Mosaic art glass, rests in this firm. The unlimited variety of magnificent color effects and art combinations that are produced by the Mosaic process, render it superior to all other methods of producing ornamental glass work. The Mosaic glass is peculiarly adapted for church windows, house decorations, window blinds, curved surfaces and all classes of interior decorations. Many of the churches, private residences and leading business houses of St. Louis were supplied with their glass by this firm. Its trade extends into Missouri, Illinois, Kansas, Colorado, Nebraska, Iowa, Arkansas, Texas, Mississippi, Tennessee, Old Mexico, the Territories of New Mexico, Arizona, Utah, Montana and Dakota. The firm are the largest importers in the city of French, English and Belgian glass, both sheet and plate, and cathedral glass. The individual members of the firm are Albert Drey, Adolph Drey, and Max. Kahn, each of whom have resided here many years, and enjoy distinguished social and commercial standing in the community.

**Mallinckrodt Chemical Works.**—Edward Mallinckrodt, President; Geo. Goerlich, Secretary.—This business was started in 1867 and from a very small beginning has grown to be one of the largest establishments of the kind in the United States, and indeed in the world. The works of the company occupy two entire city

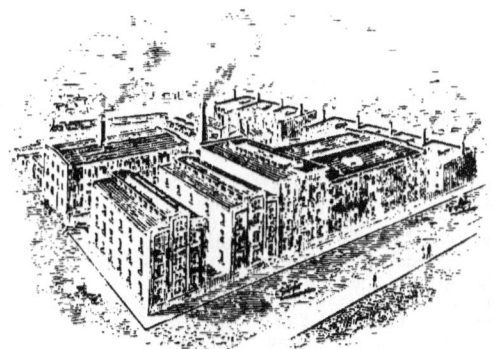

blocks, between Second, Main, Hall, Mallinckrodt and Salisbury streets, one of which only is shown in the accompanying cut. The buildings are mostly four stories in height and are equipped with the most modern and improved machinery and appliances.

This company manufactures a full line of pure chemicals for medicinal and photographic purposes, embracing over three hundred articles. A number of technical products are also made, among the most important of which are aqua ammonia and anhydrous ammonia, of which large quantities are shipped to all parts of the country, for the cooling of breweries, the manufacture of artificial ice, etc.

When we consider the large number of articles manufactured, that they are mostly high priced, some of them costing many dollars per ounce, that they are turned out by the ton and that a couple of hundred hands are employed, an idea of the extent of the business may be formed.

The Mallinckrodt Chemical Works sell their goods in every State of the Union and also export considerable to other countries, the superior quality causing a constantly increasing demand for their brand.

The Company has an office and warehouse at No. 90 William street, in New York City, where a full assorted stock of their goods is kept, and to better supply the increasing trade of the Eastern cities, they have recently bought twelve acres of land in Jersey City where they are now erecting branch chemical works.

**Hull, Steele & Company.**—Live Stock Commission Merchants; Rooms 7 and 8, Union Stock Yards.—This is an old established live stock commission house. Mr. E. B. Hull has been in the business about ten years, and in 1880 joined Mr. R. A. Steele, who had previously been engaged for about twelve years in the business, the firm becoming Hull & Steele. Mr. Steele, who was murdered in January last, was probably the oldest live stock man in the city. Mr. E. B. Hull is now the general manager of the business; Mr. Z. T. Steele, cattle salesman; Mr. C. T. Steele, book-keeper, and Mr. Charles Wells, hog salesman. The firm does a purely commission business in cattle, sheep and hogs, which they receive in large quantities from all points, and particularly from Missouri, Kansas, Arkansas, Texas, Southern Illinois, Kentucky, Tennessee, Iowa and the Western Territories. These they sell to shippers at the Union Stock Yards and the National Stock Yards in East St. Louis. The firm have an excellent reputation for the prompt and efficient manner in which they perform all commission services, and possess unsurpassed facilities for handling stock and disposing of them to the advantage of consignors. They handle over 40,000 hogs, about 10,000 head of cattle and about 6,000 sheep yearly, and pay close attention to all consignments, which should be sent to them at the Union Stock Yards.

**Consumers' Coal Company.**—Wm. Freudenau, President; A. W. Groene, Secretary and Treasurer; Miners and Wholesale and Retail Dealers in Bituminous and Anthracite Coal; 204 North Eighth street.—Mr. Freudenau, by whom this business was established, was in the milling business in this city for over twenty years. About eight years ago he became interested in coal mining and about three years later established himself as a wholesale and retail coal dealer on a large scale, prospering in the business and increasing its operations from year to year, until in October, 1886, in order to facilitate its large transactions, the present company was organized and duly incorporated under the laws of this State. The general office of the company is located at 204 North Eighth street, and it has extensive yards at

221 South Seventeenth street and at Levee and North Market street. The company are extensive miners of coal, operating one mine on the Vandalia railway, two on the O. & M., three on the L. & N.; one on the T., K. C. & St. L., and one on the C. & A. roads. They employ at the mines over one thousand men, and in this city a force of fifteen clerks and assistants. They ship coal from the mines to all points on the Missouri Pacific, Chicago & Alton, Iron Mountain and other roads, and handle fully 25 per cent. of all the coal brought to St. Louis, as well as furnishing coal in large quantities to Council Bluffs, Omaha, and other leading Western cities. They supply dealers and large manufacturers, and have established the company firmly in the confidence of the trade and the public by the merit of their goods, the reasonableness of their prices and the promptness and reliability with which they fill all orders.

**Leon Goldman.**—Stocks and Bonds; 210 North Third street.—Mr. Goldman was in the employ of the banking and brokerage firm of Donaldson & Fraley for six years prior to 1884, when upon the retirement from that firm of Mr. Moses Fraley, his uncle, he became interested in the business with Mr. John Donaldson. In January, 1886, the firm was dissolved and Mr. Goldman started for himself. He deals in stocks and bonds of all kinds, and was the first broker in the city to make a specialty of mining stocks, in which line he operates very largely and has been very successful. Although he handles all mining stocks that have a market value, the leading ones in which he deals are Granite Mountain, Small Hopes, Adams, Yavapai, Peacock, Ideal, Cleveland, Mexican Improvement, and Hope, of Montana. He possesses a very intimate knowledge of the mining stock market, and has placed several prominent mining properties on the market. He possesses facilities for advantageous dealing not excelled by any other broker in the city, and has prospered greatly in his business as a result of his sagacity and enterprise.

**Jack P. Richardson.**—Lumber Commission Merchant; 405 Walnut street.—This well-known merchant has been engaged in the lumber trade here for many years, and has built up a prosperous and extensive business in his line. He is one of the most popular merchants of the city, and has a thorough knowledge of the lumber trade, and is well posted on all the conditions of the local and general markets. His long experience, business capacity, and energetic character enable him to promptly handle large consignments of lumber, which he readily disposes of to the profit and advantage of his consignors. The business handled annually by this house amounts to about fifteen million feet. The transactions are all strictly commission business. A specialty is made of walnut, poplar, yellow pine and other hardwoods, which are received from Missouri, Arkansas, Indiana, Louisiana, Texas and all regions where the hardwoods are grown. Aside from his mercantile life Mr. Richardson is well-known and held in high esteem. He is very prominent in the Masonic order and holds the highest office in St. Louis Commandery No. 1, (The Old Guard), Knights Templar. He is actively identified with all movements pertaining to the prosperity of the city, and has several times had his name suggested for public positions. Thus far he has declined all political honors, much to the regret of his many friends.

**James A Wright & Sons Carriage Company.**—J. P. Wright, President; L. H. Wright, Vice-President; F. L. Wright, Secretary and Treasurer; Manufacturers of Carriages, Etc.; Washington avenue, corner of Nineteenth street.—One of the oldest, best known and most successful carriage manufactories in the city is that of the James A. Wright & Sons Carriage Co. It was originally established in 1847 by Mr. James A. Wright, later becoming James A. Wright & Sons, and finally being incorporated under its present style. The company's factory and salesrooms occupy a five-story and basement building, 100x150 feet, which is outfitted with all the necessary plant for the successful prosecution of the business, and gives employment to a force of seventy-five skilled workmen. The company also have a branch house at Chicago, and are extensively engaged in the manufacture and sale of every style of first-class light and heavy carriages, buggies, etc. The specialty of the company is the quality of its work and none but the best materials are used. Careful supervision is exercised over every detail to secure, in each vehicle turned out at the works, a careful adhesion to the high standard of excellence which has made the products of this factory famous. The company does a very large business, extending from the Lakes to the Gulf and including all west of the Ohio River.

**D. E. Garrison & Co.**—Manufacturers' Agents for Bessemer Steel Rails, etc.; 221 Olive street.—This business was established in 1870 by Mr. D. E. Garrison, who was joined later by his sons, Messrs. W. O. & C. K. Garrison, who, with their father, form the existing firm. They do a very large business in all the Western and Southwestern States as manufacturers' agents for the sale of Bessemer steel rails, iron rails, spikes, bolts, splices, rolling stock of all kinds and for the purchase of old iron and steel rails. Their dealings are chiefly with railroad companies for whom they make all supplies to order, as few roads use the same kinds. They represent some of the largest manufacturing concerns in their line in the country and have correspondents in all the large cities. The practical experience possessed by Mr. D. E. Garrison in all the details of this business, and the thorough business qualifications of all the members of the firm have secured for the house a large and constantly increasing patronage, for the supplying of which in a most satisfactory manner the firm possesses unsurpassed facilities.

**French Silvering and Ornamental Glass Company.**—Ewing Hill, President; W. H. Hadley, Secretary; Manufacturers of Stained Glass; Southeast Corner of Tenth and St. Charles streets.—This corporation, organized in 1882, has enjoyed a large and steadily expanding business from that date to the present. The popular culture in matters of art decoration has steadily improved in the past few

years, and in no direction has this trend toward a higher ideal been more manifest than in the use of ornamental glass. As a consequence, the manufacture of decorative glass has been encouraged, and the French Silvering and Ornamental Glass Co. has enjoyed prosperity. The company employs a force of forty skilled workmen, and manufactures all kinds of stained glass for use in churches and dwellings, and makes a specialty of embossed and sand blast glass. The quality of the product is not excelled and the demand for it extends to every part of the United States and is very large. The perfect system upon which both the manufacturing and business operations of the company are conducted has secured for it a high place among the leading establishments in the country in its line of industry.

**Heinrich Coal Company.**—John P. Heinrich, President; George Heinrich, Secretary; Office, 610 Chestnut street.—This business was established in 1865, by Mr. John P. Heinrich, the firm afterward becoming Heinrich Bros. & Co., and finally being incorporated under its present name in 1873. The company formerly owned the mines at Heinrichtown, Ill., (named after them) but sold out to the Consolidated Coal Co. in September, 1886. They still receive the output of the mines. Messrs. Heinrich Bros. brought to this city the first car load of coal ever brought over in bulk, bringing it via Venice, Madison Ferry, etc., and also brought the first wagon load of coal over the bridge. The company does a very large business with dealers, leading manufacturers and private consumers. They have railroad track depots at 1704 Clark avenue, and Levee and Convent street in this city, and at Broadway and Third street, East St. Louis. They have also a retail yard at 813 South Broadway. They deal in the best grades of anthracite coal, and in bituminous coals carry Black Diamond, St. Bernhard and Heinrich family coals; Piedmont, Big Muddy and Pittsburgh blacksmith coals and charcoal; Dutch Hollow, White Oak and other Illinois steam coals, and sell white sand, hickory, oak, and kindling wood. They have unsurpassed facilities for handling, shipment and delivery, fill all orders promptly and at the lowest market price, and have an excellent reputation for fair, square and accurate dealings.

**Ely & Walker Dry Goods Company.**—Frank Ely, President; D. D Walker, Vice-President; Patrick Baggot, Secretary and Treasurer; Importers and Jobbers in Dry Goods, Etc.; 501, 503 and 505 North Broadway.—This establishment is one of the largest jobbing houses of the many great mercantile concerns of the city. The house was established about eight years ago by Ely, Walker & Co. In 1884 the firm incorporated as the Ely & Walker Dry Goods Co., with a paid-up capital of $500,000. At the time the establishment was incorporated, a number of the employes were made stockholders. This was done from a desire upon the part of Messrs Ely and Walker to permit as great a number of the employes of the establishment as possible to participate in the profits of the business, this system of control and management enabling them to an interest in the business and make participants in the profits, a goodly number of their associates and employes, in a co-operative and mutually beneficial way. The principals of this concern have a lifetime standing in the commercial interests of the city, and a national reputation as dry goods men and as an incorporated company. This establishment has won an extended reputation for the thorough-going, liberal and progressive manner in which its business is conducted. The officers, stockholders and salesmen of the company are widely known throughout the country as gentlemen who have grown up in the trade. About twenty salesmen, all picked men, of extended acquaintance and large experience, represent the house on the road, and sell goods in all the States and Territories to the west and south of St. Louis. The house is popular and progressive, and ranks among the best on the continent.

**Chas. Niedringhaus.**—Dealer in Stoves, Furniture and all Kinds of House Furnishing Goods; 1001, 1003 and 1005 Franklin avenue.—This old-established house, which has long occupied a leading position in its line, is conducted by Mr. Chas. Niedringhaus as sole proprietor. His stocks comprise a large and varied assortment of bedroom suites, parlor suites, sideboards, fancy chairs, stoves, ranges, refrigerators, baby buggies and house furnishing goods of every description. He occupies an elegant four-story stone building, 90x150 feet, conveniently arranged for the prosecution of every department of his business, of which the first floor of 1001 Franklin avenue is the stove, range and granite ware department, the upper floor being used as sample room for refrigerators, child's carriages, fire place heaters and general stove trimmings, and at Nos. 1003 and 1005 is the furniture department, the first floor being used for bedroom suites, sideboards, extension tables, secretaries, pier mirrors, fancy cabinets, etc. The second floor is loaded down with all kinds of plain and rich parlor goods, fancy hat racks, folding beds and lounges. The third floor is stocked with a complete line of reed and rattan chairs, dining chairs in cane and leather, fancy child's beds and patent cribs. The business employs a force of fifty men, and a large trade is done in the city and all the territory tributary to it as a business center. Mr. Niedringhaus is the sole agent for the celebrated (world's best) Garland Cook Stove and Range, which commands a large trade, it being the cream of stoves, every stove being guaranteed. Close supervision of every detail of the business and square methods in all his dealings have secured Chas. Niedringhaus a constant expansion of trade and merited prosperity.

**H. L. Cornet & Co.**—House and Real Estate Agents; 110 North Eighth street.—This business was established about ten years ago by Mr. H. L. Cornet, and the firm holds a prominent position in the real estate circles of the city. They buy, sell and exchange real estate in the city and suburbs, negotiate loans on safe and favorable terms, collect rents promptly at reasonable rates, and manage several large estates. A specialty of the firm is city suburban property in the western resident quarter, which they handle largely, and they are now offering some specially desirable lots in the new residence subdivision, Clemens Place, embracing 225 lots of an average depth of 185 feet, all of them precisely at the grade established by the Board of Public Improvements, and fronting on Delmar, Goodfellow, Cates, Clemens, Von Versen and Clara avenues, in the district immediately south of Cabanne Place, west of Union avenue. These lots are offered to purchasers under building restrictions that insure the subdivision against everything of an objectionable character. Convenient to the Cable Line and the Wabash Railway, located on a natural eminence with trees, shrubbery and a perfect drainage system, the luxuries of city life are blended, in Clemens Place, with pure air and the freedom of rural attractions. Messrs. H. L. Cornet & Co. are prepared to sell these lots to eligible purchasers, and to transact every description of business pertaining to a first-class real estate agency in a manner giving entire satisfaction to those with whom they have dealings.

THE INDUSTRIES OF ST. LOUIS. 157

**Frank Paule Tailoring Company.**—Dan. Paule, President; Geo. M. Schreiner, Vice-President; Frank Paule, Secretary and Treasurer; Tailors and Importers; 722 Pine street.—This important and first-class tailoring establishment was started in 1881 by the firm of Martindale & Paule, to whom Frank Paule succeeded in 1883. The present corporation was organized in 1885, and has ever since enjoyed a prosperous and growing business. The handsome premises occupied by the company are situated at the southeast corner of Pine and Eighth streets, where is to be found a large, select and perfect assortment of the finest productions of the most noted English, French and German looms. A large force of cutters and workmen, ranging from thirty to forty in number, are employed, all of whom are skillful and artistic; none but the best workmen being suitable to the high class trade of the company. In addition to their large patronage from the most noted business and professional people of the city, the company have a large order trade from railroad officials and customers in the surrounding country. They import and deal only in fine goods and have an unrivaled reputation for the beauty, fit and workmanship of all the garments produced at this popular establishment.

**Chas. F. May.**—Architect and Superintendent; Room 50, Southeast Corner of Broadway and Olive street.—Mr. May has been established in the active practice of his profession in this city since 1879, and has achieved a reputation as a leader among the architects of St. Louis. He attends to all the details of his art and the business connected with it, gives estimates, furnishes plans, and supervises the construction of buildings from his designs. He was the architect and superintended the construction of the Concordia College in this city, built at a cost of $140,000, and also of many others among the largest and finest buildings in St. Louis, and has furnished plans, and in some instances directed the building of a number of fine churches and public school buildings at various points, including Warsaw and Boone, Iowa; Trenton and Mount Olive and many other points tributary to St. Louis. There are now being built in this city, from his plans, a number of fine residence buildings costing from $20,000 to $30,000, as well as several fine store buildings. His success in his profession has been very great and the merited result of the conscientious and skillful manner in which he has executed every commission.

**Western Bascome.**—Insurance; 309 Pine street.—Mr. Western Bascome, successor of Bascome & Munson, of 309 Pine street, St. Louis, is one of the pioneers of the insurance business. He came here in 1858, and surveyed and published the first insurance map of the city. After that he returned to New York and spent five years as general agent of one of the leading insurance companies of that city. He returned to St. Louis in 1864, and since then has been identified with the business here as general and local agent. He introduced the system of corporate bonding of employes of banks, railroads, express and other corporations, and now represents for that branch of business the American Surety Company of New York, a corporation that also is authorized to furnish court bonds, thus relieving property owners from the annoyance and anxiety of bond giving. This company has a capital of $500,000 and resources of $643,281.35. Its trustees include about fifty of the prominent capitalists of the country, three of whom are residents of this city, viz: Mr. Carlos S. Greeley, of the Greeley-Burnham Grocer Co.; Mr. George S. Drake,

158    THE INDUSTRIES OF ST. LOUIS.

Vice-President of the Boatmen's Saving Bank, and Mr. N. C. Chapman, President of the Eau Claire Lumber Co. It is exclusively devoted to suretyship, and has a force of 12,000 correspondents who give it facilities for superior information. Mr. Bascome also represents the Standard Life and Accident Insurance Company, of Detroit, Mich., for the collective insurance of employes against death and injury by accidents, thereby relieving employers from liability and the many calls for help for the injured. He introduced this new feature in accident insurance to the Western Steel Company, whose employes, to the number of about 1500, are insured under one policy in that company. As the successor of Bascome & Munson, he continues to represent the following first-class fire and marine insurance companies, who insured property in 1886 as follows: Queen Insurance Co., of Liverpool, $3,620,026; London Assurance Corporation, London, $2,106,915; Howard Insurance Co., of New York, $1,363,062; New York Equitable Insurance Co., of New York, $966,769; Boylston Insurance Co., of Boston, $696,411; North American Insurance Co., of Boston, $476,102; Louisville Underwriters, of Louisville, Ky., (marine), $871,481; and Union Marine Insurance Co., Liverpool, (marine). These corporations are all known to be solid and well managed, promptly paying all losses, and offer undoubted security for insurance on reasonable terms, consistent with legitimate and fair dealing.

**Jos. M. Hayes Woolen Company.**—Joseph M. Hayes, President; P. G. Lewis, Secretary; Importers and Jobbers of Fine Woolens and Tailors' Trimmings; 617, 619 and 621 Washington avenue.—One of the leading and most successful jobbing houses of the city is that of the Jos. M. Hayes Woolen Co. It was started by Mr. Hayes, in a comparatively small way, in 1876, and the business has steadily grown and expanded from year to year until it is now not only the largest house in its line in the city, but in the West. In extent the business done in 1886 closely approximated $1,000,000, and the territory covered by its trade includes all the country from the Lakes to the Gulf of Mexico, and from the Ohio River to the Pacific ocean. In December last, in order to facilitate his large and increasing business, Mr. Hayes had it incorporated under its present name, but still controls its destinies and directs its affairs with the same energetic and accurate methods by which it has been built up to its present vast proportions. The company occupy four floors of the elegant iron and stone buildings, 100x150 feet, forming the northeast corner of Washington avenue and Seventh street. A force of fifty clerks and assistants are employed, in addition to which fifteen traveling salesmen represent the house on the road. The company offer not only a large assortment of foreign woolens, but also the leading styles of fine and medium domestic fabrics for men's wear, while the stock of tailors' trimmings is large and complete. The house holds a substantial place in the esteem and confidence of the trade, and has earned it by the merit of its goods and the accurate system and honorable methods by which all its dealings are characterized.

**S. A. Rider & Co.**—Wholesale Dealers in Watches, Diamonds and Jewelry; 502 to 506 North Sixth street.—St. Louis has many large firms engaged in the business of jobbing watches, diamonds, jewelry, etc. to the trade of the Western and Southern States, and this is one of the many branches of trade that have been successful, and added to the prosperous character of the city. One of the most prominent and enterprising firms engaged in this trade is that of S. A. Rider & Co., who began business here in 1879, and have at present one of the largest trades of any similar establishment west of New York. Mr. S. A. Rider is the sole member of the firm which bears his name, and is a gentleman who has devoted a lifetime to mercantile pursuits. He enjoys a high reputation as a gentleman and merchant, and his integrity and reliability have caused his house to secure a large and valuable patronage. He sells all over the West and South, and includes in his territory the states and territories of Colorado, Utah, Montana, Dakota, Wyoming, Nebraska, Minnesota, Iowa, Kansas, Missouri, Illinois, Indiana, Kentucky, Mississippi, Tennessee, Arkansas, Texas and the Indian Territory. The stock carried by the house is very extensive and represents a large capital. It includes solid silver and plated ware of all kinds, a complete line of American watches, jewelry, clocks, diamonds, and articles of all descriptions, to be found in a first-class house. Mr. Rider has an office in New York City, at 14 Maiden Lane, and his facilities for purchasing and importing are not excelled by any similar establishment in St. Louis.

# THE INDUSTRIES OF ST. LOUIS. 159

**Ramsey & Swasey.**—Architects; Rooms 22 and 24, 620 Chestnut street.—Mr. Charles K. Ramsey has been established in business as an architect in this city for the past fifteen years. In 1884 he was joined by Mr. W. Albert Swasey, an architect from New York. Among the many fine buildings designed by Mr. Ramsey are those of the Krafft-Holmes Grocery Co.; the Presbyterian Church, Lucas place; Simmons Hardware Co., Catlin Tobacco Co.; many of the fine residences in Vandeventer place, including Mayor Francis' house; the Mallinckrodt Chemical Works, covering two blocks, and to which the firm are about to erect an eight-story addition. They have also designed a great many churches, Ellis Wainwright's new residence, and a large number of prominent dwellings, all in the modern designs, the proposed Tuscan Lodge, Knights Templar, etc. These fine examples of the architect's art are the best possible evidence of the skill of the gentlemen composing the firm, and show that the success they have achieved and the large and steadily increasing business they enjoy, is the result of positive and demonstrated superiority in all the details of the profession. Those who confide architectural commissions to this firm may be sure that they will be executed in the highest style of the art, combining the useful with the artistic.

**Geo. D. Barnard & Co.**—Geo. D. Barnard, E. T. Ustick, and W. K. Richards, Directors; Blank Book Makers, Lithographers, Printers and Stationers; 1101, 1103 and 1105 Washington avenue.—This corporation, eight years ago, succeeded

the firm of Van Beek, Barnard & Tinsley, under which style the business had been conducted for several years previously. They occupy a large and imposing edifice built expressly for their business, and in every way adapted to its purposes. This building has five stories and a basement, and fronts 75 feet on Washington avenue and 160 feet on Eleventh street, running back to Lucas avenue in the rear and thus having light on three sides. The company employ a force of two hundred and fifty hands, and are blank book manufacturers, lithographers, printers and stationers on a large scale. In their various manufacturing departments they employ none but the most skilled workmen, and all the blank book, lithographic and printing work done by the company is of the best style known to the art. They are large jobbers, but their main business is directly with consumers, and extends to every part of the Union. They have a number of special lines in which they excel all other houses in the volume of their business, such as legal blanks and blank books prepared to fill the requirements of the laws for a number of Southern and Western States, lithographic work for banks, etc. In stationery their stocks are immense in their proportions, and comprise everything pertaining to the line. They have eighteen shrewd, wide-awake and efficient traveling representatives, and enjoy a reputation second to no house in the country. They have gained a great and merited success by dealing in a superior class of goods and selling them at fair and reasonable prices, filling every order with promptness and fidelity and to the entire satisfaction of the customers of the house.

**Geo. A. Rubelman Hardware Company.**—George A. Rubelman, President; Henry W. Schlingman, Vice-President; Charles F. Myers. Secretary; Dealers in Cabinet Hardware, etc.; 905 and 907 North Sixth street.—This establishment was founded in 1860 by the present head of the company Mr. George A. Rubelman, whose career has been "onward and upward" since he began the battle of life over thirty years ago. In 1881 Mr. Rubelman incorporated his business under the above head. The establishment occupies the spacious premises at 905 and 907 North Sixth street, which is a four story building fronting 30 feet on Sixth street, and having a depth of 130 feet. A large stock of cabinet and general hardware is carried. The house makes a specialty of cabinet hardware, and has nearly a monopoly in that class of goods among Western cabinet makers and furniture manufacturers. Trade is located throughout that section of the West tributary to St. Louis, and reaches from the Iowa line to the State of Texas and includes Nebraska, Kansas, New Mexico and other Western States and Territories. The career of the head of the company, Mr. Geo. A. Rubelman, is an interesting one. He began work in a hardware store kept by Wm. Seaver, in 1854, when he was but thirteen years old, and four years later, when his employer failed, he was appointed by the principal creditor to manage the business. In 1860 he and his brother John G purchased the store, giving their notes for $6,500 in payment therefor. After a hard struggle they had cleared off all obligations before January 1, 1863. He sold out to his brother in 1875, and opened for himself, in a small way. but his business expanded rapidly, and he soon came into possession of a trade sufficient to justify the erection of the magnificent building now occupied. Mr. Rubelman is a director of the Fifth National Bank, and is prominently identified with other enterprises. It was principally owing to his efforts that the organization of the St. Louis Furniture Exchange was effected.

**Dennison Manufacturing Company.**—H. B. Dennison, President, Boston; Albert Metcalf, Vice-President, Boston; H. K. Dyer, Treasurer, New York; W. D. Franklin, St. Louis Manager: 404 North Third street.—This house, established by Mr. E. D. Dennison in 1844, is known and does a large business in every part of the world. The headquarters of the company are at Boston, Mass., and it has factories at Roxbury, Mass.; Brunswick, Me., and Brooklyn, N. Y., and houses at Boston, New York, Philadelphia, St. Louis, Chicago, Cincinnati and London, England. At the factories, which give employment to eleven hundred hands, are manufactured, besides the world-celebrated "Dennison's Shipping Tags," gum labels, lawyers' seals, coin wrappers, gummed paper, merchandise (string) tags, jewelers' paper boxes, morocco, plush and velvet cases, fine colored and white tissue paper and flower paper and flower paper material; sealing wax in all qualities and colors, Japanese napkins, wood boxes for mailing and express use, Dennison's Absorbent Cotton, and Denniroid (composition) and indestructible chips, also wood and paper game sets. The St. Louis house, a four-story building, 25x120 feet, at 404 North Third street, is under the efficient management of Mr. W. D. Franklin who, with twenty assistants in the house and two active travelers on the road, does a large business for the company in this city and the entire Western, Southwestern and Southern country tributary to this market.

**H. Gaus & Sons Manufacturing Company.**—H. Gaus, President; F. J. Gaus, Vice-President; Henry Gaus, Jr., Secretary and Treasurer; Manufacturers of Doors, Frames, Sash, Blinds, Packing Boxes, Etc.; Southeast Corner of Main and Clinton streets.—This company holds a prominent and important position among the industrial establishments of the city, and its development is a gratifying proof of the satisfactory results of industry, close application and honorable methods. The business had its inception in a small planing mill started by Mr. Henry Gaus in 1863 at the corner of Sixteenth street and Cass avenue. Mr. Gaus, who had previously worked at his trade as a boxmaker, brought his practical experience to bear on his independent venture, closely supervised all its operations, and saw its trade steadily grow as the result of his careful management. He trained his sons in his own ways of industry and usefulness, and in 1879, Henry Gaus, Jr., became his father's partner, the factory having then become by additions 75x150 feet and three stories high. In 1884 the mill was destroyed by fire, but with characteristic determination the firm replaced it by a larger one at the southeast corner of Main and Clinton streets. In 1885 Mr. F. J. Gaus, the younger son of Mr. Henry Gaus, Sr., having attained his majority, was given an interest in the business and the present company was incorporated. The premises owned and occupied by the company, which have been steadily added to as occasion required, now consist of two and three story factories covering an area of 240x325 feet with large lumber yards attached. The factories are completely equipped with all the necessary plant and machinery. The company manufacture doors, frames, sash, blinds, mouldings and general planing mill work, packing boxes, egg cases, chicken coops, berry trays, fruit boxes, etc. They employ from one hundred to one hundred and fifty hands, according to the season, their large box manufacturing business requiring the almost constant employment of sixty of these. They supply boxes to many large houses, including the Dozier-Weyl Cracker Co., the Simmons Hardware Co., etc. In all departments of their business they do a large trade in the city and the states tributary to it as a business center, and enjoy a prosperity which has been fairly earned by years of earnest effort.

**Buckland & Pallen (Trustees).**—Real Estate Office; Missouri avenue, Opposite Main street, East St. Louis, Illinois.—This business was established some thirty years ago by the Connecticut Land Company, Messrs. James Buckland and Selwyn B. Pallen becoming trustees several years ago, under the firm name of Buckland and Pallen. They have 7,700 feet of town lots and 83 acres in the city and 500 acres contiguous to it. They have very large railroad frontage and lands suitable for factories and railroads, all of which they are prepared to sell upon the most reasonable terms. Those desiring choice city lots in East St. Louis for business or other purposes, or farms in the neighborhood, cannot do better than to consult Messrs. Buckland & Pallen, who will be found reliable and accurate in all their dealings.

**St. Louis Hardware and Cutlery Co.**—Louis H. Kallemeier, President; Henry Garlich, Vice-President; Wm. Capelle, Secretary and Treasurer; Exclusive Jobbers of Hardware and Cutlery; 819 North Fourth street.—Prominent among the leading houses engaged as jobbers in hardware and cutlery is that of the St. Louis Hardware and Cutlery Co., which was incorporated in 1882. They occupy a spacious six-story building, with a frontage of 30 feet at 819 North Fourth street by a depth of 130 feet. Large as these premises are, they are too contracted for the rapidly increasing business of the company, to accommodate which they contemplate procuring additional warehouse facilities. Their stocks are very large and embrace everything in the line of shelf and heavy hardware, imported and domestic cutlery, etc., and this house is also the Western depot for A. B. Hendryx & Co.'s celebrated bird cages, which are admitted to be the most complete and useful article in their line ever offered to the public.

The company employs a force of twenty competent assistants in its store, in addition to which a staff of twelve energetic traveling men represent the house in its vast trade territory comprising the entire country west from Indiana to and including the Pacific Coast States, and from the Canadian line south to Louisiana. The house enjoys unsurpassed facilities for the successful prosecution of every department of its business, and by selling only honest goods and adopting fair and accurate methods in its dealings has achieved a great and merited prosperity.

**Cash, Stewart & Overstreet.**—Live Stock Commission Merchants; 15 Exchange Building, (up stairs), National Stock Yards.—No man is more intimately connected with the history of the St. Louis live stock market than is Mr. J. G. Cash, the senior member of this firm, who came to the city in 1864 and went into business as part owner of the Broadway Retail Yards, then as owner of the North Missouri Stock Yards, which he conducted for eight years, then as founder of the Union Stock Yards, which he superintended for a year; and as superintendent for two years of the National Stock Yards. Prior to the establishment of the present firm in 1884 he was connected as member, consecutively, of the firms of Moody, Cash & Co., J. G. Cash & Bro., and Cash, Stewart & Co. He is now a director of the St. Louis Live Stock Exchange and prominent in every movement looking to the improvement of the live stock interests of this market. Mr. Stewart has also a long experience in this line, having been engaged in it for the past nineteen years, first as a member of the firm of C. G. Buchanan & Co., then as a salesman for Hilliard, Manson & Co., and finally as a partner in the present firm. Mr. Overstreet has been in the live stock business since 1873, having been for eleven years a member of the firm of J. W. Overstreet & Co., and since 1884 of the firm of Cash, Stewart & Overstreet. Thus fortified by experience and having ample resources and every facility for the advantageous prosecution of the business, the firm have by strict attention to every detail and undeviating fidelity to every trust, acquired a deserved prominence in the live stock commission line and the patronage of a large number of the leading stockmen of the West and Southwest. Messrs. Stewart and Overstreet look after the business of the firm in cattle and sheep, and Mr. Cash superintends the hog department. No firm is more substantial or in better repute, and none more reliable as a medium for the prompt and satisfactory transaction of live stock business.'

**John W. Renshaw.**—Notary Public, Real Estate and Insurance Agent; Main street, East St. Louis. Ill.—Mr. Renshaw has for a number of years been recognized as one of the most prominent and popular of the citizens of East St. Louis. He was formerly for several years Chief of Police of that city, for six years School Treasurer, and at present, City Treasurer, filing a bond for each position for $100,000. Seven years ago he established himself in his present business, in which he has enjoyed a pronounced and steadily expanding success. He has a large amount of desirable property for rent and sale, and attends to all the departments of a real estate business, also making a specialty of collections. In addition to his business in this line, Mr. Renshaw is prepared to place insurance for property owners in East St. Louis in a number of the most substantial and reliable companies, of which he is the representative, on the lowest terms consistent with absolute safety. Those having business to transact in any of the lines above enumerated, will find Mr. Renshaw an efficient and attentive medium for its satisfactory performance.

**E. C. Kruse & Co.**—Commission Merchants for the Sale of Hides, Wool, Pelts, Tallow, Furs, etc.; 318 North Commercial street.—This business was established in 1873 by the firm of Evans & Huntley, to whom E. C. Kruse & Co. succeeded in 1883. Mr. Emil C. Kruse, the senior member of the firm, was with Evans & Huntley for ten years prior to the establishment of this business, and is thoroughly experienced in the business and intimately acquainted with the markets for the commodities handled by him. The firm has established the most favorable relations with buyers in the principal Eastern cities, and has unsurpassed facilities for the advantageous sale of wool, hides, furs, pelts, tallow, beeswax, feathers, rags, bones, etc. The firm has a large patronage from producers and shippers and receives large consignments from all parts of the West and South. The close attention paid to all consignments, and the promptness with which the firm makes returns on the day of sale have secured for it a high reputation and a steady increase in the volume of its business from year to year.

**A. J. Jordan.**—Manufacturer of Fine Cutlery; Factory, East India Works, 20 Radford street, Sheffield, England; Salesrooms, 612 Washington avenue and 613 St. Charles street, St. Louis.—Though a Marylander by birth and a truly representative American in every respect, Mr. A. J. Jordan finds Sheffield, England, the most favorable location for the manufacture of his specialty of fine cutlery. He owns and operates the extensive East India Works in that city, and manufactures every description of fine table and pocket cutlery, which he ships in immense quantities to his commodious salesroom in this city, having a frontage of 25 feet on Washington avenue, and running back 155 feet to a similar frontage on St. Charles street, in which is carried a large stock embracing everything in the line. The trade of the house is immense in its proportions, extending throughout the South and covering the entire range of Western States and Territories, and the Pacific Coast from Puget Sound to the Gulf of California, the services of twelve wide-awake and experienced traveling salesmen being enlisted in attending to this widely extended custom. During the past three years Mr. Jordan's time has been principally spent at the works in England, and he is there at this writing, but the business of the house prospers as usual in his absence, his brother, Mr. C. D. Jordan, a gentleman of superior business attainments, having charge of its affairs, and giving to them the close and intelligent attention which their magnitude requires. The merit of the goods manufactured by Mr. Jordan has caused the demand for them to increase steadily from the establishment of the business by him in 1872 to the present time.

## THE INDUSTRIES OF ST. LOUIS.

**Trask Fish Company.**—Rich & Co., J. M. Dutro, Proctor, Greenwood & Co., I. R. Trask & Co., Consolidated; Established 1855; Incorporated 1878; I. R. Trask, President; Ocean and Lake Fish; 523 North Second street.—The consolidation of four large firms and the incorporation of their combined interests under the name heading this account was effected in 1878. A company of unusual capital and resources was thus organized. These firms were Rich & Co., J. M. Dutro, Proctor, Greenwood & Co., and I. R. Trask & Co., the former of whom had been established so long ago as 1855. The new company was started with a capital of $50,000. Its annual trade amounts, in round numbers, to a quarter of a million dollars. The transactions are mostly in brands of the company's own preparation and packing. The bulk of the Trask Fish Company's stock is carried in their warehouse, which occupies the whole block on Front street, between Florida and Mullanphy streets. The store and office building is at 523 North Second street.

About twenty-five employes are busily engaged in caring for their stock and in looking after the demands of patrons. The house has five travelers in its service and sells goods in the following States: Missouri, Iowa, Illinois, Indiana, Kentucky, Tennessee, Alabama, Georgia, Mississippi, Louisiana, Texas, Arkansas, Indian Territory, Kansas, Nebraska, Dakota, Colorado, New Mexico and to the Republic of Mexico.

All the wholesale grocers of the territory just mentioned handle Trask's goods, and orders may be directed to them or to the company as may be most convenient.

Among the company's brands that have been approved by popular demand may be mentioned, Trask's Selected Shore

Mackerel, in barrels, half barrels and pails, also Trask's Fat Breakfast Mackerel, in barrels, half barrels and pails, now so much sought for, that imitations have been marketed, but by an injunction issued by the St. Louis Circuit Court, all persons have been enjoined from using said brands; the sales of these two brands now aggregate over 100,000 packages annually.

Trask's Georges 1-lb. Brick Codfish; these bricks are made from the very choicest Georges codfish wrapped in wax paper; their method of putting up this brand of codfish must be acknowledged by all grocers to be far superior to any other.

Trask's Cape Cod Turkey, selected from the choicest Georges codfish middles, and cut in New York style. In mackerel and codfish especially the Trask Fish Company has made every effort to put up its goods so as to make them attractive and saleable.

As intimated in this account, this company is one of strength and resources, and is thus enabled to accommodate its patrons generally.

**Huse & Loomis Ice and Transportation Company.**—W. L. Huse, President; James L. Huse, Vice-President; Wholesale Dealers in Ice; Office, 409 Washington avenue, Second Floor.—This business had its inception in the establishment of the firm of Huse, Loomis & Co., about twenty-five years ago. The present company, incorporated in 1880, has a capital, paid up, of $550,000 and employs a force of about two thousand men in winter cutting ice at Peru, LaSalle, Kingston, Beardstown, Clear Lake, Crystal Lake and Alton, Ill., at all of which points they have extensive ice houses. They have also ice houses in this city, one covering a block at the foot of Cass avenue, and another covering a block at the foot of Barton street. They have wharf boats at the foot of Clark avenue and Market street, from which they deliver ice largely to city dealers, employing in spring a force of two hundred men in unloading. They own and run the steamers Jack Frost and Polar Wave and forty barges, and frequently charter other steamers and barges to supply their large trade at all points south of St. Louis on the Mississippi River, and to which they sell ice in barge-load lots. The great volume of the company's business may be judged from the fact that they handle about 250,000 tons of ice per annum. The business has steadily grown from its inception to the present time and now exceeds in magnitude of its trade any similar concern in its line.

**Bennett & Harris.**—Successors to Thomas E. Bennett; Brokers; 305 Pine street.—This business was established by the late Thomas E. Bennett, a gentleman of long experience and intimate knowledge of financial affairs. He was cashier of a National Bank at Winona for eight years, and cashier of State banks for seven years previously. In 1885 he established this business, which he built up to a pronounced success. He was especially prominent in mining operations, in which line he conducted a number of large and important deals, being largely interested in the Silver Dell Mine, at Georgetown, N. M.; the Gold Run Mine, at Breckinridge, Col.; the Queen of the West Mine, at Kokomo, Col., and the Nay-Aug Consolidated. He was Secretary of the Silver Dell and Gold Run Companies. He greatly interested himself in the project to establish a Mining Exchange in this city on the plan of that at San Francisco, and which would doubtless, if properly inaugurated, make St. Louis the great mining center of the country. Mr. Bennett was a gentleman of the highest personal character and the most irreproachable business standing. His sudden and unexpected death, which occurred in April, took from the financial circle of the city one of its most honored and prominent figures. Mr. A. B. Bennett, his son, trained to business pursuits under his father's guidance, succeeds his father in the business, to which he brings all the qualifications necessary to success. With Mr. A. B. Bennett is associated as partner Mr. A. H. Harris, recently of San Francisco, where he was formerly a prominent mining broker. He is a heavy mine owner and thoroughly experienced in the business. The firm deals in all kinds of Government, State, County and Municipal Bonds and in stocks of every description, making a specialty of the better class of mining stocks. They pay strict attention to every commission placed in their hands and have every facility for continuing the business success which was built up by the late Mr. Thomas E. Bennett.

**Elliot Frog and Switch Company.**—H. Elliot, President; H. Elliot, Jr., Secretary; Railroad Crossings, Frogs and Switches, and Every Description of Railroad Iron Work; East St. Louis, Illinois.—This large and important manufacturing establishment has been successfully conducted since it was founded by the Messrs. Elliot in 1873, and the present corporation was organized four years ago. Their factory is fully and completely equipped with all the latest and most improved machinery and appliances adapted to the requirements of the business, and give employment to a force averaging over one hundred men. The specialty of the company is Elliot's Patent Railroad Crossings, Frogs and Switches, which are in demand in all parts of the United States, and especially in all parts of the West. They also do every description of railroad iron work. Their facilities are unsurpassed and they enjoy a wide-spread reputation for the superiority of their product. Conducting their affairs on accurate principles they have built up their business to a great and steadily growing success.

**Plant Seed Company.**—Alfred Plant, President; George Urquhart, Vice-President; Garden, Grass and Flower Seeds, Etc.; 812 and 814 North Fourth street.—The business conducted by the Plant Seed Company was originally established in 1845 by Wm. M. Plant. Fred. W. Plant. Samuel Plant and Alfred Plant, under the style of Plant Brothers. To this old established firm the present company, incorporated in 1872, are successors. The premises occupied by the company front 60 feet at 812 and 814 North Fourth street, running back 130 feet to similar frontage at 815 and 817 North Third street, the building being five stories in height. The company does a very large business as dealers in every description of garden, grass and flower seeds, all of which are grown by experts in seed culture, and in such localities and soils as suit them best, the seeds being carefully selected, and being the purest and best to be found. In addition to seeds the company sells "The Planet, Jr.," and "Fire Fly" garden and farm implements, finely formed and finished tools, unequaled for use in kitchen or market gardening. The house has, by the superior quality of its goods, made its name famous among farmers and gardeners throughout the entire Union, Canada and Mexico, and the great success of the company is due to this merit, together with the unbroken record made by this house of forty-two years of fair and honorable dealings with the purchasing public.

**John M. Sellers.**—Manufacturer of Fire and Water-Proof Gravel and Composition Roofs and Roofing Materials; Office, Southeast Corner of Fourth and Market streets.—Ever since he established his business in 1850, Mr. Sellers has been prominently identified with the building interests of St. Louis. He is extensively engaged as a manufacturer of fire and water proof gravel and composition roofs and roofing materials, his works at 613 Chouteau avenue being a two story building with 75 feet front and running back 200 feet to Papin street. He employs in this city from eighty to one hundred workmen, and has ten teams of his own, besides hiring many others. The roofing furnished by him is in high favor with the best and most experienced architects, and the large number of buildings roofed by him include many of the most prominent breweries and other business structures of the city. He has a branch house at Kansas City, which is also doing a prosperous business, and from the two houses his business extends throughout Illinois, Missouri, Kansas, Nebraska and the South

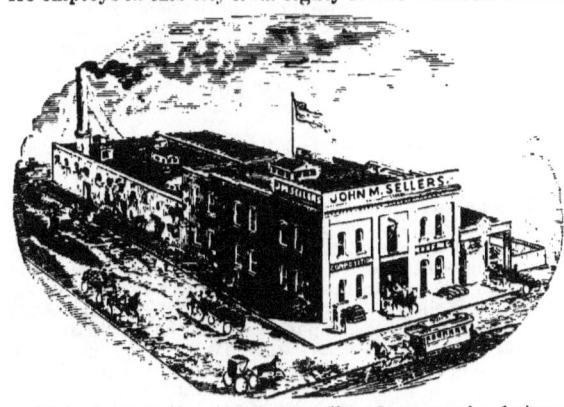

and West generally, prominent railroad companies being among his chief patrons. The uniform merit of his workmanship and materials has secured for him a large and steadily growing trade and a successful career.

**J. P. Becker.**—The Three Leading Stores: Clothing, Dry Goods and Carpet Bazaar, Corner Missouri avenue and Main street; Hat House, Main street near Missouri avenue; "Bee Hive" Shoe Store, Missouri avenue, opposite East St. Louis Bank, East St. Louis, Ill.—Mr. Becker has for twenty years occupied a leading position as a successful merchant in East St. Louis, having established himself in business in 1867. He has three stores as above enumerated, his clothing, dry goods and carpet house and his hat store, comprising a large double two story building 50x150 feet in dimensions, and his shoe establishment being 25x150 feet in area. He carries large and completely assorted stocks in all lines, selected with great care, bought direct from first hands, and not excelled in quality by any house on either side of the river. By close attention to his business, selling superior goods at reasonable prices, and fair and reliable methods in all his transactions, he has earned the confidence of the public, and a large trade in East St. Louis and the surrounding country that steadily increases from year to year.

**Woolman-Todd Boot and Shoe Company.**—J. H. S. Woolman, President; G. W. Todd, Vice-President; Francis R. Phillips. Secretary and Treasurer; Manufacturers and Jobbers of Boots and Shoes; 413 Washington avenue.—In the early part of 1885, Messrs. John Phillips. J. H. S. Woolman and G. W. Todd, all gentlemen of experience in the shoe and leather trades, united in the establishment of the firm of Phillips, Woolman & Todd, which was succeeded in January, 1886, by the present corporation. They occupy a fine five-story and basement building, 25x140 feet, and carry a large and diversified stock of everything in their line. They do a very large business, and have a staff of nine active traveling salesmen who represent the house in its extensive trade territory, embracing the States of Missouri, Illinois, Kansas, Nebraska, Arkansas, Texas, Indian Territory and the Southwest generally. The business has steadily grown from its inception and the house has established a reputation for goods of superior merit and accurate and liberal methods of dealing, which has given it a standing in the trade as one of the most popular boot and shoe houses of the West.

**Nonotuck Silk Company.**—Corticelli Silk Mills; Ira Dimock, President; E. W. Eaton, Treasurer; Corticelli Spool Silk, Etc.; C. H. Sampson, St. Louis Agent; 408 North Broadway.—The name and fame of the Corticelli Silk Mills extends to all parts of the country. These silk mills are at Florence, Leeds, and Haydenville, Mass., and are the largest of their kind in the world. The company manufactures, in addition to the world-celebrated Corticelli spool silk, Florence knitting silk, Floiselle, silk hosiery, underwear and mittens, sewings, embroideries, wash silk, braids, etc. Branch houses are established at New York, Boston, Cincinnati, Chicago, Louisville, New Orleans, San Francisco and St. Louis. In this city they occupy two floors, 25x140 feet, at 408 North Broadway, and employ thirteen assistants in the store, and eight traveling salesmen, who represent the house in the trade territory assigned to this branch, reaching west to Montana and Utah, and south to Texas and New Orleans, in which a large business is done. This branch was established in 1879, and is under the efficient management of Mr. C. H. Sampson, In his business relations his methods are of the most systematic and accurate description.

**A. Frank & Sons.**—Wholesale Dry Goods and Notions; Southwest Corner of Broadway and Washington avenue.—This mammoth wholesale establishment, which occupies the large six-story and basement iron building on the corner of Broadway and Washington avenue, was founded in 1866 by Mr. A. Frank, the senior member of the firm. That it occupies an important and commanding position in the mercantile world is best evidenced by the extent and character of its business, which covers the Western and Southern States. About one hundred men are employed, including traveling salesmen who attend to customers residing in the States of Missouri, Illinois, Kansas, Nebraska, Colorado, Arkansas, Texas, Louisiana and several of the territories. The house is very popular with the retail trade of this city and enjoys an extensive patronage from local merchants. The capital employed is upwards of $300,000, and the annual business approximates $1,500,000. Associated with Mr. A. Frank, are his sons August, Joseph and Louis, who have become members of the firm, and infused additional life and enterprise into the business. The result of the father's experience and training is to be seen in the successful career of the sons who enjoy, with their parent, a distinguished record as successful merchants.

**C. C. Daly & Co.**—Live Stock Commission Merchants; Office No. 1, Exchange Building, National Stock Yards, East St. Louis, Illinois.—For the past fifteen years this firm has successfully conducted a live stock commission business, which has steadily increased in volume from year to year since its inception. The firm has ample resources and every facility for the prompt and efficient transaction of all business in the line. All of the members of the firm are practical and experienced in all the details of the business. Mr. C. C. Daly is a Director of the St. Louis Live Stock Exchange, and prominent in live stock circles. He attends to the transactions of the firm in hogs and sheep, while Mr. E. A. Griffin is the cattle salesman, each of the members having special experience in the department assigned to his supervision. The great care and faithful attention paid by them to the interests of their patrons has secured for the firm a high standing with stockmen throughout the West and Southwest, and a prosperity which is the well-earned result of uniform accuracy and reliability in their dealings.

**Rio Chemical Company.**—Manufacturers of Medical Specialties for Physicians; Northwest Corner of Main and Locust streets, St. Louis; 16 Coleman street, London, E. C., England, and 5 Rue de la Paix, Paris, France; J. C. Richardson, President; Frank Lawrence, Vice-President; H. A. Siegrist, Secretary and Treasurer.—This well-known chemical house has been in successful existence for many years, and its physicians' specialties have given to it a world-wide reputation with the medical profession. The specialties manufactured by this company are: Celerina, aletris cordial, pinus canadensis, white and dark, and acid mannate. The sales are very large, and scattered throughout the United States and European countries. The manufactory and offices were located on Second street for many years, but the quarters having become too small for the greatly increased business, the present elegant and spacious building at the northwest corner Main and Locust streets was secured and remodeled to suit the purposes for which it is required and possession taken January 1st. The universal excellence of the preparations of this company have made them the standards in the medical world.

**H. A. Hyatt.**—Photographic Goods, Picture Frames, Mouldings, etc.: Outfits for the Professional and Amateur a Specialty; Northeast Corner of Eighth and

Locust streets.—The original establishment of this house occurred in 1848, William H. Tilford being its founder. The firm of Gatchell & Hyatt succeeded to the business in 1873 and continued until 1881, when Mr. Hyatt became sole proprietor. The business has steadily grown from year to year and now embraces, in addition to the heavy city patronage enjoyed by the house, a large trade in all the territory tributary to St. Louis as a business center. The premises occupied by the business embrace three floors of the building, 25x140 feet in area, at the northeast corner of Eighth and Locust streets. A very large stock and full lines are carried, including picture frames in approved modern and antique designs, mouldings in all styles and sizes, and a most complete assortment of all classes of goods for the use of photographers. It is the largest house in its line in the city, and few in the country can compare with it either in the extent of its stock or the volume of its business.

**Missouri Tinware Company.**—S. Baer, President; S. Adler, Vice-President; E. Adler, Secretary; 206 North Second street.—This company was only incorporated the present year, but was organized in 1883, and has been engaged in a profitable and extensive business since that year. The spacious and central location of the establishment at 206 North Second street was well chosen, and the local trade has under able and efficient management enjoyed a profitable boom. Outside of St. Louis the trade is located and scattered over the entire West and South even to extreme points. Kansas, Nebraska, Colorado, Wyoming, Montana, New Mexico, Arkansas, Texas, Louisiana, Mississippi and Southern Illinois contribute a large trade to this establishment. The already large business increased perceptibly the past year, and many new customers in New Mexico, and outlying Territories and States, were added to the books. The active management of the interests of this corporation is entrusted to Messrs. S. Baer, the President, and E. Adler, Secretary and Treasurer, both of them gentlemen of extensive acquaintance in the business community and familiar with the details of the trade. The untiring energy and industry of these gentlemen, together with their progressive business methods, have caused the Missouri Tinware Company to push well to the front as one of the leaders in that branch of industry. The large four-story establishment is at all times stocked with the choicest staples and specialties in the tinware and Japan goods line.

**Tudor Iron Works.**—T. A. Meysenburg, President; George S. Edgell, Treasurer; B. S. Adams, Secretary; Manufacturers of Railway Supplies; 509 North Third street.—The manufacturing enterprise known as the Tudor Iron Works was established in 1873 as the St. Louis Bolt and Iron Company, under which name it was conducted until it changed to its present style in 1886. The office of the company is located at 509 North Third street, and its works at East St. Louis, and a force of 500 men is employed in their operation. The company manufactures fish bars, spikes, mine rail, street rail, track and bridge bolts, nuts, etc. Its business is mainly with railroads, miners, jobbers, etc. It has unsurpassed facilities for manufacture, handling and shipment, and its goods have a standing second to none for quality. It is prepared at all times to offer the best inducements to purchasers of track fastenings and mine rail.

**Day Rubber Company.**—A. W. Day, President and Treasurer; E. B. Wilder, Secretary; Importers, Manufacturers and Dealers in India Rubber Goods; 615 North Fourth street.—This business was established in 1882 by the firm of Day Bros. & Co., the present company being incorporated in May, 1885. They do a large and steadily growing business in all parts of the country, enjoying an especially extensive patronage throughout the West, South and Southwest. They carry full and completely assorted lines of rubber and leather belting, rubber, cotton and linen hose, packing of all kinds, rawhide and tanned lace leather, carriage cloths, rubber clothing, boots and shoes, druggists' sundries, etc. They are also manufacturers' agents for many specialties of high merit, including the Cleveland Rubber Co.'s belting, hose and packing; Hoyt's celebrated oak tanned leather belting; the New Jersey Rubber Shoe Co.; the Boston Rubber Co.'s carriage cloths and the Standard Oiled Clothing Co. The company has most complete facilities for the efficient transaction of its business, occupying, in addition to its commodious office and salesroom premises at 615 North Fourth street, spacious warehouses located at 830 North Fourth street and 835 North Third street. The house has the confidence of the trade, its goods being of the best quality and its methods of the most satisfactory character. Messrs. A. W. Day and E. B. Wilder, who are respectively President and Secretary of the company, were formerly engaged in business at Hartford, Conn., and are gentlemen of superior attainments. To their careful and energetic management the prosperity enjoyed by the company is largely due.

**Henry McCabe.**—Manufacturer of Plug Chewing and Twist Tobacco; 707 North Second street.—Mr. McCabe established this business some twenty years ago, and by close attention to its details and upright and honorable dealings, has prospered and increased his business from year to year until he has built up a trade throughout Missouri, Illinois, Indiana and the South. He has for many years enjoyed a first class reputation for the superior quality of his goods, and his brands of "Eagle," "Honey Dew" and "Southern Choice" twists have for a number of years been known and regarded as standards of merit in twist tobaccos, while his plug tobaccos are also of first-class quality. Mr. McCabe employs a large force of hands, and pays strict attention to the selection and purchase of the leaf from which his product is made. Conducting his business upon fair and honorable principles, and filling all orders with dispatch and in a reliable manner, he has maintained for twenty years a prominent place in the business circles of the city.

**George H. Hewes.**—Contracting Engineer, and Manufacturers' Agent for Mining and Water Works Machinery; 811 N. Second street.—Mr. Hewes, who is a practical engineer and has been successfully engaged in his present business since 1883, is the St. Louis representative of the Webster, Camp & Lane Machine Co., of Akron, Ohio, manufacturers of mining and hoisting engines, making a specialty of their "Double Portable Band Friction Hoists," "Tail Rope Haulage Machines," and also for direct acting hoisting plants upon the most approved principles of mechanical science, such as lately contracted for by one of the largest St. Louis enterprises, the Granite Mountain Mining Co. This contract was made with Mr. Hewes. He is also the agent for the Gordon & Maxwell Co., of Hamilton, Ohio, manufacturers of steam pumping machinery for water works, mines and all other purposes, their pumps being of the duplex pattern and possessing other special features. The perfect mechanism of these machines has secured for them the strong approval of practical engineers. In addition to these agencies Mr. Hewes represents Griffiths & Wedge, manufacturers of stamp mills of the latest and most improved pattern.

**Planters' House.**—J. Gerardi, Proprietor; Fourth, Pine and Chestnut streets.—The oldest as well as one of the best of the first-class hotels of St. Louis or the West, is the Planters' House. The charter was granted by the Legislature of 1836-7, but owing to the financial troubles of that period the house was not completed till 1841, when it was opened under the management of Stickney & McKnight. Several changes in proprietorship took place before Mr. Joseph Girardi, the present proprietor, acquired it.

The house in its early history at once took the lead as the fashionable and leading hotel of the place. It was the resort of the most distinguished and wealthy visitors, and the chosen scene of the fashionable balls, parties and receptions. It gained a national reputation as one of the best hotels in the country. This it still retains under the administration of Mr. Gerardi, who has added to it many conveniences not known in that day, and called to his aid in catering to the comfort of his guests all the modern conveniences in use by the best hotels. Under his efficient and experienced supervision, the house still maintains its reputation for superior accommodation, and is still a prime favorite with the traveling public. It is conducted on the most modern plan, giving to the guest a choice between the American or European methods. In addition to the table d'hote in the grand dining room, with a menu which has no superior in any hotel in the country, either in quality or variety, three first-class restaurants are attached to the house. A force of two hundred and fifty trained and experienced employes attend to the wants of the guests, and the house has three hundred rooms, recently refitted and newly and elegantly furnished. The house is a favorite at home, having a number of the best people of the city as resident boarders, and is no less esteemed by visitors to the city as a place in which their sojourn will be made pleasant. Its location is most convenient, being directly opposite the Chamber of Commerce and in the heart of the business center, near all the leading places of amusement, and reached by street car lines from every direction. Its merited success reflects great credit on Mr. Gerardi, to whose good judgment is due the perfection of its accommodations, and also upon Mr. W. H. Cunningham, who, after twenty years of efficient service as clerk has for the past two years been installed as manager. Mr. Gerardi is also the caterer of the St. Louis Jockey Club, on the track at the Fair Grounds, in which his success is no less marked than in his excellent administration of the affairs of the Planters' House.

**The Merchants' National Bank.**—James E. Yeatman, President; James C. Moore, Cashier; Corner Third and Locust streets —One of the most prosperous banking institutions in the city is the Merchants' National Bank, located at the corner of Third and Locust streets. It does a general banking business, receiving deposits, discounting approved paper, issuing foreign exchange, etc. Its capital is $700,000, and its surplus $140,000. This bank is the successor of the old Merchants' Bank, organized in April, 1857, with John A. Brownlee as president, and Robert F. Barry as cashier. In 1865 the institution was reorganized as a national bank, with W. L. Ewing as president, and James E. Yeatman as cashier. Mr. Ewing served one year and was succeeded by Robert Campbell, who also served a year, when Mr. Ewing became President for another year. From 1869 to 1872 George L. Stansbury was president, when he retired and L. B. Parsons was chosen and served until 1874, when James E. Yeatman was promoted from cashier to president, which position he has retained ever since. Succeeding Mr. Yeatman, Robert Eagle served as cashier until 1878, when he was succeeded by James C. Moore, the present incumbent. The charter of the bank expiring in 1885, it was renewed for twenty years.

**Wittenberg & Sorber.**—Designers, Photographers and Engravers on Wood; 319 North Third street.—One of the oldest firms engaged in the business of wood engraving is that of Wittenberg & Sorber, of which Messrs. Paul Wittenberg, Carl Sorber and Richard Brown are the individual members, and which was established in 1870. The premises occupied by them are eligibly located at 319 North Third street, in the heart of the business center, and employment is given to a force of twenty workmen, thoroughly skilled in all branches of the business. The work done by this firm has a just celebrity for the beauty of its designs and the finished, artistic and rapid manner of its execution. The house enjoys a large patronage from the leading manufacturers of the city. Among its regular customers can be mentioned such firms as the L. M. Rumsey Manufacturing Co., Simmons Hardware Co., Wrought Iron Range Co., N. O. Nelson Manufacturing Co., Deere. Mansur & Co., etc., and the firm is constantly employed on work for large houses in all departments of commerce and industry, making cuts for illustrated catalogues, etc. The retention of this class of patronage is the strongest possible evidence of the high merit of their work and the promptness and reliability of their methods of business. Estimates and designs are cheerfully furnished on application.

**St. Louis Car Roofing Company.**—Henry P. Wyman, President; Geo. A. Bannantine, Vice-President and Treasurer; John C. Wands. Superintendent; "Anchor Iron Car Roofing;" "Improved Winslow Iron Roof" and "Ventilated Iron Car Roof;" Office, 216 Pine street.—This business was established in 1875 by the Standard Galvanizing Works, of which Maj. John C. Wands, Superintendent of the present company, was a member, and which was succeeded by the St. Louis Car Roofing Company on its incorporation in 1883. The office of the company is eligibly located at 216 Pine street, and it has two factories, one situated on the corner of Soulard and Main streets, and the other in Carondelet between Nagle and Robert streets. These factories are completely fitted with all the machinery and equipments requisite to the successful prosecution of the business, and give employment to a force of forty skilled workmen. This company operates the only establishment of this character west of the Mississippi, and manufactures the "Anchor Iron Car Roofing" and "Improved Winslow Iron Roof." To these standard and excellent products the company has recently added another, just invented and patented by Maj. John C. Wands, and known as the "Ventilated Iron Car Roof," a contrivance of great ingenuity and high merit, by means of which perfect and uniform ventilation is given with a strong roof guaranteed to outlast the car. This great invention will doubtless cause a large increase in the business of the company, which is already of large proportions, and numbers among its patrons the leading railroads west. north and south of St. Louis. The company's facilities for manufacture are unsurpassed, while to its perfect system and efficient management it owes, in no less degree than to the merit of its goods, its high standing and prosperity.

**Western Anthracite Coal Company.**—R. C. Kerens, President; James O. Churchill, Vice-President and Manager; Charles H. Smith. Secretary; Wholesale and Retail Dealers in Anthracite and Bituminous Coal and Coke; 311 Olive street.—The business transacted under the corporate name of the Western Anthracite Coal Co. was originally established in 1881. The company owns important interests in mines, and especially that of the Bryden Coal and Coke Co., the product of which it handles largely. The office of the company is located at 311 Olive street, and its extensive shipping yards are at Nineteenth and Twentieth streets and Spruce street. It deals wholesale and retail in anthracite and bituminous coal and coke, making a specialty of delivering at all railroad points, and having, in addition to a heavy city trade, a large patronage in the State of Missouri generally, and in Illinois, Nebraska, Iowa, Kansas, Arkansas and Texas. The company possesses unexcelled facilities for handling and shipment, and is prepared to sell in any desired quantity on the most advantageous terms. The President, Mr. R. C. Kerens, is the well-known capitalist and contractor, and the Vice-President, Col. James O. Churchill, who has the management of the company's business, is well-known and greatly esteemed in commercial circles as a business man of superior attainments. He served five years and five months in the army, and was for over three years in the Eleventh Illinois volunteers. He was appointed Captain and A. Q. M. by President Lincoln, and as Major and Lieutenant Colonel by President Johnson. serving with distinction throughout the civil war. In business life, since that unhappy period, he has shown an equal adaptation to peaceful vocations.

**Westlake & Button Novelty Works Company.**—Mrs. L. R. Westlake, President; L. K. Palmer, Secretary; M. L. Westlake, Lessee of Works; Manufacturers and Jobbers of Builders' and Contractors' Outfittings; 1201 to 1217 North Main street.—One of the oldest and most prominent of the large manufacturing

establishments of this city is that of the Westlake & Button Novelty Works Co. The business was commenced in 1855 by Messrs. J. V. Westlake and A. A. Button, and the present incorporation was formed in 1874. Upon the retirement of Mr. Button, Mr. J. V. Westlake assumed the sole control of the business, and upon the death of the latter in 1883, his widow, Mrs. L. R. Westlake, was elected president, and the works and business of the company were leased to M. L. Westlake, and run under the management of H. P. Westlake, brother of the founder, by whom they have been successfully conducted ever since. The works occupy the spacious two story building embracing an area of 180x180 feet and comprising Nos. 1201 to 1217 North Main street, the office premises being located at 1213 North Main street. The works give employment to from thirty-five to fifty skilled and experienced workmen, and its lines of manufacture include all kinds of contractors', miners' and builders' outfittings, broom-makers' machinery and plant, etc., and embrace tackle blocks, manilla and wire rope, iron blocks, sheaves, capstans, etc., pilot wheels, handbarrows, boat crabs, pumps, boom derricks, builders' derricks, foundry cranes, stone travelers, pile drivers of every description, bridge and trestle bolts, car wheels, dump, platform, coal pit and mining cars; store, sidewalk and brick and mortar elevators; baggage and express barrows, railroad, warehouse and other trucks, wheel-barrows of every description, and presses, cleaners, winders, sewers, etc., for broom makers' use, together with a vast variety of goods impossible to enumerate in the space allotted to this article. The high merit of the goods and the spirit of fairness and liberality which have ever characterized its dealings have given this house the high reputation and great success it has enjoyed for over thirty years.

**Thomas L. Fekete.**—Real Estate and Financial and Insurance Agent; 107 North Fourth street, East St. Louis, Ill.—Mr. Fekete established himself as above in 1875, since which he has enjoyed a large and steadily increasing business. He attends to all the details of a legitimate real estate business, buying and selling property, loaning money on approved security, conveyancing, preparing abstracts of titles, acting as house agent, etc. He is also a notary public and prepared to take acknowledgments of deeds and instruments, and perform other notarial acts. Mr. Fekete is also a well-known underwriter, representing the following leading and substantial companies: Ætna, of Hartford; American Central, of St. Louis; Concordia, of Milwaukee; Commercial Union, of London; Liverpool and London and Globe, of England; Milwaukee Mechanics, of Wisconsin; Niagara, of New York; Northern, of England; Phœnix, of Hartford; Hecla, of Madison, Wis.; Phenix, of Brooklyn; and United States Mutual, of New York. Through these great companies, all of the highest standing and noted as prompt payers of losses, he is prepared to offer first-class insurance at the lowest rates consistent with absolute safety. Mr. Fekete has earned the high reputation he enjoys by the accuracy and reliability of his business methods.

**Great Western Oil Works of Cleveland, Ohio.**—Scrofield, Shurmer & Teagle, Independent Refiners of Petroleum; A. Whittemore, Manager St. Louis Branch; 1045 North Levee.—This large and prosperous concern is, with the exception of the Standard Oil Co., of which it is a formidable competitor, the largest refiner of petroleum in the United States, and operates on a capital of $1,000,000. The works of the company are located at Cleveland, Ohio, where they produce illuminating and lubricating oils, naphtha and gasoline in immense quantities, including among the oils manufactured by them, the following well-known brands: Standard White, 110°; Family Headlight, 150°; Royal Headlight, 175°; Palacine (or Palace Light); Snow Drop (water white); Ruby Illuminator (red oil); 63° Deodorized Naphtha; 74° Deodorized Gasoline; XXXX Light Machine; Imperial Light Machine; Amber Light Machine; Royal Cylinder; Perfection Cylinder; Olivene Cylinder; Amber Cylinder; West Virginia Black Oil; Zero Cold Test Black Oil; 15° Cold Test Black Oil, and 25° Cold Test Black Oil. The branch in this city does a large business in all the States of the West and South, and under the efficient and experienced supervision of Mr. A. Whittemore, the resident manager, has steadily increased the volume of its trade from year to year. Mr. Whittemore is a fit representative of the great company whose interests he has in charge, and a gentleman of sterling business qualities, and honorable and reliable commercial conduct.

**McKinley & Downman.**—Miners of and Dealers in Coal; 315 Olive street.—The firm of McKinley & Downman, composed of Messrs. Crittenden McKinley and John B. Downman, was established about three years ago. They are sole agents for the city of St. Louis of the Carbondale Coal and Coke Co., miners of Big Muddy and Carterville coal and coke; and dealers in Illinois and anthracite coal, which they sell to manufacturers and consumers in the city, and also ship extensively over the Iron Mountain railroad, and to all Western points. Their office is at 315 Olive street, and they have extensive yards at Twenty-first street and Pacific railroad, Jefferson avenue and Walnut street, and on the Cairo Short Line at East St. Louis. This firm controls the output of the mines of the Du Quoin Coal Mining Co., of which Crittenden McKinley is President, located at Du Quoin Ill., which have a daily capacity of eight hundred tons. This is known as the "Vulcan" coal, and is supplied to the largest manufacturers of the city requiring a high grade fuel. It is also shipped in large quantities to the West and Northwest. They also control the output of the T. & H. mine at Wilderman, Ill., amounting to four hundred tons per day. This mine is operated by the T. & H. Mining Co., of which Crittenden McKinley is President; A. Brandenburger, Vice-President; John B. Downman, Secretary, and Wm. Tirre, Superintendent. It was started about twelve years ago by Messrs. Brandenburger and Tirre, and was incorporated in 1881, Messrs. McKinley & Downman purchasing a controlling interest in it in 1886. Mr. McKinley was agent for the Carbondale Coal and Coke Co. for four years prior to the establishment of this firm. The firm have unsurpassed facilities for the handling, shipment and sale of coal and coke, and by the uniform reliability of their methods and the reasonableness of their prices have obtained a large and constantly increasing trade.

**The Continental Bank of St. Louis.**—George A. Baker, President; J. M. Thompson, Vice-President; Charles W. Bullen, Cashier; Northwest Corner of Fourth and Olive streets.—This bank was originally chartered in February, 1865, as "The National Loan Bank of St. Louis," and organized in 1866, under the State law, but the name conflicting with the National banks the directors were required to make a change and substituted the name of "Continental Bank." During the past six years the financial history of this bank has been of the most gratifying character. At the beginning of that period the capital stock of the bank was $100,000. This, under the careful and conservative methods which mark the present management, has been doubled out of the bank's earnings, the paid-up capital being now $200,000. In 1886, the bank, after paying a dividend of 8 per cent. upon its capital stock, passed 20 per cent. to its surplus account, and its surplus fund amounted, at the opening of business for the present year, to $73,829.80. The bank is justly regarded as one of the most substantial of the financial institutions of the city, and does a live, active business, carrying the accounts of many of the leading commercial houses and manufacturing firms. The present board of directors is composed of the following substantial and prominent gentlemen: J. M. Thompson, H. A. Crawford, I. G. Baker, E. C. Meacham, C. W. Rogers, George W. Parker, Joseph Hill, C. S. Freeborn, R. C. Kerens, Chas. F. Gauss and George A. Baker.

**J. L. Woolf & Brother.**—Job Lot Emporium for Trunks, Bags, Clothing, Hats, Caps, etc.; 418 Washington avenue.—The live and energetic firm of J. L. Woolf & Bro., composed of Messrs. J. L. and George Woolf, was originally established in 1861 as merchant tailors, which they changed to their present business in 1879.  They also carried on two general stores in Missouri, two in Illinois and one in Texas until four years ago, when they consolidated all their capital and enterprise into the growing business which they have brought to a point of eminent success at the four story and basement building which they occupy at 418 Washington avenue, and which has a frontage of 25 feet by a depth of 100 feet. They do a very large business in the purchase of goods in the line of clothing, boots and shoes, hats, hosiery, gents' furnishing goods, laces, braids, corsets, etc.; notions, musical instruments, etc., at assignee, government, underwriters' and receivers' sales in every prominent city of the Union, and sell in job lots at wholesale only, at prices that cannot be duplicated. They are also agents for the St. Louis Trunk Manufacturing Co., and carry the full line of their make of trunks, traveling bags and satchels. They also act as purchasing agents, buying goods at wholesale at auction, for which they have unsurpassed facilities. They have a large patronage extending throughout Missouri, Arkansas, Nebraska, Kansas, Texas, Mississippi, Tennessee, Kentucky, Illinois, Iowa, Montana, Arizona, New Mexico and Indian Territory. They have had a phenomenal success, which they have achieved by tireless energy and a close attention to every detail of their business.

**F. W. Rosenthal & Company.**—Importers and Dealers in Wall Paper, Carpets, Rugs, Curtain Goods, Etc.; 410 and 412 North Fourth street.—This old and representative business house was established in 1854 as Zimmerman & Rosenthal, the present senior of the house, Mr. F. W. Rosenthal, being a member of the original firm, which was succeeded by F. W. Rosenthal & Co. The other principal in the house is Mr. C. W. Rosenthal, and the business is now located in the spacious five-story premises, 60x120 feet, comprising 410 and 412 North Fourth street. In the building at 410 is conducted their business as importers and dealers in fine wall paper and Lincrusta Walton, which they handle more extensively than any other concern west of New York, having an immense and steadily growing patronage in the States of Missouri, Illinois, Iowa, Nebraska, Kansas, Arkansas, New Mexico, Louisiana, Tennessee and Texas, as well as a heavy city trade. Their stock in these goods is of the finest quality and most complete assortment. At the adjoining building, 412 North Fourth street, is their wholesale and retail carpet store and warehouse, where they carry a large and thoroughly diversified stock of carpets, rugs, oilcloth, etc., of every description, chiefly of American manufacture, the domestic goods in this line being in every way equal to those of foreign make. They also carry full lines of the finest imported lace curtains, rich draperies, portieres, lambrequins and all window cornices, poles and furnishings. A force of sixty competent assistants is employed in the house, while seven wide-awake commercial travelers represent the interests of the firm on the road. The superior quality of the goods handled by this house, combined with reliable methods in the conduct of its affairs, has established for it an excellent reputation and a great and merited prosperity.

**H. Brentano & Co.**—Stock Brokers; 23 Gay Building, 204 North Third street.—A firm of stock brokers which enjoys a large patronage and does an extensive business is that of H. Brentano & Co., the office of which is eligibly located at room 23, Gay building, 204 North Third street. They deal in United States, state, county and municipal bonds, railroad, insurance, mining and miscellaneous stocks. Their facilities for advantageous dealing in these securities are unsurpassed and every commission entrusted to their hands is given close and earnest attention. A thorough knowledge of the markets enables them to embrace every opportunity to advance the interests of their customers, and to their reliable methods is due the high standing they hold in the financial circle.

**Buxton & Skinner Stationery Company.**—Charles M. Skinner, President and Treasurer; A. H. Frederick, Secretary: Artistic Lithograpers and Printers, Blank-Book Manufacturers and Stationers; 215 and 217 Chestnut street.—This is the largest and most complete establishment of its kind in the city. It was originally established in 1870 by the firm of Buxton & Skinner, the present company being organized and incorporated in 1881. The premises occupied by the company consist of a commodious six-story building 40x100 feet, with a warehouse in the rear, two stories high and covering an area of 50x100 feet. The premises are fully equipped with all the requisite modern machinery and appliances adapted to the requirements of the business, and employment is given to a force of one hundred and twenty-five skilled and experienced men. The company does all kinds of printing and lithographing, blank-book manufacturing, etc., and carries a large and thoroughly diversified stock of stationery and office supplies. This house is headquarters for mining and stock certificates and stationery supplies for mining and all stock companies, the great superiority and artistic finish of its work in this department placing in it the lead, and the company has recently printed stock certificates for some fifty different mining companies, all of which were entirely satisfactory and much commended for their workmanship. The house does a very large business in the city and also in the States of Missouri, Illinois, Kansas, Nebraska, Arkansas and Texas, in which trade territory seven active and energetic commercial travelers represent the house on the road. Conducting their business on fair and liberal principles, thoroughly systematizing their transactions and resting their reputation on the uniform superiority of their workmanship and merit of their goods, the company has attained a high standing and a permanent success.

**H. M. Blossom & Co.**—Fire and Marine Insurance; 217 North Third Street.—For over a quarter of a century Mr. H. M. Blossom has been prominently identified with the insurance interests of St. Louis, and is an officer in the St. Louis Board of Underwriters. In the fifties he was clerk and part owner in the Missouri river boats "Hiawatha" and "Polar Star," but left the river traffic in 1861 to engage in his present business. He was afterward joined by his nephew, Mr H. A. Blossom, a gentleman of high business attainments and experience, and these two form the firm of H. M. Blossom & Co., representing the following substantial and popular insurance corporations: Imperial Fire Insurance Co., of London; Commercial Union Assurance Co., of London; Phœnix Insurance Co., of Hartford; Connecticut Fire Insurance Co., of Hartford: St. Paul Fire and Marine Insurance Co., of St. Paul; Citizens' Insurance Co., of Pittsburgh; Farmers' Insurance Co., of New York; Commercial Insurance Co., of Albany; Boston Marine Insurance Co., of Boston; Phenix Insurance Co., of New York: Mercantile Fire and Marine Insurance Co., of Boston; and the Spring Garden Insurance Co., of Philadelphia. The Imperial Fire, of London, established for more than a century, has assets in the United States of $1,500,000, and took fire risks in Missouri during 1886 amounting to $2,053,892 The Commercial Union, of London, wrote risks in this State last year amounting to $4,230,128; the Phœnix, of Hartford, $7,394,211; the Connecticut, of Hartford, $4,131,375; and the other companies enumerated also carried large amounts. Those desiring insurance cannot do better than consult the firm of H. M. Blossom & Co., who do a large business, and whose relations with the insuring public have always been cordial and satisfactory.

**S. N. Long Syrup Company.**—S. N. Long, President; Geo. L. Fielding, Secretary; Syrup Manufacturers; 315 and 317 North Main street.—A very prominent establishment, having a special and valuable line of manufacture, is that of the S. N. Long Syrup Co. The business was inaugurated in 1885 and was incorporated in July, 1886. The company occupies the commodious premises at 315 and 317 North Main street, comprising two four-story buildings, each 25x150 feet, and also uses outside warehouses, to a considerable extent, for storage purposes. The company manufactures and sells to the jobbing trade and wholesale grocers, maple syrups, and also all kinds of sugar syrups, under a process of their own, which gives the syrups a specially pleasant flavor and prevents their fermenting. They also have a process for treating molasses which keeps it from fermenting. They carry the largest stock of syrups and molasses west of New York, and do an immense business in this city, Kansas City. St. Paul and all the West and Northwest, and through the large jobbing houses to all parts of the country. The great superiority of their goods and the perfect business methods of this great house have given it an unexcelled reputation in trade circles.

**The Goodyear Rubber Company.**—Principal Office, New York City; St. Louis Branch, 400 North Fourth street: Geo. B. Thomson, Agent; Manufacturers, Importers and Wholesale Dealers in Goodyear's Rubber Goods.—

The largest concern in the world in its line is the Goodyear Rubber Co., which has its principal office in New York City, and factories at Bristol, R.I.; Middleton, Ct.; Elizabeth, N.J.; Lambertsville, N. J.; San Francisco, Cal., and Harlem, N. Y., and warehouses in the principal cities of the country. The St. Louis house was established in 1866, and under the experienced and efficient management of Mr. Geo. B. Thomson has enjoyed great prosperity and a steadily increasing business in Missouri, Southern Illinois, Arkansas and the entire South. In the house here, twenty-two clerks and assistants are employed, and four traveling salesmen from this branch represent the company on the road. The premises occupied comprise a four-story building, 30x135 feet, and the stock carried embraces all lines of the Goodyear Rubber Co.'s goods, including rubber clothing, rubber boots and shoes, belting, packing, hose, druggists' rubber goods, etc. All of these goods are of the best and finest manufactured, the name of Goodyear being the recognized synonym for unequalled excellence in every description of rubber goods. Mr. Thomson, the manager of the St. Louis house, is a worthy representative of the great corporation whose interests in this section he has in charge, and throughout the period of twenty-one years, during which he has carried on this business, has enjoyed, in an eminent degree, the esteem and confidence of the business community. He is prominent in efforts to promote the commercial prosperity of the city, and by close attention to every detail of the business and fidelity to the interests of his principals has made the St. Louis house one of the most successful and popular of the company's branches.

**Krafft-Holmes Grocery Company.**—J. C. Krafft, President; J. R. Holmes, Vice-President; J. W. Scudder, Secretary; Wholesale Grocers; 614 to 620 North Fourth street; 613 to 619 North Third street.—The important wholesale grocery house, incorporated in 1884 under the style of the Krafft-Holmes Grocery Co., was originally established in 1870 by the firm of Krafft, Holmes & Co. The history of the house has been one of continuous advance, its business having steadily increased from year to year, until it now requires the services of fifty experienced clerks and assistants at its store, and eighteen active traveling men representing it in its extensive trade territory, embracing the States of Illinois, Missouri, Kansas, Iowa, Nebraska, Colorado and all west to and including the Pacific Coast States and the entire West and South. The company occupies a spacious and imposing six-story-and-basement structure fronting on three streets: North Fourth, Christy avenue, and North Third street, and covering Nos. 614 to 620 North Fourth street and 613 to 619 North Third street. This edifice was built expressly for the company by Mr. John A. Scudder, father of the Secretary, and is fitted with every convenience for facilitating the business of the house. The stock carried by the company is immense, and covers every article embraced in the lines of staple and fancy groceries and grocers' sundries and shelf goods. Messrs. Krafft and Holmes are both prominent in the commercial world and identified with many enterprises looking to the advancement of the business interests of the city, and the Krafft-Holmes Grocery Co. is distinguished by the amplitude of its resources, the wisdom and good judgment of its business management, and the accuracy which characterizes all its transactions. It enjoys its great prosperity as the legitimate result of superior goods and the uniformly satisfactory character of its relations with the trade.

**American Wine Company.**—D. G. Cook, President; H. G. Provines, Secretary; Cook's Imperial Champagne, Extra Dry and Pure Still Wines; Office, Wine House and Vaults, 3015 to 3021 Cass avenue.—That all the conditions for the production of wine of quality equal to the best made in France exist in the United States has often been declared, and that this is not the mere assertion of the theorist has been amply proved by the American Wine Company, who, in "Cook's Imperial Champagne," have produced a wine conceded by connoisseurs equal, if not superior, to the best imported article. The business was established in 1859 by Mr. Isaac Cook, the present company being incorporated in 1867. Mr. D. G. Cook, now President of the company, is the son of its founder. The company has a large press-house and wine cellars at Sandusky, Ohio, in which State the company buys its grapes, the fruit being pressed at Sandusky and thence shipped to this city for bottling. The company's wine vaults in this city are by far the largest in the United States, the cellars being fifty feet under the surface and 100x150 feet in surface dimensions, the ice cellars having a capacity of 1,000 tons. They have a capacity for 150,000 gallons at one time, and employ their own coopers, and do their washing and bottling on the premises; having all the machinery and appliances for the business and facilities for washing over 12,000 bottles daily and for corking 10,000 daily. A force of forty men is employed in the various departments during the bottling season. In addition to the vaults and cooperage facilities the company has storage capacity for one and a half million bottles, which is always full during the season. The wines produced by this company have taken many prizes at international expositions, not only in this country, but also in Europe. "Cook's Imperial Champagne" can be found on the wine list of every first-class hotel and restaurant in this country as well as in the leading hotels, clubs and private wine cellars in European countries. The trade of the company is of immense proportions, and is especially large in the country east of the Rocky Mountains. It grows annually, and the prosperity which has attended its efforts to introduce an American wine of which Americans have a right to be proud is a source of gratification to those interested in the industrial progress of the nation.

**S. G. Burnham.**—Stationer, Printer, Lithographer, etc.: 112 Olive street.—In the line of stationery, printing, lithographing, etc., Mr. S. G. Burnham has been successfully engaged since 1877. He occupies the premises at 112 Olive street, four stories high, with 25 feet front and running back 100 feet. He keeps on hand a large and completely diversified assortment of stationery goods, including blank books of all styles, sizes and bindings, letter books, pens, pencils, ink, paper and a full line of stationery sundries. He does general printing promptly and in the highest style of the art, giving employment to sixteen skilled and experienced workmen. He makes a specialty of blank books and letter copying books, for the manufacture of which his facilities are unsurpassed. He does a large and prosperous trade, the bulk of his patronage coming from city merchants, to whom he has commended himself by the merit of his work and the fairness and correct principles which characterize his dealings.

**F. H. Logeman Chair Manufacturing Company.**—F. H. Logeman, President; W. H. Logeman, Vice-President; C. A. Logeman, Secretary; Manufacturers of Chairs; 2000 to 2028 North Main street.—With an honorable and successful career of a third of a century behind it; a business amounting to a quarter of a million dollars annually with it in the living present; and a reputation and patronage giving promise of a still more prosperous future before it, no hive of industry in the city is more worthy of mention than that of the F. H. Logeman Chair Manufacturing Co. The business was established in 1853, by Mr. F. H. Logeman, now the honored President of the company. In 1855 Mr. Conrades became a member of the firm, the business being carried on as Conrades and Logeman until 1883, when, upon the retirement of Mr. Conrades, the firm took its present corporate name with F. H. Logeman as President; W. H. Logeman, his brother, as Vice-President, and C. A. Logeman, son of the President, as Secretary, with a capital stock of $200,000. The premises occupied by the company cover a whole block at the intersection of Main and Madison streets, 240x440 feet in dimensions. The office and salesrooms occupy a seven-story building 60x100 feet; the warerooms adjoining a seven-story building, 75x75 feet, and the factories and workshops adjoining fill the remainder of the block, running back to the railroad tracks. The factories, which are completely equipped with modern and improved machinery, give employment to from 250 to 300 skilled workmen, according to the season and the demand, and five energetic and experienced travelers are employed as representatives of the house. The factory is the oldest in its line in the city, and the largest in the West, and its patronage covers the entire United States, and reaches into Canada and Mexico. The company manufactures all kinds of parlor, dining, easy, rocking and every description of chairs, of which they keep an immense stock and complete assortment, and ship, principally in carload lots, in every direction. Chairs of their make have a high reputation for their superiority in materials, workmanship and finish, and to this fact, combined with the tact and judgment which characterize the business methods of the company, is due its high standing with the trade and the immensity of its business.

**Lungstras Dyeing and Cleaning Company.**—Eugene Lungstras, President and Treasurer; Charles Springe, Secretary; Works, 1300 to 1318 Park avenue; City Branch Store, 105 and 107 North Sixth street.—This establishment was founded in 1872 by Eugene Lungstras, and is the largest concern of its kind in the Western country. The works occupy nearly an entire block of ground and have a frontage

on Park avenue, Thirteenth and Linn streets. The history of this establishment is one of interest and illustrates what energy and industry will accomplish if properly applied. Mr. Lungstras was formerly a resident of Sedalia, in the western part of the State, and removed to St. Louis in 1871 and engaged in the dyeing business on a moderate scale. His knowledge and experience soon became known and business prospered with him so rapidly that his facilities were increased again and again until the works are now the most complete in the United States. In 1882 Mr. Lungstras incorporated his business under the present name, and selected as his assistant in the management of the business Mr. Charles Springe, the Secretary, who is also a gentleman of practical experience. The company are enabled to meet an extensive commercial demand for the dyeing and cleaning of goods in the piece and other wares uncut and unworn. A very large business is done in dyeing and cleaning for merchants in the city and throughout the West and South. Several new processes are employed at these works, and the cleaning and recarding of wool blankets is a specialty. The city branch or down town store is located in the elegant fire-proof building at 105 and 107 North Sixth street. The extensive patronage of this company and the enterprising character of the business exertions of President Lungstras and Secretary Springe have placed it among the leading industries of the city.

**American Refrigerator Transit Company.**—Reid Northrop, President; General Office, 100 North Third street.—This company was incorporated in 1881, and does an immense business in the transportation of all kinds of perishable freight, without transfer or delay, to the East, West, North and South, and is the only line running Local Refrigerator Cars to Texas and the seaboard. The property of the company, including cars, equipment, warehouses, etc., is valued at over $1,000,000, and its hauling capacity is 10,000 loads per annum, in the transportation of which it consumes 15,000 tons of ice. The company has a warehouse at the Iron Mountain Railroad, the largest and first erected in the country, built upon the same plan as the cars. The general office of the company is located at 100 North Third street and Mr. Reid Northrop, who was General Superintendent of the company for four years until that office was abolished, was in November, 1886, elected President of the company. Under his enterprising and able management the business of the company, already very large and extending to all parts of the Union, Canada and Mexico, is steadily increasing. The company is prepared to issue foreign and domestic bills of lading to all points and enjoys unsurpassed facilities for the transportation of perishable freight. The company has branch offices in Chicago, New York and Kansas City and representation at all prominent points in the country.

**Graham Paper Company.**—Ben. B. Graham, President; H. B. Graham, Vice-President; A. D. Cooper, Treasurer and Secretary; Wholesale Paper and Paper Stock; 217 and 219 North Main street.—Those great mercantile establishments which have thrived through good and bad seasons, and after many years have reached great size, form the worthiest monuments a city can boast. Of this class St. Louis furnishes no more striking representative than the Graham Paper Company, wholesale dealers in paper and paper stock. This business was founded in 1855, and after a successful career of twenty-five years was incorporated in 1880, since which the growth of the business has been still more marked, and their field of operations still more widely extended, until it now covers the entire territory to Portland, Oregon, and from Canada to the Gulf of Mexico. The company controls and handles the product of a number of the largest mills in the Northern and Eastern States, and carries very heavy stocks of everything in the line of paper and paper stock. The premises at 217 and 219 North Main street, being two stores, five stories, each 40x150 feet, are used by the company as salesrooms and offices. In addition to this they occupy a warehouse of two high stories, covering a quarter of a block, at 1229 to 1237 North Sixth street, which they use for their paper stock; another track warehouse, three stories high, and covering a quarter of a block, at the corner of Main and Brooklyn streets, which they use for rag storage; and premises used as a paper warehouse, occupying five floors of No. 214 and one floor of 212 North Main street, each 32x100 feet. They have a branch house at Kansas City, and agencies at San Francisco, Salt Lake City and other points. They employ over 150 experienced hands, and their annual sales amount to over $1,000,000. Their business is thoroughly systematized, and great as are its proportions is managed upon the most accurate methods, and works with the precision of a well-regulated machine.

**M. Shaughnessy & Co.**—Wholesale Wines and Liquors; 121 Locust street.—The house of M. Shaughnessy & Co., importers and dealers in wines, liquors, etc., was founded in 1880 and has enjoyed a large and steadily growing business since its establishment. The premises occupied by the firm consist of a five-story building with a frontage of 25 feet by a depth of 100 feet at 121 Locust street. The stock of the house is large and thoroughly diversified, embracing all kinds of wines and liquors, selected with reference to their purity and excellence, for which the goods handled by this house are justly celebrated. The firm does a large business with drug stores, saloons, etc. in the city, as well as in Illinois, Missouri, Kansas and all the territory tributary to the St. Louis market. The house has achieved the high reputation it enjoys and the success which has attended its career not only as a result of the merit of the goods it handles, but also in consequence of its fair and liberal treatment of its customers and the correctness of its business methods.

**Smith-Davis Manufacturing Company.**—J. G. Smith, President; H. N. Davis, Secretary; Manufacturers of Spring, Wire and Iron Beds; Office and Factory, Twenty-third street and Lucas avenue.—This large manufacturing concern was originally established in 1871, by the firm of J. G. Smith & Co., to which the present company succeeded on its incorporation in 1882. The founder of the business, Mr. J. G. Smith, still remains at the head of the company as its president, and directs its affairs with the same ability and experienced judgment that have built up the business to its present important proportions as one of the largest concerns in its line in the West. The spacious manufactory of the company is supplied with all the most modern and improved plant and appliances necessary to its successful operation, and gives employment to a force of one hundred men. The company has acquired a solid reputation for the superior merit of its manufactured products, including spring, wire and iron beds, canvas and wire cots and excelsior, and enjoys a large and constantly expanding trade which reaches every section of the Union.

**E. H. Warner.**—Wholesale Lumber Dealer; Marion and Kosciusko streets.—For the past nine years Mr. Warner has been extensively and successfully engaged in business as a wholesale lumber dealer. His yards, which cover an entire block, are completely stocked with every description of hardwood lumber as well as a very large stock of yellow pine. He has every facility for the handling, piling and shipment of lumber, and is prepared to fill orders for the largest quantities in the most prompt and satisfactory manner. He does a large trade in the States of Missouri, Kansas, Iowa, Nebraska and Illinois, in all of which he has earned and possesses a high standing in the trade for the accuracy and reliability of his business methods and the fairness and liberality by which all his dealings are characterized.

**Sect Wine Company.**—H. Koehler, Sr., President; O. C. Koehler, Superintendent; H. Koehler, Jr., Secretary and Treasurer; Champagne and Still Wines; Champagne Vaults, 2814 to 2824 South Seventh street.—This prominent and prosperous

establishment has been successfully engaged in the wine business since 1880. The wine house of the company in this city covers about one-fourth of a block and they have two stories of cellars, 40,000 square feet each, taking in the whole block, and giving them unsurpassed storage capacity. They produce and deal in champagne and still wines, their brand of champagne, "Koehler's Sect" being widely and favorably known. It is made by the French process of fermenting grape juice in the bottle, being the precise method by which all the celebrated imported brands are made. The effervescence is produced from the wine itself, and is not artificially charged, as in imitation sparkling wines. From three to four years of time are required to finish champagne in this manner, great watchfulness and skill being constantly necessary. The firm have imported several experienced men from Rheims in France. Koehler's Sect enjoys an enviable reputation, and may be found on the wine lists of all first-class hotels, restaurants and saloons in the land. Our illustration shows the racking or clearing department of the Sect Wine Co., where the champagne is cleared of sediment after fermentation. The still wines of this firm are celebrated for their great purity, and general excellence, which is easily explained on the ground that they purchase no wines, but press all grapes at their own press houses in this city, the grapes coming from different parts of the country, mostly from the islands of Lake Erie. Thirty men are employed in the vaults, and a staff of traveling salesmen represent the company on the road. The merit of their wines and the reliability of their dealings have secured for them a pronounced and steadily growing success.

**Noxon, Albert & Toomey.**—Scenic Artists; Studios Olympic Theatre and Grand Opera House, St. Louis; Chicago Opera House, Chicago; and Groves' Opera House, Cedar Rapids, Iowa.—This famous trio of scenic artists enjoy a reputation in their line second to none in America. Specimens of their artistic workmanship are to be seen in leading theatres and opera houses all over the United States. Thomas Noxon, the senior member of the firm, is a veteran painter and has resided in St. Louis for upwards of a quarter of a century. Many of the finest drop curtains, and much of the fine theatrical scenery that has been seen in the United States, have been the work of his artistic brush. He is a born artist, and is acknowledged to stand at the head of his profession. His associates, Messrs. Albert and Toomey, are also artists of rare ability. The firm is constantly occupied with work not only from local places of amusement, but from some of the largest theatres of other localities. The firm this season have received contracts for the decorations and scenery of the Bowersick Opera House, Lawrence, Kansas; John L. Park Opera House, Fort Smith, Arkansas; the New Club and Opera House at San Antonio, Texas; Vendome Theatre, Nashville, Tennessee; the elaborate scenery to be used during the famous tour of Messrs. Booth and Barrett, season commencing September, 1887; the grand spectacular productions of the Arabian Nights, intended to be the most elaborate scenic production ever on the American stage and its first production June 1st, 1887, at the Chicago Opera House, and many other places of amusement in course of erection. Among the numerous contracts secured by this firm the present year, and one that is a flattering testimonial to their merit and reliability, is that of the New Music Hall, Buffalo, New York. This magnificent structure will cost nearly $1,500,000, and the scenery alone will aggregate nearly $30,000. The competitors for this contract included the leading scenic artists of the world. The contract was obtained by Noxon, Albert & Toomey, although they were the highest bidders but one. In the test of merit they came out victorious and carried off the contract.

**Sam'l A. Gaylord & Company.**—Bankers and Brokers; 307 Olive street.— The firmly established reputation for solidity and reliability possessed by the firm of Sam'l A. Gaylord & Co., of which Messrs. Sam'l A. Gaylord and John H. Blessing are the members, has attached to this house since it began business in 1861. In that year Mr. Gaylord, with his father and brother, inaugurated this business, the firm afterwards becoming Gaylord, Leavenworth & Co., and in 1866 adopting the present style. Mr. Blessing was employed by Mr. Gaylord from 1869 to 1880, when he acquired an interest in the business. The firm has its office at 307 Olive street and does a large business in the purchase and sale of Government, State, County, Municipal, Railroad and Default Bonds, United States Land Warrants, and all leading stocks, making a specialty of "Small Hopes," "Adams" and other dividend paying mining stocks, and is also prepared to execute orders for all mining stocks that have a market value. Mr. Gaylord has been actively engaged in the banking and brokerage business in St. Louis since 1849, and the firm's operations are all conducted with experience and sound judgment. It is unsurpassed as a medium for transactions relating to the purchase or sale of investment securities.

**Fleischmann & Co.**—Original Manufacturers and Introducers into the United States of Compressed Yeast; H. C. Robinson, Agent; 17 and 19 South Eleventh street.—The art of bread-making has been greatly improved since the introduction of compressed yeast, and this service was rendered to the American people by the firm of Fleischmann & Co., whose headquarters in this country are at New York and Cincinnati. They have branches in all the leading cities of the country, the St. Louis branch having being under the faithful and efficient management of Mr. H. C. Robinson, and doing a large business in Missouri, Kansas, Arkansas, Texas, Iowa and Illinois. The Western home office at Cincinnati is in charge of Mr. Charles Fleischmann. The firm have an immense business in all quarters of the globe, their European headquarters being in London, and the St. Louis branch, which has been established fifteen years, is one of the most prosperous, employing twenty men and seven wagons and doing a large city trade in addition to its thriving business in the outside territory assigned to the management of Agent Robinson.

**E. P. Gray.**—Publisher, Importer, Bookseller and Stationer; Manufacturer of Christmas and Birthday Novelties, Valentines, Etc.; Sole Agent for the Ætna Paper and Envelope Co., and Lew. Isaacs & Co. Glucinum Pens; 501 North Fourth street.— This business was established about forty years ago by Mr. E. P. Gray. He carries complete stocks of books, periodicals, albums, bibles, praise books, fine presentation books, fine cutlery, morocco and fancy leather goods, etc. He manufactures fine Christmas, New Year, Easter and birthday novelties, valentines, school writing books, tablets, scribbling blocks, etc., handles all the latest literature in books and periodicals, fancy goods in great variety, full line of stationery of every description, and is sole agent for the celebrated Ætna paper and envelopes and Lew. Isaacs & Co.'s glucinum pens. He has a large and constantly increasing business, including, in addition to an extensive city patronage, a trade extending throughout the South and West. He has fifteen clerks and assistants and is represented on the road by a staff of traveling salesmen. The prompt and satisfactory manner in which he fills all contracts and the fair and liberal methods adopted by him in carrying on the business have secured for him a great and merited success.

**Pioneer Steam Keg Works Company.**—Wm. Brown, President; Daniel S. Brown, Vice-President; Prentiss J. Batchelor, Secretary and Treasurer; Firman Jessup, Superintendent; Stave Factory, Brownwood, Mo.; Keg Factory and Office, 2212 De Kalb street.—These works were the first of their kind west of the Mississippi, and were established in 1854 by Mr. Wm. Brown, President of the present company. The original establishment was too insignificant for comparison with the present great concern, yet it is the same, and has, under the able management of Mr. Brown, grown to its present great proportions, and, as forcibly as any other enterprise that can be named, illustrates the remarkable progress and general expansion of the manufacturing interests of St. Louis and the West. The company was incorporated in 1886, and all of the present officers were members of the firm of Wm. Brown & Co., so many years in existence. There are 225 employes in the service of the company, and the capacity of the factory is about 7,000 kegs a day. The product goes to all sections of the country, and a large part of the output is turned over to the Samuel Cupples Wooden Ware Co., who act as the jobbers in its general distribution.

**Shultz Belting Company.**—John A. J. Shultz, President; Wm. P. Mullen, Vice-President; B. C. Alvord, Secretary; Manufacturers of the Shultz Patent Fulled Leather Belting, Lace and Picker Leather, Etc.; Southwest Corner of Bismarck and Barton streets.—This important corporation has a capital stock of $300,000 and occupies spacious premises 309x307 feet in area. The works are equipped with a plant not excelled anywhere, and embracing a large amount of special machinery which is the invention of President Shultz, used by no other establishment and

specially adapted to the manufacture of Fulled Leather Belting, Lace and Picker Leather. The products of these works have attained a just celebrity for softness, pliability and elasticity combined with durability, and the superiority of this company's manufacture is attested by an annual increase in the volume of its sales, and a steady expansion in its trade territory which now embraces, as well as all the States of the Union, the Dominion of Canada and the principal countries of Europe, in which agencies are maintained in the leading cities as well as at all the important points in this country. The superiority of the company's processes of manufacture is due to the inventive genius of President Shultz, who is a practical and experienced tanner, and has devoted several years to perfecting improvements in the manufacture of belting. The company is a strong one, has ample resources and every facility and convenience for manufacturing and marketing its products. Over one hundred men are employed at the works, and the operations of the company are conducted upon a perfect and accurate system. The board of directors is composed of the following well-known and substantial business men: L. G. Kammerer, Wm. P. Mullen, S. C. Bunn, H. F. Mueller and J. A. J. Shultz.

**F. O. Sawyer & Co.**—Wholesale Paper Dealers; 301 and 303 North Second street.—The oldest paper house in St. Louis, and one of the largest and most prosperous in the entire West, is that of F. O. Sawyer & Co., which was established in 1859 by Mr. F. O. Sawyer. In 1863 the firm became Johnson & Sawyer, but in 1875 adopted its present style, which it still retains. The premises occupied by the firm comprise a roomy five-story structure, with a frontage of 50 feet by a depth of 150 feet, at 301 and 303 North Second street, where the business is conducted with the efficient aid of fifteen competent assistants. The firm deals wholesale in every description of printers' and binders' paper stock, printed wrapping papers, the best and heaviest in the market, and Western satchel-bottom paper bags which are unsurpassed, besides every article in the paper line, including the manufactures of the Globe Envelope Co., for which the firm are sole Western agents. They control the output of several of the largest and most prominent paper mills in the country, and do a very large business in this city and the entire State of Missouri as well as in Indiana, Illinois, Iowa, Kansas, Nebraska, Arkansas, Texas and other States, and keep three active and energetic commercial travelers constantly on the road in the interests of the house. Much of the trade of the house is in car load lots, and no firm or company in its line possesses better facilities for filling orders promptly and of any desired magnitude. In the whole course of the long business history of this house, its reputation has been unsurpassed for meritorious goods, strict reliability and fair and equitable methods. Its trade has steadily grown and it retains its high standing in the commercial world by a rigid steadfastness to the principles which have ever actuated its dealings.

**Hill-Settle Tobacco Company.**—Richard T. Hill, President; Thomas T. Settle, Secretary and Treasurer; Sole Manufacturers of Concentrated Extract of Tobacco, and Extract of Tobacco Salve; 114 Pine street.—This business was established in 1879 for the purpose of manufacturing a patented "Concentrated Extract of Tobacco for Sheep Dip." The firm was originally Hill, Slayden & Settle, and was afterwards incorporated as the Hill-Settle Tobacco Co., in 1882. The company are sole manufacturers and patentees of "Concentrated Extract of Tobacco for Sheep Dip," which they ship to all sheep raising portions of the country, but more largely to South Africa, South America, and Australia. In addition to the manufacture of the sheep dip they are also sole manufacturers of a "Tobacco Salve" for cuts, wounds, etc., for man or beast, largely used by stockmen, express companies, transfer companies, and livery teaming companies. Another branch of their business is the manufacture of the celebrated "Tabacan," an infallible remedy for piles, a discovery of their own, and they also deal largely in tobacco stems, which they ship east and as far south as Florida, for fertilizing purposes. The extent of their business in this line is shown by the fact that they bought from Liggett & Myers, alone 395,000 lbs. of tobacco stems last September. Their factory is situate on Theresa avenue and Missouri Pacific R. R., and is 150x150 feet in dimensions. Their office is located at 114 Pine street. Their trade is immense in its proportions, their sheep dip being far superior to any other compound manufactured for the same purpose, and their other articles equally meritorious for the purposes for which they are manufactured. The success which has attended their efforts to introduce these goods has resulted from this excellence, combined with the thorough system pervading their management of their affairs, and fairness and liberality with which they conduct their dealings with their customers in all parts of the world.

**St. Louis Tent Manufacturing Company.**—Thomas Morrison, Proprietor; Tents, Awnings, Wagon Covers, etc.; 214 North Second street.—In 1866 Mr. Thomas Morrison started in the boat store and rigging business at the corner of Pine street and North Levee. The introduction of wire rigging made this business no longer profitable, and he started, in 1874, his present business of manufacturing wagon covers, tents, tarpaulins, awnings, flags, ore bags, etc. He occupies a commodious five-story building, 25x150, at 214 North Second street, and gives constant employment to thirty girls and ten to twelve awning men. His business is very large, covering 50 per cent of the awning business of the city, and a large trade in all his other lines, especially in tents, which he sells extensively to railroad contractors. He sells as far east as Pennsylvania and New York, all south to Florida, Alabama and Texas, and west to California, Oregon and Washington Territory. His reputation for superiority in materials and workmanship is very high, and to this, combined with the marked fairness and liberality that characterize his dealings, he owes the great success he has achieved.

**Pond Engineering Company.**—Frank H. Pond, Proprietor; Engineers and Contractors of Steam and Hydraulic Machinery; Masonic Building, 707 & 709 Market street.—This house was established in 1877. During the past ten years this company has acquired a vast business, extending from Ohio to the Pacific Coast and from Canada to Mexico, in the furnishing

and erection of motive power for manufacturing establishments, water works, electric light plants, etc., including engines, boilers, furnaces, grates, heaters, pumps, injectors, valves, piping, belting, etc., which they deliver to purchasers in perfect running order, with special reference to simplicity of construction, ease of operation and economy in fuel. They have furnished the motive power to many of the largest mills and manufacturing establishments of this and other cities. They also do a large business in furnishing complete pumping plants for city water works, over a score of Western cities having been supplied with their machinery by this company, leaving them in successful operation. They have furnished a large number of electric light stations in the West, with their specialties, which are giving the best of satisfaction and most economical results. They are also prepared with all the necessary apparatus for testing the efficiency of any device or machine. Having devoted their closest attention to engineering and contracting for many years the Pond Engineering Co. is prepared to submit plans, specifications, estimates or proposals on the most advantageous terms and to execute work in their line in the most skillful and scientific manner. Every contract undertaken by them has been completed in a satisfactory manner, and they have acquired a solid and substantial reputation and a position as leaders in their line in the Western country. The Pond Engineering Co. publish each year, for free distribution, a complete illustrated catalogue of their specialties. Their 1887 catalogue is just being issued from the press, and those wishing to purchase engines, boilers, grates, heaters, pumps, injectors, valves, piping, etc., will find it to their advantage to send for this catalogue before placing their orders.

**Mutual Reserve Fund Life Association.**—New York: E. B. Harper, President; Wm. A. Brawner, General Manager Missouri and Southern Illinois Department; 718 Pine street.—This prosperous insurance corporation was organized in 1881, and has ever since done a large and steadily expanding business. The object of the association is to provide for the families of deceased members by furnishing to the policy-holders a perfect insurance at the lowest cost consistent with the greatest possible security. The system embraces an equitably adjusted Tontine Reserve Fund, made up of one-quarter of the mortuary receipts, and a number of other features peculiar to this association, and all in the direction of economy in expense and the interest of the assured. The system furnishes insurance at cost upon the actual death rate experienced, and the cost of insurance is about 60 per cent. less than in the old line companies. The Manager of the Missouri and Southern Illinois Department of the company's business is Mr. William A. Brawner, under whose experienced and efficient supervision the business of the association has greatly prospered in this region. In order to stimulate their agents to greater efforts the association offers prizes for the largest amount of business in each year. Mr. Brawner has carried off three first prizes and several second prizes. He wrote over $3,500,000 of insurance here last year, and has paid out nearly a quarter of a million dollars during his term. The association does no Southern business in yellow fever districts, and by confining its transactions exclusively to the healthy localities, and a careful selection of its risks, has a reduced death rate. At the beginning of the present year the association has assets amounting to a total of $1,586,493.55 against total liabilities of $375,700, leaving a net surplus of $1,210,793.55. The management of the association is safe and conservative, and its board of directors is composed of leading and representative business men of New York and other cities. ex-Mayor Henry Overstolz, of this city, being a member of the board. The association has earned the strong position it holds in public confidence by the uniform justice and equity of its dealings.

**W. J. Russell.**—Carriage Repository; General Agent Columbus Buggy Co., Columbus, O.; Abbott Buggy Co., Chicago, Ills.; Racine Wagon and Carriage Co., Racine, Wis.; 1514 and 1516 Olive street.—This elegant carriage repository is one of the handsomest in the city, and contains many handsome vehicles from some of the best known manufacturers in the country. Mr. Russell has conducted the business for several years and is well-known in the trade. He has the agency for the well-known Columbus Buggy Co., of Columbus, Ohio. The buggies made by this company have a national reputation, and are noted for their durability, high finish and first-class material of which they are made. They are very popular and can be found in nearly all first-class livery stables. Mr. Russell has sold many of them in this city, and has them at all times in stock. He has also the agencies of the Abbott Buggy Co., of Chicago; Racine Wagon and Carriage Co., of Racine, Wis., and Hitchcock Sleigh Co., of Cortland, New York, all of which establishments are noted for the high grade work which they manufacture. In Mr. Russell's spacious repository can always be found a large assortment of useful and stylish vehicles, including barouches, surreys, park wagons, road carts, sleighs, jump seat rockaways, and business wagons. All of his vehicles are strictly first-class, and latest designs. The trade of this establishment is in keeping with the character of its work, and it enjoys an extensive and liberal patronage.

**C. Hager & Son.**—Manufacturers of Hinges; 2427 to 2437 De Kalb street.—One of the important industries of the city is this large establishment for the manufacture of hinges. It employs constantly one hundred skilled hands, and its product is readily sold in all the Western States. The territory in which the firm has an extensive and lucrative business is from the Ohio River west to the Pacific Ocean, and from the international boundary line on the north to old Mexico on the south. The premises at 2427 to 2437 De Kalb street are 150 feet on that street and have a depth of nearly 200 feet. The establishment is equipped with all improved machinery for the manufacture of all kinds of hinges including strap, T strap, plate hinges, and washers. This successful business was established in 1857 by Mr. C. Hager, the present senior proprietor, a practical mechanic, who from a small foundation, has brought his business up to its present greatness.

**St. Louis Refrigerator and Wooden Gutter Company.**—O. G. Schulenburg, President; Louis Werner, Vice-President; W. Grayson, Secretary; Manufacturers of Refrigerators and Wooden Gutters and Dealers in Lumber; Main and Rutger streets.—This important corporation was organized in 1873, with a paid-up capital of $200,000, and has ever since carried on the business with steadily increasing success. The lumber yards and works of the company extend from Rutger to Miller, and from Main to Kosciusko streets. The works are the largest of their kind in the United States, and a large force of workmen are employed, the factory being fitted with all the necessary machinery of the most improved make. The refrigerators, wooden gutters, etc., turned out at these works are noted for their superior workmanship and materials, and their perfect adaptability to the purposes for which they are designed, the "Centennial Refrigerators" made by this company being accorded the palm of unequaled merit, and being constructed on the most approved principles. The company's saw mills are located in Arkansas, and their yards are completely stocked with yellow pine and hardwood lumber of all kinds, in which they do one of the largest trades west of the Mississippi River. The trade of the company, which is very large, embraces all the States and territories east and west of the Mississippi River. All the operations of the company are conducted upon perfect, accurate and reliable principles, and it justly enjoys a standing as one of the leading and representative manufacturing establishments of the city.

**Garrison-Chappell-Pirie Paper Company.**—O. L. Garrison, President; W. G. Chappell, Vice-President; A. H. Pirie, Secretary and Treasurer; Wholesale Paper Dealers; 312 and 314 North Third street.—This leading and successful house was established in 1882, and is located at 312 and 314 North Third street. They deal in all kinds of paper, but have an especially large business in news, print and printers' supply papers, in which lines their stocks are heavy and complete. Four competent and active commercial travelers represent the interests of the house upon the road, and the company has a very heavy patronage throughout the West and South. The house enjoys unsurpassed facilities for advantageous dealings in its line, and has a high reputation in the trade for the superiority of its goods and the correctness and reliability of its business methods.

**H. Westermann & Co.**—Wholesale Queensware, China and Glass; 514 North Main street.—Among the firms which have long been identified with the commercial history of St. Louis, is that of H. Westermann & Co., which was established in 1857, and has enjoyed a successful career ever since. The business was formerly located at 608 Washington avenue, but was removed in January, 1886, to its present commodious quarters at 514 North Main street, where it occupies a seven-story building, 20x130 feet, as salesrooms and offices. In addition, the firm has a large warehouse comprising five floors, 40x120 feet, conveniently located at 612 North Levee. The firm imports English and French queensware, china, and stoneware, and handles foreign and domestic glassware, lamps, mirrors, cutlery, etc. The stock carried is immense in its proportions and completely diversified, containing everything in the line. The long experience of the firm and the favorable relations established by it with foreign and domestic manufacturers gives it unsurpassed facilities for advantageous dealings, and enables it to offer the greatest inducements to the trade. It enjoys a large and lucrative business in the States of Missouri, Illinois and the entire West, Northwest, South and Southwest. This trade, built up during thirty years of an honorable business career, is retained and steadily added to as a result of superior merit in the goods handled, and the enlightened and correct business methods which have given this house its high standing and unexcelled reputation.

**Hudson Brothers Commission Company.**—William A. Hudson, President; B. F. Hudson, Vice-President; A. D. Scott, Secretary and Treasurer; Produce and Provisions; 212 North Second street; Warehouse 207 North Main street.—For thirty years this old and reliable house has occupied a leading position in the produce and provision trade, it having been established in 1857 by Mr. William A. Hudson, who still remains at the head of the house as the highly esteemed President of the Hudson Bros. Commission Co., incorporated in 1884. The company occupies as salesrooms and office the five-story building 25x150 feet at 212 North Second street, and as a warehouse the premises at 207 North Main, four stories, 25x150 feet. They fill orders for all kinds of produce and provisions: butter, cheese, potatoes, apples, etc., and do a very large business in all the States of the Northwest, West, Southwest and Southeast to Alabama and Florida. The trade of the house steadily increases, and it has had its share in the trade reaction of the past year, doing a heavier business in 1886 than ever before. The house long since gained the confidence of the business world by its entire reliability and correct methods, and maintains its high standing by the retention of the accurate business principles by which it has ever been actuated in all its dealings.

**Johansen Bros.**—Manufacturers of Ladies', Misses' and Children's Shoes; 1100 Olive street.—This firm is composed of Messrs. Michael and John Johansen and is one of the most prominent and prosperous in its line of industry. Mr. Michael Johansen learned his trade in Norway, coming to the United States in 1870. The firm was established in 1877 and began on a modest scale at Sixth street and Franklin avenue from whence they removed to their present quarters. They do a large business in the manufacture of ladies', misses' and children's shoes, in which line they are not excelled in the quality and workmanship of their product by any firm in the city. They give constant employment to a force of seventy-five hands and have a large trade with jobbers in the city and dealers in other parts of Missouri, Illinois, Kansas and Arkansas. Thoroughly experienced in all the departments of the business and prompt and reliable in filling orders, the firm enjoys the esteem and confidence of all with whom they have had dealings.

**New Missouri Sand Company.**—James Black, President; Wm. B. Craft, Secretary; Porter White, Treasurer. Offices: Room 40, Southeast Corner Fifth and Olive streets and foot of Chambers street.—This business was originally established in 1871 as the Missouri Sand Company, the change to its present style taking place in October, 1886. The company is extensively engaged in business as elevators and dealers in river sand, which they are prepared to furnish in any quantity by the barge or wagon-load. They have unsurpassed facilities for the successful prosecution of the business, owning the steamer Delver and barges Missouri Sand Co. Nos. 1, 2, 3 and 4. They sell sand from the barge; and dump, on the levee, for winter use. The business is managed on correct principles, and the dealings of the company with its customers are conducted in a satisfactory manner. It has a large and constantly increasing patronage, and fills orders promptly.

**St. Louis Union Stock Yard Co.**—C. C. Maffitt, President; William A. Ramsay, Secretary and Treasurer; Don Palmer, Superintendent; Office and Yards, Bremen avenue, East of Broadway.—The extent of the live stock interests of the Southwest, and the position of St. Louis as the natural depot for the trade of that section, made it necessary to provide here the requisite facilities for handling. Out of this necessity arose the organization of the St. Louis Union Stock Yards Co., with a paid-up capital of $325,000, which occurred in 1874. The company's yards, which are completely fitted up with every facility and convenience for the handling and care of stock, comprise thirty acres in the north part of the city, on Bremen avenue, east of Broadway, with all the necessary buildings, pens. etc., with additional yards, ten acres in extent, on the east side of the river. The yards at Bremen avenue are the only wholesale yards in St. Louis for the sale of all kinds of live stock. During the year 1886 there were received and handled at the yards 90,753 head of cattle, 328,028 hogs, 118,715 sheep and 13,172 horses and mules; and shipments were made to all parts of the United States and Canada. The stock came, for the most part, from Missouri, Kansas, Arkansas and Southern Illinois. President Maffitt, though yet a young man, is thoroughly identified with the business interests of St. Louis. He is President of the Chouteau. Harrison & Valle Iron Company, and a director in a number of business organizations, but, withal, never loses sight of the stock yards interests, and under his executive care the affairs of the yards have prospered. Superintendent Palmer gives efficient attention to all the details of the business, in regard to the general care of the yards and the care and handling of stock. He is thoroughly experienced in the business, and gives entire satisfaction to those having dealings with the company. About seventy-five hands are employed, and the yards are unsurpassed in the facilities offered to those having live stock for sale or transshipment. Mr. Ramsay, the Secretary and Treasurer of the company, has been identified with the company as such since its organization. He gives close attention to its interests, and has aided greatly by his efficiency in increasing its prosperity.

**J. K. Wright & Co.**—Manufacturers of Printing Inks and Colors; St. Louis Branch, E. S. Pike, Representative; 307 North Third street.—This is a prominent and substantial house. having its headquarters at Philadelphia, Pa., with branch houses at New York. Chicago and St. Louis. The house here was established ten years ago, and is under the able and efficient management of Mr. E. S. Pike, representative of the firm. under whose supervision the trade of the house in the South and the West has been largely increased. At the extensive factory at Philadelphia the firm gives employment to fifty hands, and manufactures superior printing inks and colors, which are in demand in all parts of the country, and are of the best quality manufactured. A staff of ten active and experienced traveling salesmen represent the firm in its great business, which extends to every portion of the Union. The works are known as the Fairmount Printing Ink and Color Works, and are among the largest and best in their line in the country. Mr. Pike, at the branch here, is prepared to fill all orders for the celebrated inks and colors manufactured at their works with accuracy and despatch, and at prices which, quality considered, are the lowest.

**Vane-Calvert Paint Company.**—W. H. Calvert. President; Atwood Vane, Secretary: Manufacturers of Mixed Paint: 615. 617 and 619 North Main street.—In the line of manufacture of mixed paints the great house of the Vane-Calvert Paint Co. is entitled to special and prominent mention. The house was established in 1869 as Vane. Calvert & Co., and was incorporated under its present style in 1883. The company occupies as a manufactory the large building in the rear of 615, 617 and 619 North Main street. four stories in height, and as salesrooms and office the entire four-story building. 30x110 feet. at 615 North Main street. Their manufacturing establishment is completely fitted up with all the requisite machinery and appliances for the successful operation of their business. giving employment to a force of twenty skilled workmen. The company manufactures, by a process of its own, which renders them unequaled for durability and covering capacity. all colors and shades of mixed paints. ready for immediate use. These mixed paints have attained a high reputation and a great demand from Maine to California and from Canada to the Gulf of Mexico. and the business of the house is of immense proportions. Six active and experienced travelers represent the house on the road. and the company has, by the superiority of its goods and the tact and good judgment of its business methods, achieved a great and merited success.

**Geo. F. Brunner Manufacturing Company.**—Louis Nolte, President; E. W. Dolch, Manager; Manufacturers of Bone Black, Bone Meal and Fertilizers; Second street, between Prairie and DeSoto avenues.—This important manufacturing business was established in 1864 by Mr. Geo. F. Brunner, who was succeeded by the present corporation. The works cover about half a block on Second street, between Prairie and DeSoto avenues, and are fully equipped with all the plant and machinery necessary to the successful prosecution of the business. A large force of men are employed and the company manufactures bone black, bone meal, sulphate of ammonia, fertilizers, etc., and pays cash for bones, horns, tankage, etc.

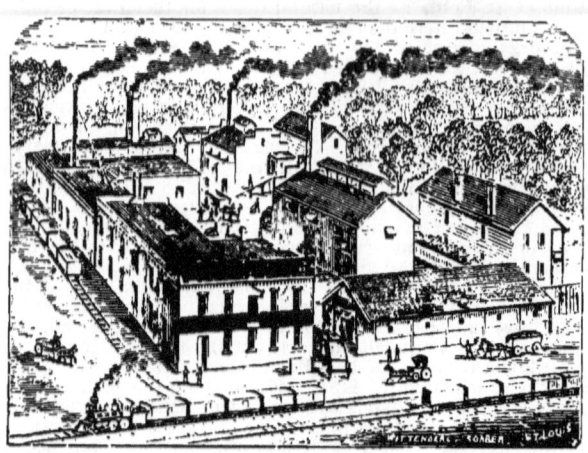

The product of these works enjoys, with merit, a reputation for superior quality, and the large trade of the company extends to San Francisco, New York, the Middle and Southern States. This large business and prominent standing is due to the high grade of the fertilizers and the splendid results obtained by their farmer patrons. The management of the company's business is in good hands, and is characterized by accurate methods. The President, Mr. Louis Nolte, is one of the leading business men of the city, and under his practical guidance the company's affairs have prospered and its trade has expanded. The efficient aid of Mr. E. W. Dolch, who manages the outside affairs of the company, has also been an important factor in its success. To the close supervision of all the manufacturing operations, and attention to every detail the company is indebted for the popularity of its product in the trade.

**George W. Godlove & Company.**—Commission Merchants in Wool, Hides, Furs. Roots, Seeds, Etc.; 114 North Main street and 115 North Commercial street.—Prominent among the best known houses in the commission business in this city, the firm of Geo. W. Godlove & Co. is deserving of especial and honorable mention. This firm has been established and actively engaged in business since 1870, and sells on commission wool, hides, peltries, furs, seeds, roots, grain, broom corn and country produce of all kinds. The premises occupied by them consist of a seven-story building with a frontage of 30 feet at 114 North Main street and running back 120 feet to 115 North Commercial street. The long and active connection of the firm with this business, and the accurate knowledge of the market gained by them in this extended experience, gives them superior advantages in the handling of consignments. The firm has achieved a high reputation for the faithful attention paid by it to the interest and advantage of the producer and shipper and has a patronage extended through Missouri, Illinois, Arkansas, Tennessee, Texas and all the States of the South and Southwest, and is annually adding to its extensive business connection.

**Klausmann Brewery Co.**—John Krauss, President and Treasurer; J. Moerschel, Superintendent; Fred. Rathgeber, Secretary; Lager and Eureka Bottled Beer; 8639, South Broadway.—This business was established in 1858, by the firm of Klausmann & Co. The founder, Mr. Charles Klausmann, died some twenty years ago, but his widow still retains an interest in the present company, which was incorporated in 1878. The company own a handsome new brick brewery, five stories high, which, with outhouses and grounds, cover over four blocks. The brewery is equipped with all the latest appliances and equipment for the manufacture of beer, and has a capacity for brewing of 60,000 barrels annually. Seventy-five men and twenty-four teams are employed, and the beer produced by the company is justly celebrated for its superior quality, and includes, besides the barrel beer, a very fine bottled article known as the "Eureka" beer. In addition to their large city trade the company has an extensive business in Missouri, Arkansas, Texas, Illinois, Louisiana and at all Lower Mississippi points. They increased their business very largely in 1886, and this year, so far, shows an increase of about 800 barrels per month in their product and sales over last year, and they expect to be soon compelled to enlarge their capacity in response to the steadily increasing demand for their beer. Adjoining their brewery premises they have a fine summer garden, beautifully situated on a plateau, with a fine river view. It is laid out with excellent taste, and is called "The Klausmann Brewery Co.'s Cave." After Mr. Krauss became connected with the business the capital was increased, and the brewery entered upon a career of enhanced prosperity. Mr. Rathgeber, the Secretary, has filled that position with great efficiency since the incorporation of the company in 1878. Mr. Nic. Eckerle was one of the original incorporators, and held the position of Superintendent until his death, when he was succeeded by Mr. J. Moerschel. The brewery has several traveling men constantly on the road, and with greatly increased facilities holds a high place in the esteem of the trade.

**A. B. Mayer Manufacturing Company.**—A. B. Mayer, President; Mrs. R. Mayer, Vice-President and Treasurer; F. Mayer, Secretary; Manufacturers of Bone Black and Fertilizers, and Dealers in Paper Stock, Scrap Iron, Bones, etc.; Office and Warehouses, 1012 to 1022 North Twelfth street.—This business was established in 1863 by Mr. A. B. Mayer, as a dealer in paper stock, scrap iron, bones, etc., and in 1873 the manufacturing department was added. The present company was incorporated in March of the present year, Mr. A. B. Mayer remaining at the head of the business as President. They own the Anchor Bone Black Works at Lowell, Mo., and the Anchor Fertilizing Works at the foot of Harrison street in this city. Their city office and warehouses are at 1012 to 1022 North Twelfth street, covering about a quarter of a block. The specialty of the company is the manufacture of the "Anchor Brand Bone Fertilizers" by their own processes. These fertilizers have been proved by the test of use to be the best in the market, and have taken prizes wherever exhibited. The company also manufacture a superior quality of bone black and still continue to deal largely in paper stock, etc. They do a large business in Missouri, Illinois, Kentucky, Arkansas, Texas, Kansas, Tennessee and the entire South and West, and in their manufactured product in all parts of the country. The house stands high in the trade and is deservedly prosperous.

**Daniel Devlin.**—Union Machine Shops, Fourth and Valentine streets.—This extensive establishment has been in existence about eight years, but its proprietor, Mr. Daniel Devlin, has for nearly forty years been engaged in the foundry and general machinery business in St. Louis. He is a native of the city, and, as a boy, learned his trade here. The works of Mr. Devlin are located on Valentine street, formerly known as Almond, and have a frontage of 160 feet, extending from Fourth street east to the alley. A force of forty men are constantly employed, and the shops are equipped with all of the latest improved machinery and apparatus. All kinds of machinery are manufactured, and the facilities for prompt and excellent work enjoyed by these shops are not excelled anywhere. During the past few years seventeen locomotives have been made at these works. Mr. Devlin is the owner of several valuable patents, one of the most prominent of which is the "Standard Brick Machine," an apparatus for making brick by hand. These machines are capable of making 4,000 bricks per day. They have become very popular in the South and West, and, with their aid, a small hand-brickyard can make the finest of pressed brick. Mr. Devlin has also recently invented a curve for cable railroads, which is an anti-friction curve, and relieves the cable of all the heavy strain usually endured in rounding curves. It is pronounced by experts to be the best cable invention yet perfected. The trade of this establishment is very large, and is located in the city and Western and Southern States. Mr. Devlin makes a specialty of second hand boilers and machinery, which he takes in exchange, and, after placing them in thorough repair, carries them in stock. He has always a number on hand.

**Parlin, Orendorff & Bauer.**—Manufacturers and Jobbers of Farm Machinery, etc.; 120 North Main street.—The house of Parlin, Orendorff & Bauer occupies a leading position among those engaged as manufacturers and jobbers of farm machinery, carriages, buggies, farm and spring wagons, phaetons, road carts, agricultural implements, etc. The firm adopted its present style in December, 1886, succeeding the firm of Bauer, Walter & Co., established in 1880, and is now composed of Mr. Ferdinand Bauer, of this city, and the Parlin & Orendorff Co., of Canton, Ill., where they operate a large plow and farming implement factory, established in 1842, and manufacture the celebrated "Canton Clipper" plows and agricultural implements, of which this house makes a specialty. In addition to the sale of its own products, the firm acts as agent for the "Bain" farm and "Racine" spring wagons, justly approved as the perfection of efficiency and durability, and many other standard machines and implements. The firm, in the several lines handled by it, takes especial care to deal only in such as have been approved by practical experience as the most useful, and its stock is large and thoroughly diversified in the best farm machinery, implements and vehicles offered to the trade. The house occupies a spacious seven-story building, 30x120 feet, and does a large and constantly growing business in all the States of the South and Southwest, in which it is regarded with the highest favor by dealers. Five active and energetic travelers are engaged to push its business, and the unsurpassed merit of its goods, and the uniform fairness of its dealings, have achieved for it a high reputation with the trade and the agricultural community.

**Stark Nut-Lock Co.**—F. G. Stark, President; W. T. Haarstick, Vice-President; George Minch, Secretary and Treasurer; Manufacturers of the Stark Nut-Lock; Office, 918 and 920 North Second street.—Of the new enterprises in St. Louis there is none that has met with more marked success than the Stark Nut-Lock Company. Although only incorporated in the latter part of 1885, they have succeeded in introducing their patented device on over sixty leading railway systems, and wound up the year of 1886 by taking orders in the month of December for 165,000 track lock-nuts and receiving orders to equip 1,700 cars. The device mentioned is the Stark Patent Nut-Lock, a simple and ingenious contrivance for fastening securely nuts to bolts of all kinds, and which is patented by Mr. F. G. Stark, President of the company. The company has a capital stock of $100,000 and its offices are located at New York, St. Louis and Chicago, while its works are at New York and St. Louis. The office and workshops of the company in this city are at 918 and 920 North Second street, and fully equipped with all requisite machinery and appliances for the business. The trade of the company extends to every part of the country, and is steadily increasing as the merits of its device obtain a wider celebrity. The President of the company, Mr. Stark, resides in New York; Mr. Haarstick, the Vice-President, is President of the Mississippi Valley Transportation Co., in this city, and Mr. Minch, the Secretary and Treasurer, has for years been engaged in the grain and flour trade in this city. All are business men of high attainments, and with their efficient management the success already achieved by the company will doubtless double and quadruple itself in the near future.

**Bishop & Spear.**—Recleaners of Peanuts and Pecans, and Proprietors of the "Parrot" and "Boss" Brands of Peanuts; 510 and 512 North Second street.—The firm of Bishop & Spear, of which Messrs. R. P. Bishop and G. B. Spear are the members, removed to this city from Cincinnati in 1884, because of the superior facilities here for carrying on their trade. They deal exclusively in peanuts and pecans, receiving peanuts chiefly from Virginia and Tennessee, and pecans from Texas. This is the largest house of its line in the country, their stock of peanuts alone frequently amounting to upward of $100,000 in value. They occupy the two five-story iron buildings, 60x150 feet, at 510 and 512 North Second street, which are fitted up with all the requisite machinery for cleaning six hundred bags or 3,000 bushels of peanuts per day. They make a specialty of hand-picked nuts, and do an immense business, keeping a number of buyers on the road, but no salesmen, as they sell through brokers exclusively. Their trade extends from the Atlantic to the Pacific, and is especially large in the Northern, Western, and Southern States. The great success they have obtained is due to their intimate and special knowledge of their line of business, the care given to the processes of selection and cleaning and in keeping their brands up to a high and uniform standard.

**Steinwender & Sellner.**—Importers, Distillers and Dealers in Fine Kentucky Whiskies, Wines, etc.: 117 South Broadway.—This firm, which is composed of Messrs. H. A. Steinwender, A. C. Sellner and G. A. Steinwender, was established in 1870, and is one of the largest, most prosperous and most prominent houses of the city in its line. The specialty of the house is in fine Kentucky Whiskies. The firm are the sole agents for and control the output of the Old Oscar Pepper Distillery, Woodford County, Kentucky, which occupies the original site of the distillery in which James Crow made the whisky which became celebrated as the best in the world. The process of distillation (hand-made sour mash) is the same as employed by James Crow, and the water used being from the same spring only, the whiskey produced is of equal purity and like flavor. The firm are also the largest direct importers in the city of such high-class wines as Cruse et Fils Freres and Barton & Guestier clarets; Pommery Sec, G. H. Mumm, Dry Monopole and other choice champagnes; fine French brandies, ports, sherries, liqueurs, etc. They carry a large stock of complete assortment and unsurpassed quality in all lines. They occupy a spacious and elegant six-story building, 30x150, in addition to which they store their imported liquors largely in customs warehouses, and their whiskies in bond and free warehouses in Kentucky. Sixteen clerks and assistants are employed in the house, and eight traveling salesmen represent the firm on the road. The high merit of their goods has secured for them a large city business with clubs, fine hotels, jobbers, etc., and a heavy trade in Missouri, Illinois, Arkansas, Texas, Kansas, Iowa, Nebraska, and all the West and Northwest.

**James F. Ewing.**—Agent for the Michigan Salt Association, the Michigan Dairy Salt Co., and the Celebrated Michigan Salt Association Dairy Salt; 105 North Third street, Chamber of Commerce Building.—The Michigan Salt Association is one of the most prominent of the corporations of the country, and was organized in 1876 to effect a unity of interest among the salt manufacturers of Michigan. The charter of the Association expiring in 1881 it was at once reorganized under the name of the "Salt Association of Michigan," and last year it was again reorganized under its old name of the "Michigan Salt Association." The corporation handles the product of the manufacturers, taking their salt as fast as made, making liberal advances thereon, placing it in the market and paying for it in full when sold. The potency of the Association is shown by the fact that of a total product in Michigan in 1886 of 4,097,943 barrels of salt, the Association controlled all but about 600,000 barrels. The headquarters of the Association are at East Saginaw, Michigan. The Michigan Dairy Salt Company is also a Saginaw institution, and sells its product through the Michigan Salt Association. During 1886 the works of this company produced 75,000 barrels of dairy salt, the quality of which is not surpassed by any manufactured. The principal agencies of the Michigan Salt Association are at Chicago, St. Louis, Milwaukee, Duluth, Louisville, Cincinnati, Toledo, Nashville and Sandusky. The St. Louis branch was established in 1881, in which year Mr. Ewing was a manufacturer and jobber of salt of many years' experience. He does an immense business throughout the States of Kentucky, Tennessee, Mississippi, Alabama, Southern Illinois, Missouri, Kansas, Colorado, Arkansas, Texas and the Indian Territory. He makes a specialty of dairy salt, which is of a particularly fine quality, and made expressly for use in butter and cheese manufacture. It is put up in linen bags of 224 lbs. each, and quarter-bags of 56 lbs. each. Mr. Ewing stands high in the business community, and his methods are such as to commend him to the respect and confidence of the trade.

**James Whitelaw.**—Printers' Machinist; 107 Market street.—Mr. Whitelaw was for nineteen years general foreman for the St. Louis Type Foundry before establishing this business, of which he has made a signal success. He makes a specialty of improving and repairing printers', bookbinders', and lithographers' machinery, and also shafting, pulleys, hangers, stamping dies, gear cutting. The business has steadily grown from its inception to the present time, and the trade of Mr. Whitelaw includes, besides a heavy city patronage, a business extending throughout Southern Illinois, Missouri, Kansas and the South and West generally. Only the most skilled labor is employed at this establishment, and it enjoys an excellent reputation for superior workmanship. Mr. Whitelaw is now adding to his facilities a department for the manufacture of novelties and light machinery, and is now manufacturing a new and improved style of type-writers, telegraphic instruments, bank check punches, etc., and can undertake contracts for the manufacture of new inventions. He is a thoroughly reliable and successful business man.

**Riches & Co.**—Engravers on Wood; 304 and 306 Olive street.—In the artistic branches of industry St. Louis holds a prominent position among the leading cities of the country. In designing and engraving on wood, an art which combines, more perhaps than any other, the merits of beauty and utility, no firm in the city can show superior excellence in its achievements than that of Riches & Co. This firm has been steadily increasing its trade from the inception of their business connection, the finished and conscientious work turned out by them securing for the firm, at all times, a continuance of patronage from those who give them a trial. They make a specialty of commercial work, and design and execute labels, trade marks, letter head cuts, and all work for business catalogues and price lists in the highest and most perfect style of this most difficult and exacting art. They are also the publishers of the Poultry Record, a periodical devoted to the interests of the poultry raisers of the country, and which is an acknowledged authority on the subject. Messrs. Riches & Co. have built up an excellent reputation for their work in wood-engraving by the promptness and reliability with which they fill every order as well as by the intrinsic merit of their work.

**H. H. Bothe.**—Manufacturer of Omnibuses, Street Cars, Express, Mail and Business Wagons New York Trucks, Etc.; 1317, 1319 and 1321 North Ninth street.—This large and prosperous manufacturing establishment has been successfully conducted since 1876 when it was started by Mr. Bothe. The extensive premises, 100x150 feet, occupied by the factory, which is two stories in height, are completely equipped with all necessary plant and machinery and give employment to a force of from fifty to sixty skilled and experienced workmen. Here are manufactured omnibuses, street cars, express, mail, stake, baggage, grocers', cracker, dry goods, delivery, beer and pleasure wagons, New York trucks, etc. Mr. Bothe manufactures all the wagons and does all the repairing for the Pacific Express Co., has large orders from the American Express Co., Chicago, and made the large vans for the Cruttwell Storage and Moving Co., and the New York Storage Warehouse and Furniture Company of this city. He makes all kinds of heavy work and in all his departments the vehicles turned out by him are acknowledged to be first-class in every respect, and never fail to give satisfaction to his customers. His trade is very large and extends West, North and South to all States and Territories.

**Cole Brothers Commission Company.**—Nathan Cole, President; A. B. Cole, Vice-President; W. H. Sears, Secretary and Treasurer; E. H. Cole; Commission, Grain, Flour, Provisions, Wool, etc.; 213 North Second street.—This leading and representative commission house was established over thirty years ago as Cole Brothers, and has had a busy and prosperous career. The premises occupied by the company are commodious, with 30 feet frontage by a depth of 140 feet, and centrally located at 213 North Second street. They deal largely in options, grain, flour, provisions, wool and everything usually handled by a commission house, receiving large consignments from all parts of Missouri, Illinois, Iowa, Kansas, Nebraska, Texas, Arkansas, Kentucky and other States, and selling on 'Change. The house has long held a high place in the esteem and confidence of the commercial world, as a result of close and prompt attention to all business entrusted to its care, and the perfect reliability of its business methods. Experience and a close knowledge of the markets, and just and equitable treatment of their customers, are the means by which the house has achieved its great success, which it maintains by a close adherence to the high principles by which its transactions have ever been characterized.

**Deere, Mansur & Co.**—Deere & Co., Moline, Ill.; A. Mansur and L. B. Tebbetts, St. Louis; Farm Machinery, "John Deere" Plows and Cultivators, Etc.; 515 and 517 North Main street.—This establishment is the St. Louis branch of the John Deere Moline Plow Works, and was opened in 1874 as a medium for the sale of the plows and other farm implements made at the factory at Moline, Illinois, founded in 1847 by Mr. John Deere. The St. Louis house is under the management of Messrs. A. Mansur and L. B. Tebbetts, who, with the firm of Deere & Co., of Moline, form the firm of Deere, Mansur & Co. This house does a large business in the plows and implements manufactured at the Moline works, supplying Indiana, Southern Illinois, Missouri, Kansas and the entire South and Southwest with the "John Deere" implements, including plows, planters, cultivators, etc., and doing an annual business in these goods amounting to about $1,000,000. Prominent among the goods handled by the firm may be mentioned the following: The "John Deere" plows, leading all others in strength, durability, lightness of draft, quality of workmanship and ease of management. The "Gilpin" sulky plow, a prime favorite with large farmers, and which is in great demand, is also of the Moline make, as are also the "Deere" spring cultivators, the "Sylvan" cultivator and the all-iron "Columbia" cultivator. Another leading product of this factory is the "New Deal" wheeled walking plow, built with either one, two, three or four plows, throwing the weight of the furrows on the wheels, and with the frame of the machine made as light as is compatible with sufficient strength. This plow is a great labor saver, and although only introduced two years ago, has already attained great popularity and an enormous sale.

*John Deere*

PIONEER WESTERN PLOW MANUFACTURER, AND FOUNDER OF THE LARGEST STEEL-PLOW FACTORY IN THE WORLD.

They also sell the "Deere" rotary drop corn planters, the pioneers in successful rotary drops and still unequaled; the "Deere" and "Moline" stalk cutters, and the "Hoosier" drills, all of which have proved the superiority of their merits by the test of use. Besides the line of "John Deere" farming implements, Deere, Mansur & Co. do a very large business in farm and spring wagons, buggies, carriages, carts, track sulkies, buckboards, mountain wagons, jump seats, etc., in which their stock is very large and complete, and without a competitor anywhere in the West. The firm controls the sale, in the entire Southwest, of the "Mitchell" farm wagons, and many other first-class makes of vehicles. In hay machinery their line is complete and selected from the best known and most valuable of the inventions in this department. In sorghum machinery they also offer a choice among the best machines in the market. In cane mills they have the "Charter Oak," the "Samson," the "New Amber" and the "Monitor." Without further enumeration, which would trench too much on space, it may be said in brief that the stock of this great house is enormous as to size and complete as to assortment. They occupy, as salesrooms and offices, the two five-story stores at Nos. 515 and 517 North Main street, having a frontage of 60 feet by a depth of 150 feet. In addition to this they have a large two-story warehouse at the corner of Ninth and Spruce streets, where they carry constantly over 100 carloads of goods. They employ fifty experienced men and are represented by eight travelers. During the season of 1887 the firm has noted a gratifying increase in the volume of its sales. The great popularity and high reputation of this house is due not only to the acknowledged superiority of its goods, but also to the systematic correctness of its methods, the spirit of fairness and liberality which prevades its dealings and its prompt attention to orders.

**W. B. Westcott & Co.**—Commission; Hay, Grain, Flour, etc.; 202 North Main street and 203 North Commercial street.—A firm of commission merchants which has a deserved prominence is that of W. B. Westcott & Co. The house was established in 1872 as Westcott Bros., became Westcott and Hall, composed of Messrs. W. B. Westcott and W. R. Hall, in 1882, and in 1886, on the death of Mr. Hall, assumed its present style. The firm occupies a seven-story building, 30x120 feet, at 202 North Main street, running back to 203 North Commercial street. They deal in and handle on commission hay, grain, flour, wool, hides, peltries, furs, feathers, cotton, butter, eggs, game, etc., in all of which lines they do a large business, extending through the States of Missouri and Illinois, and all the States of the South and Southwest, and eastward as far as Pennsylvania, and also to some extent in New York and Canada, and for the last five years have been the leading house in selling dried fruit on commission. The firm has established a deservedly high reputation among shippers and producers, and by close attention to every detail of its business has secured the extensive patronage which it now enjoys.

**Charles W. Melcher.**—Mining and Quarrying Machinery; 811 North Second street.—Mr. Melcher is the Southwestern agent of a number of the best known Eastern manufacturers of this class of machinery. Among these is the Ingersoll Rock Drill Company, of New York, manufacturers of air compressors, rock

drills, stone channeling machines, and other special mining and quarrying machines. No stronger proof of the intrinsic value and real merit of the Ingersoll machinery is needed than the fact that it is preferred, even at higher prices than other similar machinery is offered, on every public work of any magnitude now under construction in the United States. Nineteen of the twenty-three large tunnels which have been driven with machine drills in this country have employed the Ingersoll drill. Mr. Melcher is also agent for J. S. Mundy, of Newark, N. J., builder of hoisting machinery for mines, quarries and contractors. These machines are widely and favorably known throughout the United States, and are preferred by engineers and contractors to other machines of similar character. He also represents I. B. Davis & Son, of Hartford, Conn., manufacturers of the Berryman feed water heater and purifier, the simplest, most efficient and durable heater manufactured to-day. In handling the above first-class machinery, Mr. Melcher has secured a large patronage, extending over the entire southwestern country, and to his industry and close attention to the interests of his principals, combined with the merits of the machines themselves, he owes the great success which he has achieved.

**Swan, Duncan & Co.**—Brokers—Mining Stocks and Lands a Specialty; Southern Hotel, 102 South Broadway.—The mining industries of the West have received of late much attention from St. Louis people, who have invested large amounts in Western mines. Many of the investments have brought large returns, and several millions of dollars are annually paid out in dividends to fortunate local holders of mining stocks. The better class of brokers whose attention has been diverted to mining matters, are careful of their clients' interests in such investments, and seek to encourage only first-class properties. One of the best known and highly respected firms doing business in this city is that of Swan, Duncan & Co. This firm was organized in 1886, by W. B. Swan and E. W. Duncan, and have elegant offices and parlors at 102 South Broadway, in the Southern Hotel block. They have with them gentlemen of large experience in the profession, and practically familiar with the value of mining claims and Western lands, who give their personal attention to all matters of that kind, and acquire a thorough knowledge of the value and character of the investment sought for. Messrs. Swan, Duncan & Co. have placed successfully some of the finest mining properties in the country, and have a long list of patrons for whom they act. They have made some of the heaviest investments that have been made of late years for local and Eastern capitalists, and their thorough reliability, as well as ability, has been long established.

The Missouri Safe Deposit Company.—James J. Hoyt, President; Henry G. Marquand and George D. Capen, Vice-Presidents: George D. Capen, Treasurer; Justin S. Kendrick, Secretary; Edw. A. Smith, Superintendent of Safes; Equitable Building, Sixth and Locust streets.—The organization of safe deposit companies dates back but a few years, and was effected in response to the imperative demands of the people to have protection for their wealth and valuables. Burglary had attained practically to a rank among the sciences, and no safe or vault seemed secure against the onslaughts of the expert burglar. Finally it became an absolute necessity to recognize these facts, and to devise means to protect property from these depredations, and make it absolutely secure. Safe deposit companies sprang into existence, and have practically solved the problem. As they are incorporated companies of large resources, they have been enabled to experiment and perfect the most improved safeguards that science has created, and to-day they are virtually invulnerable. No safe deposit company has ever suffered a loss from burglary. The Missouri Safe Deposit Company was organized during 1886, and has one of the most complete and secure establishments that unlimited money can procure, or human ingenuity devise. It is located on the ground floor and sub-basement of the elegant and imposing Equitable building, at the northwest corner of Sixth and Locust streets. This immense edifice is of iron and stone,

and is absolutely fire-proof. The vaults of the company are perfectly burglar-proof, and the handsomest and most complete in the world. The entrance is from the main hall of the building, through steel-barred gates that it would be impossible to pass without the permission of the attendants. Every appliance and mechanism that can be of service to the company, or improve the safety of its vaults, has been adopted. The main vault is the second largest vault in the world, that of the New York Produce Exchange being the only one that excels it in dimensions, and that by only a few inches. It is of chrome steel and iron, nine inches thick, and has three inches of fire-proofing surrounding it. The foundations are of brick, in the formation of arches, and 100,000 bricks were used in its construction. The vault is so constructed that watchmen can pass around it on all sides, under and over it. During the day attendants are constantly about, and at night armed police patrol the premises at all times, registering every half hour their trips to each part of the vaults on a watchman's clock. The vault contains 1,000 boxes or compartments, each provided with its own lock, to open which requires not only the subscriber's key but that of the official in charge as well. There is room for 8,000 boxes in the vault, and they will be put in as rapidly as they are required. Each entrance has double doors, with time-lock combinations, and, in addition, four other combinations. Two of these latter combinations are held by the president, and two by the superintendent, so that the presence of both is required to open the vault. Electric bells are placed over the entire establishment, so that an attack in any part of the place could be instantly communicated over the entire premises, and every attendant be notified of the exact place of attack. Wires also connect with police headquarters, and any tampering with the vaults would bring a large squad of police upon the scene. The boxes vary in size, and command from $10 to $350 per year rental. Reception rooms, reading rooms, parlors for ladies, and private rooms for box-holders are provided. There are about forty of these small rooms for the accommodation of patrons. Comfort and elegance, as well as absolute safety, are included in the arrangements. The board of directors of the company is composed of the following well-known and substantial citizens: Messrs. Louis Fitzgerald, Henry G. Marquand, Henry B. Hyde, George D. Capen, George W. Allen, D. K. Ferguson, Henry C. Haarstick, James J. Hoyt and William Nichols. The officers and directors of the company are business men of the highest standing, and enjoy the esteem and confidence of the people of St. Louis.

**The De La Vergne Refrigerating Machine Company.**—Ruemmeli & Rassbach, General Western Agents; Room 507 Granite Building, Corner Fourth and Market streets.—This business, established in 1878 by John C. De La Vergne, was incorporated under its present style in 1881. The headquarters and works of the company are in New York, and its business has grown to large proportions, the demand for their machines rapidly increasing from year to year. They are manufacturers of refrigerating and ice-making machines, which have been demonstrated by the actual experience of the largest brewers, packers, ice manufacturers, etc., to be the best devices of the kind ever made. Up to April 1st, 1887, from the date of its incorporation, the company had erected 141 machines, equivalent in capacity to the melting of 5,880 tons of ice each day, all of which machines are now in successful operation. Among these are one 110-ton machine in use by the Anheuser-Busch Brewing Association in this city, which also has a machine at Kansas City; one 75-ton machine used by the Hyde Park Brewery Co.; two 50-ton machines used by the Wainwright Brewery Co.; two 50-ton machines by the Jos. Schnaider's Brewing Co.; one 50-ton machine by the H. Grone Brewery Co.; one 64-ton machine used by the St. Louis Beef Canning Co., at East St. Louis, and one 9-ton machine used by the M. A. Seed Dry Plate Co. in their works at Woodland.

In addition to the above-mentioned plants already in operation in this city and vicinity, the company has a large force of workmen employed erecting ammonia expansion piping to cool 600,000 cubic feet of space in the Anheuser-Busch Brewery; and have lately contracted to erect an extensive condensing apparatus for Chas. G. Stifel's Brewing Co. The company manufacture their own pipe work, which, together with the machines, is shipped direct from the shops, and Messrs. Ruemmeli & Rassbach superintend the erection. The works of the company, situated at Bank street and North River, New York, and occupying nearly the whole of a large block, are kept running to their full capacity, day and night, in order to supply the demand. By the use of these machines solid blocks of crystal ice can be manufactured cheaper than they can be supplied by the ice companies, and cold storage space, as required in many industries, can be maintained at any degree of temperature with exactness and economy not attainable by the use of natural ice. These machines have always given entire satisfaction to their owners, and work more evenly and reliably than any others, avoiding the annoyances caused by break-downs and stoppages so often experienced by those using inferior machines. The great demand and steadily increasing popularity of these machines is the result of their marked superiority of construction and mechanism. Messrs. Ruemmeli & Rassbach, the general Western agents, are prepared to supply these machines and anhydrous ammonia in any quantity promptly, and to put up the plants in perfect working order.

**The Dr. Harter Medicine Company.**—S. K. Harter, President; F. M. Sterrett, Secretary and Manager; A. S. Hallock, Treasurer; Proprietary Medicines; 213 North Main street.—Of all the business names associated with St. Louis none is more widely or more favorably known than that of Dr. Harter, the founder of the business now conducted by The Dr. Harter Medicine Company. Dr. Harter, who established the business in 1854, was one of the most learned and successful physicians of the Southwest, and graduated with distinction from six of the leading medical colleges of the country. He managed the business with great ability and signal success until his decease some years ago. The present company was incorporated April 9, 1873, under the laws of Missouri, and occupies a spacious five-story building, 30x150 feet, at 213 North Main street and also has a store room on Chestnut street, two stories, 30x150 feet. The company manufactures all of Dr. Harter's celebrated preparations, including Dr. Harter's Iron Tonic, Dr. Harter's Fever and Ague Specific, Dr. Harter's Liver Pills, Dr. Harter's Soothing Drops, Dr. Harter's Vermifuge Candy, Dr. Harter's Liniment, Dr. Harter's Lung Balm, Dr. Harter's Wild Cherry Bitters, Dr. Du Choine's Nerve Pills, Dr. Du Choine's Female Regulating Pills, etc. These medicines have, most of them, been before the public for over thirty years, and all of them are well-known. That they possess genuine merit is completely and satisfactorily attested by the fact that the demand for them has shown a steady and healthy increase from year to year, the demand extending to every part of the country and the sales of these goods equaling, and probably excelling, those of any proprietary medicines in the world. The company sells direct to dealers in the States of Missouri, Illinois, Nebraska, Iowa, Minnesota, Wisconsin, Michigan, Ohio, Indiana, Kansas, Arkansas, Texas, Louisiana, Mississippi, Alabama, Georgia, Florida, North Carolina, South Carolina, Tennessee and Kentucky, in all of which the company has its regular travelers. They also do a very large business in the East through jobbers in New York, Boston and other cities. The president of the company, Mr. S. K. Harter, lives at Troy, Miami County, Ohio, and is prominent in business and financial circles, being the largest land owner in the county and an extensive holder of bank stock. The business of the company is managed by Mr. F. M. Sterrett, its efficient secretary. Mr. Sterrett is a native of Clark County, Ohio, and is now forty-one years of age. Receiving the solid foundation of a liberal public and high school education, he went to the Ohio Wesleyan University, from which he joined the Fifth Regiment of Ohio Cavalry, in which he served with honor for thirteen months, returning to finish his education, and then took an extensive foreign tour. Returning to this country he engaged in business as a commercial traveler until 1879, when he was appointed Postmaster of Troy, Ohio. In April, 1885, he tendered his resignation, which was not accepted until October of that year. He then came to this city, having accepted his present position as secretary and manager of the vast business of The Dr. Harter Medicine Co., for which his great business attainments and high personal character so thoroughly qualify him. His capacity for the management of affairs of magnitude has been shown by the good judgment and accurate methods which characterize his conduct of this business and by which its patronage has been increased, and the relations of the company with its customers have been maintained upon a mutually satisfactory basis.

**Berry Brothers.**—Manufacturers of Varnishes, Detroit, Michigan; St. Louis Branch, E. P. Davenport, Manager, 402 North Second street.—The importance of St. Louis as a center for the distribution of goods in the South and Southwest is recognized by manufacturers everywhere, and the great houses of the country generally maintain branches in this city. Prominent among these is the firm of Berry Brothers, established in 1858, whose mammoth establishment at Detroit, Mich., is the most extensive varnish factory in the world. They have branch houses in Boston, New York, Philadelphia, Baltimore, Rochester (N. Y.), Cincinnati and Chicago, as well as their establishment in this city, which is located at 402 North

Second street, and is under the management of Mr. E. P. Davenport. From these houses the products of the factory are distributed to every part of the Union, besides which they do a large export trade with Canada, South America and Europe. The varnishes manufactured by this house, have, by their superior quality, gained a merited pre-eminence. The hard oil finish, the only preparation adapted for use on pianos, organs, desks, mouldings and furniture generally, was originated by this firm, and although many attempts have been made to imitate it, none have been successful. The St. Louis branch, which has been established fifteen years, has a large trade in the city and the States tributary to its market. Manager Davenport was formerly a varnish manufacturer in Cincinnati, and has special qualifications for his present position, in which he has acquitted himself with credit and efficiency, giving satisfaction alike to the great house he represents and their customers in the territory allotted to this branch.

**Senter & Co.**—Cotton Factors and Commission Merchants; Northwest Corner of Third and Walnut streets.—This house is the largest handler of cotton in St. Louis, enjoys a high reputation among St. Louis merchants, and all with whom it has dealings. The house was established in 1864 by the present members of the firm, who came to St. Louis from the South, where for many years they were prominent and successful business men. The firm at present is composed of Wm. M. Senter and W. T. Wilkins, and transacts a general commission business in cotton, wool, hides, etc., all of which receives the special attention of the house, and its aggregate volume is enormous.  The long experience of the members of this firm, their extensive connections, and first-class facilities give to them an advantage that is thoroughly appreciated by the Southern shippers, who are not slow to consign to them their cotton and other produce. The house has large financial resources, and their prompt and liberal advances, quick sales and remittances have placed them to the front among the cotton factors of the country. The house receives cotton from every State and Territory contiguous to St. Louis and readily disposes of it to advantage on this market. This firm is held in the highest esteem for their business and personal qualities by the mercantile community. W. M. Senter is the President of the St. Louis Cotton Compress Co., the largest concern of its kind in this country.

**The Paddock-Hawley Iron Company.**—Gaius Paddock, President; C. K. Paddock, Secretary; Wholesale Hardware, Iron, etc.; 806 to 816 North Main street — The enormous business of this company entitles it to conspicuous mention in a work detailing the industrial history of the city. The business was established in 1872, succeeding the firm of Speer and Crawford with the style of Paddock, Leahy & Co., and subsequently changing to its present corporate name. The company does a large wholesale business in iron, steel, nails, carriage and heavy hardware, trimmings, wood material, etc. Their salesrooms and offices occupy five buildings, each five stories high, with a frontage of 125 feet by a depth of 125 feet, together with an extensive warehouse, five stories, 50x100 feet, and the basement of four adjoining stores, 100x125 feet, giving them about 122,000 square feet of floor room. In addition to this they also occupy a large warehouse for the accommodation of their surplus stock, at the corner of Poplar and Eighth streets, which covers half a block, 150x300 feet. The operations of the company are aided by a force of sixty experienced employes, while ten active and energetic travelers represent the interests of the house on the road. The volume of its trade is enormous, its sales aggregating over $1,000,000 annually and extending over the entire South, Southwest, Northwest and westward to the Pacific. The magnitude of the business gives them unsurpassed facilities, enabling them to offer superior inducements to the trade, and they are Western agents for the following leading manufacturing companies: Sandusky Wheel Company, Ullin (Ill.) Wood Work Company, Vernon (Ind.) Wood Work Company, Fairfield (Conn.) Rubber Company, Rhode Island Horse Shoe Company, Champlain Horse Nail Company, Cleveland Spring Company, Concord Axle Company, Norway Iron and Steel Company (Boston Mass.), National Tubular Axle Company (McKeesport, Pa.), Pennsylvania Tube Works (Pittsburgh), and the Cleveland Rolling Mill Company. The vast business of the company has been built up by the superiority of its goods, the enterprise of its management, and the systematic thoroughness of its business methods.

## THE INDUSTRIES OF ST. LOUIS. 199

**Wickham & Pendleton**—Wholesale Grocers: 204 and 206 North Main street and 205 and 207 North Commercial street.—The important firm of Wickham and Pendleton, which occupies a prominent position among the large wholesale grocery and commision houses of the city, has been identified as a representative house since 1865. The members of the firm are Messrs. W. L. Wickham, A. B. Pendleton, W. F. Kropp, and J. V. Doniphan. The premises occupied by the firm consist of a large five-story building, fronting 40 feet at 204 and 206 North Main street, and running back 120 feet, through to 205 and 207 North Commercial street. They are fully stocked with every article usually dealt in by first-class wholesale grocery houses, flour, meal, whiskies, tobacco, cigars, provisions of all kinds and grocers' specialties in complete assortment. The trade of the house extends to all the States of the South, West and Southwest. The firm also deals largely in horses, mules, wagons and all kinds of plantation supplies. In the long and successful career of this house, it has ever maintained with its customers the highest reputation for the fairness and liberality of its dealings, promptness and exactness in filling orders, and the uniform excellence of its goods.

**The Heine Safety Boiler Company.**—E. D. Meier, President; John W. Meier, Secretary and Treasurer; Boiler Manufacturers; 102 North Main street.—Great as are the advantages which have accrued to civilization from the introduction of steam power, the dangers to life and property were 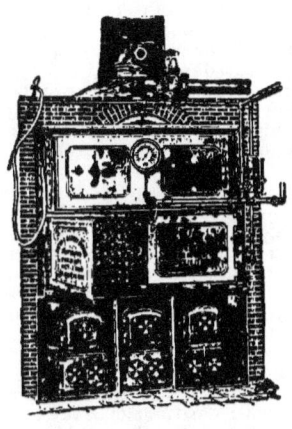 greatly increased by the imperfect boilers which were first used. It was to banish these elements of danger that the Heine Safety Boiler was invented. The first of these boilers made in America was built in 1882 by the firm of Adolphus Meier & Co., of this city. So great was the success of the experiment that a demand for these valuable boilers was soon created, and on January 1, 1885, the Heine Safety Boiler Co. was formed. These boilers are built upon perfectly scientific principles, and their principal advantages are a positive circulation, avoidance of incrustations, steady pressure, a great saving in fuel and freedom from explosions. They are used for all purposes in which steam is required: water works, gas works, heating buildings, iron works, electric light plants, etc. The increase in the demand for them has been remarkable, the sales for 1886 being treble those of the preceding year, and practical engineers, without exception among those using them, attesting their superiority over other boilers, and the trade of the company extends to every part of the Union.

**The F. H. Thomas Law Book Company.**—F. H. Thomas, President; J. G. Lodge, Vice-President; A. M. Thomas, Secretary; Publishers and Dealers in Law Books; 9 South Fourth Street.—This prominent and prosperous corporation is well and favorably known to the legal profession in all parts of the United States as one of the leading law book houses in the country. The business was originally started in 1869 by the firm of Soule, Thomas & Windsor, which afterwards became Soule, Thomas & Wentworth, then F. H. Thomas and Co., and finally, in 1885, the present company was incorporated. Their store at 9 South Fourth Street is completely stocked with everything in the literature of law, including all the text books, original and reprint English and American reports, including those of the Supreme Court of the United States, and courts of last resort in all the States, and such *nisi prius* courts as are reported. The business of the house extends to every part of the Union, and four traveling salesmen represent them on the road. No firm in the country excels them in facilities for filling orders for law books, and the promptness and accuracy with which their business is conducted has secured for them a high reputation and a great business success. A further credit should attach to the enterprise of this house through their efforts in securing the trade of the law department of the Imperial University of Tokyo, Japan, whose orders they now command. Their monopoly of the large library patronage which they control is due to their specialty in the sale of the statutes and session laws of the different States and Territories, which no other law book house attempts to traffic in.

**Jos. Winkel Terra Cotta Works.**—Manufacturers of Architectural and Horticultural Terra Cotta: Works at Cheltenham; Office, 1121 Market street, Room 522.—To Mr. Joseph Winkel, the proprietor of these works, must be accorded the honor of having built up an important industry in St. Louis. The works were established in 1883, at Cheltenham, where the raw material for the manufacture of terra cotta of a superior quality is found in generous quantities on the premises. Employment is given to a force of fifty workmen and work is executed in strict accordance with designs furnished by architects, with a perfection of workmanship, uniformity of color, and of materials which for durability are not excelled by any manufactory in the country. Mr. Winkel keeps constantly on hand and promptly fills all orders for skewbacks for 9 and 13 inch arches, keys, window caps, diaper tile of all sizes, string courses, panels, etc.; also chimney tops of various designs. He is prepared to furnish estimates for anything in the line, and the high merit of the workmanship and materials turned out at these works has secured for him not only a heavy city business, but also a trade extending throughout Missouri, Kansas, Texas, Iowa, Minnesota, Arkansas and all parts of the South and West.

**Blattner & Adam.**—Practical Opticians, Mathematical and Electrical Instrument Makers; 22½ North Fourth street.—The business conducted by the firm of Blattner & Adam, composed of Messrs. Henry Blattner and Frank Adam, was established in 1840 by Mr. Jacob Blattner, father of the present head of the house. The existing firm was formed in 1870, and is located at 220 North Fourth street. They have a large business as dealers in every line of optical goods, and in mathematical and electrical instruments, making a specialty of surveying instruments, which they manufacture upon the most modern and approved principles, and sell largely to railroad companies, and to official and private surveyors in all parts of the country. In all its lines this firm sustains an excellent reputation for the perfect mechanism and accuracy of its instruments and the business, which has steadily grown during the forty-seven years of its existence, is now one of the most prosperous in its line in the West.

**Merkel Brothers.**—Designers and Engravers: 45 McLean Building, Fourth and Market streets.—The firm of Merkel Bros., of which the individual members are Messrs. C. F. M. and B. M. Merkel, has only been in existence about a year, but 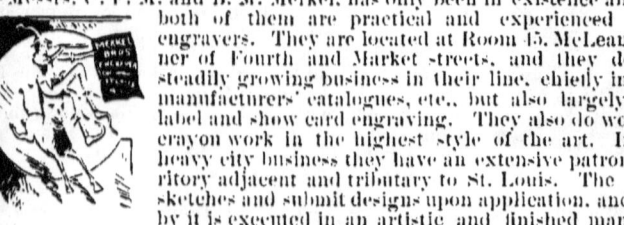 both of them are practical and experienced designers and engravers. They are located at Room 45, McLean building, corner of Fourth and Market streets, and they do a large and steadily growing business in their line, chiefly in wood cuts for manufacturers' catalogues, etc., but also largely in landscape, label and show card engraving. They also do wood carving and crayon work in the highest style of the art. In addition to a heavy city business they have an extensive patronage in the territory adjacent and tributary to St. Louis. The firm will make sketches and submit designs upon application, and all work done by it is executed in an artistic and finished manner. The firm has gained an excellent reputation for the appropriateness and beauty of its designs and its promptness in filling orders, and has fairly started upon a successful business career.

**Glendale Zinc Works.**—S. C. Edgar, Lessee; Manufacturer and Refiner of Spelter; Plow street, South St. Louis.—Prominent among the large manufacturing establishments of the city is the Glendale Zinc Works, belonging to the Glendale Zinc Co., by whom they are leased to Mr. S. C Edgar. These works, which are the largest in their line in the country, cover over three acres at South St. Louis, between the railroad tracks and the river, and give employment to a force of 250 men. They are equipped with a plant which is not surpassed by any in its completeness, and here all the operations pertaining to the manufacture and refining of spelter are carried on. The works have every facility and convenience for the handling and receipt of the raw material, and the shipment of manufactured product by rail or river, and do a prosperous business in all the States East to the Atlantic Ocean, the entire product being sold by Mr. Edward F. Byrne, of No. 54 Cliff Street, New York, who acts as Mr. Edgar's sales agent. Mr. Edgar is a thorough business man, experienced in all the details of this line of manufacture, and holds the foremost position he has attained in the trade by the exercise of experienced judgment and perfect system and accuracy in all his transactions.

**Charles Galle.**—Engraving on Wood and Advertising Signs; 110 Locust street.—Mr. Galle has been successfully engaged in the wood engraving business since 1883, and has been without a partner, except for about eight months in 1886, when the firm was Chas. Galle & Lange Engraving Co. (not incorporated). Mr.

Galle is a practical engraver and printer. He occupies premises, 25x100 feet, at 110 Locust street, and designs attractive engravings for advertisers, color plates for fine color plate printing, etc. In addition to this line Mr. Galle has another branch, of which he makes a specialty; this is the manufacture of the "Enameled Wood Pulp Sign" and the "Patent Protecting Sign Frame." The enameled wood pulp sign is made of a compressed sheet of pulp material, saturated and coated with water-proofing compounds, printed from engraved plates in rich colors and highly enameled. This sign is much superior to tin or iron signs, as temperature has no effect on it, and is largely in demand, especially by brewers and large manufacturers. It is made only in quantities of one hundred and upward, in any desired size, design, or color, and for convenience, cheapness and durability is much preferred by those who have used it to any other kind offered. Mr. Galle's business is very large, both in the city and the territory tributary to its market, and his patronage is steadily increasing as a result of the merit of his work and the prompt and accurate filling of orders.

**Massa, Lewis & Co.**—Importers and Jobbers in Watch Material, Jewelers' Supplies, etc.; 210 North Fourth street.—The house of Massa, Lewis & Co. does a very large business as importers and jobbers in every description of watch material, jewelers' supplies, tools, spectacles, etc. In addition to their house here the firm has a prosperous branch at 293 Sixteenth street, Denver, Colorado, which is managed by Mr. T. J. Lewis, of the firm, the house here being under the supervision of Mr. Edwin Massa, the senior partner. A staff of active and experienced travelers is employed at each branch, and the house has an extensive patronage in all the territory east to Indiana, and west to the Pacific Ocean, and all between these boundaries, north and south. In the Pacific Coast region the house has a representative constantly traveling, with headquarters at San Francisco. The stock carried at each of their houses is large and thoroughly diversified, selected with judgment and of the best foreign and domestic makes, and its trade shows annually a steady and healthy increase.

**Wilson, Nichols & Co.**—Wholesale Provisions and Packers of Dried Beef; 215 North Second street.—Although its members are still in the vigorous prime of life the firm of Wilson, Nichols & Co. is an old one. In 1858 Mr. H. L. Wilson, then 22 years old, came to St. Louis and went to work as a clerk. The following year he went into business with Mr. W. Nichols, and they have been together ever since. They first began business at 214 North Second street, where they remained nineteen years, at the expiration of which they removed across the street to their present location, at 215 North Second street, a commodious five-story building, 30x160 feet, conveniently equipped for the requirements of their business, and having a hydraulic elevator, which renders their top floor as useful as their main one. They carry a very large stock, comprising everything in the line of provisions, and also do a very extensive business as packers of dried beef. Their trade extends all over the West, Southwest and South, and in their long and honorable business career they have acquired a fine reputation, and the esteem and confidence of the trade, by the uniform excellence of their goods, and the fair and liberal spirit which actuates them in all their dealings. Their business, although it has for many years been large, is steadily growing from year to year, and the prosperity of the firm in the future bids fair to surpass its success in the past.

Chas. Ehlermann Hop and Malt Company.—Chas. Ehlermann, President and Treasurer; Otto Giesecke, Secretary; Wm. H. Beneke, Assistant Treasurer; Brewers', Distillers' and Bottlers' Supplies; Twenty-Second street and Scott avenue.—

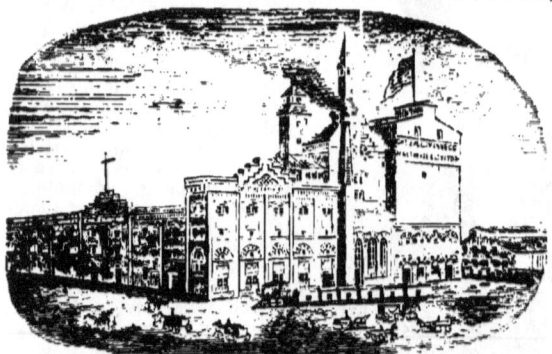

This establishment is the largest as well as one of the oldest in its line west of the Mississippi River. It was originally founded in 1859 by the firm of Wattenberg & Busch, Mr. Wattenberg being the uncle of Mr. Chas. Ehlermann. Chas. Ruepple & Co., of which Mr. Ehlermann was a member, afterward succeeded to the business, and the firm later became Chas. Ehlermann & Co., by whom the business was conducted until the present corporation was organized in 1886. The premises occupied by the company cover half a block and have a capacity, in malt house and elevator, of 400,000 bushels. Twenty-five men are employed and the company does a large business as maltsters and dealers in hops and brewery, distillery and bottlers' supplies. They have always on hand, in immense supply, complete stocks of malt, hops, rice, malt sugar, glucose, isinglass, pitch, rosin, varnish, bungs, shovels, kegs, barrels, brooms, pumps, faucets, brewers' and bottlers' machinery, and every description of goods in their line. Their trade extends not only all over the United States, but also to Central and South America and, in some lines of brewers' supplies, to Europe. The steady growth of the business of the company is the result of close attention to every detail of the business. Mr. Ehlermann has been trained to the business from his youth and is thoroughly experienced in all its branches. To his energy and enterprise the great prosperity enjoyed by the house is largely due.

B. Harris & Co.—Commission Merchants; Dealers in Hides, Wool, Furs, Etc.; 118 North Main street.—This firm, which has recently located in St. Louis, occupies eligible premises, consisting of a five-story building, 30x125 feet in dimensions, at 118 North Main street. The members of the firm are Messrs. Ben. Harris, Marcus Harris and Lewis Harris, and are brothers. The business was originally established at Warrensburg, Mo., where it was conducted by their father and themselves, with steady success, for sixteen years. The business field at Warrensburg, however, proved too restricted for them, and this spring they removed their headquarters to St. Louis, retaining their Warrensburg establishment as a branch house and leaving it in charge of Mr. Lewis Harris, while the St. Louis house is under the management of Messrs. Ben. and Marcus Harris. The members of the firm have a long experience in the business and a thorough knowledge of the markets in wool, hides, furs, pelts, etc., in which line they solicit consignments. Close attention is paid by them to the interests of those sending them consignments, for the advantageous sale of which they possess unsurpassed facilities. Possessed of ample means, and conducting their business on accurate and reliable methods, they have long enjoyed a merited reputation for their fidelity to the interests of shippers, which by the adoption, in the wider field they have now chosen for their business operations, of the high principles which have actuated their commercial conduct in the past, will doubtless result in still greater prosperity. Those placing business in the hands of this firm will find them worthy of confidence and patronage.

**A. G. Hulbert.**—Manufacturer of Wire and Iron Fences.—The illustration accompanying this article is a faithful portrait of Mr. A. G. Hulbert, the leading manufacturer of wire and iron fences, whose factories are in the western part of the city, and office at 904 Olive street. Eleven years ago, Mr. Hulbert began the manu‑

facture of wire fencing at Marshalltown, Iowa, with branch factories in Kansas and Texas, and in 1880 established the business in St. Louis, which he has built up to a leading position among the industries of its kind in the West. Being one of the most extensive advertisers of farm fences, there are few readers of agricultural papers who are not familiar with his name and manufactures. He is the sole proprietor of all the wire netting patents in the United States and Canada, and is the only manufacturer of the improved heavy grades suitable for farm fences, and altogether owns sixteen valuable patents covering barbed and tablet wire, iron posts, gates, fences and fence-making machinery, affording solid protection to his business and a marked advantage over competitors. He has always opposed monopoly pools, and has effected many reductions in the cost of barbed wire, in his various connections with its manufacture as senior member of the firm of Hulbert Brothers for eight years, and Hulbert & Gould six years and stockholder in three of the oldest incorporated fence and wire companies of Iowa, aside from the manufacturing business here, which he owns individually. His line of manufacture includes, with its several specialties, the making or handling of all goods belonging to fencing and wire trade. One of his latest introductions is the "Inflexible" wire netting, made with straight parallel wires running through all the meshes, making a substantial fence, and retaining under heavy strain its full width between posts, even when set fifteen to twenty feet apart, and as it costs no more it effectually throws out of market the old style nettings, which required top and bottom nail for support. His patent spiral steel lattice is a new article of manufacture for gates, fences, windows and tree guards, etc., being made of half-inch galvanized ribbon steel, it affords a more durable and handsome substitute for heavy wire work. Mr. Hulbert is favorably known among St. Louis publishers, as the founder of an agricultural paper now in its eighth volume, with a circulation accredited in all standard lists higher than any other of its class here. His tenth annual catalogue just issued, although a condensed pocket edition, contains more novel designs and solid information for buyers and users of fencing, than any other pamphlet in print; it is mailed free in response to letters of inquiry averaging from 50 to 100 daily, from all parts of the United States. We are satisfied that few other St. Louis industries give as flattering promise of rapid and permanent growth as the manufacturing business of A. G. Hulbert.

**Hirschl & Bendheim.**—Manufacturers of Fine Cigars, and Wholesale Dealers in Pipes, Tobaccos and Smokers' Articles; 409 North Third street.—The firm of Hirschl & Bendheim, of which Messrs. Solomon Hirschl, Myer H. Bendheim and Carl Bendheim are the individual members, was founded in 1871, and is one of the most prosperous in its line in the city. They are manufacturers of cigars, their factory being in New York, and their specialty fine goods, and are also extensive importers of Havana cigars, and wholesale dealers in pipes, tobaccos and all smokers' articles. They are also sole agents for H. Tibbe, Son & Co.'s Missouri Meerschaum Patent Corn Cob Pipes, which are well known to smokers and the trade as the best articles of the kind offered to the public. The firm employs twenty men at its commodious premises at 409 North Third street, and has eight commercial travelers on the road. It enjoys an extensive patronage in Missouri, Illinois, Kansas, Arkansas, Nebraska, Colorado, New Mexico, Texas, Mississippi, Tennessee, Kentucky, Indiana, Iowa, Michigan, Wisconsin, Minnesota and States on the Pacific Coast, and carries a large and thoroughly diversified stock of every article in the smokers' line. Its standing in the trade is very high, and its methods of dealing fair and liberal.

**Murphy & Company, Varnish Makers.**—Location of works, Newark, N. J., and Cleveland, Ohio; St. Louis Department, 300 South Fourth street.—This company, which is incorporated under the laws of the State of Ohio, is the largest manufacturer of varnish in America. In addition to their factories in Newark and Cleveland, and the department in St. Louis, the company has departments and salesrooms in New York and Chicago. The works of the company are so large and its facilities so great, that a year's supply of crude materials can be carried. The storage capacity of the varnish tanks at Newark is 235,000 gallons; at Cleveland 204,000; and at St. Louis and Chicago 50,000 gallons. And even this has been found insufficient for their rapidly growing business, and large additions are at present being made. The factory at Cleveland is devoted to the production of wagon, implement, and cabinet varnishes; while the main establishment at Newark is engaged with the manufacture of all the fine, high grades of carriage and car varnishes. The total running capacity of the Newark works is over 2,000 gallons of varnish and japan per day—a half a million gallons per year, consuming five hundred tons of copal and corresponding amounts of linseed oil and turpentine. The St. Louis house was established in 1883. The firm occupies, here, one of the most elegant and attractive buildings in the city, located at the southeast corner of Fourth and Clark avenue, which is admirably suited and adapted for its requirements. The St. Louis department is in charge of Mr. M. H. Stearns, who has had ten years' experience in the business. The A. B. C. System of Surfacers recently introduced by this company has been a great success with car builders and leading carriage manufacturers. Murphy & Company are very enterprising, and their salesmen visit every State and Territory in the Union. Knowing that in the end the people will be educated to appreciate the choicer grades of varnish, their brand on a package always means that it contains the best varnish that can be made of that particular grade. They do not take advantage of the general lack of information among consumers of varnish, to cheapen quality, in order to meet competition, and, as they frequently remark, make varnishes to be used as well as sold.

**T. Greer Russell.**—Brokerage and Commission; 300 North Main street.—Prominent among the leading and old established brokerage and commission merchants of the city is Mr. T. Greer Russell, who has been continuously engaged in this business since 1860. In the period of over a quarter of a century of active and honorable business life, he has succeeded in building up a large trade and a reputation unsurpassed by any merchant in his line. He makes a specialty of filling orders for pecan nuts, dried fruit, hemp seed, Virginia peanuts, etc., in round lots, selling only to jobbers and the wholesale trade, and having a very extensive patronage East, North, and West. His long experience in this line gives him a knowledge of the market for the commodities in which he deals, and facilities for their profitable handling and disposition equaled by few and surpassed by none, and he has held for many years a high place in the esteem and confidence of the trade, as a legitimate result of his close attention to business and the uniform fairness and accuracy of the methods employed by him in all his dealings.

**Winn Boiler Compound Company.**—D. R. Boogher, President; J. C. Weigand, Secretary; Manufacturers of Winn's Vegetable Boiler Compound; 106 and 108 Olive street.—This company was formed in 1882 for the purpose of manufacturing a valuable invention of Mr. J. C. Winn, known as Winn's Vegetable Boiler Compound. From that time to the present the demand for this article has been steadily growing, as its merits have become known over an extended field. The compound prevents the formation of scale and sediment in boilers, or, when applied to boilers in which scale has already formed, removes it effectually. It does not injure iron, saves fuel and labor, prevents foaming and explosions, and affords a safe and inexpensive method of keeping boilers clean and in good condition. This compound has long since passed out of the range of experiment and become an assured success, as is fully attested by the universal approbation of practical engineers and the constant increase in the demand for it, which now extends to all parts of the country, and has necessitated the establishment of agencies at St. Paul, Kansas City, Boston, New Orleans, Leadville, Chicago, and Columbus, O. The factory, warerooms and office of the company are eligibly located at 106 and 108 Olive street.

**A. Levy & Co.**—Agents of the Cyclostyle, and The Addressing, Duplicating and Mailing Co.; 21 North Second street.—Mr. A. Levy is the sole member of this firm, which has for fourteen years conducted a successful business as brokers and representatives of Eastern manufacturers. Recently Mr. Levy has obtained the Western control of the famous Cyclostyle, a copying machine from which 2,000 impressions or copies can be made from one writing.

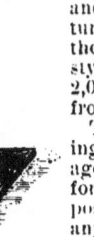

The Addressing, Mailing and Duplicating Co., for which Mr. Levy is also the agent, is a New York enterprise, formed for the purpose of addressing envelopes, postal cards, newspaper wrappers, etc., to any trade, profession or private individual in the United States. Accurate lists have been compiled of the names of residents in every county of each State. The facilities for accomplishing this work are very complete, and letters, price-lists, etc., can be duplicated and addressed to the extent of 100,000 copies per day. The plan is of great convenience to the merchants and business community, and is one of the most useful of the many improvements of the age in which we live.

**Clarksville Cider and Vinegar Company.**—Wm. H. Avis, President; Geo. Keightley, Vice-President; Charles J. Blake, Secretary and Treasurer; Pure Apple Cider, Vinegar and Syrup; 505 North Second street. The Clarksville Cider and Vinegar Co., which has its works at Clarksville, Pike county, Missouri, and its depot at 505 North Second street, this city, is the only concern west of New York of any considerable size, and the only one in the Mississippi Valley that makes pure, straight cider, cider vinegar and cider syrup. The company was formed in 1884, and has ever since endeavored strenuously to educate the people up to using pure, straight cider and cider vinegar in place of the inferior and often deleterious compounds of the artificial cider makers. In this laudable enterprise the company has succeeded so well that their trade has rapidly increased, the sales from this point in 1886 being 200 per cent. larger than those of 1885, and the prospects being bright for the season's sales in 1887 being double those of last year. The works at Clarksville have been in successful operation for more than twenty years, under the management of its founder, Henry S. Carroll, afterward Carroll, Wirrick & Co., to which firm the present company succeeded. Clarksville is located in the very center of the apple belt of the country, in the eastern part of Pike county, about one hundred miles above St. Louis, and the works have a capacity of 40,000 bushels per season, and are equipped with three of the largest and most powerful presses made, which are kept running day and night. The goods of this company are slightly higher priced than imitations, but they are successfully warring against and rapidly displacing artificial cider and cider vinegar. Mr. Avis, the president, is a citizen of St. Louis, resides here and manages the business of the company at this end, the other members being at the factory. The high merit of the company's goods and the thoroughness of its business principles have secured for it a great and growing success.

**Royal Cigar Company.**—Oscar Pryibil, President; Charles Knetzger, Secretary and Treasurer; Charles Schiele, Vice-President and Superintendent; Manufacturers of Cigars. Exclusively; Northwest Corner Main and Market streets.—This company removed its headquarters, in 1886, from Illinois to this city, where it occupies commodious premises, 25x100 feet, at the northwest corner of Main and Market streets. Their business is exclusively that of manufacturers of cigars, in which business they are extensively engaged, giving constant employment to a force of twenty-five skilled and experienced workmen. Their goods are all first-class, both in material and workmanship, and their specialties, "The Royal Cheroot" and "New Cable" have taken a fast hold upon public approval and are in very large and constantly increasing demand in Southern Illinois, Missouri, Kentucky, Arkansas, Tennessee and Indiana, in which states they do a large business. Resting their claims to success upon the merit of their goods, they have achieved a high reputation and an assurance of a prosperous business career.

**F. E. Little & Co.**—Feathers; 701 and 703 North Main street.—In the special line of feathers, the firm of F. E. Little & Co. occupies a foremost position. The business was established in 1884 by Little & Ely, to whom the present firm succeeds. Mr. Frank E. Little having bought out Mr. Ely's interest in December, 1886. The premises occupied by the firm consist of two stores at 701 and 703 North Main street, five stories high, with a frontage of 40 feet by a depth of 140 feet. They deal in feathers very largely, cleaning about 250,000 lbs. of feathers per annum, and manufacture the celebrated "Star" brand of odorless feathers and pillows. They also deal in mattress moss. Their trade covers a vast territory, west, north, northwest and east, and their shipments to Boston, Philadelphia and San Francisco are especially large. With an extensive knowledge of everything pertaining to their line the facilities of the house for handling this description of goods are unsurpassed, and the accuracy of their methods has given the firm a high standing and reputation.

**Walter S. Bartley.**—Provision, Tallow, Flour and Grain Broker; 216 Pine street.—For the last fourteen years Mr. Walter S. Bartley has been engaged in business in this city as a broker in provisions, tallow, flour and grain. He occupies an office at 216 Pine street, conveniently located in the heart of the business center of the city, and handles the class of goods mentioned in round lots only, shipping them to all parts of the Union and to Europe. During his long and honorable business career he has ever maintained a high reputation for the close attention given by him to the details of his business and the perfect system and correct methods by which all his transactions are characterized. His ripe experience, superior intimacy with the markets in the commodities which he handles, and the unsurpassed facilities he possesses for advantageous dealing, have secured for him a large patronage and great business success.

**William Sessinghaus & Co.**—Millers; 116 and 118 North Second street.—The mill of William Sessinghaus & Co., used in the manufacture of a superior article of corn meal, occupies the two four-story buildings with a frontage of forty feet at 116 and 118 North Second street by a depth of sixty feet. In addition to the manufacture of corn meal, which is the specialty of the house, the firm deals in flour and feed and handles every description of feed goods on commission. Mr. Sessinghaus is a practical and experienced man in every department of the corn meal, flour and feed business, and by close attention to every detail, just and liberal methods in his dealings with his customers, and promptness in filling orders, he has secured a large and steadily increasing trade in the city and surrounding country, and a high reputation which gives assurance of the continuance of the success he has achieved.

**William N. Tivy.**—General Commission Merchant; 424 North Second street.—One of the oldest commission houses in the city is that of Mr. William N. Tivy, who has been successfully engaged in the business since 1853. He occupies the four-story building, 25x100 feet, at 424 North Second street, with the basement of the adjoining building, which is completely equipped for use as a refrigerator. He deals extensively, on commission, in butter, cheese. lard, eggs, honey, dried fruit, wool, hides, etc., receiving butter and cheese from Northern Illinois, Wisconsin and Iowa, and the other lines in which he deals from all the States in the West, Southwest, and South tributary to the St. Louis market. In the long period of a third of a century in which Mr. Tivy has been engaged in business pursuits, he has ever maintained a high reputation for the close attention paid by him to the details of every transaction placed in his hands and the reliability and accuracy of his methods of dealing. He sells principally to shippers in this city, and has the confidence of the trade in an eminent degree.

**A. Oakes & Co.**—Manufacturers of Pure Home-Made Candies and Fine Confections; Factory, 819 St. Charles street; Office and Salesroom, 307 North Broadway.—No firm in St. Louis is better known or enjoys the distinction that this firm does in the confection and candy line. The house was established by Peter Oakes in 1865, since which time the name of Oakes has become a household word in connection with candy. For many years he maintained a place on Olive street, just west of Fourth, that secured a large and fashionable patronage. The elegant and spacious salesroom at 307 North Broadway was secured several years ago, and it is one of the most popular establishments of the city. Mr. Peter Oakes, who is the company of the firm title, is an artist of many years' experience in the candy trade, and the fine bon bons, choice caramels, and other dainty bits of confection that are so temptingly displayed are all made under his personal supervision, and nothing but the best and purest ingredients are allowed to enter into their manufacture. The demand for Oakes' celebrated candies is not confined to local residents but extends to all States directly tributary to St. Louis. Shipments are made to California, Texas, Louisiana and other Western and Southern States, and the trade with Missouri, Kansas, Nebraska, Arkansas, Illinois and the Territories is always large. Oakes and his candies have a high reputation.

**O. M. Schmidt & Co.**—Wholesale Grocers, Liquor Dealers and Commission Merchants, 117 North Second street.—The prominent and prosperous firm of O. M. Schmidt & Co. is composed of Messrs. O. M. Schmidt, Frank Hassendeubel, and E. H. Schmidt. It was established in 1876, and occupies the large five-story building 30x140 feet, at 117 North Second street, which is conveniently and centrally located. They carry on an extensive business as wholesale grocers and liquor dealers, and have a large and thoroughly diversified stock of staple and fancy groceries, grocers' sundries and shelf goods, as well as a complete and carefully assorted stock of the best known brands of liquors of every description. They employ three active and energetic commercial travelers to represent the house, and enjoy a large and extensive patronage in the States of Missouri and Illinois and other territory adjacent to this market. They also do a flourishing business as commission merchants, and have an excellent reputation with shippers and producers, possessing every facility for the profitable handling of consignments. The business has steadily grown since its inception, and was specially large during the season of 1886; while the outlook for the present year promises a still greater increase in the volume of the trade. The high standing of the house has been fairly earned by the uniform merit of its goods and the correctness of its business methods.

**Huttig Sash and Door Company.**—William Huttig, Jr., President; F. Huttig, Treasurer; C. F. W. Huttig, Secretary; C. H. Huttig, Manager; Manufacturers of Sash, Doors and Blinds, and Wholesale Dealers in Mouldings, Stair Work, etc.; Warehouse, Dock and Main streets; Factory, Tenth and Mullanphy streets. —This substantial and representative house, recognized as one of the most prominent and prosperous in its line in the West, was established in this city in 1885. The parent house is at Muscatine, Iowa, where it was established twenty years ago by the firm of Huttig Bros., and is now doing a heavy business as the Huttig Bros. Manufacturing Co. They have also a house, established five years ago, at

Kansas City, where the style of the company is the Western Sash and Door Co. From St. Louis the company has a very heavy and constantly increasing trade in all the country tributary to this market. Their warehouse covers half a block, is a handsome and substantial brick structure and is completely stocked with sash, doors, blinds, mouldings, stair work, etc. Their factory, covering a half block at Tenth and Mullanphy streets, is a late acquisition, and is used for the manufacture of special sizes of sash, doors, and blinds, interior finish and fancy work of this description, the stock work being supplied from the Muscatine factory. In mechanical equipment and every convenience and accessory calculated to facilitate their business operations, they have no superior in the country, and their product is known to the lumber trade of the Northwest, West and South for its superior workmanship. Railway tracks, convenient to both warehouse and factory, give them first-class facilities for handling and shipment and enable them to fill all orders with dispatch. Sound judgment and intelligent methods of management, combined with the utmost financial stability and an accurate knowledge of the requirements of the trade, are prominent among the elements that have contributed to give this house its solid reputation and a steady expansion of trade from year to year.

**Herman Levy & Co.**—Commission Merchants and Dealers in Hides, Furs, Wool, Pelts, Deer Skins, Tallow, Ginseng, etc.; 20 North Main street.—This successful and representative house was established by Mr. Herman Levy in 1882. The firm occupies commodious premises conveniently and centrally located at 20 North Main street and does a general commission business, making a prime specialty of furs, in which line they are leading dealers in the West. They have a large and annually increasing patronage in Illinois. Missouri, Arkansas, Indian Territory, Mississippi, Louisiana and Texas, and have a high reputation among shippers and producers, whose esteem and confidence they hold as a result of faithful attention to every consignment. Their facilities for the advantageous disposition of goods shipped to them is unsurpassed, their knowledge of the market being close and accurate and their commercial attainments giving them a foremost standing in trade circles.

**J. C. C. Waldeck Provision Company.**—J. C. C. Waldeck, President and Treasurer; General Dealers in all Kinds of Fresh and Cured Pork; 111 Market street.—This business was established in 1880 as Jacob C. C. Waldeck & Co., to which the present company are the successors, Mr. Waldeck, the founder of the house, remaining President and Treasurer of the incorporation, which occupies commodious premises, 25x75 feet, at No. 111 Market street. The business of the house is very large, not only in the city, but also in the country contiguous to it and in the Southern States In the summer season the trade in provisions and hams is made a specialty, and in winter fresh meats. The house makes a specialty of fresh spare ribs, tenderloins, sausage meat in season, tongues, check meat and neck roll. The facilities of the house for the delivery of goods to any part of the city and their shipment to the country are unsurpassed, while the reputation they have gained for the superior merit of their goods is such that their business shows an annual increase; and the fair and liberal methods adopted by the company in all its dealings have contributed in a large degree to bring about the merited success it has achieved.

**R. L. Coleman & Co.**—Hot and Cold Blast Iron, etc.; Office, 120 North Third street.—This business was established about ten years ago by the firm of R. L. Coleman & Bro., under which name it was successfully conducted until 1886, when, upon the death of his brother, Mr. R. L. Coleman continued the business alone, adopting the above title. He has his office at 120 North Third street, and also has two yards for storage purposes, one of which is located on North Main street and the other on Twenty-first street. He does the largest pig iron trade in the city, and has, at this writing, orders on hand for 30,000 tons. He deals chiefly in Tennessee, Alabama, Texas, Ohio and Missouri iron, and also largely in rails, car wheels, car axles, etc. He does a very large trade, his business territory extending west to California, south to Texas, north to Iowa, and east into Illinois. His facilities for handling and transportation are unexcelled, and the goods handled by him are of the best quality. He has a high reputation in the commercial world, and does a successful and prosperous business. At present he finds trade particularly good, the rapid increase in prices having caused a great improvement in the iron business during the past few months. Mr. Coleman has a long and practical experience in this line, and, by the fairness and liberality of his dealings, retains all his old customers and gains new ones with each succeeding season.

**Nathan & Lierow.**—Fire and Marine Insurance; 222 Pine street.—This prominent firm of underwriters was formed in 1884, but the members of the firm had previously been engaged in the business: Mr. Nathan for three years, and Mr. Lierow for twenty-four years. Thus fortified with valuable experience, and bringing to the business every qualification for its successful prosecution, the firm has built up a valuable business connection, and justly holds a high place in the confidence of the insuring public. They are agents for the German Fire Insurance Co., of Freeport, Ill., with $2,000,000 capital, and which wrote risks in Missouri during 1886 to the amount of $6,484,290. This company is the largest in resources and the volume of its business of any west of the Alleghenies. It leads all other companies in business transacted in Kansas, Missouri and Illinois, and does a specially large business insuring farms in all Western States. It is prompt in the payment of losses, and fair and liberal in all its relations with its policy-holders. Other solid companies for which Messrs. Nathan & Lierow are agents are the American Insurance Co., of Newark, N. J., with $600,000 capital, $346,264.98 surplus, and which did Missouri business last year amounting to $1,809,000 in risks written; the Hanover Fire Insurance Co., of New York, with a capital of $3,000,000, and which wrote Missouri risks last year amounting to $4,164,978; and the Clinton Fire Insurance Co., of New York, capital $500,000, which did Missouri business in 1886 amounting to $744,611. Through these first-class companies the firm are prepared to offer insurance on good risks at the lowest terms consistent with absolute safety. These companies are all in every respect reliable, and Messrs. Nathan & Lierow, by the accuracy of their business methods, have earned the prosperity they enjoy, and have written and are now carrying a large number of risks upon much of the best business and residence property in St. Louis.

LACLEDE BUILDING COR. FOURTH & OLIVE STS.

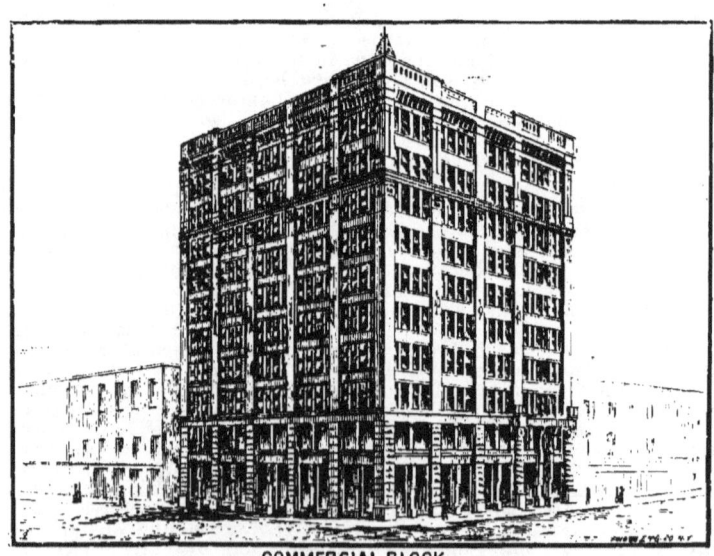

COMMERCIAL BLOCK.

**E. S. Warner & Co.**—Real Estate and Financial Agents, 205 North Eighth street.—The real estate business in St. Louis has assumed large proportions in the last five years, and much outside capital has sought investment in local property. Much of this is due to the push and energy of E. S. Warner, the head of the prominent firm which bears his name. He has resided in St. Louis for many years, and has been prominently identified with the real estate business for the past twenty-five years. His knowledge of property values is very extensive, and his judgment is relied upon by many of the largest investors. Several years ago he foresaw the grand possibilities of the West End becoming the fashionable and popular residence section of the city, and at once commenced to boom that locality. The success of the West End is due largely to his efforts. He was one of the first to urge the improvement of West Pine street from Cabanne Place to Vandeventer avenue. He was also one of the committee of citizens who raised the fund necessary to grade Lindell avenue, and his associates on the committee attribute to him a large share of the glory for its success. Mr. Warner conducted the negotiation for the lease of the property at the southwest corner of Fourth and Olive streets upon which the magnificent ten-story Laclede Building will be erected, also the lease of the property at the southeast corner of Sixth and Olive streets for a term of ninety-nine years, upon which a ten-story building will be built this fall, and which two buildings are shown in the illustrations on the opposite page. He makes a specialty of the purchase and sale of real estate.

**Burd-Stuyvesant Glue Company.**—Wm. Burd, President; M. S. Stuyvesant, Secretary and Treasurer; Glue, etc.; 6 North Main street.—This business was established in 1877 by Mr. William Burd, the firm becoming first Burd & Morton, then Burd & Little, and finally adopting the present style upon the incorporation of the company in 1885. The premises occupied by the company are eligibly located at 6 North Main street, having a frontage of 40 feet and running back 140 feet, six stories in height. The company deal in glue, moss, curled hair, ground flint, sandpaper, glycerine for printers' rollers, etc. The company control the annual product of several of the oldest and largest glue manufacturers in Europe and the United States, and for this reason do not manufacture themselves. The trade of the house is immense in its proportions, extending over the entire United States and the Dominion of Canada. The business of the company is largest in its specialty of glue, but it also has a large trade in its other lines which is rapidly increasing. The special facilities enjoyed by the company enable it to distance its competitors in the advantageous terms it is enabled to offer to the trade, and the accurate methods which it employs in all its transactions have given it an unsurpassed reputation and an assurance of a continuance of the success it has achieved.

**Geo. J. Fritz.**—Central Iron Works; Patentee and Builder of Steam Engines, Boilers, Doctors, Pumps, Seed Meal Molders, Barrel Trusses, etc.; 2018, 2020, 2022, 2024, 2026 and 2028 South Third street.—These works were established by Mr. George J. Fritz in 1874 upon a very modest scale, the original premises having but forty-four feet of front. The steady perseverance and energy of the proprietor has caused an expansion of the business which has necessitated additions from time to time, and the works now cover an area of 200x150 feet, are two stories high, and are fitted up with all the latest and most improved machinery and plant adapted to the business, and employment is given to a force of about one hundred men, all of whom are skilled mechanics. All the operations of the works are conducted under the close personal supervision of Mr. Fritz, who is a thoroughly practical and experienced man in the

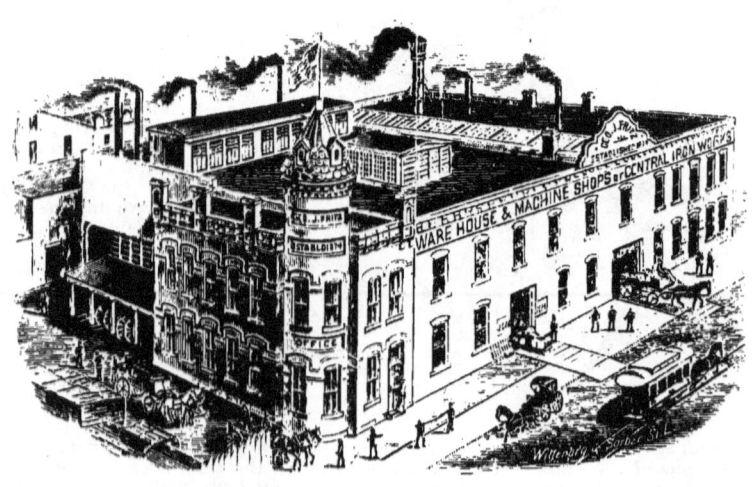

business. The range of manufactures carried on at the works is a wide one, embracing engines, boilers, doctors, crushing rolls, electric light engines, cotton seed hullers, pumps, seed meal molders, barrel trusses, brewers', bottlers' and coopers' machinery, butchers' machinery, laundry machinery, shafting, pulleys, hangers, mill gearing and mill supplies, brass goods of all kinds, pipe and pipe fittings, pipe-fitters' tools, belting, hose, packing, etc., in fact, all kinds of machinery. A specialty of the works is a rapid speed engine for dynamo-electric lights and other purposes, the invention of Mr. Fritz, who is also the designer and inventor of a number of the other machines produced at these works. Many of the largest and most important manufacturing establishments of the city have been supplied and fitted with machinery from these works, among others the improvements in the brewery of the Anheuser-Busch Brewing Association and that of William J. Lemp; also all of the machinery of the new Wainwright brewery. Special attention is given to repairing all kinds of machinery, for which these works are unsurpassed in facilities. A large business is done at these works in regrinding and corrugating millers' rolls, in order to adapt them to the new roller process, for which business Mr. Fritz has a special plant, which is not excelled by any house in the country. The trade of the house is very large, and stretches to every part of the United States, and it is especially great in the States of the South and West; the works having a widespread reputation for superior workmanship and facilities, and Mr. Fritz enjoying the respect and confidence of the trade, to which he has commended himself by the perfect accuracy and reliability by which his transactions are characterized. He issues a handsome catalogue, giving detailed information in regard to his manufactures, which those who are interested in machinery would do well to send for.

**Anthony & Kuhn Brewing Company.**—Henry Anthony, President; Francis Kuhn, Treasurer; Fred. G Schoenthaler, Secretary; Brewery, Sidney and Buel streets; Depot and Salesroom, 110 and 112 North Broadway.—Among the larger brewing establishments of St. Louis none enjoys more prosperity or a better reputation than the Anthony & Kuhn Brewing Company. The business was established twenty years ago, upon a comparatively modest scale, by Messrs. Henry Anthony and Francis Kuhn. Both being experienced brewers they brought to the business a fund of practical knowledge which, combined with enterprise and honorable business methods, has brought the establishment to its present condition of success. The business expanded to such an extent that in 1883, in order to carry it on more advantageously, the present company was formed. Their brewery, which covers more than a block, is one of the best equipped in the country, containing every facility and convenience for the business, and the latest and most approved inventions in refrigerating machinery. Over one hundred men are employed by the company, and the product of the brewery is of such excellent quality that the XXX brand is in large demand, not only in the city and surrounding country, but the bottled goods are sold all over the Union, and also exported in large quantities.

The XXX beer is a healthy and nutritive family beverage, made from the choicest materials the market affords. It contains only a small percentage of malt spirit, such as is absolutely necessary to the keeping qualities of the article, while in nutritious properties it exceeds any other brand in the market, and is preferable to the various malt extracts and similar preparations put upon the market of late years, which contain a large percentage of alcohol and have a nauseating effect upon the stomach. These statements are supported by an analysis recently made from samples out of the stock of the brewery by Messrs. Weinerth & Heckelmann, the well-known analytical chemists of this city, who found the beer an effervescing liquid of amber color, pleasant aromatic odor, agreeable bitter taste, very palatable, and perfect clearness, containing by chemical examination the following ingredients: total solid extractive matter, 8.97 per cent.; bitter extract of hops, 0.19 per cent.; nitrogenous constituents, 0.97 per cent.; phosphates, 0.29 per cent.; malt spirit, 4.50 per cent. The beer has taken a large number of premiums at exhibitions and fairs, and the trade of the company increases steadily from year to year. Managed with perfect system and upon liberal and honorable principles, the company is a representative one in every respect.

**P. Burns & Co.**—Manufacturers and Wholesale Dealers in Saddles, Harness, etc.; 705 and 707 Lucas avenue.—This firm was established thirty years ago in a small town in Cooper county, Missouri, and, seeking a larger field, they removed to St. Louis twenty-four years ago. The firm has been a prominent factor in the building up of the market of St. Louis in saddlery and harness to its position as the largest in the world in that line. They are extensively engaged in the manufacture of saddles, harness, collars, etc., and as dealers in saddlery, hardware, whips, etc., carrying very large and complete stocks in all lines. They occupy an elegant six-story and basement building, 30x125 feet, which they erected a year and a half ago, and which is expressly adapted to their business. At these premises they employ a force of nearly one hundred skilled and experienced workmen. They have a very large trade, covering the States of Illinois, Missouri, Kansas, Iowa, Nebraska, Arkansas, Texas, Indian Territory, and several of the Southern States. Six traveling salesmen are employed, and the house holds a high position in the esteem and confidence of the trade, its goods being of the best quality, the finest workmanship, and made in the most attractive and popular styles. The firm makes a specialty of buggy harness, in which department it excels. In the history of the house, covering nearly a third of a century, its dealings have always been characterized by fairness and accuracy, and the result has been a steady expansion in its business, and a success which is the well-earned result of merit.

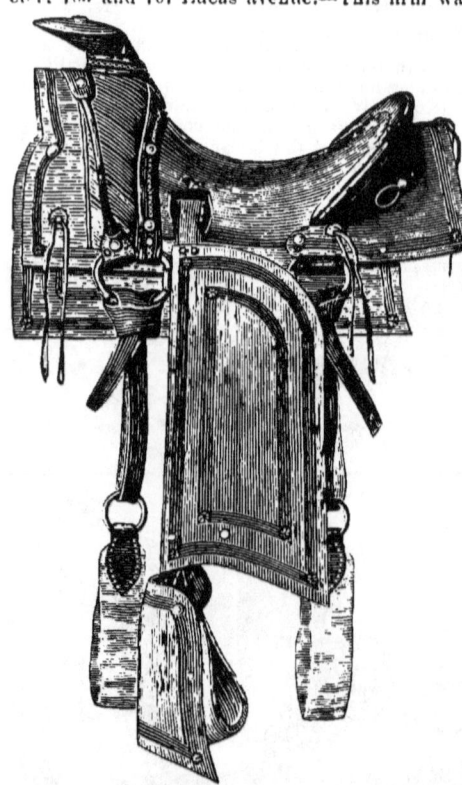

**The Mutual Life Insurance Company of New York.**—Richard A. McCurdy, President; Byron Sherman, General Agent. St. Louis; 300 North Fourth street.—The benefits of life insurance are recognized by all intelligent people, and in making this beneficent provision for the family the main problem is the selection of the company in which to procure a policy. Among the best insurance corporations of the country The Mutual Life Insurance Company holds a prominent and distinguished position. It was organized in 1842, and throughout the long period from that year to the present time has maintained, by the accuracy and reliability of its methods, a foremost place in public confidence. Its board of trustees is composed of thirty-six of the most substantial business men of New York, and its assets at the beginning of the present year amounted to $114,181,963.24. It had policies and annuities in force, Jan. 1, 1887, amounting to $393,809,202.88, its premium income for 1886 was $15,634,720.66, and it had a reserve for policies in force and risks terminated of, $108,460,120.25, and a surplus, at 4 per cent., of $5,643,568.15. The company issues policies on all the usual life plans, and in addition has a new policy, combining all the good features that have been approved by experience, and offering every advantage to the assured consistent with the certainty of meeting the obligations incurred. This policy is free from all provisions that could in any case lead to the contesting of the claim, has no restrictions upon travel or foreign residence; has all the advantages claimed for the "Tontine" insurance without the offensive gambling features; it is paid immediately upon the presentation of proofs of death; and cannot be forfeited after three annual payments. Should death occur during the first dividend period of ten, fifteen or twenty years, the company pays not only the face of the policy, but in addition returns all the premiums paid to that date. At the end of dividend period the insured receives his dividend in cash or in paid up insurance, as he may prefer. He also has the privilege of surrendering his policy for a guaranteed cash value at that time or later. In safety, equity and absence of restrictions this policy is without doubt unexcelled in liberality to the insured, and is, in fact, the ne plus ultra of a life insurance contract. The general agency of the company in St. Louis was established in 1867, although they had maintained a sub-agency in the city for several years prior to that date. Mr. Byron Sherman, the general agent of the company here, is justly looked upon as an authority upon life insurance, and to his energy and close attention to business the company owes a steady increase in its business in this section. Parties contemplating insurance would do well to apply to the general agency for detailed information, which will be cheerfully furnished on application.

**Clarkson & Wagner.**—Hamilton-Corliss and Stationary and Portable Engines, Saw Mills, Gang Edgers, Lath Machines, Wood-Working Machinery, Belting and Mill Supplies; 709 North Second street.—In 1881 Messrs. James Clarkson and H. C. Wagner, who had been for many years with Owens, Lane & Dyer,  struck out for themselves and established this business, and have met with great success ever since. They occupy the spacious five-story building, 30x130 feet, at 709 North Second street, and have a large patronage extending east to Pennsylvania and covering the entire Northwest, Southwest, and South. They deal in the celebrated Hamilton-Corliss engine, which is unsurpassed in economy in fuel, close regulation, strength, workmanship, finish and smoothness of action. The firm also deals in every description of stationary and portable engines, saw mills, gang edges, lath machines, wood-working machinery, belting and mill supplies. They have a deservedly high reputation and a great success as the result of the superiority of their goods and their close attention to every detail of their business.

**Henry & Co.**—Manufacturers of Excelsior; 1100 North Main street.—An industry of comparatively recent growth, but which has already attained great importance, is the manufacture of excelsior, and in this line the firm of Henry & Co., located at 11'0 North Main street, occupy a prominent and leading position. The members of the firm are Messrs. P. Henry, F. Tieman and F. Uetrecht, and their premises are eligibly located at No. 1100 North Main street, covering an area of 120x 130 feet. The factory is fitted up with improved excelsior cutting machines of Mr. Henry's own patent, which are iron frame, double upright machines. Mr. Henry has a long experience in this line, having been engaged in the manufacture of horizontal excelsior cutting machines in Cincinnati as early as 1866. The excelsior manufactured by this firm is only of the best quality, being made from cottonwood, which is at once the lightest and most durable. It is made in three grades: coarse, medium and fine, and the works have a capacity of over seven tons per day and give employment to a force of about forty skilled hands. The business was established by the present firm in 1874 and has grown year by year until it has assumed immense proportions, finding a large patronage, not only in this city, but also in all the States of the West, South and Southwest. It is sold to upholsterers, mattress makers, carriage makers, undertakers and also for packing purposes. Mr. Henry also manufactures and sells his excelsior machine, of which he is the sole inventor and which is acknowledged to be the most complete offered to the public. The superiority of the goods manufactured by this firm has given them a high reputation and has secured for them a large and valuable trade.

**Parker, Ritter, Nicholls Stationery Company.**—Stationers, Office Outfitters, Blank-Book Manufacturers, Printers and Lithographers; 400 and 402 North Third street.—Some business houses seem to obtain a hold on the community from the day they start, others attain popularity by slow and weary steps. The subject of this sketch, the Parker, Ritter, Nicholls Stationery Co., seemed in some unusual manner to spring into public favor and patronage at once. Its unprecedented success is due to close attention to business, a thorough acquaintance with the needs of the business public and a careful endeavor to always furnish the best only in each line. It was started in 1881 by Mr. J. A. Parker, who soon associated with himself Mr. E. P. V. Ritter, Treasurer of Famous Shoe & Clothing Co. Not long after, Mr. F. S. Parker, his brother, (now Treasurer of the St. Bernard Dollar Store Co.) gave his personal help, and a little later Mr. C. C. Nicholls, Secretary of the Beard & Bro. Safe and Lock Co., and now secretary of several of the most successful building associations, entered the company, and the firm was incorporated under its present name. In all its rapid strides forward, this live concern has been assisted by competent and gentlemanly salesmen and managers of the different departments of the business. This house was the first in the stationery business to take hold of such specialties in office outfitting as the caligraph writing machine, stenograph shorthand machine, the Amberg's cabinet letter file, Shea Smith's letter books, ready addressed circular envelopes, etc. And their numerous specialties, all the very best in their line, that they now have and control for a number of States, show their thorough knowledge of business men's needs, and success in supplying the same.

They are leaders in almost every particular, other houses adopting their methods. The business they have built up in special appliances for the dictation and writing of letters, by the use of the marvellous stenograph shorthand machine (far superior and more accurate than old style shorthand), is surprising. The "caligraph," the latest improvement in writing machines, has made a wonderful revolution in the correspondence of the country. This firm are general agents for it in the Southwest. The large business they have built up in the proper appliances for the copying of letters by the blotter bath, specially adapted inks, the unequaled Shea Smith copying books, with all their peculiar advantages, has greatly increased the importance of their concern in the eyes of business men. The latest thing to mention is the proper filing of letters by Amberg's directory system of cabinet letter files. Hardly a large business house in the country but has this indispensable office fixture and this enterprising firm has obtained the exclusive agency for it. Of course we must not omit to mention that this concern has also every known article in the category of office supplies, blank-books, inks, pens, pencils, paper, baskets, presses, etc., etc., and they have special facilities for supplying banks and business men with everything in the line of lithography, printing and blank books, and are constantly filling orders from all parts of the South and West. Their location is one of the best in the city.

**Pentland & Hahn.**—Block and Pump Makers; 944 North Main street.—An old established and popular house in the line of block and pump making is that of Pentland & Hahn, which was founded in 1856 by Messrs. F. M. Thompson and W. J. Pentland. In 1858 the firm became W. J. Pentland alone, and in 1865 he was joined by Mr. M. Hahn, adopting the present firm name. They occupy commodious premises, 25x120 feet, at 944 North Main street, which are fully equipped with all the machinery and appliances requisite to the proper prosecution of their business. They manufacture tackle blocks, hoisting wheels, crabs, stone derricks, log pumps, tenpin balls, rope and iron strapped blocks of all kinds, wire rope fastenings, etc. They constantly carry a large and diversified stock of every description of article pertaining to their line, and in addition are prepared to do turning, rigging, blacksmithing and repairing of all kinds in the most workmanlike manner and on short notice. In the long and honorable career of this house it has established a high reputation for the excellence of its goods and the superiority of its workmanship, and it enjoys a large and steadily growing patronage.

**The United States Stenograph Company.**—Joseph Specht, President; J. A. Parker, Vice-President; E. P. V. Ritter, Secretary and Treasurer; H. C. Wright, General Manager; 402 North Third Street.—This company was incorporated in 1881 for the purpose of manufacturing and introducing that wonderful invention of Mr. M. M. Bartholomew, the Stenograph, a most useful machine for writing a system of shorthand, as rapid as any other, noiseless in operation, the most exact and uniform, the least trouble in practice, and by far the most quickly and easily

learned, and bears to shorthand the same relation as the type-writer does to long hand. The work done by the stenograph is always legible and can be read by anyone who understands its alphabet. The machine consists of five writing keys, each carrying a marker, a spacing key, a paper guide, an inked ribbon, with reels for holding it, and a device for moving the paper forward and a reel for holding the same. The demand for the instrument is very large and steadily increasing, and agencies and schools are being rapidly established in every part of the United States, Canada and Mexico. The Stenograph is the equivalent in saving time, money or labor in office work, to other remarkable machines in more material fields. For court work it is unexcelled for accuracy and speed. The officers of the company are men of large business experience and responsibility in other departments of trade.

**C. E. Udell & Co.**—Cheese Dealers; 114 Pine street.—This business was established in 1873 as S. R. Udell & Co., changing to its present style of C. E. Udell & Co. some five years ago, Messrs. C. E. Udell and T. F. Jones composing the firm. They occupy the four-story and cellar building, 25x120 feet, at 114 Pine street, which is fully and completely stocked with every description of cheese, in which line they deal exclusively. The firm receives most of its full cream cheese from Wisconsin, where it keeps an experienced buyer permanently stationed, and receives other grades of cheese from points in Illinois, Ohio, New York and abroad. The trade of the house is confined to sales to jobbers, with whom it has extensive dealings in all parts of the South and West. The firm received its share of the benefits of the business reaction noticeable during the past year, having had a larger trade in 1886 than in any previous season. Devoting its attention exclusively to one line, in which the members of the firm have a special experience and knowledge, and dealing upon a scale of unsurpassed magnitude, the facilities of the house are unexcelled, and its business course is characterized by a spirit of fairness and liberality, which has secured for it a high standing and a prosperous career.

**Eagle Machine Works Manufacturing Company.**—H. S. Albrecht, President; Wm. Grundeler, Vice-President and Secretary; Manufacturers of Engines and General Machinery; 940 to 942 North Main street.—This large and important business, which was formerly conducted by the firm of Dvorak & Voita, was incorporated under its present name in 1883. The company occupies as works a commodious three-story building, 56x150 feet, and the machinery equipment includes all the most modern and improved devices and appliances for the prosecution of their manufacturing operations, including a 35-horse-power engine, lathes of great capacity and of the most improved pattern and make, and a pattern shop fully and completely stocked with all the necessary tools, and containing all patterns of engines, trucks, low cars, coal mine trucks, etc. They manufacture all kinds of engines and general machinery, platform and grain elevators, pulleys, shafting and hangers, etc. They also manufacture the "Lone Star" brick-making machine, with a capacity of 15,000 per day, and which bears a high reputation with brick makers for the perfection of its mechanism. The works give employment to twenty-five of the most skilled and experienced workmen, and every engine and article of machinery produced by this company is made of the best materials and of the most complete style of workmanship, the company having acquired its high reputation and maintained it from the inception of the business to the present time, by reason of the superiority of its products, to which, combined with the enterprise of its management and the perfect system maintained in its transactions, is due its great success and its high position in the business world.

**Rhodus Commission Company.**—Thomas Rhodus, Manager; Commission: Furs, Hides, Wool, Game and Country Produce; 314 North Commercial street.—Occupying a very prominent position among the commercial houses whose enterprise and industry have combined to make this city a great mart for the disposition of the products of the field and farm, is that of the Rhodus Commission Co., of which Mr. Thomas Rhodus is the manager. The firm is located in the commodious six-story building, 125x40 feet, at 314 North Commercial street; the main floor of which they occupy, renting the remainder of the building to other parties. They do a large and constantly growing trade, dealing in all kinds of raw furs, hides, wool, game and all kinds of country produce. The firm make liberal advances on consignments, which they receive in large quantities from all points and dispose of chiefly in this city. Mr. Rhodus, the manager, possesses a large practical experience and a close and intimate knowledge of the market. Every transaction receives his careful attention, and by his judicious management and devotion to the interests of those sending consignments he has established this house in the confidence of producers and shippers and earned for it the success which is the reward of industry and fidelity.

**James A. Quirk.**—Manufacturer and Wholesale and Retail Dealer in Trunks, Valises and Satchels; Southwest Corner Second and Walnut streets.—This is an old house which has sustained for many years an excellent reputation for the quality of its goods and the accurate methods by which its transactions are characterized. Mr. Quirk has been engaged in business in this city for the past thirty years, during which he has built up a large trade extending east to Indiana and to every part of the South and West, as well as having some Northern trade. He occupies two spacious five-story buildings, including his box shops in the southern part of the city, and gives employment to forty skilled and experienced workmen, besides twelve trunk box makers. He manufactures and deals in every description of trunks, valises and satchels, all of the best workmanship and made of the best and most serviceable materials. One of the houses is devoted to the wholesale trade, while the other is used for the retail department of Mr. Quirk's business, and enjoys a heavy city patronage. He has three travelers representing him on the road, and enjoys success as the result of a long and honorable business history.

**T. B. Boyd & Co.**—Importers, Manufacturers and Jobbers of Men's Furnishing Goods and Shirts; 309 North Fourth street.—The firm of T. B. Boyd & Co., composed of Messrs. T. B. Boyd and George D. Bennett, are successors to Wilson Brothers & Boyd, and occupy the whole of the spacious four-story building at 309 North Fourth street. They have a force of seventy skilled employes, and manufacture, import and deal in every description of men's furnishing goods and shirts, and carry a stock which for extent and variety is not excelled in this city or the West. The house, which has been established ten years, has steadily increased in its business from its inception to the present time, and now enjoys a generous and appreciative custom in every part of the Southern and Western country, throughout which territory it has acquired a deserved popularity by the uniform reliability of its dealings. The firm also has a retail department which is highly regarded by residents of and visitors to the city. Both members of the firm are capable and experienced, thoroughly conversant with the line in which they are engaged. By careful and attentive supervision of all its details they have built their business up to its present proportions, and have achieved an unqualified success as the result of earnest effort and honorable and enterprising business methods.

**Foerstel, Heibeck & Co.**—Practical Engravers, Lithographers and Printers; 400 North Third street.—This business was established in 1878 by Messrs. J. Foerstel and R. Heibeck, who were joined in 1883 by Mr. G. Menk, when the firm assumed its present name. They are practical engravers, lithographers, and commercial printers, and their premises at 400 North Third street are fitted up with all the necessary plant and machinery adapted to the requirements of their business. The firm has a very high reputation for the superiority of its workmanship, every order being filled promptly and executed in the most perfect and finished manner known to art. As a consequence of this artistic merit the firm enjoys a large patronage, working chiefly on city orders, but also having a considerable business in the States tributary to St. Louis as a commercial center. The business has steadily grown since its inception, and its success has been due in no less degree to correct business methods than to meritorious workmanship.

**F. A. Bensberg & Co.**—Wholesale Liquor Dealers; Fine Kentucky Whiskies; 208 Walnut street.—This business, which took its present style in 1880, was originally established in 1852 by the father of the present proprietor, Mr. Ferdinand A. Bensberg. The premises occupied by the business comprise a five-story building, 25x125 feet, fitted up with every convenience for the successful prosecution of the business, and completely stocked with a fine assortment of all kinds of liquors of the best quality. The firm are large handlers of fine Kentucky whiskies, controlling the '87 crop of the Old W. S. Stone's distillery in Daviess county, Kentucky, where is produced a fine grade of hand made sour mash whisky that is in high repute for its superior quality in all parts of the country. They do a large business shipping direct from the distilleries to all parts of the Union. From their establishment here they sell to dealers in the city and all the States and Territories tributary to its market. The house has for many years held a high place in the esteem and confidence of the trade, the merit of their goods, the reliability of their methods of dealing and their promptness and accuracy in filling orders having placed them among the leading houses in their line.

**H. & L. Chase.**—Wholesale Bags and Bagging; 8 to 16 North Main street.—One of the largest and oldest houses in the country in the line of bags, bagging, burlaps, flour bags, twine, etc., is that of H. & L. Chase, the members of which are Mr. W. L. Chase, of Boston, and Mr. F. H. Ludington, of St. Louis. They occupy four large five-story buildings fronting twenty-five feet each at Nos. 8 to 16 North Main street, and running back 110 feet each. Every description of domestic and foreign bagging material and bags is carried in their stock, which is of immense proportions, and with unsurpassed facilities for manufacturing and printing. The trade of the firm extends to every part of the country. The ample capital of the firm and the magnitude of its operations enable them to offer unsurpassed inducements to dealers and the jobbing trade, with whom the house, by the accuracy of its methods and the uniform merit of its goods, has maintained its deserved reputation as a leading establishment in its department of commerce.

**Messmore, Gannett & Co.**—Commission Merchants; 510 Chamber of Commerce.—Although the firm of Messmore, Gannett & Co. has only existed about two years, all its members, including Messrs. T. B. Morton, A. L. Messmore, and John M. Gannett, have been actively engaged in business as commission merchants for fourteen or fifteen years. Their office is at 510 Chamber of Commerce, and they have a warehouse at 10 South Commercial street, 20x120 feet and four stories high. They do a commission business in grain, flour and seeds only, and have an extensive patronage, the house enjoying an excellent reputation among the shippers and producers of the articles in which they deal in all the territory tributary to the St. Louis market. By close attention to the details of every transaction placed in their hands, and the satisfactory manner in which they perform commission services, they have built up a large patronage and a prosperous and steadily increasing business

**Adams Commission Company.**—Commission Merchants; 928 North Third street.—The firm doing business under the style of Adams Commission Co. is composed of Messrs. J. B. Retallack and J. Lyon. The business was established in 1881 by Mr. James Cummisky, later becoming J. C. Adams & Co., to whom the present firm are the successors. They occupy a commodious four-story building, fronting 30 feet at 928 North Third street and running back 100 feet. They do a strictly commission business, their chief lines in winter being hides, wool, furs, poultry, game, eggs, and dried and green fruits; and in early summer strawberries and all small fruits. Later they make a specialty of watermelons from Georgia and Southeast Missouri, which line they handle as largely as any house in the West, and also handle peaches and grapes, of which they receive consignments amounting to many carloads from the States of Ohio and New York. The firm has a large and valuable patronage among shippers and producers in Arkansas, Indian Territory, throughout Missouri and in Southern Kansas, Southern and Southeastern Illinois and part of Mississippi, selling the goods consigned to them chiefly in this city. The close attention paid by the firm to the details of every consignment sent them, and the uniform fidelity to the interests of their customers which they display, has given them a prominent position among the commission houses of the city and a justly deserved prosperity.

**Wyckoff, Seamans & Benedict.**—Dealers in Standard Type-Writers and Type-Writer Supplies of Every Kind; 308 North Sixth street.—The invention of the type-writer takes high rank among the leading discoveries of the nineteenth century, and its merits are fully acknowledged. A type-writer is now justly regarded as an indispensable requisite in every business, and these machines are now in general use throughout the country. The Remington Standard Type Writer is the best device of the kind invented, and for these the firm of Wyckoff, Seamans & Benedict are the sole proprietors. Their St. Louis branch has charge of a large territory west of the Mississippi, in which they have had great success in introducing these standard type-writers, which are manufactured by the Standard Type Writer Company at Ilion, N.Y. The St. Louis house is under the efficient management of Mr. Fred. Sholes, to whose close attention to all the details of the business is due in a great measure the large trade in these type-writers and in type-writer supplies of all kinds in the Southwestern country. The machines always give satisfaction, and those who use them are unanimous in their praise.

**Flesh & Mook.**—Manufacturers of Signs of Every Description, Painters, etc.; 414 North Third street.—This firm was established in 1867, succeeding the firm of Flesh & Greenwood. In that year Mr. M. M. Flesh bought out Mr. Greenwood, his partner, and was joined by Mr. George J. Mook, forming the present firm. They carried on business at 513 North Third street for several years, but in 1885 removed to their present premises at 414 North Third street, three floors, 20x160 feet. They have every facility for the successful prosecution of their large business, which gives employment to a force averaging seventy-five men; but in the busy season to a much greater number. The business of the firm is the manufacture of signs, house painting, decorating, etc. In their great specialty of signs, they are not surpassed by any house in the West, and they make them in every useful style: metal, brass, copper and silver signs; wire signs, white letter signs, pictorial and illustrated signs, and also manufacture parade floats, Sunday school, society and political flags, banners and regimental standards, in silk and bunting; drop curtains, scenery and show painting, etc. The business of the house is very large, extending throughout the States of Missouri, Illinois, Kansas, Iowa, Nebraska, Arkansas, Texas and all Northwest, Southwest and South and into Mexico. The firm has experienced a steady and healthy growth throughout the twenty years of its busy career, and sustains a high reputation for the great superiority of its workmanship, its promptness in filling orders and the reliable manner in which its business is conducted.

**Larkin & Scheffer.**—Manufacturing Chemists; Office and Laboratory, Main and Anna streets.—A trade which reaches to every portion of the United States; to Canada, Mexico, Havana, Peru, and other South American countries, and to England, is enjoyed by this establishment, which is one of the largest in its line in the country. The business was established in 1871 by Larkin & Scheffer, and has since been largely increased and extended owing to its rapid growth and spread of its transactions. The firm of Larkin & Schetter consists of Messrs. E. H. Larkin, H. W. Scheffer, and Thomas H. Larkin, gentlemen of many years experience in this line of business, who have earned by industry and enterprise the success which has crowned their efforts. The specialties of the firm are ammonia, ethers and chloroform, and all chemicals. The laboratory and works cover nearly a block of ground, are provided with all improved facilities and apparatus, and have from their location transportation advantages, both by rail and water, that are not excelled by any manufacturing enterprise.

**M. & J. Rumely.**—Threshing Machinery and Engines; Works at La Porte, Ind.; St. Louis Branch Office, Corner Tenth and Spruce streets; F. M. Foy, Manager. —The large and important works of M. & J. Rumely, at La Porte, Ind., of which Mr. Meinrad Rumely is now proprietor, have been successfully operated since their establishment in 1853, in the manufacture of a superior line of threshing machinery, long acknowledged to be the best in their line, and in great demand in all sections of the country. The works have been many times enlarged, and a number of improvements have been added to the machines since the foundation of the business.

The machinery turned out at these works are the most complete offered for the use of threshermen and farmers. Among the machinery manufactured by the firm may be enumerated the new Rumely Separator, combining in itself all the good points of the "Vibrator and Agitator" and "apron" threshers, and surpassing any other made in fast and clean threshing; the Rumely Portable Engine, strong, durable, simple in construction and easy to manage; the Rumely Traction Engine and Boiler; the New Rumely Traction; the Rumely Patent Straw Burner Boiler; the Rumely Spark Arrestor, etc. The merit of these machines is evidenced by a steadily increasing demand for them and the uniform satisfaction they give to those who use them. The St. Louis branch office was established in 1885, and placed in charge of Mr. F. M. Foy, a gentleman who has been engaged in the business for twenty-one years, and is thoroughly experienced in all its details. He has ample storage and shipping facilities in the Pacific Warehouse, where his office is situated, and has exclusive control of a territory embracing Southern Illinois, Missouri and Kansas, in which he has a staff of traveling salesmen. The merit of the machines and the thorough and accurate business methods of Mr. Foy have caused a large increase in the sales of these goods in the territory assigned to his painstaking and efficient management.

**Henry Bromschwig & Co.**—Importers and Jobbers of Tailors' Trimmings; 604 North Fourth street and 603 North Third street.—The firm of Henry Bromschwig & Co. is composed of Messrs. Henry Bromschwig and Clem. Landzettel, who have been connected in this business since 1874. The premises occupied by the firm front 25 feet at 604 North Fourth street, running back 125 feet to a similar frontage at 603 North Third street. This is the only *exclusively* tailors' trimming house in the city, and deals in every article used by tailors except the cloth. Their business is very heavy, and covers a wide territory, extending east to Indiana, and all Northwest, West, Southwest, and South, requiring the services of a staff of eight active and experienced traveling salesmen. Confining themselves strictly to this line the firm have acquired the confidence and patronage of the trade, with which their dealings are conducted on a most satisfactory basis and upon a scale which increases yearly the prosperity enjoyed by the house.

**W. W. Judy & Co.**—Dealers in Poultry and Game; 704 North Broadway and Union Market.—The firm of W. W. Judy & Co., composed of Mr. Judy and Mr. James T. Farrell, was established in 1865, at first occupying a location opposite the old post office. In 1876 they removed to their present stand at 704 North Broadway, a three-story and basement building, 25x60 feet, and now occupy in addition the basement adjoining, under the Fifth National Bank, which they have fitted up as a refrigerator. They have also two other stores in Union Market, one at the corner of Broadway and Christy avenue, and the other at the corner of Sixth and Morgan streets. They have the largest business in their line in the West, including, in addition to their immense local patronage, a large shipping business. They receive poultry and game from all points, and have representatives in all the game districts buying direct from the hunters. They ship poultry to Boston, New York and all Eastern markets, and export to Europe venison, bear, wild turkeys, quail, prairie chickens and game of all kinds, sending them by express to New York, and thence by Cunard steamers to England. The name of the firm is as well and favorably known in Leadenhall market, London, as in St. Louis, and their facilities for the preparation and shipment of game are not excelled by any house in the country. Their business has steadily grown, and the reputation which the house has acquired has been earned by years of energetic application to every detail. In addition to this business, in which a force of about forty men are employed, the house has the agency for Palmer's fireworks, manufactured at Rochester, N.Y., in which line they also have a large trade.

**Brook & Co.**—Manufacturers of Trunks, Traveling Bags, Sample Cases, etc.; 304 North Fourth street.—This well known and popular establishment was founded in 1855, and is the oldest trunk house in the city. The firm enjoys an unsurpassed reputation for the superior quality and workmanship of their goods. They are manufacturers of trunks, traveling bags, sample cases, cutlery rolls, etc., of every description, and sole manufacturers of the Rawhide Fibre sample trunk, of which they make a specialty. This trunk is the lightest durable trunk in the world, and is guaranteed to give better satisfaction than any Eastern or patent trunk costing double the money. Only the best materials are used and skilled labor employed in the manufacture of their goods, and by selling them at the most reasonable prices, they offer the greatest inducements to purchasers. The excellence of their sample trunks has secured for them a large business, including among their patrons the most prominent manufacturing and jobbing houses in the city. They are prepared to fill all orders in a prompt and satisfactory manner. They refer by permission to the following well known firms, of different lines of business, as to their reliability: Simmons Hardware Co., Witte Hardware Co., Richardson Drug Co., C. & W. McClean, Reinhard, Dinkelman & Co., A. J. Jordan, L. Banman Jewelry Co., Missouri Glass Co., Parson & Co., Geo. Gog Boot and Shoe Co., T. C. Hanford & Co., Hughitt & McCarthys, Bremen Tanning Co., Dozier-Weyl Cracker Co., Massa, Lewis & Co., S. H. Banman & Co., and Henry Bromschwig & Co.

**E. G. Willis & Brother.**—Leather, Hides and Wool; 518 North Main street.—In the list of the commercial houses of St. Louis, that of E. G. Willis & Bro. holds a deservedly prominent position. The business was established in 1870 by the firm of Willis & Burnett, and on the death of Mr. Burnett in the following year the firm became Willis, Kimball & Co., changing in 1880 to its present style. The members of the present firm are Messrs. Edward G. and Fred. C. Willis, and they occupy as salesrooms and offices a commodious six-story building, eligibly located at 518 North Main street, and in addition have spacious warehouses at 514 North Levee and 518 North Commercial street. The specialty of the firm is leather, which they carry in large quantities and every variety. In addition to this business they deal largely in hides, and have a branch at New Orleans devoted exclusively to this branch of their business. They also deal very extensively in wool in its season, so extensively that in November, 1886, they sold 250,000 lbs. of wool in one invoice. Their trade is very large and extends to all parts of the Union, their facilities for large transactions being unsurpassed, and their reputation being firmly established as among the leading houses of the country in their line.

**St. Louis Mantel and Grate Company.**—S. Hand, President; F. A. Smith, Secretary; Manufacturers of Marble, Iron and Slate Mantels, Enameled Grates, Encaustic Tile, Etc.; 24 South Eleventh street.—This business was started in Cincinnati thirty-five years ago by the firm of S. Hand & Co., who also established the St. Louis house in 1873. The Cincinnati house is still retained and there the manufacture of the enameled grates is carried on. The company has also an interest in a house in Chicago. The corporation was organized ten years ago, and does a large and steadily increasing business. They make a specialty of marbleized and art painted slate mantels. They buy slate very largely from the Vermont quarries, and have it shipped to them, already dimensioned, in carload lots, doing their marbleizing, oil painting and finishing here. They own and occupy spacious premises 75x153 feet, for their works here, which they are now increasing by the erection of an addition. They employ thirty-five skilled Eastern workmen and have a large business in the States of Missouri, Iowa and Illinois (including Chicago), and in all the Western country to the Pacific and south into Mexico. Upon the first establishment of the works in St. Louis the step was regarded as experimental and a conservative course was pursued, but experience having demonstrated the great advantages of St. Louis as a distributive point, the company are now pushing their business with steadily increasing success. Their marble, iron and slate mantels, enameled grates, and American and English encaustic tile are of the finest quality manufactured, their stock is very large, and their facilities for handling and shipment first-class in every respect. They are prepared to fill all orders in a prompt and satisfactory manner.

**Cox & Gordon.**—Pork Packers, Curers of the Missouri Ham, and Jobbers in Pork, Lard, Bacon, etc.; 1019 to 1025 South Third street.—This firm occupy the large packing house located on South Third street, from No. 1019 to 1025, which is located on the railroad tracks and has every convenience and facility for the advantageous prosecution of business. The establishment was founded in 1877 by the firm of Morris, Cox & Co. In 1880 it was changed to Chas. A. Cox & Co., and in 1881 it became Cox & Gordon. The firm consists of Chas. A. Cox and Samuel Gordon, Jr. During the year 1886 they have added largely to their building and put in refrigerating machinery for curing during the summer months. They handle and deal in all kinds of hog products and have a very large trade both to the north and south of St. Louis. The Missouri hams, which this house cure, are considered the best in the market and are a credit to the State, whose name they bear, and the city of St. Louis. Mr. Cox and Mr. Gordon are recognized as bright, enterprising business men of extended experience in their line, and have a strong hold upon the provision trade of this city. Their business has steadily increased from its inception, the uniform reliability of the goods handled by the firm and their fair and accurate dealings having brought them the prosperity due to industry and enterprise.

**American Shade Company.**—W. W. Carpenter, President; F. S. Carpenter, Vice-President; H. N. Carpenter, Secretary and Treasurer; Window Shades, etc.; 610 North Second street.—This business was established in 1874 by Mr. W. W. Carpenter, who is now the highly esteemed President of the corporation, which was formed in 1883. The premises occupied by the company consist of three commodious floors, 25x150 feet, at 610 North Second street. The company is largely engaged in the manufacture of window shades and opaqued hollands, in all colors and every style, and also makes a specialty of fine ornamental dadoes and lettering in gold or colors. A large force of competent and skilled workmen is employed in the manufacturing operations of the company, while five active and experienced traveling men are engaged in pushing the trade of the house, which is very large and covers a wide range of territory, including, besides a large patronage in the city, a prosperous business in Missouri, Illinois, Kansas and the entire West and South. The superiority of the goods manufactured by the company, and the correct business methods adopted by it in all its dealings have secured for it a great and steadily growing patronage and merited success.

**H. O. Pope Produce Company.**—W. S. Forbes, President; Frank E. Ritchie, Vice-President; H. O. Pope, Secretary and Treasurer; Wholesale Produce, Fruits and Vegetables; 1130 and 1132 North Third street.—The corporation known as the H. O. Pope Produce Co., was organized and incorporated in January of the present year, succeeding to the business successfully conducted for six years previously by the firm of H. O. Pope & Co. They occupy the main floors, basements and cellars of the two commodious buildings, with a frontage of 60 feet, at 1130 and 1132 North Third street, and running back 120 feet. They do a large business as wholesale dealers in produce, making a specialty of fruits and vegetables. In the early part of the year they do a large shipping trade in New York seed potatoes, amounting to about fourteen carloads per day, and in the summer season they handle vegetables, small fruits, garden truck, etc. They enjoy facilities surpassed by none for the efficient carrying on of their business, which they conduct upon methods which have secured it success and an excellent standing with the trade.

**Annan, Burg & Co.**—General Commission Merchants; 2 South Commercial street.—This house was established some years since by Messrs. Roger P. Annan, Henry Burg and Daniel E. Smith, who formed a co-partnership under the above firm name.

The members of the firm are all gentlemen of wide and extended experience in the commission business and occupy prominent positions in the front rank of St. Louis mercantile circles. Although engaged in the transaction of a general commission business the house devotes its special attention to grain and flour, in which particular line it has unequaled facilities, and it handles large and numerous consignments from all Western and Northwestern points. The output of many of the best mills of Colorado, Nebraska, Kansas, Minnesota, Iowa, Illinois and Missouri is handled by this firm. A perfect knowledge of market values at all times and the condition of trade, together with prompt attention to all consignments directed to their care, have given to this firm a commanding influence among the Western producers and in the business world.

**Bellefontaine Cemetery Association.**—James E. Yeatman, President; George S. Drake, Vice-President; Samuel Copp, Secretary and Treasurer; A. Hotchkiss, Superintendent; Office, 302 North Fourth street, Northeast Corner of Olive.—In no way can the virtues of a community be more justly judged than by the measure of the respect shown to the memory of its dead. A city's cemeteries show the extent to which the finer and nobler sentiments are imbedded in the hearts of its citizens. Judged by this standard, St. Louis takes a foremost position among the cities of the Union. In none of them can be found a more beautiful or better kept spot, set apart as the "silent city of the dead" than is found here in Bellefontaine Cemetery, the property of the Bellefontaine Cemetery Association. It was originally dedicated May 15th, 1850, the tract then embracing about one hundred and thirty-eight acres, to which additions have been made from time to time, the present area occupied being three hundred and thirty-two and one-half acres. The original name of the association, under its charter of 1849, was the Rural Cemetery Association, the present name being conferred by amendments made in the charter March 1st, 1851. The lots are secured by the charter for cemetery purposes forever, and are free from taxation, and also free from levy under executions. The cemetery grounds are eminently adapted for the purpose, being undulating, and have been beautified until they form a fitting resting place for the honored dead. Among the monuments and tombs are works of the highest art in marble and granite, and art and nature have made it the equal of any cemetery known in the diversification and beauty of its scenery. A large force of men is employed to keep the grounds in order, and the management of its affairs reflects high credit upon its officers and board of trustees, the latter consisting of fifteen of the most prominent and respected citizens of St. Louis.

**Patrick Fox.**—Catholic Publisher and Importer of Church Goods; 14 South Broadway.—This house was established about thirty-five years ago, by its present proprietor, and has always been recognized as one of the leading houses in its line west of New York. All of the publications of the Church and Catholic literature of all kinds are kept in stock and published by Mr. Fox, who also carries a large stock of church and altar goods of all descriptions. Mr. Patrick Fox is well known to the people of the city of St. Louis and neighboring States, and is held in high esteem by all, including the leading dignitaries of the Church, who have for years endorsed his goods and publications. Many of the churches of the West and South have been supplied by Mr. Fox, and his trade is very extensive in all parts of the Western States. As a citizen and prominent resident of the community, he is well known to all St. Louisans, and is identified with many interests. He is a leading stockholder in the great Whalen Copper Mining Company, whose property is considered among the most valuable in the country.

**St. Louis Corset Company.**—Wm. McCable, President; A. Davis, Secretary; Manufacturers of Corsets; Twenty-first and Morgan streets.—This company was organized in the early part of the present year for the purpose of manufacturing corsets, for which their two-story premises at Twenty-first and Morgan streets, covering an area of 60x150 feet, are completely equipped with all the latest and most improved machinery and appliances adapted to the business. A large force of employes have been engaged and placed under intelligent supervision, and the company has already secured a large trade from all parts of the country, which is rapidly expanding and increasing in volume. The company makes a specialty of an overlaid side extension corset, with a non-breakable side and extending back, which, for elegance in form, ease of fit and durability in wear, is not excelled by any manufactured, and is rapidly growing in the favor of the ladies of the country. President McCable, who occupies elegant offices in the building, is a sagacious, energetic and enterprising business man, and the merit of the company's manufacture and the ability of its management will doubtless secure for it a steadily increasing prosperity.

**Deming Commission Company.**—F. L. Deming, President; E. B. Deming, Vice-President; Charles Deming, Secretary and Treasurer; Brokerage and Commission; 507 North Second street.—This prominent and representative house was established in 1872 as F. L. Deming & Bro., and was incorporated under its present title in 1885. The company occupies a five-story building, 25x120 feet, at 507 North Second street, and handles all kinds of canned goods in vegetables, fruits, sardines, fish, etc., also raisins, California fruit, foreign fruits, nuts and everything in that line. The house receives consignments from all points and sells chiefly to city jobbers and also to some jobbers in Texas and the intermediate territory. The house received its full share of the benefits arising from the general revival in trade noticed in the season of 1886, and that of the present year bids fair to rival its predecessor. The company has a very high standing in trade circles, and an unsurpassed reputation for the accuracy of its business methods and the high principles by which its dealings are governed, and enjoys a merited success as the result of its industry and close attention to business.

**Muldoon & Sharp.**—Pork Packers and Wholesale Dealers in Provisions; 904 to 912 South Second street.—This prominent and prosperous firm, of which Messrs. Patrick Muldoon and James Sharp are the individual members, has been established for more than a quarter of a century, and during that entire period has held the highest standing in the trade. They have extensive slaughter and packing houses at Canton, Mo., employing sixty men, and twenty-five more are engaged at their warehouses in this city, 100x200 feet, fronting on Second street and running back to Risley street. They are extensive packers of all descriptions of pork products, and curers of the celebrated "Four Ace" hams, which are the favorites with consumers and in large and steadily increasing demand by the trade. Their stock in all these lines is very large and their business is of immense proportions, extending over all the Southern States and being particularly large in Texas. They have built up and sustained their business by the quality of their product and the uniform fairness and accuracy of their dealings. All orders sent them are attended to with fidelity and dispatch and are filled in a satisfactory manner.

**David G. Evans & Co.**—Importers and Jobbers of Teas, Coffees, etc.; 504 North Second street.—The house of David G. Evans & Co. has been successfully conducted ever since its establishment in 1865, in the business of importers and jobbers of teas, coffees and spices, and manufacturers of ground spices, mustard, cream tartar, baking powder, roasted and ground coffees, etc. They import teas direct in very large quantities, and their premises, a four-story building, 30x150 feet, are fully equipped with all the necessary machinery and appliances for roasting and grinding coffees and grinding spices. They give employment to thirty-five competent assistants and have twenty-five active and energetic commercial travelers representing the house on the road. Their trade extends to Indiana, Illinois, Missouri, Kansas, Iowa, Nebraska, Minnesota, Colorado and the entire Southwest. The house has long had a high standing by reason of the exceptional excellence of its goods and still continues to hold the esteem and confidence of the trade by a strict adherence to the honorable and liberal methods which have ever characterized its business dealings.

**M. W. Alexander.**—Druggist and Pharmacist; Northwest Corner of Broadway and Olive street.—Prominently located in large and spacious quarters, at the junction of the two leading retail streets of the city, is the old and prominent retail drug house of M. W. Alexander. The house was established by Mr. Alexander in 1856, at the corner of Fourth and Market streets, and became at once the leading and most reliable house in the city. Its reputation for the purity of its goods, and compounding of prescriptions, has never been excelled. All old residents of the city, and prominent medical practitioners, unhesitatingly recommend in flattering terms this old and prominent establishment. Mr. Alexander continued business at the old location until 1880, when he disposed of that store. During the centennial year of 1876 he opened the magnificent drug palace, which he now conducts, at the northwest corner of Broadway and Olive streets. The place was destroyed by fire in December, 1878, and reopened in December, 1879. The store is one of the most elegantly appointed in the entire country.

**Miller & Worley.**—Tobacco Manufacturers; Pine street, between Second and Third streets.—Prominent among the large firms in the city engaged in the tobacco manufacturing business, is that of Miller & Worley, composed of Messrs. A. Miller and C. Worley, and which was established ten years ago. They occupy a five-story building, 55x85 feet, situated on Pine street, between Second and Third streets, fitted up with all the latest and most improved machinery and plant applicable to their business, and giving work to a force of fifty employes. They manufacture plug tobaccos of a superior grade, including the following well-known and celebrated brands: "Purity," "Owl," "Bengal," "Famous," "Welcome," and "Missouri Seal;" as well as the "Premium Hard Pressed," "Premium Light Pressed," "Coronet" and "Bon Ton" brands of natural leaf tobaccos. All of these are favorites with consumers and in demand by the trade, with which this house does an extensive business covering a large territory including the States of Missouri, Illinois, Indiana, Kansas, Nebraska, Arkansas, Texas, Louisiana, Tennessee, and the entire South and West. Using only the best tobacco in their manufacture, and exercising the closest supervision over every detail of their business, this firm enjoys that prosperity which is the reward of honest goods and fair dealing.

**Herman Eisenhardt.**—Manufacturer of Candles, Soap and Lard Oil; Office and Warerooms, 14 South Second street; Factory and Works, 2715 to 2729 Columbus street.—The important manufacturing concern now owned and operated by Mr. Eisenhardt was founded in 1860 by Mr. E. Anheuser, the celebrated brewer, by whom it was carried on until 1867, when it was acquired by Mr. Eisenhardt, under whose experienced and systematic management its trade has steadily increased. The works on Columbus street have a frontage of 200 feet by a depth of 150 feet, and are fully equipped with all the plant and machinery necessary to the successful prosecution of the business. Thirty men are constantly employed and the product of candles, soap and lard oil is very large. At the salesrooms a large and complete stock is carried and Mr. Eisenhardt, in addition to a heavy business with city jobbers, sells largely in the States of Louisiana, Mississippi, Tennessee and the entire South. His facilities for manufacture and the filling of orders are unsurpassed, and he maintains a substantial hold upon a large and steadily increasing trade by superior goods and reliability in all his transactions.

THE INDUSTRIES OF ST. LOUIS.     227

**The Gage & Horton Manufacturing Company.**—Charles Gage, President and Treasurer; Chas. L. Gage, Vice-President; Wm. M. Horton, Secretary; Manufacturers of Stoves, Ranges, Marbleized Iron and Slate Mantels and Grates, Etc.; Factory, 4010 Manchester road; Office and Salesroom, 1231 Olive street, St. Louis.—This establishment, which is one of the most prominent and prosperous in its line in the entire West, was originally founded in 1859, the present corporation, however, having been organized in 1882. The extensive factory of the com-

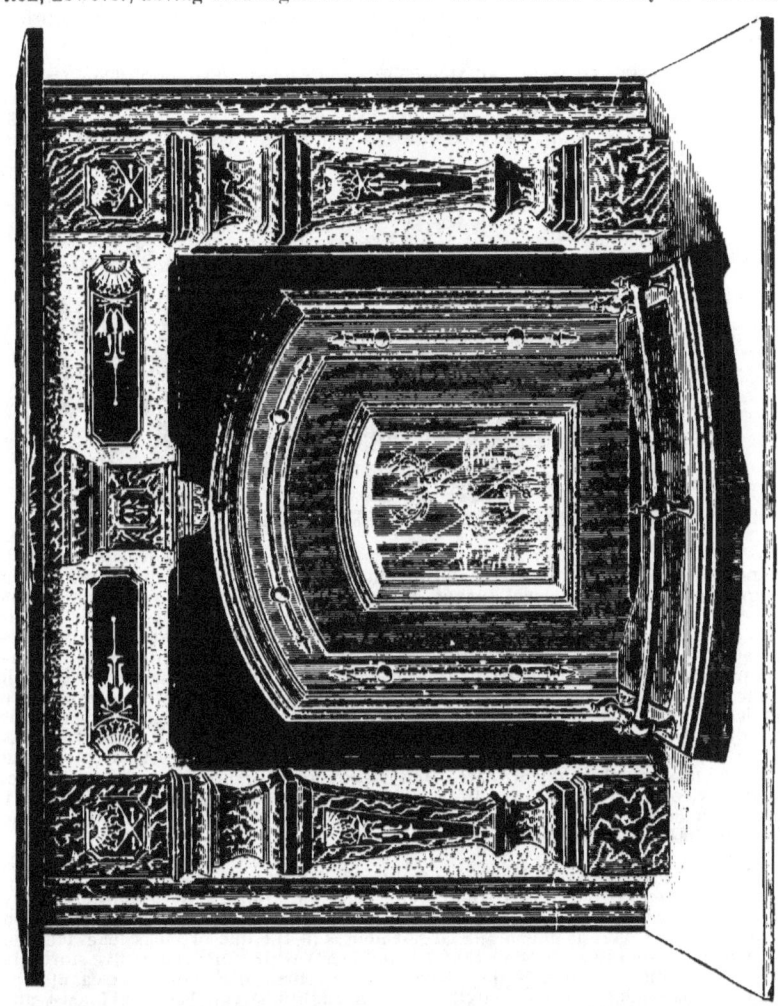

pany, located on Manchester road, near Chouteau avenue, is equipped in the most complete manner with all the latest and most improved plant and machinery adapted to the successful prosecution of the business, and gives employment to a large number of skilled and experienced workmen. Here is carried on, upon a large scale, the manufacture of the superior "Kitchen Gem" line of stoves and ranges, and the unapproachable marbleized iron and marbleized slate mantels and grates, for which this company has gained a wide celebrity for superior quality, low prices and a generous trade extending west to the Pacific Ocean and embracing in its scope all the States and Territories of the West and South, from the Canadian line to the Gulf of Mexico; and the country east to Indiana. In addition to the articles of their own manufacture the company deal extensively in hard wood mantels, and the celebrated "Economy" hot air, and combination hot air and steam furnaces. They carry large and completely diversified stocks of all goods manufactured or handled by them, and by the fairness and accuracy of their dealings and the superior advantages which they are able to offer to customers, command a steadily increasing trade and a pronounced success which is the result of well directed energy and enterprise. Write them for catalogues and price lists.

**Henry Heil.**—Importer and Manufacturer of Chemical Apparatus and Chemicals, and Materials for Smelters, Assayers. Miners and Jewelers; 212 South Fourth street.—This is the largest house of its kind in America, and was established in 1866 by the late Theodore Kalb, who died in 1883. After the decease of its founder the

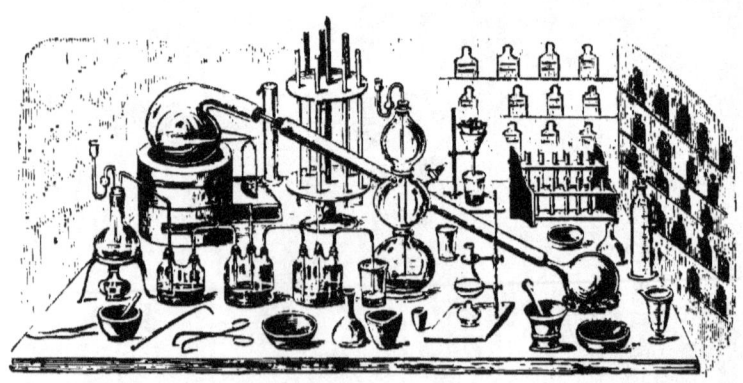

house was purchased by Mr. Henry Heil, who had been in this business for many years. The importance of this establishment has been forcibly demonstrated by the progress of the mining development of the West, as it is fully a thousand miles nearer the mining camps than the Eastern markets, and it can reach them several days earlier than Eastern establishments possibly can. The resources of this house are such that all kinds of chemical apparatus and chemicals are either manufactured or imported direct from European factories in large quantities, and all of the supplies which enter into the processes of assaying and smelting minerals are carried in stock. A very large and complete stock of chemicals, the rarest not excepted, from the renowned factory of E. Merck, Darmstadt, is carried by this house, and buyers of this class of goods will find it to their interest to correspond with the firm on the subject. Mr. Heil issues an elegant illustrated catalogue, descriptive of his stock, which will be mailed on request. His trade reaches every part of the country, and excels all others in the competition for the business of the Western States and Territories.

**Max Judd & Co.**—Cloak Manufacturers; 710 and 712 Washington avenue.—This firm, composed of Max Judd and Isidore I. Judd, has been successfully engaged in business for the past fourteen years and has established a reputation throughout the West as one of the largest houses in the line of cloak manufacture. They occupy premises, 60x80 feet, at 710 and 712 Washington avenue, five stories in height, in addition to which they have now in course of erection an elegant five-story and basement building, 60x130 feet, on Eighth street, between Locust and St. Charles streets. They employ a force of one hundred and eighty hands in their manufacturing operations, in addition to which they have seven shrewd and active traveling men who represent them in their extensive trade territory embracing the States of Missouri, Illinois, Kansas, Colorado, Utah, California and the entire West and Southwest. Their business is immense in its proportions, and their stock includes cloaks in all the latest styles and most fashionable materials. The house has a first-class standing in the trade and is managed with perfect system and fair and accurate methods.

**James Hanley.**—Carriages, Buggies, Phaetons, Surreys, and Spring Wagons; 900 to 904 Clark avenue.—Mr. Hanley took the proprietorship of this business in 1886, as successor to the Papin Buggy Manufacturing Co., by which it was conducted for over fifteen years, and with which Mr. Hanley was connected prior to purchasing the business. He occupies spacious premises, 100x200 feet, completely supplied with all the necessary plant and equipment for the successful prosecution of the business, and gives employment to a force of twenty-five of the most skilled and

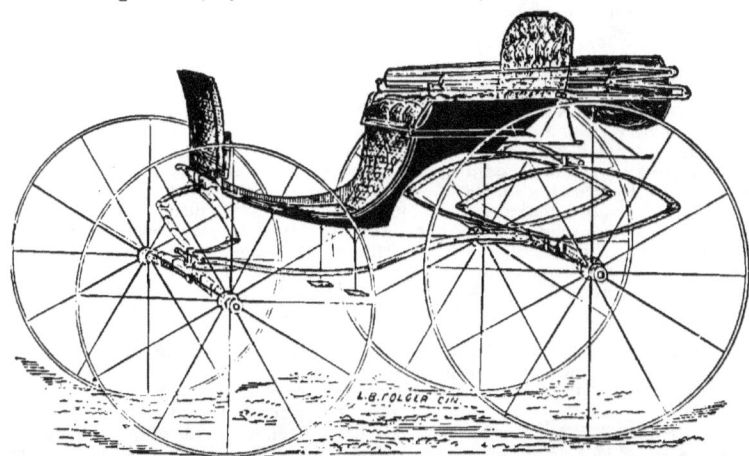

experienced workmen. He manufactures every description of carriages, buggies, phaetons, surreys and spring wagons, and makes a specialty of sewing machine wagons, which are the best made, and in which he does a business extending to all parts of the country, and has a large trade in Old and New Mexico. In all the departments of his business the product of his works are unsurpassed in the excellence of materials used in their construction and in the superiority of their workmanship and finish. He does a large trade in all parts of the West and South, and for the whole period of sixteen years of his experience in the business has enjoyed a first-class reputation for the fairness of his dealings and the promptness and reliability with which he fills every order.

**Jacob Kaiser & Co.**—Upholsterers, Manufacturers of Mattrasses, etc.; 204 South Fourth street.—This house was established fourteen years ago by Mr. Jacob Kaiser, the present proprietor, who is acknowledged as one of the prominent representative men in his line. In this establishment the finest of upholstery work, by the most skillful workmen, is done, and the character of it has firmly established the high reputation for merit which the house has always possessed. One of the leading and most important features connected with this first-class establishment is the manufacture of mattrasses and bedding. A large force of hands are employed, and vast quantities of hair mattrasses and bedding of every description are constantly turned out. The successful and extensive trade built up by Mr. Kaiser is located throughout the Western and Southern States.

**Orr & Lindsley Shoe Company.**—William C. Orr, President; D. B. Lindsley, Vice-President; G. H. Moll, Secretary; Wholesale Dealers in Boots and Shoes; 519 Washington avenue.—This prominent house is one of the oldest and most extensive engaged in the boot and shoe line, and has a large and prosperous trade with the States and Territories that are contiguous to St. Louis markets. The house was founded in 1851 by Mr. William C. Orr, the President of the present company, who has been in business continuously since that time. Mr. D. B. Lindsley, his partner, has been associated with him for many years, and both gentlemen enjoy the highest standing in commercial and financial circles. The trade established and fostered by this house had grown to such an extent, that last year the firm incorporated as the Orr & Lindsley Shoe Co., in order to better handle the largely increasing business. The officers of the company are gentlemen of wide experience, whose knowledge of the trade and energetic business methods have continued to secure to their house a trade that is not surpassed by that of any similar concern in St. Louis. The traveling salesmen of the Orr & Lindsley Shoe Co. visit the States and Territories of Missouri, Illinois, Kansas, Nebraska, Colorado, New Mexico, Arizona, Arkansas, Texas, Indian Territory, Louisiana, Mississippi, Kentucky and Tennessee, in each of which the house has many customers. The business location of the firm, at 519 Washington avenue, is central and convenient, and is one of the most desirable in the wholesale district, and has ample facilities for the quick handling of goods.

**Whitney & Weston.**—Real Estate and Financial Agents; 816 Pine street.—This firm, of which Messrs. C. M. Whitney and J. F. Weston are the members, was established in 1885. Mr. Whitney was formerly a lawyer in good practice, and for several years Surveyor of Customs and United States Disbursing Agent in this city, and both he and Mr. Weston are gentlemen of experience in all matters pertaining to St. Louis real estate. They have built up a large and steadily growing business, and buy and sell real estate, negotiate loans, take charge of estates, make disbursements and pay taxes, draw deeds, wills and contracts, and attend to all matters pertaining to a legitimate real estate and financial agency business. The members of the firm are well-known citizens, and have an excellent standing in the community. Every interest entrusted to their care is guarded with attentive fidelity, and they possess superior advantages for the profitable and prompt negotiation of transactions in relation to real estate.

**Holt, Payne & Co.**—Live Stock Commission Merchants; Union Stock Yards.—This firm, composed of Messrs. John J. Holt, J. C. Payne and Hugh M. Watson, was established in 1877, although the members had been engaged in the live stock business for about ten years previous to that.

Mr. Holt attends to the office and financial affairs of the firm. Mr. Payne is the cattle salesman and Mr. Watson the hog salesman. These gentlemen attend personally to the interests of the customers, engaging in no speculations, but devoting their means and energies to the commission business. The salesmen, being principals in the firm, are interested in giving satisfaction to their customers, and by their close attention have secured for the firm a large patronage from Missouri, Illinois, Arkansas, Kansas, Iowa and Tennessee. They hold no stock unless compelled to do so, but sell on first feed and water, if possible. They honor drafts on consignments to the amount of two-thirds of the value of the stock, when a bill of lading accompanies the draft. The firm handles a very large number of hogs and cattle, and their annual transactions reach in the neighborhood of $1,500,000. They have a branch at the National Stock Yards, East St. Louis, and stock consigned to either yards will be promptly and efficiently attended to by the firm.

**Weinheimer & Opp.**—Importers of Havana, and Wholesale Dealers in Seed Leaf Tobacco; 206 Walnut street.—This firm, established in 1883, at once took rank among the leading houses in its line in the West and has maintained that position by the enterprise of its methods. The firm maintain the most favorable relations with producers, buying their native tobaccos for cash and direct from farmers in Connecticut, Pennsylvania, Wisconsin and New York State, and doing their own packing. They are also large importers of Havana tobacco for filling and Sumatra leaf for wrappers. They handle only cigar leaf, and do a large and satisfactory business with jobbers and cigar manufacturers in Illinois, Missouri, Kansas, Iowa, Wisconsin, Minnesota, Nebraska, Colorado, etc. They carry a large stock, and occupy a spacious five-story building. They are prepared to fill all orders in a prompt and reliable manner, and to offer unsurpassed inducements, both in quality and price, to their customers. The members of the firm are thorough business men and by judicious management have secured a substantial and steadily growing trade.

**Charles Thuener & Co.**—Manufacturers of Galvanized Iron Cornices, etc.: 8 and 10 South Jefferson avenue.—This firm, of which Messrs. Charles Thuener, John H. Lippelmann and Paul Herchenbach are the individual members, have been

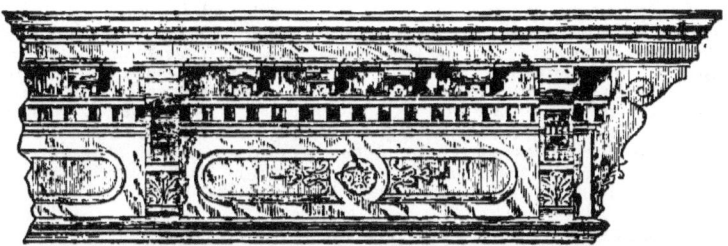

successfully engaged for ten years in this business. They manufacture galvanized iron cornices of standard and ornamental designs, guttering, spouting, skylights, ventilators, metal roofing, etc. The premises occupied by them, consisting of a two-story building, 60x120 feet, are completely fitted and supplied with all the most improved plant and equipments appropriate to the business, and give employment to a force of thirty skilled workmen. The superior quality of the product of these works has attracted to them the approval and patronage of the trade, including builders, contractors, etc., in this city and throughout Missouri, Southern Illinois, Arkansas and other states, tributary, in a commercial sense, to St. Louis. The great care taken in the selection of the best materials and superior workmen, and the close and intelligent supervision of every detail of their business, have caused it to prosper and enjoy a steady growth. They furnish estimates on buildings promptly upon application and solicit correspondence in regard to business in their line.

**Parisian Cloak Company.**—F. Seigel Bros., Proprietors; Importers and Manufacturers of Ladies', Misses' and Children's Cloaks and Suits; Sam Schroeder, St. Louis Representative; Northeast Corner Broadway and Washington avenue.— The headquarters of this important house is at 120 Market street, Chicago, the house here being established in 1885. Under the experienced and efficient management of Mr. Schroeder the business of the St. Louis house has prospered and now includes, in addition to a large retail business in the city, an extensive trade in Missouri, Southern Illinois, Arkansas, Texas, Louisiana and the entire South. It is the only exclusive cloak house in the city, and the leader in styles, and by honorable methods of dealing, adherence to one price, and making no misrepresentations, it has acquired the confidence of the public and a steadily increasing patronage. They carry a large and full stock, embracing everything in their line; occupy elegant salesrooms, eligibly located on one of the best corners in the city, and possess every facility for carrying on the business. Mr. Schroeder, the manager, is a gentleman of superior business attainments, and to his prompt and reliable methods is largely due the great success achieved by the St. Louis house.

**Green & Clark.**—Manufacturers of and Wholesale Dealers in Missouri Cider and Vinegar; 2000 to 2010 Pine street.—The largest cider-making establishment in the city or State is that owned and conducted by Messrs. O. F. Green and J. E. Clark, under the firm style of Green & Clark. The business was established in 1867, in a comparatively modest way, on Market street, but soon attracted the attention of the trade by the superiority of its product, until "Missouri Cider," the trade-mark of the firm, came to be acknowledged as an unequaled product, and the steadily increasing demand compelled the firm to seek new quarters. They now occupy an entire building of four stories, and 90x109 feet in dimensions, completely equipped with every facility and convenience for manufacturing, barreling, bottling and storing their product of Missouri cider and cider and wine vinegar. They employ a force of seventy-five hands, and have, in addition to a heavy city business, a trade extending through the States of Missouri, Illinois, Kansas, Arkansas, Texas, Mississippi Tennessee, Louisiana, and the Southwest and South generally. Messrs. Green and Clark are both old residents, members of the Merchants' Exchange, stockholders in the Exposition company, and prominent and esteemed in the business community.

**H. A. Mussman, Jr.**—Importer and Wholesale and Retail Dealer in Cigars, Tobacco, Cigarettes and Smokers' Articles: 128 Olive street.—Mr. Mussman established his present business in 1882 at 124 Olive street, succeeding Stickney & Ellis, whose stock he purchased at that time. He enjoys a large and prosperous retail trade and is also a jobber and manufacturer in cigars, and imported and domestic tobaccos. Mr. Mussman is a thoroughly practical man at the business, having been in this line for some ten years. As a manufacturer he only began in January of the present year, but has already built up a good trade which is steadily on the increase. He is a thorough St. Louisan and takes an abiding interest in everything tending to promote the interests of the city. A self-made man, he has earned by industry and superior business attainments a high place in popular esteem. He takes a live interest in political affairs and is a prominent member of a number of leading political organizations. Fair and liberal in all his dealings he is doing a prosperous business and is on the high road to a great and merited success.

**B. Loeblein.**—St. Louis Collar and Whip Factory; 1900 Franklin avenue.—For over a third of a century Mr. Loeblein has been successfully engaged in this business, which he established in 1852. In addition to the premises occupied by him at the corner of Franklin avenue and Twentieth street, he has an extensive whip factory on Spring avenue, near St. Louis avenue. Employment is given to from thirty-five to forty skilled workmen, and the collars and whips manufactured at these works have long been noted for their superiority in materials and workmanship, and are in demand and command a large trade in all parts of the West and South. Mr. Loeblein has carried on this business constantly and consecutively since his beginning in 1852, and is the largest and only exclusively whip manufacturer in the Mississippi Valley. He has his own tannery and makes his own leather, twenty different kinds, for his work. The merit of his goods and the accuracy and entire reliability of his business methods are strongly shown in the fact that during the entire history of his long and prosperous business career, he has always stood high in the trade, and the volume of his transactions still steadily increases from year to year.

**Gauss-Shelton Hat Company**—Charles F. Gauss, President; Theodore Shelton, Vice-President; F. J. Langenburg, Secretary; Wholesale Hats, Caps, Gloves, Valises, etc.; 414 and 416 North Broadway.—This business was established in 1860 by Mr. Charles F. Gauss, and was incorporated in 1881 as the Gauss-Hunicke Hat Co., the name being changed to the present style previous to the death of Mr. H. A. Hunicke in June, 1886. The company occupy a large and elegant store fronting 60 feet at Nos. 414 and 416 North Broadway, by a depth of 120 feet, the six stories of which are crowded with an immense stock of hats, caps, gloves, valises, etc., which they sell wholesale to a large trade in the territory embracing Missouri, Southern and Central Illinois, Tennessee, Kentucky, Mississippi, Arkansas, Louisiana, Texas, Kansas, Iowa, Nebraska, Minnesota, Colorado, New Mexico, Arizona, Nevada, Utah, Wyoming, Idaho and Montana. They have a force of fifty assistants engaged in their store, while twenty active and experienced travelers represent them on the road. The house enjoys the confidence of the trade for the reliability of its goods and the uniform accuracy which characterizes its dealings.

**Hewit, Sharp & Co.**—Commission Merchants; 210 and 212 North Commercial street.—A firm which has established an enviable reputation and a position among the leading commission houses of the city is that of Hewit, Sharp & Co., composed of Messrs. O. Hewit and C. Sharp. Their premises consist of four stories, fronting 40 feet on North Commercial street, and running back 125 feet to North Levee. The firm was established in 1879 and has had a large and steadily increasing business from that date up to the present, and now receives consignments from an extensive area of country, both north and south. The firm makes a specialty of grain, but also handles all kinds of produce, hides, furs and all lines usually sold through commission houses. The firm possesses superior facilities for the advantageous handling of consignments, and a long practical experience in the business has given its members an accurate knowledge of the market. By close attention to all the details of their business and a strict fidelity to the interests of those making consignments to them, they have acquired an unsurpassed reputation for correct business methods and the confidence of shippers and producers. The extensive patronage they enjoy has been achieved as a consequence of industrious and faithful attention to the advantage of their customers.

**A. Shattinger.**—Wholesale and Retail Dealer in Pianos and Musical Instruments; Agent Weber Pianos and Clough & Warren Organs; 10 South Broadway.—This well-known house was established some fifteen years ago by its present proprietor, and has an extensive and prosperous trade among the musically inclined people of Missouri and Illinois. Not only are the home sales in this city very large, but the house enjoys a large business throughout this State and Illinois. The house for several years has had the agency of the world-famous Weber Pianos, and has largely introduced them in Missouri and Illinois. The house also has the agency for the Peek & Son Pianos, and the Clough & Warren Organs. A full line of sheet music, and all musical goods are carried in stock at all times, sufficient to supply the demands of the trade. The great success of the house is the result alone of the experience and energy of the proprietor, Mr. A. Shattinger, who is a business man of liberal and progressive ideas, and has worked hard for the prosperous condition to which he has brought his business.

**W. P. Shryock & Co.**—Wholesale Dealers in Notions, Hardware, Glassware, etc.; 417 Washington avenue.—Mr. Shryock, a merchant for over thirty years in St. Louis, established his present business under the firm style of W. P. Shryock & Co., in 1882, and has had a large and steadily growing trade from that time to the present. He occupies a spacious five-story building, 25x130 feet, at 417 Washington avenue, and carries a very large stock of notions, hardware, glassware, tin and stamped ware, towels, table linen, toys, etc. He makes a specialty of 5, 10 and 25 cent counter goods, which he sells at wholesale in a general way, and also puts up well assorted cases of 5c, 10c and 25c counter goods to merchants throughout Missouri, Kansas, Nebraska, Illinois, Iowa, Dakota, Colorado, New Mexico, Indian Territory, Washington Territory, Arizona, Oregon, California, Nevada, Mississippi, Louisiana, Texas and the entire South. The house employs no travelers, doing its business through catalogues, of which 50,000 are issued three or four times a year, with about 500 electrotype illustrations. A force of thirteen clerks and assistants are employed at the store, and are kept busy supplying the large custom attracted to it by the unparalleled bargains which it carries in immense stock and great variety. The business is managed by Mr. Shryock with a perfect system, and his success is the legitimate result of his push and enterprise.

**M. Ehret & Co.**—W. E. Campe, Resident Manager; Manufacturers of Roofing Pitch, Tarred Felts, Paints, etc.; Location of Works, Philadelphia, Pa.; St. Louis Branch, 113 North Eighth street.—This establishment occupies almost an exclusive field, because of the wide-spread popularity and reputation of the roofing and building materials manufactured by Messrs. Ehret & Co. This firm is the sole manufacturer of the famous "Black Diamond E" prepared roofing, which has been introduced extensively, and become a great favorite as an excellent roofing material. The St. Louis branch is under the control of Mr. W. E. Campe, whose experience and enterprising business methods have enabled him to push the business of his principals to a very satisfactory result. St. Louis is the point of supply for all of the territory on the west and south, and portions of Illinois and Indiana. The display arranged by this house at the last Exposition attracted considerable attention, and was one of the most interesting features of the great exhibition. The business of the branch house in this city has become very large, and now almost equals that of the parent house at Philadelphia.

**Wm. Prufrock.**—Manufacturer of Parlor Suits, Lounges and Mattrasses; 1431 to 1437 North Sixth street.—The premises occupied by the factory of Mr. Prufrock consist of four two-story buildings located at 1431, 1433, 1435 and 1437 North Sixth

street, which have a frontage of 100 feet and a depth of 150 feet, in addition to which he has a factory at 1610 North Eighth street, and a spacious warehouse at 1620 North Eighth street. Mr. William Prufrock established his business in 1869, and by industry, close application, mechanical ability and great knowledge of the trade, has expanded his establishment far beyond its original capacity, until it has become one of the largest west of the Mississippi River. He has constantly in his employ 170 hands, and manufactures a line of goods in parlor suits and upholstery work that are not surpassed for beauty, finish and durability. His trade, which is very extensive, is located in the Western and Southern States, Mexico, New Mexico and California, and reaches east as far as the State of Ohio. He has twelve traveling salesmen constantly on the road, and his sales steadily increase in volume from year to year. The trade from local dealers is also very large, and the work of this maker has a high reputation among all furniture men. He issues a catalogue which is very comprehensive and a marvel of beauty, and a necessity to all engaged in the line. The prosperity he enjoys is the well-earned result of many years of honorable and reliable dealings.

**M. Eisenstadt Jewelry Company.**—Meyer Freide, President; Samuel Eisenstadt, Vice-President; E. Achard, Secretary; Wholesale Dealers in Watches, Diamonds and Jewelry; 409 North Eighth street.—This establishment is one of the oldest in its line in the city, and was originally founded by M. Eisenstadt in 1853. Years afterward the firm became known as M. Eisenstadt & Co., and in 1883 was incorporated as the M. Eisenstadt Jewelry Co. Only the finer grades and qualities of watches and jewelry are handled by the firm, which transacts a very large business with the retail dealers of the South and West. In the volume of annual trade the company is exceeded by no one engaged in the same line, and its popularity and high reputation extend to all parts of the country. All of the officers of the company are men of great experience in the business, and favorably known to the trade. The diamond sales of this house are very large, and the facilities enjoyed by the company are so excellent as to enable them to purchase and import choice stones and place them on the market at reasonable figures.

**M. Cohen & Co.**—Manufacturers and Jobbers of Staple Clothing; 709 and 711 Washington avenue.—This firm, composed of Messrs. M & H. Cohen, was established three years ago. Prior to that time Mr. M. Cohen was of the firm of Kamintzer, Cohen & Prinz, and Mr. H. Cohen was in the retail business. The firm occupy a three-story building, 50x110 feet, and employ six skillful cutters, and fifty workmen in the house, while they have a force of one hundred and fifty outside workmen who are also employed by them. They manufacture men's, youths', boys', and children's suits, and pants in jeans, cotton, worsteds, satinets, union cassimeres, all-wool cassimeres, corkscrews, fancy worsteds, imported moleskins, cottonades, etc. They carry a large and complete stock in all styles and sizes, and have an immense patronage in the States of Missouri, Illinois, Kansas, Iowa, Nebraska, Minnesota, Colorado, the Territories, Texas. Arkansas, Tennessee, Louisiana and the entire West and South, and have four traveling salesmen who represent them on the road. The business has steadily grown from its inception, the season of 1886 having proved a very prosperous one for the business, and the present year giving every indication of proving even more satisfactory in the volume of its sales. The house has a high standing in the trade, and its goods are of superior quality and are sold at prices which exclude competition.

**Fred. Yeakel Carriage Company.**—Fred. Yeakel, Vice-President and Manager; August Wachter, Secretary; Manufacturers of Fine Carriages. Rockaways, Barouches, Phaetons, Business Trucks and Wagons, etc.; 1326 to 1334 Merchant street.—Many of the finest vehicles to be seen upon the streets of St. Louis have the name-plate or imprint of this company upon them, its facilities being such as to permit of the manufacture of the finest work, from the light and

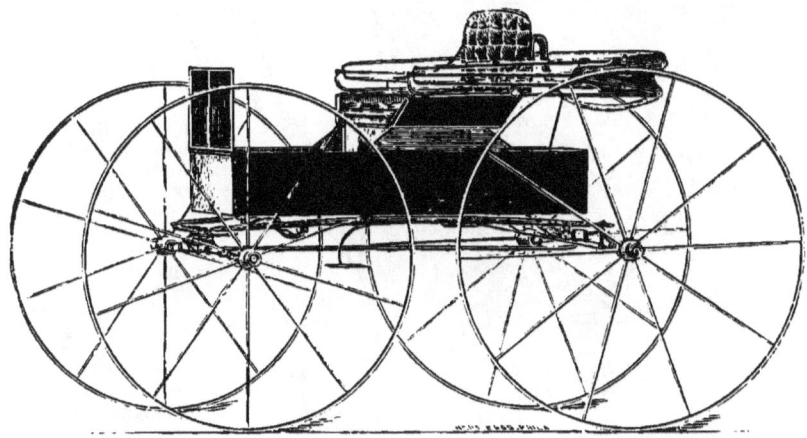

elegant buggy to the heaviest business wagons and trucks. The establishment has a frontage of 100 feet on Merchant street, and extends back to Third street, a distance of 200 feet. During busy seasons, which is pretty much all of the time, a force of seventy-five hands are employed. The company manufacture all of the finer grade of vehicles, and also give special attention to repairs. Its reputation for good, durable work, in which only the best material is used, has given to this company an established trade, not only in the city, but in all of the Western and Southern States.

**The Moser Cigar and Paper Box Co.**—Otto Moser, President; 208 to 214 Elm street.—This establishment, which is the oldest and largest factory in its line in the West, was founded in 1853, by Mr. J. D. Moser, father of the President of the present company. On the death of the founder in 1874, the firm became Moser, Bull & Co., composed of Messrs. Otto Moser and F. D. Bull, under which style the business was continued until the present corporation was organized in January, 1886. The factory, a four-story and basement building, 50x120 feet, with a two-story building adjoining, also 50x120 feet in area, is completely equipped with the most improved plant and machinery, and every facility for the manufacture of cigar boxes and paper boxes on a large scale, giving employment to a force of one hundred and thirty employes. The company has long held a superior reputation for the quality of its product, and does an immense business in the sale of cigar boxes in Illinois, Missouri, Kansas, Texas, Arkansas, etc., as well as having a large city trade in paper boxes of every description. Throughout its successful career of over one-third of a century, this establishment has held a high place in the confidence of the trade by the probity of its dealings and the efficiency of its management.

**Pelton Bros. & Co.**—Manufacturers of the Finest Electro Silver-Plated Ware: 717 South Sixth street.—This firm commenced business at Middletown, Conn., in 1854, and removed to St. Louis in 1872. The establishment occupies premises on South Sixth street, about 100 feet front, with a depth of 200 feet. The building is three stories in height. The employes number forty, and include the most skilled workmen. The firm consists of Frederick W. and Oliver Z. Pelton, both of whom are gentlemen of many years practical experience in their line. To their knowledge of the trade is added rare judgment and business capacity, and they have firmly and securely gained a position and reputation for their establishment that puts it among the leading concerns of its kind in America. Their foresight in realizing the advantages of St. Louis, and removing their establishment to this city has proven correct, and their central position enables them to reach all sections of the country.

**S. Di Franza & Co.**—Wig Manufacturers and all Kinds of Hair Work; 507 North Fourth street.—This firm has been established in this city for twenty years. Their late place of business was at 319 North Broadway, but they moved in January last to their present location, 507 North Fourth street, and are prepared for a large business. In 1884, V. Podesta, an experienced adept in the business, became a partner in the firm. Wigs, bangs, braids, etc., and hair work of any and all descriptions are done in the latest style, first quality goods and workmanship guaranteed; and they are also importers of human hair and all kinds of hair bleach. Robare's L'Aureline, and Per-Oxide of Hydrogen (which is sold by the ounce at half the cost of any preparation and is equally harmless). All goods sold by them are guaranteed to be as good as represented, work done promptly in the best manner, bangs and hair-cutting a specialty, by first-class artists. Persons not living in the city can order by mail and receive entire satisfaction. They keep constantly on hand a large assortment of fine hair ornaments, Rhinestone, amber, cut steel, etc.

**Gus A. Milius.**—Importer and Dealer in Fine Cigars; Northeast Corner of Sixth and St. Charles streets.—The proprietor of this establishment was for many years a member of the traveling fraternity, and packed his sample trunks to all sections of the country in the interests of one of the largest jobbing establishments in the United States. In 1886 he retired from the road, and embarked in business on his own account. His establishment at Sixth and St. Charles streets, under the Hotel Barnum, is one of the finest and most elegant in the city. In connection with his retail business Mr. Milius has an extensive jobbing trade in the city and the Southern and Western States, throughout which he is well known. He is a direct importer of the finest grades of Havana cigars, and dealer in the finer brands of Key West and domestic cigars. He has the exclusive agency of the "Autocraticus," a favorite imported brand; Las Lomas, a Key West cigar, and the celebrated domestic brand, Las Rivales. A full line of all standard brands of fine cigars are always kept in stock.

**Degnan-Maginnis Saddlery Company.**—Manufacturers of Saddlery, Harness, etc.; 509 North Main street.—The large manufacturing business in the line of saddlery, harness, etc., now operated by the Degnan-Maginnis Saddlery Co., was established in 1864 by the firm of Burns & Degnan, who continued until 1886, when the house changed to its present style. The company manufactures all kinds of saddlery, harness, collars, whips, etc., and are wholesale dealers in every description of saddlery hardware. The house makes a specialty of stock saddles and light harness, and carries a full line of horse clothing. The building occupied by the firm as a harness factory, salesrooms and offices, is conveniently located at 509 North Main street, and is six stories high, having a frontage of 30 feet by a depth of 150 feet. The firm gives employment to seventy-five skilled and experienced workmen, and has the advantage of the services of seven active and energetic traveling men, who represent its interests on the road. The trade of the house extends throughout the States of Missouri, Illinois, Indiana, and the entire West, Northwest, Southwest and South, and is very large in all portions of this vast territory, the superiority of its goods having given it a wide-spread reputation for perfect and finished workmanship, and the accuracy of its business methods having commended it to the esteem and confidence of the trade.

**S. Bienenstok & Co.**—Wool, Hides, Broom Corn, etc.; 222 and 224 North Main street.—As a receiving market for wool St. Louis has no equal in the country, and in this important branch of industry the largest dealers in the city are the firm of S. Bienenstok & Co. The house was established in 1836 by Mr. Simon Bienenstok, father of the present head of the firm, and he still gives the business here his supervision. The present firm consists of Mr. Sigfried Bienenstok and Henry Mitchell. They occupy as salesrooms and offices five floors, fronting 50 feet, at 222 and 224 North Main street, and running back 120 feet to another frontage at 223 and 225 North Commercial street. They also have warehouses at 209, 211 and 213 North Commercial, twelve floors 20x100 feet each. At all these premises they deal in and handle on commission wool, hides, peltries, furs, tallows, etc.; in all of which lines they operate very largely. In wool their business is the largest in the West, handling over $3,000,000 worth of the staple annually. Mr. Sigfried Bienenstok makes his headquarters at Chicago, where the firm has a house at 192 and 194 Michigan street. The firm also deals largely in broom corn, carrying on that branch of its business in a separate store at 307 North Main street. They buy their goods in all the States of the West, Northwest, Southwest and South, and sell principally in Eastern markets. The ample capital of the firm, the magnitude of its operations, its long and practical knowledge of the markets and the perfect system upon which its operations are conducted has given it a leading position in its line, and facilities for advantageous dealing which are unsurpassed.

# THE INDUSTRIES OF ST. LOUIS.

**A. P. Erker.**—Practical Optician; 204 North Broadway.—Mr. Erker established himself in this business in 1880, and being thoroughly experienced and skilled in his business has built up a large patronage in the articles in which he deals, including spectacles, eye glasses, opera and field glasses, telescopes, microscopes, drawing instruments, artificial eyes, etc. He makes a specialty of filling the prescriptions of oculists, which he does in the most accurate manner. He has an unexcelled reputation for the merit of his goods, his practical knowledge of the business giving him facilities not surpassed by anyone in his line. He is prepared at all times to fill orders at prices which cannot be duplicated for goods of equal merit.

**The MacMurray-Judge Architectural Iron Company.**—A. J. Judge, President and General Manager; J. W. MacMurray, Vice-President; William Lennox, Treasurer; F. W. Judge, Secretary; Office and Works, Southeast corner of Twenty-First and Papin streets; Branch Office, 902 Chestnut street.—This large and representative manufacturing concern dates its history back to 1832, when it was established in a comparatively modest scale by the firm of MacMurray & Judge, to whom the present company are the successors. The works cover a block, and are completely equipped with all the latest and most approved appliances and machinery adapted to the business. The company employs one hundred men and does an immense business in the city and in all the States of the South and West, and in some of its lines all over the Union. The company manufacture iron house and store fronts in standard and ornamental patterns, and every variety of iron work required in stores and dwellings, including roof crestings, columns, lintels, sills, girders, iron railing for fences, roofs and balconies, guards for windows and doors, iron shutters and doors, bank vaults and entrances, sewer castings of all kinds, hitching posts, extension folding gates and guards, illuminated sidewalk lights, coal vault rings and chutes, sash weights, hinge eyes, jail work, etc. They are sole manufacturers of Farrelly & Co.'s patent double portable book case, shelf and pigeon hole case, suitable for custodians of valuable public and private books and documents, and sole agent for the Pigott burglar and fire proof-shutters, which, while they are burglar proof, open automatically when a stream of water strikes them. The company make a specialty of house and store fronts, in which they are not excelled by any concern in the country. The product of these works is noted for superior quality, and the establishment for over fifty years has ranked high among the leading industries of the city.

**The Ten Broek Agency.**—Gerrit H. Ten Broek, Manager; Albert H. Engel, Assistant Manager; Phillips & Stewart, Counsel; Collectors and Mercantile Adjusters; Rooms 65, 66 and 68 Turner Building, 304 North Eighth street.—This is the leading-collection office of the West, and one of the strongest in the country. It was established in 1880 by Mr. G. H. Ten Broek in conjunction with Messrs. Phillips & Stewart, attorneys, who withdrew in 1882, the firm becoming Ten Broek & Jones.

In 1885 Mr. Ten Brock sold his interest to Jos. S. Jones & Co. and started the present firm, and associated with him, shortly after, Mr. Albert H. Engel, who had been chief clerk for the old firm. In November, 1886, they bought out Jos. S. Jones & Co., consolidating the two agencies, and again associating with them Messrs. Phillips & Stewart as consulting counsel and attorneys for the agency. They have correspondents in all parts of the country, and although their chief business is collecting for St. Louis merchants, they have a large clientele in other cities. Their facilities for carrying on the business are unexcelled and the uniform fidelity with which they discharge every trust has given the Ten Brock Agency a foremost place in the confidence of the business community.

**Kitzinger, Tuholske & Frohlichstein.**—Manufacturers of Jeans and Staple Clothing; 419 Washington avenue.—This business establishment was founded in 1879 by Mr. H. Kitzinger, who conducted it alone until 1884, when he admitted Messrs. M. Tuholske and I. W. Frohlichstein to partnership, and the present firm was formed. They occupy a spacious five-story and basement building, fronting 25 feet at 419 Washington avenue, and running back 120 feet. They employ six skillful cutters and fifty regular hands who work by single dozens, but the great bulk of their manufacture is given out in 20-dozen lots to other shops. The house carries an enormous stock of every description of jeans and staple clothing, and has a large trade with dealers in the States of Missouri, Illinois, Kansas, Arkansas, Iowa, Mississippi, Tennessee, Nebraska, Texas, and the entire West and South, having every facility for successful dealing, and enjoying an unexcelled reputation in the trade for the prompt and close attention bestowed by them on every order.

**Smith-Davis Manufacturing Company.**—J. G. Smith, President; H. N. Davis, Secretary; Manufacturers of Spring, Wire and Iron Beds; Office and Factory, Twenty-third street and Lucas avenue.—This large manufacturing concern was originally established in 1871 by the firm of J. G. Smith & Co., to which the present company succeeded on its incorporation in 1882. The founder of the business, Mr. J. G. Smith, still remains at the head of the company as its President, and directs its affairs with the same ability and experienced judgment that has built up the business to its present important proportions as one of the largest concerns in its line in the West. The spacious manufactory of the company is supplied with all the most modern and improved plant and appliances necessary to its successful operation, and gives employment to a force of one hundred men. The company has acquired a solid reputation for the superior merit of its manufactured products, including spring, wire and iron beds, canvas and wire cots and excelsior, and enjoys a large and constantly expanding trade which reaches every section of the Union.

**Newcomb Brothers Wall Paper Company.**—George A. Newcomb, President; Frank S. Newcomb, Secretary; Dealers in Wall Paper, Curtain Materials and Art Decorations; 303 and 305 North Broadway.—This is one of the prominent business firms of the city, and no house in its special line has been more successful, or enjoys to a higher degree the confidence and esteem of the public. It was established in 1852, and has earned a reputation for merit and artistic designs and workmanship, that has largely contributed to its successful patronage. After many years of success, the firm was incorporated as the Newcomb Bros. Wall Paper Co. in 1884. The stock carried is at all times large, and embraces, besides the leading popular designs in wall papers, window shades, curtain materials, etc., many original novelties in the way of interior decorations. Mr. George A. Newcomb, the senior member of the firm, and now President, is the active manager, and thoroughly understands the requirements of his business. His high conception of merit, and his artistic taste, have combined to produce many delightful effects in decorations. The work of this popular house is to be seen in many of the private homes and public places of the city, which have received their embellishment from Newcomb Brothers. The specialty of the company is the decoration of interiors, and whether for residences, hotels, clubs or private edifices, their designs and workmanship are unexcelled.

**Gus. Frey.**—Blank Book Manufacturer, Lithographer and Printer; 316 and 318 North Third street.—This business was established by Mr. Frey eight years ago, and the steadily increasing success he has enjoyed is a practical demonstration of the merit of his workmanship and the accuracy and reliability of his business methods. He carries on all the various departments of blank book manufacture, lithographing and printing, employing sixty skilled and experienced workmen. The premises occupied by him, embracing an area 60x160 feet, are fully outfitted with all the most improved modern machinery and appliances appropriate to his business, and all the work turned out at the establishment is executed in the best and most perfect manner. This merit has secured for him a large city patronage, and a trade extending north, south and west in all the States tributary to St. Louis in a commercial sense. A number of traveling salesmen represent the house on the road, and every order is filled with dispatch and gives complete satisfaction. In addition to his other departments Mr. Frey does general binding in the most perfect and improved styles of the art. In resources and facilities, and in every element which goes to make up a perfect adaptability to every demand of this branch of productive industry, the establishment of Mr. Frey is without a superior in the city or the West.

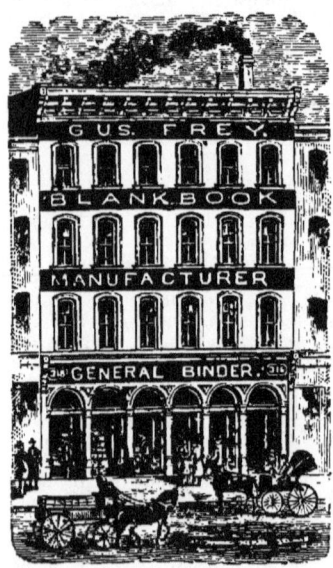

**Charles E. Lewis.**—Wholesale Dealers in Undertakers' Trimmings and Cabinet Hardware; 615 and 617 North Eighth street.—Mr. Lewis has conducted this business for a number of years, and is known to the undertaking and cabinet-making trade in the city and throughout all the Southern and Western States as having the largest and best stock of undertakers' trimmings and cabinet hardware to be found in this city, carrying everything that pertains to the line, and occupying a large double building, six-stories in height and embracing an area of 50x100 feet. Mr. Lewis is an experienced and practical man in the business, and devotes his entire time and attention to its details. He has a very large business, which he has secured by the merit of his goods and the uniform accuracy and reliability of his business methods.

**James Stewart & Co.**—Architects, Builders and Contractors; Fourth and Market streets.—Mr. James Stewart, the head of this firm, established himself in business in this city in 1866, when he came from Ottawa, Canada, where he and Mr. Alexander Mackenzie, afterwards Premier of Canada, were Crown Commissioners to adjust accounts and receive from the contractors the Parliament Buildings. He comes of a family of architects and builders for generations, and his brothers in Scotland are eminent in the profession. Mr. Stewart is the only American honorary member of the Edinburg Architectural Association. Since coming to St. Louis he has held a foremost position among the leading architects of the city. He built the Music Pavilion at Forest Park, the Retreat at Lafayette Park, Dr. McLean's Tower Block, at the corner Fourth and Market streets, and many other noted buildings. A few years ago his son, Mr. Alexander M. Stewart, became a member of the firm. During the past year they erected for the Merchants' Elevator Co. a river annex at the foot of Florida street, 70x200 feet, with five elevators, and a capacity of 500,000 bushels. In this building, which cost $860,000, a new system of spouting was used, being the first introduction, south of Minneapolis, of the "Hughes System of Revolving Spouts" of which the firm has sole control. This building has the lowest rate of insurance of any elevator in St. Louis. They also built last year, for Haydock Bros., carriage manufacturers, a building 80x140 feet, six stories high, at the corner of Thirteenth and Papin streets, being a wing only of the main building, which is to be erected the present year. This building is the best and strongest example of the "slow burning construction" principle west of New York. All the floors are of 6-inch thick yellow pine with a $1\frac{1}{4}$-inch wearing floor, and the building which cost $45,000, is insured at 30 cents on the $100, a striking example of what can be done in the way of low insurance by erecting good manufactories. By this method of construction all joisting of floors is avoided. No connection is made between the different floors, and the power is carried from floor to floor in brick shafts or chambers provided for that purpose. The St. Louis Cable and Western Railroad building, which was burned on the night of December 5th, was rebuilt by this firm in seventeen working days. The building was 106x135, two stories high, and cost $22,000. Other buildings erected by this firm last year were: Twelve-room residence for J. C. Love, Esq., in Vandeventer place, with front of Dunreath red sandstone, at a cost of $13,000, and a residence of seven rooms on Olive street, near Sarah street for $5,500; for James A. Gregory, twelve-room residence at the corner of Channing avenue and Morgan street, costing $10,500; for Dr. S. L. Niedelet, late coroner, nine-room building, flat system, on Ewing avenue, near Pacific street, for $5,500. In January last they built for the Merchants' Elevator Co. a corn crib of 160,000 bushels capacity, 45x54 feet and 80 feet high—the highest in the world—at a cost of $16,000. The firm has plans now ready for main building for Haydock Bros., corner of Thirteenth and Papin streets, 90x250, six stories high, to cost $75,000, similar to the building erected for them last year; for Milburn Carriage Manufacturing Co., a six-story factory, 70x137 feet, at corner of Cass avenue and Seventh street, similar in style to the Haydock building, and to cost $30,000; for Merchants' Elevator Co. a new annex, 50x90 feet, of 150,000 bushels capacity, to cost $20,000; for Sedalia, Mo., a grain elevator, 35x80 feet, of 90,000 bushels capacity, to cost $16,000, and residences for E. P. V. Ritter, James A. Gregory, John Bauman, A. M. Stewart and J. C. Stewart. The firm gives special attention to the erection of grain elevators, mills and warehouses, and do a very large business in all lines of the profession. In 1886 they opened the quarries of the Dunreath Red Stone and Quarry Co., at Dunreath, Iowa, of which corporation Mr. James Stewart is President; William McMillan, Vice-President; and A. M. Stewart, Secretary and Treasurer. The company has a paid-up capital of $150,000, and while as yet only in its infancy, has erected complete quarry machines, steam channelers, etc., and has employed since its opening about sixty hands. By July 1st of the present year fully one hundred men will be employed, and the shipping capacity will be eight cars per day. This stone is pronounced by all architects and experts the best red sandstone ever found in America.

**G. H. Diederich Furniture Company.**—Mrs. G. H. Diederich, President; Henry Diederich, Secretary; Manufacturers of Furniture; Second and Tyler streets.—This prominent and prosperous manufacturing establishment was founded twenty years ago by Mr. G. H. Diederich, under whose experienced and careful management the business steadily grew. Shortly before his death, two years ago, the present company was incorporated, and after he died his widow became President of the company, and his son, Mr. Henry Diederich, Secretary. The company's factory is a three-story structure, 60x100 feet in dimensions, and, with their adjoining lumber yards, etc., cover an area of 240x160. The factory is completely equipped with all the latest and most improved machinery and appliances for the purposes of their business, giving employment to a force of fifty skilled and experienced workmen. They manufacture every description of chamber furniture, making a specialty of bedsteads, for which the company has acquired a wide celebrity as the result of superior workmanship and materials. They have a large assortment of tables, lounges, cribs, bedsteads, wardrobes, etc., constantly on hand, which they are prepared to offer at the most reasonable prices. Their business is very large, and extends over the States of Arkansas, Missouri, Texas, Kansas, New Mexico, Colorado, and the South and West generally, employing a staff of three active and experienced traveling salesmen. The active management of the business devolves upon Mr. Henry Diederich, who has received a thorough training in all its details, and is an energetic and enterprising manufacturer, and manages the affairs of the house upon the most accurate methods.

**Reade Manufacturing Company.**—Manufacturing Chemists, Druggists and Distillers of Fruit Essences. Makers of Specialties for the Various Requirements of the Trades and of Manufacturers; 323 Clark avenue.—This concern was established in St Louis in 1883 by W. J. Reade and an associate since retired. Mr. Reade has been for twenty-five years practically engaged in the manufacturing and wholesaling of chemicals and drugs for every conceivable sort of trade, for every variety of purpose, and for every quarter of the globe. Such an experience and practice has well qualified him to furnish materials and advice in the chemical and drug department, to both merchants and consumers. The productions of his English firm have been imported by American jobbers and manufacturers for the last seventy years, so that now, when such goods are obtainable at home, free from the costs, delays and difficulties of importation, their friends all over the continent will readily recognize the important advantages derived from the location of such a firm in so central a city as St. Louis.

**The Bryant Carriage Company.**—C. J. Bryant, Proprietor; Vehicles and Harness and other Horse Trappings; 1009 and 1011 Locust street.—This business was recently established by Mr. Bryant, who has the agency for the Buckeye Buggy Co., of Columbus, Ohio, and for Studebaker Bros., Chicago, Ill., and South Bend, Ind., the largest house in its line in the world. The Bryant Carriage Co. handles the full line of buggies, phætons, etc., manufactured by the Buckeye Co., and the fine carriages of the Studebaker make. They carry full lines of fine vehicles of both makes, and deal in

fine harness, saddlery, lap robes, and all horse trappings. Mr. Bryant is a practical carriage builder, and is widely known, having been for years in the city collector's office, and filled other important positions of public trust. He is a Union veteran, and served through the civil war, and is a prominent member of the Grand Army of the Republic. He is a thorough business man, and attends closely to every detail, managing his affairs on correct and reliable methods, with the valuable assistance of Mr. Fotheringham, a gentleman of superior business attainments. The premises occupied by the business comprise a fine three-story building, 60x160 feet in dimensions, eligibly and centrally located, and the business has already assumed prosperous proportions, the goods being in demand in the city and surrounding country.

**E. W. Horstman & Co.**—Wholesale Produce and Vegetables; 813 North Third street.—This business was established about twenty years ago by Mr. C. Horstman, by whom the business was conducted until 1881, when he was succeeded by the present firm of E. W. Horstman & Co., composed of Messrs. E. W. Horstman and Wm. H. Redemeyer, Jr. They do a large and steadily increasing wholesale business in produce and vegetables of every description, making a specialty of potatoes, apples, onions, cabbage and kraut, receiving goods from the East and North and shipping them South, and also selling them largely to shippers. They have unsurpassed facilities for handling, shipping and dealing in produce and vegetables, and especially for the procurement of early vegetables, maintaining the most favorable relations with producers, and being enabled to offer the most advantageous terms, both in price and quality, to their customers. Conducting their business on fair and liberal methods they enjoy an annually increasing patronage and deserved prosperity.

**Knickmeyer & Co.**—Wholesale Dealers in Liquors and Wines; 917 North Fourth street.—This business was established in 1849 by the firm of Nulsen & Co. Messrs. F. and H. H. Knickmeyer were with that firm for about fourteen years prior to 1882, when they succeeded to the business under the firm style of Knickmeyer & Co. They occupy a commodious three-story building at 917 North Fourth street, and do an extensive business as wholesalers and rectifiers of liquors, wines, etc., enjoying a large and steadily growing patronage, including, in addition to a heavy city trade, a considerable business in the States of Missouri, Illinois and Arkansas. The excellent reputation of the goods sold by this house, which has attached to it for the many years of its history, has been sustained under the able management of the present firm, and they carry a large and completely assorted stock of liquors and wines, embracing everything pertaining to their line. Their dealings with their customers have always been characterized by fairness and liberal methods, and the business enjoys an annual and steady expansion.

**Varney Carriage Company.**—Zenas Varney, President and Treasurer; John W. Bowen, Secretary; Manufacturers of Carriages and Buggies; 2017 and 2019 Morgan street.—This establishment is well known in the city on account of the excellence of its manufactures, and the many high class vehicles it has turned out during its existence. The factory was established in 1868 by Mr. Varney, who is thoroughly and practically familiar with the carriage business, and well understands the wants of the people of St. Louis regarding pleasure vehicles. The business was incorporated in 1883 with Zenas Varney as President and John W. Bowen as Secretary. The company occupy a large, elegant building on Morgan street, near Twentieth, where its factory and salesroom are located. The annual trade is very large, located principally in the city and surrounding towns. Many of the stylish and elegant equipages seen upon the streets and boulevards of St. Louis are from this establishment, and the name plate of the Varney Carriage Co. upon any vehicle is a guarantee of its excellence and general superiority.

**Raymond & Torwegge.**—Manufacturers of Fine Silk, Cassimere, Pull-Over, Beaver, Otter and Fine Flexible Stiff Hats; 722 North Fourth street.—This business was established about twenty-five years ago as Raymond & Torwegge. Mr. Raymond died about seven years afterward but the name was retained, the present members of the firm being Messrs. J. L. Rose and H. J. Torwegge. They have their factory and salesrooms at 722 North Fourth street, occupying the upper half of the building, and giving employment to a force of fifty men. They manufacture fine hats of the varieties mentioned in the headlines of this sketch, and have a large trade, extending east to Ohio, and all South, North and West. The uniform merit of their manufacture is well known to the trade, and they have maintained throughout the long and prosperous history of the house a leading position in this department of industry. Their facilities for manufacture are not surpassed in the West, and the close attention given by them to every detail of the business has caused their relations with the trade to be of the most satisfactory and gratifying character.

**L. Garvey & Co.**—Wholesale Produce Dealers and Commission Merchants; 1 and 3 South Main street.—Under this style Mr. L. Garvey has been successfully engaged in business for the past eleven years. He deals wholesale in produce and provisions, butter, cheese, dried fruits, etc., and also does a general commission business. He has a full staff of buyers and salesmen on the road, and receives produce, provisions, etc., from New York, Michigan, Wisconsin, Iowa, Illinois, Missouri and Ohio, and sells in the city and in Texas, Arkansas, Indian Territory, Kansas, New Mexico, Louisiana, Mississippi, and Tennessee. He enjoys a large trade in all the lines in which he deals, and also has a heavy commission business, his accurate knowledge of the markets, and close attention to the details of every transaction placed in his hands having secured for him an excellent standing with and large patronage from producers and shippers. He has first-class facilities for the transaction of every department of his business, and has earned his present prosperity by the fairness and accuracy of his business methods.

# EAST ST. LOUIS.

## THE THRIVING CITY ON THE ILLINOIS SIDE OF THE RIVER—ITS MUNICIPAL GOVERNMENT.

EAST ST. LOUIS had its origin in a settlement made by Capt. James Pigott, who, in 1797, established a ferry at this point between the east and west banks of the river. Illinoistown, as East St. Louis was originally named, was laid out in the autumn of 1817, and in November of that year a number of lots in the town were disposed of at auction and private sale. This town is now the southeast portion of the city of East St. Louis. Many new divisions were added from time to time, and at an election held April 1, 1861, the citizens changed the name of the town from Illinoistown to East St. Louis. In 1865 the government of the town was changed by the adoption of a city charter, and J. B. Bowman was elected the first mayor on April 3d of that year.

The city has enjoyed a steady and healthy growth in industrial importance and material prosperity. It is the center of a vast railroad system, radiating in all directions, and connected by means of the great Mississippi bridge with St. Louis, with which it is identified by a strong community of interests, and to the prosperity and commercial importance of which it is a large contributor. Many large manufacturing establishments are located in East St. Louis, which has all the advantages and resources for the successful prosecution of every description of industrial enterprises.

The present officers of the City of East St. Louis are M. M. Stephens, Mayor; John W. Renshaw, Treasurer; John Meyer, City Clerk; Michael Walsh, Marshal; James W. Kirk, City Auditor, and E. R. Davis, City Attorney. The legislative government of the city is vested in a city council, over which the Mayor presides, and composed of eight aldermen, the present incumbents being as follows: First Ward—D. C. Marsh and W. W. Russell; Second Ward—Louis Menges, Jr., and Dr. C. F. Strecker; Third Ward—Robert Cunningham and Martin Egan; Fourth Ward—Mark Bird and John V. Tefft. The stated sessions of the Council occur on the second Tuesdays of April, June, August, October and December. The regular standing committees of the XXIII Council are as follows: Ways and Means—Messrs. Tefft, Russell, Strecker, Menges, Jr.; Claims—Messrs. Marsh, Strecker, Tefft, Cunningham; Streets and Alleys—Messrs. Russell, Strecker, Egan, Bird; Police—Messrs. Strecker, Marsh, Egan, Tefft; Fire and Water—Messrs. Egan, Russell, Strecker, Menges, Jr.; Railroads—Messrs. Tefft, Strecker, Egan, Marsh; Public Buildings and Grounds—Messrs. Russell, Egan, Strecker, Bird. Litigation—Messrs. Marsh, Strecker, Tefft, Cunningham.

The Mayor, Mr. M. M. Stephens, was elected to his position in response to a demand for reform in the financial administration of the city, and is devoting his attention, with efficient aid from the Council, to the task of retrenchment, the solution of the debt problem, and the development of the material interests of the city.

# INDEX.

## REPRESENTATIVE HOUSES.

| | PAGE |
|---|---|
| Adams Commission Co., commission merchants | 220 |
| Alexander, M. W., druggist and pharmacist | 226 |
| American Carbon Co. (See Heisler Electric Light Co.) | 95 |
| American Cotton Oil Co | 134 |
| American Refrigerator Transit Co | 177 |
| American Shade Co., window shades, etc. | 223 |
| American Wine Co., "Cook's Imperial Champagne," extra dry and still wines | 176 |
| American Wood Preserving Co., wood preserving by zinc-gypsum process | 139 |
| Anchor Line, The, St. Louis to Vicksburg and New Orleans | 73 |
| Annan, Burg & Co., general commission merchants | 224 |
| Anthony & Kuhn Brewing Co | 213 |
| Barnard, Geo. D., & Co., blank book makers, lithographers, printers and stationers | 159 |
| Barnhart Mercantile Co., wholesale dealers in fancy groceries, foreign and domestic fruits, etc. | 91 |
| Bartley, Walter S., provision, tallow, flour and grain broker | 206 |
| Bascome, Western, Insurance | 157 |
| Becker, J. P., the Three Leading Stores, East St. Louis | 165 |
| Bellefontaine Cemetery Association | 224 |
| Bemis Bro. Bag Co., manufacturers of bags and burlaps | 124 |
| Bennett & Harris, brokers | 164 |
| Bcusbery, F. A., & Co., wholesale liquor dealers; fine Kentucky whiskies | 219 |
| Berry Bros., manufacturers of varnishes | 197 |
| Bethesda Mineral Water, Chas. Moss & Co., agents (See also advertisement, page 253) | 115 |
| Bienenstok, S., & Co. wool, hides, broom corn, etc. | 237 |
| Billingsley & Nanson Commission Co., grain, hay, flour, etc. | 122 |
| Bishop & Spear, recleaners of peanuts and pecans, and proprietors of the "Parrot" and "Boss" brands of peanuts | 190 |
| Blakely, Sanders & Co., live stock commission merchants | 120 |
| Blattner & Adam, practical opticians, mathematical and electrical instrument makers | 200 |

| | PAGE |
|---|---|
| Blossom, H. M., & Co., fire and marine insurance | 174 |
| Booth, Barada & Co., real estate agents | 149 |
| Bothe, H. H., manufacturer of omnibuses, street cars, express, mail and business wagons, New York trucks, etc. | 192 |
| Boyd, T. B., & Co., importers, manufacturers and jobbers of men's furnishing goods and shirts | 218 |
| Branch-Crookes Saw Co., manufacturers of all kinds of saws, planing knives, etc. | 92 |
| Brentano, H., & Co., stock brokers | 173 |
| Brockman, P., & Co., general commission merchants | 132 |
| Bromschwig, Henry, & Co., importers and jobbers of tailors' trimmings | 221 |
| Brook & Co., manufacturers of trunks, traveling bags, sample cases, etc. | 222 |
| Brown-Desnoyers Shoe Co., manufacturers of boots and shoes | 122 |
| Brownell, B. H., tailor and importer | 85 |
| Brownell & Wight Car Co., manufacturers of street cars | 119 |
| Bryant Carriage Co., The, vehicles and harness and other horse trappings | 242 |
| Brunner, Geo. F., Manufacturing Co., manufacturers of bone black, bone meal and fertilizers | 188 |
| Buckland & Pallen (Trustees), real estate office | 161 |
| Burd-Stuyvesant Glue Co | 211 |
| Burnham, S. G., stationer, printer, lithographer, etc. | 176 |
| Burns, P., & Co., manufacturers and wholesale dealers in saddles, harness, etc. | 214 |
| Buxton & Skinner Stationery Co., artistic lithographers and printers, blank book manufacturers and stationers | 174 |
| Byrne, John, Jr., & Co., real estate agents | 85 |
| Cafferata, A., Sons & Co., importers and wholesale dealers in tropical fruits, Florida and California oranges, etc. | 98 |
| Capitain & Steinmann, architects | 114 |
| Carter, C. B., & Co., wholesale dealers in provisions | 142 |
| Cash, Stewart & Overstreet, live stock commission merchants | 161 |
| Catlin Tobacco Co., manufacturers | 90 |

## THE INDUSTRIES OF ST. LOUIS.

| | PAGE |
|---|---|
| Chamberlain, F. B., Commission Co., commission merchants | 90 |
| Chase, H. & L., wholesale bags and bagging | 219 |
| Cherokee Brewery Co., brewers of the renowned "Herold's superior bottled lager beer," ales and porter | 147 |
| Chester & Keller Manufacturing Co., manufacturers of hickory handles, spokes, and wagon and buggy woodwork | 133 |
| Citizens' Savings Bank | 131 |
| Clarkson-Christopher Lumber Co., wholesale commission lumber dealers | 129 |
| Clarkson & Wagner, Hamilton-Corliss and stationary and portable engines, saw mills, gang edgers, lath machines, wood-working machinery, etc. | 215 |
| Clarksville Cider and Vinegar Co., pure apple cider, vinegar and syrup | 205 |
| Cleary & Co., Redmond, commission merchants | 119 |
| Cobb, S. W., & Co., commission merchants | 87 |
| Coffin—Thomas Coffin & Co., Limited, manufacturers of fire-brick, etc. | 77 |
| Cohen, M., & Co., manufacturers and jobbers of staple clothing | 234 |
| Cole Brothers Commission Co., commission, grain, flour, provisions, wool, etc. | 192 |
| Cole & Glass, Star moulding, turning and planing mill | 112 |
| Coleman, R. L., & Co., hot and cold blast iron, etc. | 209 |
| Collins, Martin, insurance | 86 |
| Comfort, C. D., manufacturer of hosiery, overalls, etc. | 108 |
| Consolidated Coal Company of St. Louis | 125 |
| Consumers' Coal Co., miners and wholesale and retail dealers in bituminous and anthracite coal | 153 |
| Continental Bank of St. Louis, The | 172 |
| Cook, W. H., & Co., brokers in cotton, coffee, grain and provisions | 115 |
| Cornet, H. L., & Co., house and real estate agents | 156 |
| Corticelli Silk Mills (Nonotuck Silk Co.,) Corticelli spool silk, etc. | 166 |
| Covenant Mutual Life Insurance Co., The | 111 |
| Cox & Gordon, pork packers, curers of the Missouri ham, and jobbers in pork, lard, bacon, etc. | 223 |
| Crescent Furniture and Lumber Co., manufacturers of kitchen safes, tables, wardrobes, etc. | 97 |
| Crown Metal Perforating Co. | 145 |
| Cummiskey, James, real estate | 133 |
| Cunningham—The James Cunningham, Son & Company, builders of high grade carriages | 127 |
| Daly, C. C., & Co., live stock commission merchants | 166 |
| Dauernheim, Chas., paper hangings, window shades, weather strips, wire screens, etc. | 113 |
| Day Rubber Co., importers, manufacturers and dealers in India rubber goods | 168 |
| Deere, Mansur & Co., farm machinery, "John Deere" plows and cultivators, etc. | 193 |
| Degnan-Maginnis Saddlery Co., manufacturers of saddlery, harness, etc. | 237 |
| Deliner-Wuerpel Mill Building Co., millwrights and machinists, builders of complete mills and manufacturers of general motive power, etc. | 150 |
| DeLaVergne Refrigerating Machine Co., The. Ruemmeli & Rassbach, general western agents | 196 |
| Deming Commission Co., brokerage and commission | 225 |
| Dennison Manufacturing Co. | 160 |
| Devlin, Daniel, Union Machine Shops | 189 |
| Diederich, G. H., Furniture Co., manufacturers of furniture | 241 |
| Di Franza, S. & Co., wig manufacturers and all kinds of hair work | 236 |
| Domestic Sewing Machine Co. | 121 |
| Donk Bros. & Co., miners and dealers in bituminous and anthracite coal | 123 |
| Donovan, J. T., & Co., real estate and financial agents | 125 |
| Drach, Charles A., & Co., electrotypers and stereotypers | 79 |
| Drey & Kahn, importers and dealers in plate, window and stained glass, etc. | 152 |
| Druhe Hardwood Lumber Co., wholesale dealers in hardwood lumber | 100 |
| Dun, R. G., & Co., The Mercantile Agency | 109 |
| Eagle Machine Works Manufacturing Co., manufacturers of engines and general machinery | 217 |
| Edgar, S. C., lessee Glendale Zinc Works | 300 |
| Edwards, Jas., & Co., stock and bond brokers | 136 |

| | PAGE |
|---|---|
| Ehlermann, Chas., Hop and Malt Co., brewers', distillers' and bottlers' supplies | 202 |
| Ebret, M., & Co., manufacturers of roofing pitch, tarred felts, paints, etc. | 233 |
| Eisenhardt, Herman, manufacturer of candles, soap and lard oil | 226 |
| Eisenstadt, M., Jewelry Co., wholesale dealers in watches, diamonds and jewelry | 231 |
| Eliot Frog and Switch Co., railroad crossings, frogs and switches and every description of railroad iron work | 164 |
| Ely & Walker Dry Goods Co., importers and jobbers in dry goods | 156 |
| Engelke & Feiner, proprietors of Southern Roller Mills | 128 |
| Equitable Life Assurance Society of the United States, The | 72 |
| Erker, A. P., practical optician | 238 |
| Evans, David G., & Co., importers and jobbers of teas, coffees, etc. | 226 |
| Evens & Howard, manufacturers of fire brick, gas retorts, sewer pipe and other fire clay goods | 83 |
| Everett & Post, pig lead, spelter and ingot copper | 76 |
| Ewing, James F., agent for the Michigan Salt Association, the Michigan Dairy Salt Co., and the celebrated Michigan Salt Association dairy salt | 191 |
| Fabricius Toy and Notion Co., importers and dealers in toys, fancy goods, notions, etc. | 122 |
| Fallon, John F., carriage builder | 113 |
| Faust, A. E., wholesale and retail dealer in fresh oysters, sea fish, celery and other foreign and domestic delicacies | 93 |
| Fehlig Bros Box Manufacturing Co., Southern Box Factory | 115 |
| Fekete, Thomas L., real estate and financial and insurance agent | 171 |
| Fleischmann & Co., original manufacturers and introducers into the United States of compressed yeast | 180 |
| Flesh & Mook, manufacturers of signs of every description, painters, etc. | 220 |
| Foerstel, Helbeck & Co., practical engravers, lithographers and printers | 219 |
| Fox, Patrick, Catholic publisher and importer of church goods | 225 |
| Frantz Toy and Notion Co., importers of fancy goods, toys, notions, etc. | 122 |
| Francis—D. R. Francis & Bro., Commission Co. | 80 |
| Frank, A., & Sons, wholesale dry goods and notions | 166 |
| Frankenthal, A., & Brother, manufacturers and dealers in men's furnishing goods | 98 |
| French Silvering and Ornamental Glass Co., manufacturers of stained glass | 155 |
| Frey, Gus, blank book manufacturer, lithographer and printer | 240 |
| Fritz, Geo. J., Central Iron Works, patentee and builder of steam engines, boilers, doctors, pumps, seed meal molders, barrel trusses, etc. | 212 |
| Fruin-Bambrick Construction Co., contractors, builders of railroads, water works, etc. | 86 |
| Gage & Horton Manufacturing Co., The, manufacturers of stoves, ranges, marbleized iron and slate mantels and grates, etc. | 227 |
| Gaiennie, Frank, commission merchant | 74 |
| Galle, Charles, engraving on wood and advertising signs | 201 |
| Gamahl, John J., Lumber Co., dealers in pine, poplar, cedar and hardwood lumber | 86 |
| Garrison, D. E., & Co., manufacturers' agents for Bessemer steel rails | 153 |
| Garrison-Chappell-Pirie Paper Co., wholesale paper dealers | 184 |
| Gartside Coal Co., Illinois and Big Muddy coal | 136 |
| Garvey, L., & Co., wholesale produce dealers and commission merchants | 213 |
| Gans, H., & Sons Manufacturing Co., manufacturers of doors, frames, sash, blinds, packing boxes, etc. | 160 |
| Gauss-Shelton Hat Co., wholesale hats, caps, gloves, vallses, etc. | 232 |
| Gaylord, Sam'l A., & Co., bankers and brokers | 180 |
| Geisel, A., manufacturer of tinware of all descriptions and wholesale dealer in tin plate and metals | 113 |
| Gerber & Signaigo, fruit and general commission merchants | 94 |
| Ginocchio Brothers & Co., wholesale dealers in foreign, California and tropical fruits | 145 |
| Glaser Brothers, importers and manufacturers of gents' furnishing goods and notions | 121 |
| Glendale Zinc Works, S. C. Edgar, Lessee, manufacturer and refiner of spelter | 300 |

# THE INDUSTRIES OF ST. LOUIS. 247

Glover & Flukenam, manufacturers of and dealers in artists' materials, studies, etc ... 138
Godlove, George W., & Co., commission merchants in wool, hides, furs, roots, seeds, etc. 188
Gog—Geo. Gog Boot and Shoe Manufacturing Co., manufacturers of men's and boys' boots and shoes.......... 130
Goldman, Leon, stocks and bonds.......... 151
Goodyear Rubber Co., The, manufacturers, importers and dealers in Goodyear's rubber goods .......... 175
Graham Paper Co., wholesale paper and paper stock .......... 178
Gray, E. P., publisher, importer, bookseller and stationer .......... 180
Great Western Oil Works of Cleveland, Ohio, Scofield, Shurmer & Teagle, independent refiners of petroleum .......... 172
Great Western Planing Mill Co., manufacturers of sash, doors, blinds, mouldings, etc .......... 135
Green & Clark, manufacturers of and wholesale dealers in Missouri cider and vinegar .......... 231
Hager, C., & Son, manufacturers of hinges .......... 184
Halliday, G. V., & Co., safes, time locks and vault doors .......... 129
Hamilton Brown Shoe Co., manufacturers and jobbers of boots and shoes exclusively for cash .......... 75
Hanley, James, carriages, buggies, phaetons, surreys and spring wagons .......... 229
Harnett, J. A., & Co., lumber dealers and commission .......... 146
Harris, B., & Co., commission merchants; dealers in hides, wool, furs, etc .......... 202
Harter—The Dr. Harter Medicine Co., proprietary medicines .......... 197
Hartford Silver Plate Co., The .......... 78
Haydock Brothers, wholesale carriage manufacturers .......... 103
Haydock, D. W., wholesale manufacturer of carriages, buggies, surreys, etc .......... 128
Hayes—Jos. M. Hayes Woolen Co., importers & jobbers of fine woolens and tailors' trimmings 158
Haynes, W. J., & Co., commission merchants; wool, hides, furs and general produce .......... 135
Heil, Henry, importer and manufacturer of chemical apparatus and chemicals and materials for smelters, assayers, miners and jewelers .......... 228
Heine Safety Boiler Co., The, boiler manufacturers .......... 199
Heinrich Coal Co .......... 155
Heisler Electric Light Co., manufacturers and patentees of arc and incandescent dynamo machines and lamps; also of Heisler electric bells, burglar alarms, annunciators, etc., also American Carbon Co., manufacturers of carbons for electric lights, also St. Louis Illuminating Co .......... 95
Heller & Hoffman, manufacturers of chairs .......... 111
Henry & Co., manufacturers of excelsior .......... 215
Hewes, George H., contracting engineer, and manufacturers' agent for mining and water works machinery .......... 168
Hewitt, Sharp & Co., commission merchants .......... 232
Hill-Settle Tobacco Co., sole manufacturer of concentrated extract of tobacco, and extract of tobacco salve .......... 182
Hirsch & Bendheim, manufacturers of fine cigars, and wholesale dealers in pipes, tobaccos and smokers' articles .......... 203
Holt, Payne & Co., live stock commission merchants .......... 230
Hopkins, H. S., Bridge Co., general contractors 132
Horstman, E., & Co., wholesale produce and vegetables .......... 242
Hudson Brothers Commission Co., produce and provisions .......... 185
Hulbert, A. G., manufacturer of wire and iron fences (see also advt. p. 255.) .......... 203
Hull, Steele & Co., live stock commission merchants .......... 153
Humphrey, F. W., & Co., clothing, hats and furnishings, (see also outside page, back cover) 96
Hunter Brothers, flour, grain and feed; shipping and commission .......... 109
Hinse & Loomis Ice and Transportation Co., wholesale dealers in ice .......... 164
Huttig Sash and Door Co., manufacturers of sash, doors and blinds and wholesale dealers in mouldings, stair work, etc .......... 208
Hyatt, H. A., photographic goods, picture frames, mouldings, etc .......... 167
Hydraulic Press Brick Co., The .......... 99
Isaacs, H. G., architect .......... 136
Isaacs, J. L., Wall Paper Co., interior decorations and fresco painting .......... 150

Johansen Bros., manufacturers of ladies', misses' and children's shoes .......... 185
Jordan, A. J., manufacturer of fine cutlery .......... 162
Judd, Max, & Co., cloak manufacturers .......... 228
Judy, W. W., & Co., dealers in poultry and game .......... 221
Kaiser, Jacob, & Co., upholsterers, manufacturers of mattresses, etc .......... 229
Kauffman, F. A., manufacturer of vinegar and sauer kraut and wholesale dealer in Ohio and New York country cider .......... 111
Kelcher, P. F., & Co., stock and bond brokers. 119
Kellogg, Charles P., & Co., clothing and furnishing goods .......... 150
Kennard, J., & Sons' Carpet Co., carpets, curtain goods, oil cloths, etc .......... 131
Kimball, Benj., licensed broker for the assured 105
Kingsland & Ferguson Manufacturing Co., agricultural and saw-mill machinery .......... 71
Klitzinger, Tuholske & Frohlichstein, manufacturers of jeans and staple clothing .......... 239
Klausmann Brewery Co., lager and "Eureka" bottled beer .......... 188
Knickmeyer & Co., wholesale dealers in liquors and wines .......... 243
Koenig, Wm., & Co., reapers, mowers, binders, threshers and Canton engines .......... 99
Kohn & Co., bankers and brokers .......... 104
Koken, E. E., manufacturer and dealer in barbers' furniture, perfumery and cutlery .......... 134
Kraft-Holmes Grocery Co., wholesale grocers. 175
Kruse, E. C., & Co., commission merchants for the sale of hides, wool, pelts, tallow, furs, etc .......... 162
Laclede Mutual Fire Insurance Co .......... 127
Lambert Pharmacal Co., manufacturing chemists; pharmaceutical specialties exclusively for physicians .......... 76
Larkin & Sheffer, manufacturing chemists .......... 221
Laughlin & Blakely, proprietors of Planters' House Warehouse .......... 141
Legg, J. B., architect .......... 104
Levy, A., & Co., agents of the Cyclostyle and The Addressing, Duplicating & Mailing Co. 205
Levy, Herman, & Co., commission merchants and dealers in hides, furs, wool, pelts, deer skins, tallow, ginseng, etc .......... 208
Lewis, Charles E., wholesale dealer in undertakers' trimmings and cabinet hardware 240
Liggett & Myers Tobacco Co., manufacturers of plug chewing tobacco .......... 78
Lippincott & Co., manufacturers of soda water apparatus, soda and mineral waters, syrups, extracts, etc .......... 151
Little, F. E., & Co., feathers .......... 206
Liverpool and London and Globe Insurance Co., The .......... 119
Loehlein, B., St. Louis Collar & Whip Factory 232
Logeman, F. H., Chair Manufacturing Co .......... 176
Long, S. N., Syrup Co., syrup manufacturers 174
Ludlow-Saylor Wire Co., manufacturers of and dealers in wire and wire goods .......... 109
Lungstras Dyeing and Cleaning Co .......... 177
MacMurray-Judge Architectural Iron Co., The .......... 238
Mallinckrodt Chemical Works .......... 153
Mammoth Stables and Broadway Mule Yards, The, Reilly & Wolfort, proprietors .......... 149
Massa, Lewis & Co., importers and jobbers in watch material, jewelers' supplies, etc .......... 201
Maxwell & Crouch, mule market .......... 141
May, Charles F., architect and superintendent 157
Mayer, A. B., Manufacturing Co., manufacturers of bone black and fertilizers, and dealers in paper stock, scrap iron, bones, etc .......... 189
McCabe, Henry, manufacturer of plug chewing and twist tobaccos .......... 168
McKinley & Downman, miners of and dealers in coal .......... 172
Mechanics Bank, The .......... 94
Meier, E. F. W., china, glass, queensware, etc 87
Melcher, Charles W., mining and quarrying machinery .......... 194
Mercantile Agency, The, R. G. Dun & Co., proprietors .......... 109
Merchants' National Bank, The .......... 169
Merkel Brothers, designers and engravers .......... 200
Merrill, J. S., Drug Co., wholesale dealers in drugs, druggists' sundries, medicines, etc. 105
Messmore, Gannett & Co., commission merchants .......... 219
Metcalf, Moore & Co., live stock commission merchants .......... 149
Metropolitan Life Insurance Co .......... 115
Meyrose, F. & Co., proprietors Western Railroad Lamp and Lantern Manufactory .......... 85

## THE INDUSTRIES OF ST. LOUIS.

| | PAGE |
|---|---|
| Miller & Worley, tobacco manufacturers | 226 |
| Milius, Gus A., importer and dealer in fine cigars | 230 |
| Mississippi Glass Co., manufacturers of rough and ribbed plate glass | 98 |
| Mississippi Iron Works and Foundry. Pullis Bros., proprietors, architectural and ornamental iron work | 140 |
| Missouri Safe Deposit Co., The | 195 |
| Missouri Tinware Co. | 167 |
| Moller, L., & Co., builders of first-class carriages, rockaways, barouches, surreys, phaetons, buggies, etc. | 36 |
| More, Jones & Co., manufacturers of car and engine brasses, babbitt metal, solder, bar lead, etc. | 129 |
| Morrison, Thomas, proprietor St. Louis Tent Manufacturing Co. | 182 |
| Moser Cigar and Paper Box Co., The | 235 |
| Moss, Chas., & Co., agents Bethesda Mineral Water | 115 |
| Mound City Mutual Fire Insurance Co. | 141 |
| Muldoon & Sharp, pork packers and wholesale dealers in provisions | 225 |
| Mullally, Jos. J., broker | 92 |
| Murphy & Co., varnish makers | 204 |
| Murphy, P. C., manufacturer and wholesale and retail dealer in trunks and travelling goods | 105 |
| Mussman, Jr., H. A., importer and wholesale and retail dealer in cigars, tobacco, cigarettes and smokers' articles | 232 |
| Mutual Life Insurance Co., of New York, The | 214 |
| Mutual Reserve Fund Life Association | 183 |
| Nathan & Licrow, fire and marine insurance | 209 |
| Neath Gold Mining Co., The | 80 |
| Newcomb Brothers Wall Paper Co., dealers in wall paper, curtain materials and art decorations | 239 |
| New Home Sewing Machine Co. | 130 |
| New Missouri Sand Co. | 185 |
| Niedringhaus, Chas., dealer in stoves, furniture and all kinds of house furnishing goods | 156 |
| Sonotuck Silk Co., Corticelli Silk Mills | 166 |
| Noxon, Albert & Toomey, scenic artists | 179 |
| Oakes, A., & Co., manufacturers of pure home-made candies and fine confections | 207 |
| O'Connor & Harder Furnace and Range Co., manufacturers of and dealers in furnaces, ranges and house furnishing goods | 121 |
| Orr & Lindsley Shoe Co., wholesale dealers in boots and shoes | 229 |
| Pacific Oil Co., producers and manufacturers of lubricating, valve and railway oils | 91 |
| Paddock-Hawley Iron Co., The, wholesale hardware, iron, etc. | 198 |
| Parisian Cloak Co., importers and manufacturers of ladies', misses' and children's cloaks and suits | 231 |
| Parker, Ritter, Nicholls Stationery Co., stationers, office outfitters, blank-book manufacturers, printers and lithographers | 216 |
| Parker-Russell Mining and Manufacturing Co., The, manufacturers of Oak Hill gas retorts, fire brick and other fire clay products | 131 |
| Parlin, Orendorff & Bauer, manufacturers and jobbers of farm machinery, etc. | 190 |
| Paule, Frank, Tailoring Co., tailors and importers | 157 |
| Pauly Jail Building and Manufacturing Co., The | 82 |
| Pelton Bros. & Co., manufacturers of the finest electro silver-plated ware | 236 |
| Pennsylvania Lumber Co., manufacturers and wholesale dealers in yellow pine lumber | 110 |
| Pentland & Hahn, block and pump makers | 216 |
| Petton & Kloegel, manufacturers of carriages, barouches, buggies, trucks, spring wagons, etc. | 111 |
| Philibert & Johanning Manufacturing Co., manufacturers of sash, doors, blinds, etc. | 91 |
| Pioneer Steam Keg Works Co. | 181 |
| Plant Seed Co., garden, grass and flower seeds, etc. | 165 |
| Planters' House | 109 |
| Planters' Tobacco Warehouse, Laughlin & Blakely, proprietors | 140 |
| Platt & Thornburgh Paint and Glass Co. | 123 |
| Pond Engineering Co., engineers and contractors of steam and hydraulic machinery | 183 |
| Pope, H. O., Produce Co., wholesale produce, fruits and vegetables | 224 |
| Prufrock, Wm., manufacturer of parlor suites, lounges and mattresses | 234 |
| Pullis Bros., proprietors Mississippi Iron Works and foundry | 140 |
| Quernheim, W. H., & Bro., galvanized iron and copper cornices | 146 |

| | PAGE |
|---|---|
| Quirk, James A., manufacturer and wholesale and retail dealer in trunks, valises and satchels | 213 |
| Ramsey & Swasey, architects | 159 |
| Raymond & Torwegge, manufacturers of fine silk, cassimere, pull-over, beaver, otter and fine flexible silk hats | 243 |
| Reade Manufacturing Co., manufacturing chemists, druggists and distillers of fruit essences, makers of specialties for the various requirements of the trades and manufactures | 242 |
| Redfield, H. A., & Co., commission merchants and dealers in provisions | 107 |
| Regina Flour Mill Co | 147 |
| Reilly & Wolfort, proprietors of the Mammoth Stables and Broadway Mule Yards | 149 |
| Renshaw, John W., notary public, real estate and insurance agent | 162 |
| Rhodus Commission Co., commission, furs, hides, wool, game and country produce | 218 |
| Rice, Stix & Co., jobbers and wholesale dealers in dry goods, notions, etc. | 81 |
| Richardson, Jack P., lumber commission merchant | 154 |
| Riches & Co., engravers on wood | 192 |
| Rider, S. A., & Co., wholesale dealers in watches, diamonds and jewelry | 158 |
| Rio Chemical Co., manufacturers of medical specialties for physicians | 167 |
| Rohan Bros. Boiler Manufacturing Co. | 120 |
| Rosch, artistic photographer | 148 |
| Rosebrough, R. L., Sons, marble and granite works | 77 |
| Rosenthal, F. W., & Co., importers and dealers in wall paper, carpets, rugs, curtain goods, etc. | 173 |
| Rosenthal, I. B., & Co., importers, manufacturers and jobbers of millinery goods | 92 |
| Royal Cigar Co., manufacturers of cigars exclusively | 206 |
| Rubelman, Geo. A., Hardware Co., dealers in cabinet hardware etc. | 150 |
| Ruemmelli & Rassbach, general western agents of the De LaVergne Refrigerating Machine Co | 196 |
| Rumely, M. & J., threshing machinery and engines; F. M. Foy, Manager St. Louis branch | 221 |
| Ramsey, L. M., Manufacturing Co., manufacturers and jobbers of agricultural implements, pumps, wood and iron working machinery, plumbers', steam and gas-fitters' supplies | 143 |
| Russell, T. Greer, brokerage and commission | 204 |
| Russell, W. J., carriage repository, general agent Columbus Buggy Co., Columbus, Ohio | 184 |
| Safe Deposit and Trust Company of St. Louis | 151 |
| Sawyer, F. O., & Co., wholesale paper dealers | 182 |
| Scherpe & Koken, Enterprise architectural iron works and foundry | 112 |
| Schmidt, Chas., Toy and Notion Co., importers and jobbers | 78 |
| Schmidt, O. M., & Co., wholesale grocers, liquor dealers and commission merchants | 207 |
| Scholten, John A., artist and photographer | 133 |
| Schotten, Wm., & Co., importers, manufacturers and wholesale dealers in teas, coffees, spices and grocers' sundries | 79 |
| Schulenburg & Boeckeler Lumber Co. | 81 |
| Schwab Clothing Co., manufacturers of clothing | 100 |
| Sect Wine Co., champagnes and still wines | 179 |
| Seed, M. A., Dry Plate Co. | 142 |
| Sellers, John M., manufacturer of fire and waterproof gravel and composition roofs and roofing materials | 165 |
| Senter & Co., cotton factors and commission merchants | 198 |
| Sessinghaus, William, & Co., millers | 206 |
| Shapleigh, A. F., & Cantwell Hardware Co. | 107 |
| Shattinger, A., wholesale and retail dealer in pianos and musical instruments; agent Weber pianos and Clough & Warren organs | 213 |
| Shaughnessy, M., & Co., wholesale wines and liquors | 178 |
| Sheridan & Ryan, wholesale dealers in hay, grain and mill stuffs | 111 |
| Shrimpton, Alfred, & Sons, needle manufacturers, Redditch, England; A. A. & J. W. Wright, St. Louis representatives | 136 |
| Shryock, W. P., & Co., wholesale dealers in notions, hardware, glassware, etc. | 233 |
| Shultz Belting Co., manufacturers of the Shultz patent fulled leather belting, lace and picker leather, etc. | 181 |
| Smith-Davis Manufacturing Co., manufacturers of spring, wire and iron beds | 239 |
| Smith, Jas. A., & Sons Ice and Fuel Co., wholesale and retail dealers in ice and fuel | 97 |

# THE INDUSTRIES OF ST. LOUIS. 249

Southern Box Factory, Fehlig Bros. Box Manufacturing Co.,................................ 115
Southern Roller Mills, Engelke & Feluer, proprietors; manufacturers of corn meal, pearl grits and hominy........................ 128
Southern White Lead Co., manufacturers of white and red leads, litharge, etc............ 144
Speer, Jones & Co., manufacturers of machinery oils, greases, etc........................ 113
Stamm Brothers, wholesale bottles and bottlers' supplies; also proprietors of Eclipse Bottling Co., manufacturers of the celebrated "Eclipse Tonic Beer" and ginger ale........ 110
Stauard, E. O., Milling Co., manufacturers of roller process flour........................ 73
Stark Nut-Lock Co., manufacturers of the "Stark" nut-lock........................ 190
Starr Safe Co, safes, locks, etc............ 111
Steinwender & Sellner, importers, distillers and dealers in fine Kentucky whiskies, wines, etc................................ 191
Stewart, James, & Co., architects, builders and contractors........................ 240
Stifel's, Chas. G., Brewing Co............ 144
St. James Hotel, Thomas P. Miller, proprietor,. 135
St. Louis Ammonia and Chemical Co, manufacturers of fine ammonia for chemists' and druggists' use and refrigerating purposes.... 128
St. Louis Bagging Co., manufacturers of "Phœnix" and "Globe" jute bagging............ 145
St. Louis Bank Note Co., engraving, printing, steel plate and lithography................ 88
St. Louis Bridge and Iron Co , bridge builders and contractors........................ 88
St. Louis Car Roofing Co........................ 170
St. Louis Coal Tar Co , manufacturers of roofing and paving materials, coal tar, etc..... 123
St. Louis Corset Co........................ 225
St. Louis Dairy Co........................ 125
St. Louis Flagstone Co., stone sidewalks....... 134
St. Louis Glass Works........................ 90
St. Louis Hardware and Cutlery Co., exclusive jobbers of hardware and cutlery............ 161
St. Louis Illuminating Co., see Heisler Electric Light Co........................ 95
St. Louis Manufacturing Co., manufacturers of sash, doors, blinds, etc.................. 108
St. Louis Mantel and Grate Co., manufacturers of marble, iron and slate mantels, enameled grates, encaustic tile, etc................ 223
St. Louis and Mississippi Valley Transportation Co........................ 152
St. Louis Moulding and Frame Factory, J. R. Webber & Co., proprietors................ 89
St. Louis National Stock Yards Co............ 148
St. Louis Refrigerator and Woolen Gutter Co.. 184
St. Louis Shot Tower Co , manufacturers of shot and bar lead........................ 101
St. Louis Tent Manufacturing Co., Thomas Morrison, proprietor; tents, awnings, wagon covers, etc................................ 182
St Louis Transfer Co........................ 137
St. Louis Type Foundry, type founders, printers' machine works, and wholesale paper warehouse........................ 109
St. Louis Union Stock Yards Co............ 187
Straus, Jacob, Saddlery Co., wholesale manufacturers of saddlery and jobbers of saddlery hardware................................ 142
Strauss, S., & Co., wholesale millinery, fancy goods and notions........................ 137
Swan, Duncan & Co., brokers; mining stocks and lands a specialty........................ 194
Taussig Bros & Co., wholesale dealers in wool and woolen goods........................ 151
Taylor, Geo., & Co., cotton factors and general commission merchants........................ 82
Ten Broek Agency, The, collectors and mercantile adjusters................................ 238
Terry & Scott, real estate and financial agents... 146
Thalmann, B., St. Louis Printing Ink Works (see also advertisement, page 252)........ 89
Thomas Law Book Co., The F. H., publishers and dealers in law books................ 199
Thuener, Chas., & Co., manufacturers of galvanized iron cornices........................ 231

Tiemeyer, John C., packer of seed leaf and importer of Havana tobacco........................ 130
Tivy, William N., general commission merchant 207
Trask Fish Co., ocean and lake fish............ 163
Triplett, John R., insurance agency............ 117
Tudor Iron Works, manufacturers of railway supplies................................ 168
Udell, C. E., & Co., cheese dealers............ 217
United States Stenograph Co., The........ 217
Vauc-Calvert Paint Co., manufacturers of mixed paints........................ 187
Varney Carriage Co., manufacturers of carriages and buggies........................ 243
Virdeu, Samuel, & Co., commission merchants in hay................................ 121
Voelker, O , & Co., commission merchants.. 124
Wahl, John, & Co , commission merchants.. 131
Waldeck, J. C. C., Provision Co., dealers in all kinds of fresh and cured pork......... 209
Warner, E. H., wholesale lumber dealer......... 173
Warner, E. S., & Co., real estate and financial agents................................ 211
Water, Light and Power Co., The, engineers and contractors........................ 73
Waters-Pierce Oil Co........................ 118
Wear, J. H., Boogher & Co., importers and jobbers of dry goods, etc................ 106
Webber, J. R., & Co., proprietors of St. Louis Moulding and Frame Factory........... 89
Weinheimer & Opp, importers of Havana and wholesale dealers in domestic leaf........ 230
Wescott, W. B., & Co., commission: hay, grain, flour, etc........................ 194
Westermann, H., & Co., wholesale queensware, china and glass........................ 185
Western Anthracite Coal Co., wholesale and retail dealers in anthracite and bituminous coal and coke........................ 170
Western Railroad Lamp and Lantern Manufactory, F. Meyrose & Co., proprietors........ 85
Westlake & Button Novelty Co., manufacturers and jobbers of builders' and contractors' outfittings................................ 171
Wheeler, James, & Co., live stock commission merchants................................ 146
Whitelaw, James, printers' machinist............ 192
Whitman Agricultural Co., manufacturers of buy presses, agricultural implements, etc.. 116
Whitney & Weston, real estate and financial agents................................ 230
Wickham & Pendleton, wholesale grocers..... 199
Wiggins Ferry Co........................ 76
Willis, E. G., & Bro , leather, hides and wool. 222
Wilson, H. McK., & Co., improved apparatus and supplies for cheese factories, creameries and dairies........................ 112
Wilson, Nichols & Co , wholesale provisions and packers of dried beef................ 201
Wilson & Toms Investment Co., farm mortgages................................ 129
Winkel, Jos., Terra Cotta Works, manufacturers of agricultural and horticultural terra cotta................................ 200
Winn Boiler Compound Co., manufacturers of Winn's Vegetable Boiler Compound........ 205
Wittenberg & Sorber, designers, photographers and engravers on wood................ 170
Wolff, M. A., & Co., real estate agents........ 117
Wood, Walter A., Mowing and Reaping Machine Co........................ 88
Woolf, J. L., & Brother, job lot emporium for trunks, bags, clothing, hats, caps, etc..... 173
Woolman-Todd Boot and Shoe Co., manufacturers and jobbers of boots and shoes....... 166
Wright, James A., & Sons Carriage Co., manufacturers of carriages, etc................ 154
Wright, J. K., & Co., manufacturers of printing inks and colors........................ 187
Wrought Iron Range Co., manufacturers of ranges and furnaces........................ 96
Wyckoff, Seamans & Benedict, dealers in standard type-writers and type-writer supplies of every kind................................ 220
Yeakel, Fred., Carriage Co., manufacturers of fine carriages, rockaways, barouches, phætons, business trucks and wagons..... 235

## ADVERTISERS' INDEX.

Carlisle, David, manufacturer of crushed feed for horses and cattle.......... 257
Cornwall, Dr. J., National Tonic Beer; soda and mineral water bottling establishment .... 260
Cruttwell Storage, Packing and Moving Co..... 252
Deane Steam Pump Co., manufacturers of steam pumping machinery........... 253
Eddy & Eddy, manufacturing chemists........ 259
Eisner, J. M., & Co., publishers........... 255
Gerst Bros. Manufacturing Co., Cass avenue Iron works and Foundry.................. 256
Glenny Brothers Glass Co., dealers in American window glass and importers of foreign glass.............. 257
Gooch Freezer Co., Cincinnati, O.; patent ice cream freezers........ 255
Haskell Engraving Co., designers, general engravers, and manufacturers of seals, medals, badges, etc................. 258
Hulbert, A. G., manufacturer of wire and iron fences, (see also page 203 )........ 255
Humphrey, F. W., & Co., (see also page 96,) .......... outside back cover
Jones, Robt McK., & Co., dry goods commission merchants.......... 254
Leschen, A., & Sons Rope Co., manufacturers of steel and iron wire rope........ 259
Levison & Blythe Stationery Co............ 251
Lewis, O. J., & Co., auctioneers and commission merchants............ 260
Manewal-Lange Cracker Co., crackers, cakes and jumbles............. 254
McCormick, R. S., & Co., grain............ 256
Meagher & Nagle, real estate and house agents........... 258

Merchants Manufacturing Association, manufacturers of baking powder, druggists' and grocers' specialties................. 258
Moss, Charles & Co., agents for Be-thes-da Mineral Spring Co. (See also page 115)........ 253
Mullally, John, Commission Co., hay and grain. 259
Overstreet, J. W., & Co., live stock commission merchants................. 252
Phoenix Iron Works, foundry and machine shops, Wm. Ellison & Son............ 258
Poultry Record, The. (See also Riches & Co., page 192)......... 256
Roesslein & Robyn, general insurance agents... 260
Seidel & Winkler, manufacturers of bank, store, office, bar, and drug fixtures............ 257
Spurgin, James L., photographic backgrounds and accessories............. 254
Steinwender, Stoffregen & Co., importers of and jobbers in tea and coffee.............. 259
St Louis and San Francisco Railway, (See also page 29).............. inside front cover
St Louis Grain Elevator Co..... inside back cover
Thalmann, H. St. Louis Printing Ink Works, (See also page 80)........... 252
Thomas, Seth, Clock Co., clocks and watches., 258
Tinker & Smith Malting Co............... 257
Union Sign Works Co, stained glass.......... 259
Warren, Samuel D., & Co., felt and gravel roofs and roofing materials........ 253
Wieder Paint Co, manufacturers of white lead and colors, etc................. 256
Zittlosen, Martin, awnings, tents, tarpaulins, wagon covers, etc............ 254

# LEVISON & BLYTHE STATIONERY CO.,

### 213 and 215 North Third Street,

ST. LOUIS, MO.

Levison's Champion Violet Ink.

Levison's Blue-Black Fluid Ink.

Levison's Railroad Copying Ink.

Levison's Champion Scarlet Ink.

Levison's Pure Gum Mucilage.

## LEVISON & BLYTHE STATIONERY CO.,

### 213 AND 215 NORTH THIRD STREET,

MANUFACTURER OF

## BLACK AND COLORED
# PRINTING AND LITHOGRAPHIC INKS,
### Varnishes, Plate Oils, Etc.

#### 210 OLIVE STREET.

B. THALMANN'S INK USED ON THIS PUBLICATION.

---

J. W. OVERSTREET.       E. A. PEGRAM.       J. A. McNEILEY.

# J. W. OVERSTREET & CO.,
Commission Salesmen and Forwarding Agents for all kinds of

# LIVE STOCK.
Office Nos. 1 and 2, Union Stock Yards,

### ST. LOUIS, MO.
Cash advances made on consignments.

---

H. A. MORSMAN, P est.       F. P. WHERRY, Vice-P est.       C. H. SMITH, Sec. & Treas.

### Cruttwell Storage, Packing and Moving Co.
**JULIAN CRUTTWELL, Manager.**

Furniture, Pianos, Crockery & Household Goods of Every Description.
Estimates furnished at residences, for packing, hauling, shipping, moving and storage.
Also for the unpacking, repairing and cleaning of furniture and carpets.

**REFER TO**
Burrell, Comstock & Co.
A. G. Peterson.
Trorlicht, Duncker & Renard.
C. S. Freeborn, Agt. Star Union Line.     **Telephone 3179.**

*2004, 2006 and 2008 Morgan St.*

ST. LOUIS, MO.

## CHARLES MOSS & CO.
### 119 N. Second St., St. Louis, Mo.
#### AGENTS FOR
# Be-thes-da Mineral Spring Co.

### PRICE LIST.

Be-thes-da Mineral Water.
IN BULK.
Barrel, containing 42 gallons ........$8 00
Half Barrel, containing 20 gallons . 5 00
☞The barrels are lined with paraffine so prepared as to preserve the purity and perfection of the water..☜

**Still Water.**
In Cases, 10-gallon bottles............$4 50
In Cases, 20-half-gallon bottles ...... 5 00

Be-thes-da Mineral Water.
CARBONATED.
In Cases, 50 quarts ............per case, $7 00
In Cases, 100 pints ............per case, 9 00

**Be-thes-da Ginger Ale.**
In Cases, 50 quarts ........... per case, $8 50
In Barrels, 120 pints ..........per bbl., 10 00
**DELIVERED FREE OF DRAYAGE.**

### IMPORTANT CAUTION.

Like all standard and valuable articles, BE-THES-DA has experienced annoyance from impostors. Certain parties have been induced by the world-wide fame it has attained, to foist Waukesha Water on the market. The term "Waukesha Water" is calculated to deceive. When Waukesha Water is offered to you for BE-THES-DA, do not take it. To those who have not learned its great worth, this caution is necessary.

Telephone No. 977.

## The Deane Steam Pump Co.
Holyoke, Mass. and 615 N. Main St.,

ST. LOUIS.

MANUFACTURERS OF

# STEAM PUMPING MACHINERY
OF EVERY VARIETY AND FOR ALL DUTIES.

**Water Works Pumping Engines a Specialty.**

SAMUEL D. WARREN.  **ESTABLISHED 1848.**  P. S. MARQUIS.

## SAMUEL D. WARREN & CO.
MANUFACTURERS OF
# FELT AND GRAVEL ROOFS AND ROOFING MATERIALS.
OFFICE, No. 10, S. E. COR. BROADWAY AND OLIVE STREET,

TELEPHONE No. 401.  ST. LOUIS. MO.

**SPECIAL ATTENTION PAID TO WORK OUT OF THE CITY.**

☞Beware of persons claiming to put on this same Roofing, as we are the only parties in the West and South dealing in the genuine "Warren's Roofing."

## Manewal-Lange Cracker Co.

MANUFACTURERS OF EVERY VARIETY OF

### Crackers, Cakes and Jumbles,

Cor. 6th & Cass Avenue.

ST. LOUIS, MO.

**TO THE TRADE.**

Our goods are offered to you with the guarantee that they are equal to if not superior to the same grade of any other manufacturer. If, upon examination, they do not prove to be so, they may be returned at our expense for freight both ways. This applies to all goods, whether purchased direct from us or from the wholesale grocer, provided claim is made within ten (10) days from date of goods leaving our factory. If you have never used our goods, we respectfully ask that you give them a trial.

**MANEWAL-LANGE CRACKER CO.**

---

## Robt. McK. Jones & Co.

### DRY GOODS,

### Commission Merchants

AND

Manufacturers' Agents,

618 LOCUST ST.,

ST. LOUIS.

James L. Spurgin,
216 N. 10TH STREET,
ST. LOUIS, MO.
Photographic Backgrounds
AND
ACCESSORIES.

---

## MARTIN ZITTLOSEN,

**MANUFACTURER OF AND WHOLESALE DEALER IN**

### Awnings, Tents, Tarpaulins, Wagon Covers,

Water-Proof Horse Covers, Flags, Dray Covers, Rope Splicing.

**OILED CLOTHING A SPECIALTY.**

Corner Main and Walnut Streets,

Office, 27 South Main Street,    ST. LOUIS, MO.

# THE GOOCH PATENT ICE CREAM FREEZERS.

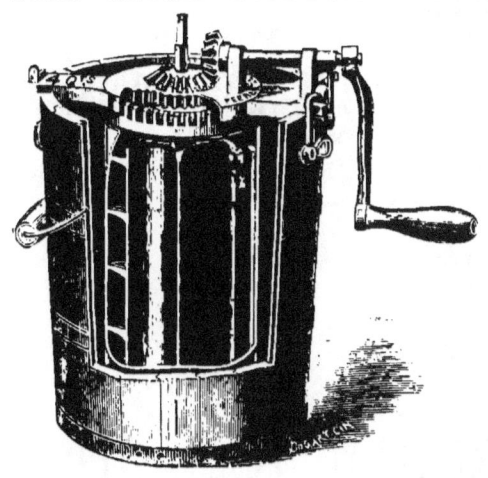

These Freezers are entirely different from any other make in the market. By their simplicity of construction and perfect adaptability to the process of making all kinds of Ice Cream, Sherbets, Frozen Fruits, etc., they have taken the front rank in the market and are universally acknowledged THE BEST FREEZERS MADE.

Dealers are constantly taking up the sale of them, and are discarding inferior Freezers heretofore thought good ones. Our increase of sales has been NINE HUNDRED PER CENT. SINCE 1879, thus showing their great popularity.

The "Peerless" are made 3-quart to 10-quart for family use; the "Giant," with fly-wheel, 14-quart to 42-quart for confectioners and hotels.

For Sale by the Leading St. Louis Hardware and Queensware Trade.

## THE GOOCH FREEZER CO.
### CINCINNATI, O.

---

# J. M. ELSTNER & CO.
## PUBLISHERS

| | |
|---|---|
| The Industries of San Francisco, Cal. | The Industries of Houston, Tex. |
| The Industries of Cincinnati, O. | The Industries of St. Louis, Mo. (1887.) |
| The Industries of St. Louis, Mo. (1885.) | The Industries of Chattanooga, Tenn., In Preparation. |
| The Industries of New Orleans. | |
| The Industries of Minneapolis, Minn. | The Industries of Detroit, Mich., In Preparation. |
| The Industries of St. Paul, Minn. | |
| The Industries of Grand Rapids, Mich. | The Industries of Montgomery, Ala., In Preparation. |
| The Industries of Atlanta, Ga. | |
| The Industries of Savannah, Ga. | |

### 210 and 212 North Third Street,
### ST. LOUIS, MO.

---

DON'T BUY FENCING Until you get my prices. I will save you money on Farm, City & Grave-Yard Fences, Iron Posts, Gates, Barb-wire, &c. Netting and Picket Fencings, or Licenses and Supplies for home manufacture. My patent netting with parallel wires, never sags between posts. 16 patents. Goods warranted. Establ'd 1876. Catalogue FREE. A. G. HULBERT, 904 Olive St. ST. LOUIS, MO.

FRED GERST, Pres.   **ESTABLISHED 1849.**   JNO. F. GERST, Sec'y

## GERST BROS. MF'G CO.,
# Cass Avenue Iron Works and Foundry,
**Manufacturers of All Kinds of**
IRON RAILINGS, GREY IRON AND ORNAMENTAL CASTINGS,

*Window Shutters, Balconies, Iron Bedsteads and Chairs, Doors, &c., Warehouse Gratings, Bank Vaults, and General Blacksmithing.*

**AGENTS FOR THE CHAMPION FENCE CO.**

800 to 806 Cass Avenue,                ST. LOUIS.

---

R. S. McCormick.                                    W. L. Green, Jr.

# R. S. McCORMICK & CO.
### GRAIN.

GAY BUILDING.                                    ST. LOUIS, MO.

*A Journal devoted to the interest of all who keep Poultry, Pigeons and Pet Stock.*

**SUBSCRIPTION, FIFTY CENTS PER YEAR.**

Address: **POULTRY RECORD,**
304 OLIVE STREET.                    ST. LOUIS, MO.

# WIEDER PAINT CO.
**MANUFACTURERS OF**
## WHITE LEAD AND COLORS,
JOBBERS OF
### PAINTS, OILS AND PAINTERS' SUPPLIES,
OFFICES: 704 and 706 North Fourth St.    **ST. LOUIS.**

Only makers of St. Louis Villa and Cottage Mixed Paints.

E. L. SEIDEL.                                    F. A. WINKLER.
# SEIDEL & WINKLER,
Manufacturers of
# BANK, STORE, OFFICE, BAR and DRUG
# FIXTURES

Railings, Mantels, Shelvings and Mirrors.

**Office, 517 Locust St.**     **Factory, S. E. Cor. Linn & Soulard Sts.**
ST. LOUIS, MO.

| GEO. TINKER, | WM. SMITH, | Z.W. TINKER, |
|---|---|---|
| Pres. | V. P. & Treas. | Sec'y. |

ESTABLISHED 1852.     INCORPORATED 1879.

TINKER & SMITH

Malting Company,

CAPACITY 225,000 BUSHELS.

Spring Water Malt House:
   Nos. 32, 34 and 100, 102, 104, 106
       SOUTH SEVENTEENTH ST.

Franklin Malt House,
   In Block between Ninth and
   Tenth Sts., Franklin Ave. and Wash St.

**ST. LOUIS, MO.**

# DAVID CARLISLE,
MANUFACTURER OF
# CRUSHED FEED
—FOR—
## HORSES AND CATTLE.

Nos. 114 & 116 Chestnut St.
**ST. LOUIS.**
TELEPHONE NO. 577.

## GLENNY BROTHERS GLASS CO.
—DEALERS IN—
# AMERICAN WINDOW GLASS
AND IMPORTERS OF
German Looking Glass Plates, French Window and Picture Glass,

Car, Coach, Photo, Colored, Cathedral, Ground, Embossed, Cut, Enameled, Rough & Fluted Glass.

Sole Agents for St. Louis for the Genuine French Mirror Plates.
**Nos. 217 and 219 South Sixth St., Cor. Clark Ave.   -   -   ST. LOUIS, MO.**

## HASKELL ENGRAVING COMPANY,

**DESIGNERS, GENERAL ENGRAVERS**

AND MANUFACTURERS OF

SEALS, MEDALS, BADGES, RUBBER STAMPS, &c.,

713 OLIVE STREET,

ST. LOUIS, MO.

## MERCHANTS MFG. ASSOC'N,

J. T. CADWALLADER & CO. Managers,

MANUFACTURERS

### SHAW'S SNOW PUFF
### AND MERCHANTS
## BAKING POWDER,

Druggists' and Grocers' Specialties,

117 NORTH MAIN STREET.

ST. LOUIS.

---

Wm. A. Meagher.   Jno. M. Nagle.

## MEAGHER & NAGLE,

### Real Estate

AND

### House Agents.

*Rent Collections a Specialty.*

Office, S. E. Cor. Ninth and Chestnut Sts.,

ST. LOUIS, MO.

Negotiators of Loans and General Collectors. Take Charge of Estates, Make Disbursements, Pay Taxes, &c

---

# Seth Thomas Clock Co.,
## CLOCKS AND WATCHES,

No. 1003 Olive Street,   -   ST. LOUIS, MO.

---

### Phoenix Iron Works, Foundry and Machine Shops,

**WM. ELLISON & SON,**

MANUFACTURERS OF

## PORTABLE AND STATIONARY ENGINES,

Boilers, Steam and Hand Elevator of an Improved Pattern, Saw Mill, Flour and Mining Machinery, Pulleys, Shafting and Hangers, Iron and Brass Castings made to order.

913 North Main Street,   ST. LOUIS, MO.

Repairing Promptly Executed.

HENRY LESCHEN, President.    EDWARD M. VOSSLER, Vice Pres't.    JOHN A LESCHEN, Sec. and Treas.

## A. Leschen & Sons Rope Co.
### MANUFACTURERS OF
**STEEL**　**WIRE ROPE**　**IRON**
### OF EVERY DESCRIPTION.
OFFICE AND WAREHOUSE:
903 & 905 N. Main Street,　　　　　　ST. LOUIS, MO.

---

J. STEINWENDER.　　　　　　　　　　　C. STOFFREGEN.
## STEINWENDER, STOFFREGEN & CO.
### —IMPORTERS OF AND JOBBERS IN—
# TEA AND COFFEE,
805, 807 & 809 N. Third St.,　　　No. 130 Front Street,
**ST. LOUIS.**　　　　　　　　　　**NEW YORK.**

---

ESTABLISHED 1867.　　　　　　　　　　INCORPORATED 1883.

# STAINED GLASS,
**FOR CHURCHES, DWELLINGS, PUBLIC BUILDINGS, ETC.**
DESIGNS AND ESTIMATES FURNISHED.

UNION SIGN WORKS CO., A. SUTTER, Manager,
115 and 117 Washington Avenue,　　　　　**ST. LOUIS.**

---

EDDY'S RELIABLE BAKING POWDER.
　　ANCHOR BAKING POWDER.
　　　　CHOICE BIRD FOOD.
　　　　　　FINE FLAVORING EXTRACTS.
CONDENSED WASH BLUE.　　　　STRICTLY PURE SPICES.

## EDDY & EDDY,
*Manufacturing Chemists,*
709 & 711 N. MAIN STREET,　　　　　**ST. LOUIS.**

---

# JOHN MULLALY COMMISSION CO.,
## HAY AND GRAIN.

—OFFICE:—
ROOMS 405 AND 406 CHAMBER OF COMMERCE.

# DR. J. CORNWALL,
## National Tonic Beer,
## Soda and Mineral Water
### BOTTLING ESTABLISHMENT.
### 1209 North Fifth Street, St. Louis, Mo.

The most powerful Apparatus in the United States has been put up for charging FOUNTAINS with SODA WATER and the following MINERAL WATERS:

| | | | |
|---|---|---|---|
| KISSINGEN | SELTZER | CARLSBAD | BASSANG |
| VICHY | MAGNESIAN | SPA | LEAMINGTON |
| CONGRESS | PULLNA | SEDLITZ | NAPLES |

## ROESLEIN & ROBYN,
## General Insurance Agents

### COMPANIES REPRESENTED.

| | | | |
|---|---|---|---|
| City of London, | - - England | Michigan F. & M. - | - Michigan |
| Farragut Fire, | - - New York | Newark Fire, | - New Jersey |
| Fire Ins. Ass'n, | - - London | Rochester-German, - | - New York |
| Germania, | - - New Orleans | Security. - - | - Conn |
| Hamburg-Bremen, - | - Germany | Union, - - | - Philadelphia |
| Merchants, | - - New Jersey | Westchester - | - New York |
| | New Hampshire, | - - New Hampshire. | |

### 223 and 225 Chestnut Street, ST. LOUIS, MO.

## O. J. Lewis & Co.
AUCTION SALES OF BOOTS AND SHOES,
TUESDAYS AND FRIDAYS.

## AUCTIONEERS AND COMMISSION MERCHANTS,

### 417 NORTH BROADWAY & 510 ST. CHARLES STREET,

www.ingramcontent.com/pod-product-compliance
Lightning Source LLC
Chambersburg PA
CBHW021355230426
43666CB00006B/533